THE NEW CHRISTIANITY

Nonviolence: A Christian Interpretation

The World of Pop Music and Jazz

THE NEW CHRISTIANITY

*An Anthology of the Rise
of Modern Religious Thought*

EDITED AND WITH INTRODUCTIONS BY

WILLIAM ROBERT MILLER

DELACORTE PRESS / NEW YORK

230
M

*Grateful acknowledgment is made to the following for
permission to reprint copyrighted material:*

"The Absolute Paradox" by S. Kierkegaard: Reprinted from *Philosophical Fragments* by S. Kierkegaard, translated by D. F. Swenson.
Reprinted by permission of Princeton University Press.

"The Antichrist" by Friedrich Nietzsche: Copyright 1920 by Alfred A.
Knopf, Inc.; renewed 1948 by H. L. Mencken. Reprinted by permission of the publishers from *The Antichrist* by Friedrich Nietzsche, translated by H. L. Mencken.

"Sunday Morning" by Wallace Stevens: Copyright 1923 by Wallace
Stevens; renewed 1951. Reprinted by permission of Alfred A. Knopf,
Inc., from *Collected Poems of Wallace Stevens*.

"The Future of an Illusion" by Sigmund Freud: From *The Future of
an Illusion* by Sigmund Freud. By permission of Liveright, Publishers, N. Y. Used with the permission of Sigmund Freud Copy-
rights Ltd., Mr. James Strachey and the Hogarth Press Ltd., from
The Future of an Illusion, Volume XXI of the Standard Edition of
The Complete Psychological Works of Sigmund Freud.

"Biology and Metabiology" by John Middleton Murry: From *God*.
Used by permission of Jonathan Cape Ltd. and the Society of Au-
thors as the Literary representatives of the estate of the late John
Middleton Murry.

"Religion and Modern Thinking" by Martin Buber: From *Eclipse of
God* by Martin Buber. Copyright 1952 by Harper & Row, Publishers,
Inc. Used by permission of the publishers.

"Theism Transcended" by Paul Tillich: Reprinted by permission of

ACKNOWLEDGMENTS

Yale University Press from *The Courage to Be* by Paul Tillich, pp. 182–190. Copyright © 1952 by Yale University Press.

"Ontology and the Question of God" and "God As Man's Ultimate Concern" by Paul Tillich: Reprinted from *Systematic Theology*, Volume I, by permission of the University of Chicago Press. Copyright 1951 by the University of Chicago.

"The Idea of God and Modern Man" by Rudolf Bultmann: From *Translating Theology into the Modern Age*. Copyright © 1965 by J. C. B. Mohr (Paul Siebeck), Tübingen, and Harper & Row, Publishers, Inc., New York. Used by permission of Harper & Row, Publishers, Inc.

"Atheism as a Purification" by Simone Weil: Reprinted by permission of G. P. Putnam's Sons from *Gravity and Grace* by Simone Weil. Copyright 1952 by G. P. Putnam's Sons.

"Last Letters from a Nazi Prison" by Dietrich Bonhoeffer: Copyright 1953 by the Macmillan Company. Reprinted by permission of the Macmillan Company from *Letters and Papers from Prison* by Dietrich Bonhoeffer. Reprinted by permission of SCM Press Ltd.

"Can a Truly Contemporary Person *Not* Be an Atheist?" by John A. T. Robinson: From *The New Reformation?* by John A. T. Robinson. Copyright © 1965 by SCM Press Ltd. Published U.S.A. 1965 by the Westminster Press. Used by permission. From *Honest to God* by John A. T. Robinson. Copyright © 1963 by SCM Press Ltd. Published U.S.A. 1963 by the Westminster Press. Used by permission. Used by permission of SCM Press Ltd.

"The Death-of-God Theology" by William Hamilton: First appeared in *The Christian Scholar* (Vol. 48, No. 1; Spring 1965) and printed here with the permission of the editor and the author.

"Christianity in a Post-Christian Era" by Gabriel Vahanian: From *Wait Without Idols* by Gabriel Vahanian. Reprinted by permission of George Braziller, Inc.

"The Self-Annihilation of God" by Thomas J. J. Altizer: From *The Gospel of Christian Atheism* by Thomas J. J. Altizer. Copyright © 1966 by W. L. Jenkins. The Westminster Press. Used by permission.

For Louise

1 COR. 13

Contents

III. THE NEW ATHEISMS

IV. THE GOD BEYOND GOD

CONTENTS

Introduction

THE ADVENT of the post-Christian era may be seen as comprising two major phases. Twentieth-century man recognizes an affinity between himself and such men as Galileo and Leonardo da Vinci —an affinity that does not extend, say, to Roger Bacon. For Bacon's science was in some sense anomalous, while that of Galileo and Leonardo corresponded to the spirit of the age in which they lived—an age in which the European intellect freed itself from the theological matrix that had formerly confined it. For much the same reasons, we draw a dateline between Groote, Wyclif and Hus as "precursors" and Luther, Calvin and Zwingli as the actuators of the Reformation. Is it only a coincidence that the latter happened to be contemporaries of Leonardo?

The meaning of the Renaissance is complex. It was a period of exploration and discovery, having extraordinary implications for literature and the arts. But it is increasingly recognized today that the period from 1500 to 1700 or 1800 is above all the era of the scientific revolution. As Herbert Butterfield observes, this development "outshines everything since the rise of Christianity and reduces the Renaissance and the Reformation to the rank of mere episodes."[1]

The episodic nature of the Protestant Reformation has barely begun to be assessed, and this is hardly the place to consider it, but it is at least worth noting its divisive and destructive impact as well as its creative and liberating effect. Its first fruit was a vicious intolerance, manifested in the German Peasants War dur-

---

[1] Herbert Butterfield, *The Origins of Modern Science* (New York: Macmillan, 1952), p. viii. See also Bronowski and Mazlish, *The Western Intellectual Tradition* (New York: Harper, 1960), pp. 107–126.

ing Luther's time and resulting in the brutal slaughter of radical
Christians such as the Anabaptists.[2] The evolution of religious
liberty, even for professed Christians, owes more to the kindness
of humane princes such as Philip of Hesse than to the Reformers
themselves. The religious situation in Europe a century after
Luther was one in which new currents of reform and dissent
arose out of the carnage of the Thirty Years War and the tragic
disaster, in the British Isles, of the Cromwellian dictatorship.
Religious thought during the eighteenth century was fragmented
into rationalism, deism, spiritualism and pietism, all reacting
against a hidebound Establishment, whether Catholic, Reformed
or Orthodox. From Paris to St. Petersburg, the educated classes
turned to the deism of the Enlightenment while maintaining
formal ties to the state religion, and among the peasantry and
artisans sectarian dissent flourished in numerous forms—quietistic, chiliastic, perfectionist.

Among the voices of the Enlightenment were such men as
Reimarus (1694–1768), who upheld Christian morality but rejected miracles and argued that the men who wrote the Bible
were dishonest and selfish; and Lessing (1729–1781), who held
that Christianity belonged to the past and had been superseded.
Even many defenders of orthodox Christianity, such as William
Paley (1743–1805), showed strong deistic influences.

In an important sense, however, the era of the scientific revolution may be regarded as merely a prelude to the truly modern
era. The secular age did not fully dawn until the scientific spirit
began to have widespread effect through applied technology. The
mechanistic images of deism were appropriate to men of pragmatic ingenuity for whom science was not merely a game of wits
but a means of subjugating nature and increasing the production
of iron and textiles. From a twentieth-century vantage point it is
Adam Smith and Benjamin Franklin who typify the "new man"
of the industrial revolution—and not only in their economic
views. It is a fitting coincidence that Smith's *Wealth of Nations*

---

[2] See Franklin H. Littell, *The Origins of Sectarian Protestantism* (New York:
Macmillan, 1964). Also, George H. Williams, *The Radical Reformation*
(Philadelphia: Westminster, 1962).

was published in 1776, the year of the world's first democratic revolution. Among the consequences of that revolution were the disestablishment of religious institutions and the inauguration of rapid economic growth along the lines proposed by Smith.

For Western civilization, however, it is the year 1789 that signals the beginning of the secular age, with the simultaneous downfall of the French monarchy, landed aristocracy and established church. For more than a generation thereafter, in however attenuated form, the ideas of the French Revolution were sown throughout Europe. In England, the Victorian era coincided with the rise of the middle class to economic and political ascendancy. In the century from Waterloo to Sarajevo, Europe became industrialized and emerged from feudalism into a predominantly urban, technological society based on unbridled competition, corporate finance and the dual exploitation of factory labor and overseas colonies. In the half-century since World War I, middle-class democracy has given way to a variety of mass societies, either democratic or totalitarian, and technology has extended its influence into every aspect of everyday life, from Edison's humble incandescent bulb to Telstar and Enovid—not to mention the capacity of nuclear weapons to annihilate life on earth. There are men today landing on the moon whose great-grandfathers were superstitious and illiterate serfs.

What has been the fate of Christianity in this secular age? Was Lessing right? In the heyday of the middle class, church membership and attendance reached unprecedented heights throughout Europe. But it was now a new form of establishment, no longer compelled by the state but dictated by status and propriety. Official Christianity became a posture, a matter of convention, a religious commodity like the factory-made bric-a-brac that adorned the typical Victorian home. As Kierkegaard wrote, "parsons canonize bourgeois mediocrity";[3] "official Christianity is both aesthetically and intellectually ludicrous."[4]

In its time (the 1850s), Kierkegaard's prophecy of a "frightful reformation" when "men will fall away from Christianity by the

[3] Soren Kierkegaard, *Journals* (New York: Oxford University Press), p. 1134.
[4] Quoted in Walter Lowrie, *A Short Life of Kierkegaard* (Princeton University Press, 1942), p. 246.

millions"[5] was greeted with smug derision by the prosperous churches. Yet by the first decade of the twentieth century the churchgoing portion of Europe's population had shriveled to a minority,[6] and after World War I vast numbers of people not only abandoned the churches but ceased to think of themselves as Christians even in a vestigial sense. Piety had become an anachronism, doctrine an absurdity, worship a waste of time. A tabulation of religious affiliations in Germany a century after Schleiermacher would indicate, first of all, that secular ideologies such as Social Democracy, Nazism and Communism claimed the loyalty of the great unchurched majority. Of those who styled themselves adherents of the church, a majority were "German Christians" who put loyalty to the Nazi state above loyalty to Christ. It is probably an understatement to say that for each Christian who opposed Hitler there were a dozen Marxists who did so, not to mention secular humanists of other kinds.

In broad outline, the secular age is a period in which Western culture ceased to be Christian, and in which the churches lost their grip on the world. The greatest names in the development of liberal theology—Schleiermacher, Ritschl, Harnack, Loisy, Gore—do not figure at all in the intellectual history of the era, and the champions of conservatism during the same period—such men as Jabez Bunting, Klaus Harms and C. H. Spurgeon—represent little more than curiosities to the church historian. The conservatives are deservedly forgotten. The task of the liberals, however, was more problematical. It was Schleiermacher who set the tone by addressing his discussions of religion to "its cultured despisers." The significance of Ritschl is that he devised a formula to defend a cluster of doctrine from the critical assaults of radicals like Strauss, thus enabling Christians to adjust to the modern world but not really confronting modern man with Christianity.[7] As Karl Jaspers stated in 1930,

---

[5] *Ibid.*
[6] See R. Mudie-Smith, ed., *The Religious Life of London* (London: 1904), ch. VII. Also, E. R. Wickham, *Church and People in an Industrial City* (London: Lutterworth, 1957), pp. 166–213.
[7] See Arthur W. Robinson, *The New Learning and the Old Faith* (London: Longmans, Green, 1928), referring to the direction of liberal biblical studies after Strauss and Renan: "On the whole, and even more remarkably in the

Religion as the historical basis of human existence has become, so
to say, invisible. . . . Nowadays the great traditions of the
Churches have often become nothing more than a futile attempt
to restore their irrevocable past, side by side with a broad-
minded adoption of all kinds of modern thought.[8]

One of the concomitants of this development, hastened by both
liberal and conservative teachings, was a steady drift away from
traditional faith. As one careful English observer noted,

The tide is ebbing within and without the churches. The drift is
towards a non-dogmatic affirmation of general kindliness and
good fellowship, with an emphasis rather on the service of men
than on the fulfilment of the will of God. . . . The children are
everywhere persuaded to attend the centres of religious teaching,
everywhere, as they struggle to manhood and womanhood in a
world of such doubtful certainties, they exhibit a large falling
away.[9]

In the aftermath of World War I came a dramatic transformation in theology, marked by the resurgence of dogmatics. Such
thinkers as Karl Barth and Emil Brunner curtly dismissed the
work of Schleiermacher, Ritschl and Harnack and returned to
the classic doctrines of Augustine, Anselm and Calvin, affirming
the absolute otherness of God and the primacy of the Bible as the
sole source of God's revelation to man. Unlike the conservatism of Bunting and Harms, the neo-orthodoxy of Barth and
Brunner was highly sophisticated. It accepted the facts of secular
life pragmatically and made use of modern scholarship in determining the meaning of biblical statements, but it made faith in
the traditional dogmas the criterion of interpretation. It was then,
too, that Kierkegaard began to be translated and read, for he
shared Barth's tough-minded seriousness about what it means to
be a Christian. Neo-orthodoxy was the theology of men who had

---

case of the New Testament, the tendency has been to return by degrees to
the traditional positions." (p. 9) Dr. Robinson was the father of the author
of *Honest to God.*
[8] Karl Jaspers, *Man in the Modern Age* (Garden City: Doubleday, 1957),
p. 152.
[9] C. F. G. Masterman, *The Condition of England* (London: 1909), p. 269.

witnessed the cataclysm of the war, and it developed further under the impact of the Depression and the rise of Fascism. Its proponents, in affirming the biblical God as "Lord of history," rejected the God of the middle class as an idol. Its chief spokesman in the United States was Reinhold Niebuhr, who considered himself, during the 1930s, a Marxist as well as a Christian. His active support of the labor movement was an instructive contrast to the sentimental and patronizing bourgeois utterances of such champions of the workers as Washington Gladden.

In the end, however, neo-orthodoxy has proved to be a stopgap. The "leap of faith" that it demands is no longer a live option for secular man, whose universe has no place for either a metaphysical or a biblical God. Since the end of World War II, owing partly to neo-orthodoxy's legacy of serious-mindedness and precision in dealing with the fundamental problems of human existence, a new generation of theologians has been impelled to reopen the ultimate questions that Barth and his generation considered closed. Why should twentieth-century man accept doctrines fashioned in the totally different intellectual worlds of the first or fourth or sixteenth centuries? If, as the neo-orthodox insisted, Christianity had become so badly distorted in the nineteenth century, might it not be possible that it also did so at other times? The radical theologian of today confronts a world that is not of his own making; moreover, he has become painfully aware that much of the Christian tradition he has inherited is spurious and irrelevant. Many of its assumptions are false or dubious, and much of its vocabulary has lost its meaning. To maintain his integrity as a mature man, he must either find a viable way to "make it as a Christian," as William Hamilton says, or else abandon Christianity.

Perhaps, as Lessing believed, Christianity has had its day. If so, will it yield to another form of faith, perhaps now evolving? If not, what are the necessary conditions of its reform and renewal if it is to survive? What is to be its relationship to secular ideologies—and must it not itself become secular in a secular age?

We have already sketched very briefly the course of bourgeois Christianity. Parallel with its development came characteristically modern competitors—the positivistic philosophy of Auguste Comte, the synthetic "New Christianity" of Saint-Simon, theosophical or "divine science" movements and the various atheisms of historical materialism, nihilism, existentialism and the like. To a large degree, liberal theology arose in response to one or another of these currents. But always present in the changing pattern was a succession of viewpoints located, so to speak, on the perimeter between the church and the world, or between Christianity and something else.

All of the writers represented in this volume, with three exceptions, were born Christians. The other three were born Jews and were variously influenced by Christianity. Whatever their intentions, whether to demolish or to reform, each represents a notable contribution to the transformation of Christianity—in sum, to opening the way to a new Christianity. Not all of the selections are of equal value, nor does each display the same degree of radicalism. I have attempted to provide some assessment of their significance in the biographical notes that precede the selections themselves, and to provide enough intellectual history there to relate each thinker to his time and to the general stream of religious thought.

The idea for this anthology arose in conversation with Richard Huett, quite fortuitously, as we were talking about the cover story "Is God Dead?" in *Time* Magazine (April 8, 1966), which was just out. I soon realized the extent to which my own experiences and studies had been preparing me for just such a project. Barely three months earlier I had amassed notes based on intensive study of William Blake and his interpreters, as well as on related readings in the economic and social history of the industrial revolution. My study of Blake was the direct outgrowth of correspondence with Thomas Altizer, who had sent me the manuscript of his own book on Blake. Last spring, partly as a result of conversations with William Hamilton, I had made a careful study of Bonhoeffer's prison letters, comparing the English translation with the German original, and during a visit to London that summer had an unusually fruitful discussion of this book with David L. Edwards, its English publisher. It was in London too that I discovered Middleton Murry's neglected book, *God*.

Paul Tillich's *The Courage to Be* helped make it possible for me to become a Christian again when I read it a dozen years ago. As it happened, I had only recently finished Freud's *The Future of an Illusion*. As an undergraduate at Columbia College in 1948, I was a thoroughgoing Marxist and an atheist. It was Mark Van Doren who, in that year, enabled me to read the Bible with the same kind of seriousness I was then devoting to Kafka and to Engels' *Dialectics of Nature*. Later, studies with W. T. Stace and Walter Kaufmann readied me for Tillich. I discovered Kierkegaard in the bosom of the church, in a series of small-group discussions on "the roots of faith"; for this I am indebted to my friends Robert Thomason and John Mills, who also acquainted me with Rudolf Bultmann's writings. It is to Maurice Friedman that I am indebted for my knowledge of Buber, initially resulting from my asking Friedman to write an article for a magazine I edited. It was about that time, too, that I first encountered the writings of Simone Weil in back issues of *Politics*. My first dabbling in Nietzsche goes back to prep-school days; I must credit Walter Kaufmann and Arthur A. Cohen with nudging me to the reading I did for this book. In many ways, I have learned new things in the course of choosing the selections and writing the biographical notes. I had not intended to include Hegel, who was known to me only as the philosopher whom Marx had "stood right-side up," until I was urged to do so by Harvey Cox and William Hamilton, as well as by Altizer. Schleiermacher, Strauss and Renan were known to me only at second hand when I first drafted my outline.

There is no end to giving credit. Woven into the above paragraphs are glimpses of autobiography that suggest something of what this book means to me and what I mean to it. I have no credentials as a professional theologian; my academic studies were chiefly in psychology and in literature, as befits a man of the secular age. Yet the impact of life experiences drove me to the Bible, drove me into correspondence and conversation with theologians, and into considerable reading—just as it drove me to Marx and Mannheim, to Freud, Köhler and Horney. For me,

editing this volume was only partly an exercise in objective scholarship, and I have tried to perform it with care. But the deeper
caring is in the commitment that this book represents, for to the
selections reproduced here I can feel that I have added my own
contribution to the new Christianity.

WILLIAM ROBERT MILLER

New York City,
August 1966

I

THE FORGOTTEN ANCESTOR

William Blake

[1757–1827]

WILLIAM BLAKE was a boy of twelve when James Watt patented his steam engine. A hosier's son, he was apprenticed to an engraver and supported himself by this craft throughout his life. He was born in the heart of London and lived his whole life there except for three years on the Sussex coast. Little is reliably known of his family background. Biographers describe his father as a "Nonconformist," which could mean Baptist, Presbyterian or a number of other things. Blake's friendship with Tom Paine, who was raised in a Quaker school, suggests one interpretation; his preoccupation with Milton suggests another. Some of his patrons and close associates were Swedenborgians. In point of fact, Blake was married and buried in the Church of England. His writings show many diverse religious influences, including ancient Celtic mythology, Gnostic and cabalistic motifs; and there are allusions to the mysticism of Jakob Boehme and the occultism of Agrippa von Nettesheim, whose *Vanity of the Arts and Sciences* asserted the need for imaginative interpretation of the Bible.[1] To a truly astonishing degree, Blake's religious thought is a synthesis of the most revolutionary ideas, overleaping the rigid categories of "Catholic" and "Reformed" and embodying an apocalyptic, visionary form of Christianity dating from the Renaissance or earlier.

What is interesting about Blake, however, is that his works do not merely sum up a body of ancient wisdom; they profoundly reflect the travail of the modern, revolutionary age. It was more

[1] See Northrop Frye, *Fearful Symmetry: A Study of William Blake* (Princeton University Press, 1947), p. 151. Also Denis Saurat, *Blake and Modern Thought* (London: Constable, 1929), pp. 91ff.

than a century after his death that the depth of his genius began to be understood and a man thought mad by his contemporaries was found to be a bearer of rich insight. The stature of Blake consists in the fact that he was so thoroughly a man of his day and yet transcended his own time. He was an ardent republican who greeted the American and French revolutions with enthusiasm; and the vision of his great prophetic books was compounded with a commitment to peace and liberty and human fulfillment during an era of imperialist war and industrialization. Blake's *Songs of Experience* coincide with a period of economic distress and social unrest, marked with riots and a virtual uprising. His references to "dark, satanic mills" are partly explained by the proliferation of iron-producing furnaces in England from 59 in 1740 to 364 in 1825; and his lament for the "daughters of Albion," tuned to the whir of looms, is documented by a rise in the consumption of raw cotton from 1.6 to 261.2 million pounds during the same period.

Yet a simple economic explanation will not do. Blake anticipates Marx and Engels in his understanding of modern alienation under capitalism and the factory system. He also anticipates them and Hegel as well in his notion of dialectic. And despite the baffling complexity of his prophetic books, they evince a visionary insight into human nature.

Thomas Aquinas distinguished between *ratio*, or reason, as a form of human work, and *intellectus*, as an "angelic faculty," essentially superhuman, given to man as *simplex intuitus* or, as Josef Pieper terms it, "that simple vision to which truth offers itself like a landscape to the eye."[2] This is the source of Blake's unremitting attack on the abstract *ratio* of sense perception as reflected in the rationalism of Bacon and Locke, and in the abstract God of Deism whom he calls Urizen ("your reason"). What Blake calls "intellectual genius" we today would call "insight," but by whatever name it points to the dialectical opposite of Urizen. This opposite is given a variety of names, but perhaps the central concept is "the human form divine" or the "divine humanity," which Blake discerns in the figure of Jesus as one

[2] Josef Pieper, *Leisure, the Basis of Culture* (New York: Mentor-Omega, 1963), p. 26. Cf. Thomas Aquinas, *Quaestiones Disputate*, 1,1.

particular instance, a symbolic individual showing what every individual may become.

Integral to Blake's vision is his insistence not only on political liberty but that there is a complex relationship between the individual and the community. Mere juridical equality is preferable to despotism, but the fulfillment of man's potential can occur only through a recognition that "one law for the lion and ox is oppression"—no two people are alike. Hence Blake rejects not only Urizen but his Old Testament counterpart, the giver of external rules. *The Everlasting Gospel* is Blake's simplest and most mature expression of his consequent view of Jesus as incarnate and living God. When he says, "Thou art a man, God is no more," it is his purpose to assert that "the divine humanity" of Jesus exhausts the relevant meanings of God. There may be such a thing as imperfect man, man without God; but a God apart from man, over against man, is a deceptive abstraction.

What is really real, says Blake, is individuality—the "minute particulars" of actual existence that make up the world of the person. According to the *ratio*, objective reality is limited and measurable. Such a perspective has its uses, but it does not begin to encompass the fullness of human experience. Consider, for example, the length of a measured hour of time. Besides the uniformity given by the clock, there is the very different way in which we experience it—its leanness or fullness. One hour may simply elapse, while another may burgeon and overflow with a whole lifetime's meaning. There are moments of ordinary happening, and there are moments that are full of life, suffused with infinity—moments of ripeness, of discovery, of crucifixion and resurrection. The potential divinity of man, prefigured in Jesus, cannot be turned into an axiom of reason. Rather, Blake sees it as a discoverable reality to be sought through an enhanced perception of what we experience. The *ratio* tells us that a grain of sand is merely an object, and it implies that man too can be reduced to a similar kind of definition. Hence Blake's insistence that vision can disclose "a world in a grain of sand," that insight can penetrate beyond the body, which is the rind of the soul, and encounter the infinite vastness within.

There Is No Natural Religion may be regarded as Blake's first important religious writing. In its first version, 1788, he attacks deism and Locke's notion that the idea of God is constructed from sensory data. The central idea in the *Songs of Experience*, which had preceded it, was essentially a naïve expression of the Quaker doctrine of the "inner light." Now Blake asserts a more articulate extra-organic sensibility, "the Poetic or Prophetic character." In the second version, a year later, he adds a further distinction, between limited and unbounded or infinite sense perception, emphasizing the actual experience of the "Infinite" in man and the world.[3]

All Religions Are One signifies, says Northrop Frye, "that the material world provides a universal language of images and that each man's imagination speaks that language with his own accent. Religions are grammars of this language. Seeing is believing, and belief is vision . . ."[4]

It is in *The Marriage of Heaven and Hell* that the Blakean dialectic comes to the fore. Implicit to it is the notion, manifested in his later writings, that "innocence becomes experience by energy; and to that end must submit to becoming guilty."[5] J. Bronowski compares this process to the "plain negation" of experience characteristic of John Wesley's view of innocence, as in Wesley's hymn:

> O hide this self from me, that I
> No more, but Christ in me may live;
> My vile affections crucify,
> Nor let one darling lust survive;
> In all things nothing may I see,
> Nothing desire or seek but thee.

Wesley is by no means alone in seeing innocence as a gift of grace from on high, given to passive man. Yet on its face, it identifies innocence with what Freud would call repression; it is predi-

---

[3] See E. D. Hirsch Jr., *Innocence and Experience* (New Haven: Yale, 1964), p. 12.
[4] Frye, *op. cit.*, p. 28.
[5] J. Bronowski, *William Blake and the Age of Revolution* (New York: Harper & Row, 1965), pp. 163, 165.

cated not on the expansion of vision but on its narrowing—it is a counsel of immaturity. Norman O. Brown sees a close parallel between Blake's "energy" and Freud's "libido":

> Freud and Blake are asserting that the ultimate essence of our being remains in our unconscious secretly faithful to the principle of pleasure, or, as Blake calls it, delight. To say this is to call in question the psychological assumptions upon which our Western morality has been built. For two thousand years or more man has been subjected to a systematic effort to transform him into an ascetic animal.[6]

Again, referring to Blake's phrase "Exuberance is Beauty," Brown sees that "the self-activity and self-enjoyment of the narcissistic Eros must consist in an overflow outward into the world"[7] —a humanistic parallel to Luther's interpretation of God's creativity as "*quellende Liebe.*"[8]

The Marriage of Heaven and Hell takes the form of a polemical satire on Swedenborg; hence its wisdom is offered as "infernal," and allowances must be made for inconsistencies here since some of Blake's usages are straightforward while others are ironic and inverted. The net effect, however, is a protest not only against Swedenborg but against every static and authoritarian conception of religion, be it rationalistic deism or "state religion." Such a conception is that of "official Christianity," which preaches blind obedience to an external God of the *status quo* and prescribes that very "slave morality" which Nietzsche was later to excoriate.

There are striking affinities between Nietzsche and Blake. The subject of *The Marriage of Heaven and Hell* could well be called "beyond good and evil," and there is a psychological kinship between the will to power and the act of vision; each asserts a form of self-transcendence from within, the affirmation of existence through self-awareness. And yet it is Blake who achieves a vitally humanistic perspective centering on a radically new under-

---

[6] Norman O. Brown, *Life Against Death* (New York: Vintage, 1959), p. 31.
[7] *Ibid.*, p. 49.
[8] See Anders Nygren, *Agapé and Eros* (Philadelphia: Westminster, 1953), p. 729.

standing of Jesus, which is most simply expressed in *The Ever-lasting Gospel*. As Frye points out, for Blake the final revelation of Christianity is not that Jesus is God, but that God is Jesus, "the universal Man who is the unified form of our scattered imaginations," hence "a compelling Word who continually recreates an unconscious floundering universe into something with beauty and intelligence."[9] The image of Jesus that we find in *The Everlasting Gospel* is not foreign to that of the New Testament, particularly the writings of John, but it is elucidated by Blake's psychological insight that humanity is, by definition, creative and "supernatural." It is by man's vision, by his creative imagination, that he transcends nature and is able to transform it into civilization. We are able to regard the world that we see as "fallen" because our imagination discloses one that is better and more real.[10] What man has elevated to the stature of God is, to the eye of unfettered vision, a perception of Man—or as Frye puts it, "we perceive *as* God; we do not perceive God. . . . as we cannot perceive anything higher than a man, nothing higher than Man can exist. . . . There is no form of life superior to our own; and the acceptance of Jesus as the fullness of both God and Man entails the rejection of all attributes of divinity which are not human."[11]

Blake is indeed a forgotten ancestor. None of the writings in this anthology owes anything to his influence until we come to Altizer. And yet his writings are a veritable seedbed of the same kinds of developments in religious thought that came to fruition in the course of the nineteenth and twentieth centuries. We may, for example, trace the idea of "the eternal Now" to the aphorisms of Lavater, which Tillich read a century after Blake; but not every such coincidence will find so convenient an explanation. Perhaps it would make more sense to see in Blake a prototype of discovery and response to characteristically modern experiences that have been repeated in different forms and at different levels as a spiral of revolutionary change embracing recurrent impacts of urbanization, secularization and the hope of liberty

[9] Frye, *op. cit.*, p. 52.
[10] Cf. Harvey Cox's remark about imagination in relation to the "theology of the future" in his essay in this anthology, p. 388.
[11] Frye, *op. cit.*, p. 32.

amid advancing threats of depersonalization—to mention only some of the salient features of our age. Despite the proliferation of Blake studies during the past decade or two, we are far from having plumbed his depths or having fully assessed his seminal influence for tomorrow's thinking.

The spelling, punctuation and arrangement of the following selections are those found in David V. Erdman, ed., *The Poetry and Prose of William Blake* (Garden City: Doubleday, 1965), which painstakingly reproduces the original. Any oddities or irregularities are Blake's own.

THERE is NO Natural Religion

The Author & Printer W Blake

[a]

The Argument.   Man has no notion of moral fitness but from Education. Naturally he is only a natural organ subject to Sense.

I   Man cannot naturally Percieve. but through his natural or bodily organs.

II   Man by his reasoning power. can only compare & judge of what he has already perciev'd.

III   From a perception of only 3 senses or 3 elements none could deduce a fourth or fifth

IV   None could have other than natural or organic thoughts if he had none but organic perceptions

V   Mans desires are limited by his perceptions. none can desire what he has not perciev'd

VI   The desires & perceptions of man untaught by any thing but organs of sense, must be limited to objects of sense.

Conclusion.   If it were not for the Poetic or Prophetic character the Philosophic & Experimental would soon be at the ratio of all things, & stand still unable to do other than repeat the same dull round over again

THERE is NO Natural Religion

[b]

I   Mans perceptions are not bounded by organs of perception. he percieves more than sense (tho' ever so acute) can discover.

II   Reason or the ratio of all we have already known. is not the same that it shall be when we know more.

[III lacking]

IV   The bounded is loathed by its possessor. The same dull round even of a univer[s]e would soon become a mill with complicated wheels

V   If the many become the same as the few when possess'd, More! More! is the cry of a mistaken soul, less than All cannot satisfy Man.

VI   If any could desire what he is incapable of possessing, despair must be his eternal lot.

VII   The desire of Man being Infinite the possession is Infinite & himself Infinite

Application.   He who sees the Infinite in all things sees God. He who sees the Ratio only sees himself only.

Therefore God becomes as we are, that we may be as he is

ALL RELIGIONS are ONE

The Voice of one crying in the Wilderness

The Argument.   As the true method of knowledge is experiment the true faculty of knowing must be the faculty which experiences. This faculty I treat of.

PRINCIPLE 1st   That the Poetic Genius is the true Man. and that the body or outward form of Man is derived from the Poetic Genius. Likewise that the forms of all things are derived from their Genius. which by the Ancients was call'd an Angel & Spirit & Demon.

PRINCIPLE 2^d As all men are alike in outward form, So (and with the same infinite variety) all are alike in the Poetic Genius

PRINCIPLE 3^d No man can think write or speak from his heart, but he must intend truth. Thus all sects of Philosophy are from the Poetic Genius adapted to the weaknesses of every individual

PRINCIPLE 4.   As none by travelling over known lands can find out the unknown. So from already acquired knowledge Man could not acquire more. therefore an universal Poetic Genius exists

PRINCIPLE. 5.   The Religeons of all Nations are derived from each Nation's different reception of the Poetic Genius which is every where call'd the Spirit of Prophecy.

PRINCIPLE 6   The Jewish & Christian Testaments are An original derivation from the Poetic Genius. this is necessary from the confined nature of bodily sensation

PRINCIPLE 7th As all men are alike (tho' infinitely various) So all Religions & as all similars have one source.

The true Man is the source he being the Poetic Genius

THE MARRIAGE of HEAVEN and HELL

PLATE 2

The Argument.

Rintrah roars & shakes his fires in the burdend air;
Hungry clouds swag on the deep

Once meek, and in a perilous path,
The just man kept his course along
The vale of death.
Roses are planted where thorns grow.
And on the barren heath
Sing the honey bees.

Then the perilous path was planted:
And a river, and a spring
On every cliff and tomb;

And on the bleached bones
Red clay brought forth.

Till the villain left the paths of ease,
To walk in perilous paths, and drive
The just man into barren climes.

Now the sneaking serpent walks
In mild humility.
And the just man rages in the wilds
Where lions roam.

Rintrah roars & shakes his fires in the burdend air;
Hungry clouds swag on the deep.

PLATE 3

As a new heaven is begun, and it is now thirty-three years since
its advent: the Eternal Hell revives. And lo! Swedenborg is the
Angel sitting at the tomb; his writings are the linen clothes folded
up. Now is the dominion of Edom, & the return of Adam into
Paradise; see Isaiah xxxiv & XXXV Chap:
Without Contraries is no progression. Attraction and Repulsion,
Reason and Energy, Love and Hate, are necessary to Human
existence.
From these contraries spring what the religious call Good &
Evil. Good is the passive that obeys Reason[.] Evil is the active
springing from Energy.
Good is Heaven. Evil is Hell.

PLATE 4

The voice of the Devil

All Bibles or sacred codes. have been the causes of the following Errors.
1. That Man has two real existing principles Viz: a Body & a
Soul.
2. That Energy. calld Evil. is alone from the Body. & that
Reason. calld Good. is alone from the Soul.

3. That God will torment Man in Eternity for following his Energies. But the following Contraries to these are True

1 Man has no Body distinct from his Soul for that calld Body is a portion of Soul discernd by the five Senses, the chief inlets of Soul in this age

2 Energy is the only life and is from the Body and Reason is the bound or outward circumference of Energy.

3 Energy is Eternal Delight

PLATE 5

Those who restrain desire, do so because theirs is weak enough to be restrained; and the restrainer or reason usurps its place & governs the unwilling.

And being restraind it by degrees becomes passive till it is only the shadow of desire.

The history of this is written in Paradise Lost. & the Governor or Reason is call'd Messiah.

And the original Archangel or possessor of the command of the heavenly host, is calld the Devil or Satan and his children are call'd Sin & Death

But in the Book of Job Miltons Messiah is call'd Satan.

For this history has been adopted by both parties

It indeed appear'd to Reason as if Desire was cast out, but the Devils account is, that the Messi[PL 6]ah fell. & formed a heaven of what he stole from the Abyss

This is shewn in the Gospel, where he prays to the Father to send the comforter or Desire that Reason may have Ideas to build on, the Jehovah of the Bible being no other than he, who dwells in flaming fire. Know that after Christs death, he became Jehovah.

But in Milton; the Father is Destiny, the Son, a Ratio of the five senses. & the Holy-ghost, Vacuum!

Note. The reason Milton wrote in fetters when he wrote of Angels & God, and at liberty when of Devils & Hell, is because he was a true Poet and of the Devils party without knowing it

A Memorable Fancy.

As I was walking among the fires of hell, delighted with the enjoyments of Genius; which to Angels look like torment and insanity. I collected some of their Proverbs: thinking that as the sayings used in a nation, mark its character, so the Proverbs of Hell, shew the nature of Infernal wisdom better than any description of buildings or garments.

When I came home; on the abyss of the five senses, where a flat sided steep frowns over the present world. I saw a mighty Devil folded in black clouds, hovering on the sides of the rock, with cor[PL 7]roding fires he wrote the following sentence now percieved by the minds of men, & read by them on earth.

How do you know but ev'ry Bird that cuts the airy way,
Is an immense world of delight, clos'd by your senses five?

Proverbs of Hell.

In seed time learn, in harvest teach, in winter enjoy.
Drive your cart and your plow over the bones of the dead.
The road of excess leads to the palace of wisdom.
Prudence is a rich ugly old maid courted by Incapacity.
He who desires but acts not, breeds pestilence.
The cut worm forgives the plow.
Dip him in the river who loves water.
A fool sees not the same tree that a wise man sees.
He whose face gives no light, shall never become a star.
Eternity is in love with the productions of time.
The busy bee has no time for sorrow.
The hours of folly are measur'd by the clock, but of wisdom: no
      clock can measure.
All wholsom food is caught without a net or a trap.
Bring out number weight & measure in a year of dearth.
No bird soars too high. if he soars with his own wings.
A dead body. revenges not injuries.
The most sublime act is to set another before you.

If the fool would persist in his folly he would become wise
Folly is the cloke of knavery.
Shame is Prides cloke.

PLATE 8

Prisons are built with stones of Law, Brothels with bricks of
    Religion.
The pride of the peacock is the glory of God.
The lust of the goat is the bounty of God.
The wrath of the lion is the wisdom of God.
The nakedness of woman is the work of God.
Excess of sorrow laughs. Excess of joy weeps.
The roaring of lions, the howling of wolves, the raging of the
    stormy sea, and the destructive sword. are portions of eter-
    nity too great for the eye of man.
The fox condemns the trap, not himself.
Joys impregnate. Sorrows bring forth.
Let man wear the fell of the lion. woman the fleece of the sheep.
The bird a nest, the spider a web, man friendship.
The selfish smiling fool. & the sullen frowning fool. shall be both
    thought wise. that they may be a rod.
What is now proved was once, only imagin'd.
The rat, the mouse, the fox, the rabbet; watch the roots, the lion,
    the tyger, the horse, the elephant, watch the fruits.
The cistern contains: the fountain overflows
One thought. fills immensity.
Always be ready to speak your mind, and a base man will avoid
    you.
Every thing possible to be believ'd is an image of truth.
The eagle never lost so much time. as when he submitted to learn
    of the crow.

PLATE 9

The fox provides for himself. but God provides for the lion.
Think in the morning, Act in the noon, Eat in the evening, Sleep
    in the night.

He who has sufferd you to impose on him knows you.

As the plow follows words, so God rewards prayers.

The tygers of wrath are wiser than the horses of instruction

Expect poison from the standing water.

You never know what is enough unless you know what is more
than enough.

Listen to the fools reproach! it is a kingly title!

The eyes of fire, the nostrils of air, the mouth of water, the beard
of earth.

The weak in courage is strong in cunning.

The apple tree never asks the beech how he shall grow, nor the
lion. the horse, how he shall take his prey.

The thankful reciever bears a plentiful harvest.

If others had not been foolish, we should be so.

The soul of sweet delight, can never be defil'd,

When thou seest an Eagle, thou seest a portion of Genius. lift up
thy head!

As the catterpiller chooses the fairest leaves to lay her eggs on, so
the priest lays his curse on the fairest joys.

To create a little flower is the labour of ages.

Dam. braces: Bless relaxes.

The best wine is the oldest. the best water the newest.

Prayers plow not! Praises reap not!

Joys laugh not! Sorrows weep not!

PLATE 10

The head Sublime, the heart Pathos, the genitals Beauty, the
hands & feet Proportion.

As the air to a bird or the sea to a fish, so is contempt to the
contemptible.

The crow wish'd every thing was black, the owl, that every thing
was white.

Exuberance is Beauty.

If the lion was advise'd by the fox. he would be cunning.

Improve[me]nt makes strait roads, but the crooked roads without
Improvement, are roads of Genius.

Sooner murder an infant in its cradle than nurse unacted desires
Where man is not nature is barren.
Truth can never be told so as to be understood, and not be
believ'd.

Enough! or Too much

PLATE 11

The ancient Poets animated all sensible objects with Gods or
Geniuses, calling them by the names and adorning them with the
properties of woods, rivers, mountains, lakes, cities, nations, and
whatever their enlarged & numerous senses could percieve.
And particularly they studied the genius of each city & country.
placing it under its mental deity.
Till a system was formed, which some took advantage of &
enslav'd the vulgar by attempting to realize or abstract the mental
deities from their objects; thus began Priesthood.
Choosing forms of worship from poetic tales.
And at length they pronounced that the Gods had orderd such
things.
Thus men forgot that All deities reside in the human breast.

PLATE 12

A Memorable Fancy.

The Prophets Isaiah and Ezekiel dined with me, and I asked
them how they dared so roundly to assert. that God spake to
them; and whether they did not think at the time, that they would
be misunderstood, & so be the cause of imposition.
Isaiah answer'd. I saw no God, nor heard any, in a finite organi-
cal perception; but my senses discover'd the infinite in every
thing, and as I was then perswaded, & remain confirm'd; that
the voice of honest indignation is the voice of God, I cared not
for consequences but wrote.
Then I asked: does a firm perswasion that a thing is so, make
it so?

He replied. All poets believe that it does, & in ages of imagination this firm perswasion removed mountains; but many are not capable of a firm perswasion of any thing.

Then Ezekiel said. The philosophy of the east taught the first principles of human perception   some nations held one principle for the origin & some another, we of Israel taught that the Poetic Genius (as you now call it) was the first principle and all the others merely derivative, which was the cause of our despising the Priests & Philosophers of other countries, and prophecying that all Gods [PL 13] would at last be proved to originate in ours & to be the tributaries of the Poetic Genius, it was this. that our great poet King David desired so fervently & invokes so patheticly, saying by this he conquers enemies & governs kingdoms; and we so loved our God. that we cursed in his name all the deities of surrounding nations, and asserted that they had rebelled; from these opinions the vulgar came to think that all nations would at last be subject to the jews.

This said he, like all firm perswasions, is come to pass, for all nations believe the jews code and worship the jews god, 'and what greater subjection can be.

I heard this with some wonder, & must confess my own conviction. After dinner I ask'd Isaiah to favour the world with his lost works, he said none of equal value was lost. Ezekiel said the same of his.

I also asked Isaiah what made him go naked and barefoot three years? he answered, the same that made our friend Diogenes the Grecian.

I then asked Ezekiel. why he eat dung, & lay so long on his right & left side? he answerd. the desire of raising other men into a perception of the infinite   this the North American tribes practise. & is' he honest who resists his genius or conscience. only for the sake of present ease or gratification?

PLATE 14

The ancient tradition that the world will be consumed in fire at the end of six thousand years is true. as I have heard from Hell.

For the cherub with his flaming sword is hereby commanded

to leave his guard at tree of life, and when he does, the whole creation will be consumed, and appear infinite, and holy whereas it now appears finite & corrupt.

This will come to pass by an improvement of sensual enjoyment.

But first the notion that man has a body distinct from his soul, is to be expunged; this I shall do, by printing in the infernal method, by corrosives, which in Hell are salutary and medicinal, melting apparent surfaces away, and displaying the infinite which was hid.

If the doors of perception were cleansed every thing would appear to man as it is, infinite.

For man has closed himself up, till he sees all things thro' narrow chinks of his cavern.

A Memorable Fancy

I was in a Printing house in Hell & saw the method in which knowledge is transmitted from generation to generation.

In the first chamber was a Dragon-Man, clearing away the rubbish from a caves mouth; within, a number of Dragons were hollowing the cave,

In the second chamber was a Viper folding round the rock & the cave, and others adorning it with gold silver and precious stones.

In the third chamber was an Eagle with wings and feathers of air, he caused the inside of the cave to be infinite, around were numbers of Eagle like men, who built palaces in the immense cliffs.

In the fourth chamber were Lions of flaming fire raging around & melting the metals into living fluids.

In the fifth chamber were Unnam'd forms, which cast the metals into the expanse.

There they were reciev'd by Men who occupied the sixth chamber, and took the forms of books & were arranged in libraries.

PLATE 16

The Giants who formed this world into its sensual existence and now seem to live in it in chains, are in truth. the causes of its life & the sources of all activity, but the chains are, the cunning of weak and tame minds. which have power to resist energy, according to the proverb, the weak in courage is strong in cunning.

Thus one portion of being, is the Prolific. the other, the Devouring: to the devourer it seems as if the producer was in his chains, but it is not so, he only takes portions of existence and fancies that the whole.

But the Prolific would cease to be Prolific unless the Devourer as a sea recieved the excess of his delights.

Some will say, Is not God alone the Prolific? I answer, God only Acts & Is, in existing beings or Men.

These two classes of men are always upon earth, & they should be enemies; whoever tries [PL 17] to reconcile them seeks to destroy existence.

Religion is an endeavour to reconcile the two.

Note. Jesus Christ did not wish to unite but to seperate them, as in the Parable of sheep and goats! & he says I came not to send Peace but a Sword.

Messiah or Satan or Tempter was formerly thought to be one of the Antediluvians who are our Energies.

A Memorable Fancy

An Angel came to me and said   O pitiable foolish young man! O horrible! O dreadful state! consider the hot burning dungeon thou art preparing for thyself to all eternity, to which thou art going in such career.

I said, perhaps you will be willing to shew me my eternal lot & we will contemplate together upon it and see whether your lot or mine is most desirable

So he took me thro' a stable & thro' a church & down into the church vault at the end of which was a mill: thro' the mill we went, and came to a cave. down the winding cavern we groped our tedious way till a void boundless as a nether sky appeard beneath us. & we held by the roots of trees and hung over this immensity, but I said, if you please we will commit ourselves to this void, and see whether providence is here also, if you will not I will? but he answered, do not presume O young-man but as we here remain behold thy lot which will soon appear when the darkness passes away

So I remaind with him sitting in the twisted [PL 18] root of an oak. he was suspended in a fungus which hung with the head downward into the deep;

By degrees we beheld the infinite Abyss, fiery as the smoke of a burning city; beneath us at an immense distance was the sun, black but shining[;] round it were fiery tracks on which revolv'd vast spiders, crawling after their prey; which flew or rather swum in the infinite deep, in the most terrific shapes of animals sprung from corruption. & the air was full of them, & seemd composed of them; these are Devils. and are called Powers of the air, I now asked my companion which was my eternal lot? he said, between the black & white spiders

But now, from between the black & white spiders a cloud and fire burst and rolled thro the deep   blackning all beneath, so that the nether deep grew black as a sea & rolled with a terrible noise: beneath us was nothing now to be seen but a black tempest, till looking east between the clouds & the waves, we saw a cataract of blood mixed with fire and not many stones throw from us appeard and sunk again the scaly fold of a monstrous serpent[.] at last to the east, distant about three degrees appeard a fiery crest above the waves[.] slowly it reared like a ridge of golden rocks till we discoverd two globes of crimson fire, from which the sea fled away in clouds of smoke, and now we saw, it was the head of Leviathan, his forehead was divided into steaks of green & purple like those on a tygers forehead: soon we saw his mouth & red gills hang just above the raging foam tinging the black deep with beams of blood, advancing toward [PL 19] us with all the fury of a spiritual existence.

My friend the Angel climb'd up from his station into the mill; I remain'd alone, & then this appearance was no more, but I found myself sitting on a pleasant bank beside a river by moon light hearing a harper who sung to the harp, & his theme was, The man who never alters his opinion is like standing water, & breeds reptiles of the mind.

But I arose, and sought for the mill, & there I found my Angel, who surprised asked me, how I escaped?

I answerd. All that we saw was owing to your metaphysics: for when you ran away, I found myself on a bank by moonlight hearing a harper, But now we have seen my eternal lot, shall I shew you yours? he laughd at my proposal; but I by force suddenly caught him in my arms, & flew westerly thro' the night, till we were elevated above the earths shadow: then I flung myself with him directly into the body of the sun, here I clothed myself in white, & taking in my hand Swedenborgs volumes sunk from the glorious clime, and passed all the planets till we came to saturn, here I staid to rest & then leap'd into the void, between saturn & the fixed stars.

Here said I! is your lot, in this space, if space it may be calld, Soon we saw the stable and the church, & I took him to the altar and open'd the Bible, and lo! it was a deep pit, into which I descended driving the Angel before me, soon we saw seven houses of brick, one we enterd; in it were a [PL 20] number of monkeys, baboons, & all of that species chaind by the middle, grinning and snatching at one another, but witheld by the shortness of their chains: however I saw that they sometimes grew numerous, and then the weak were caught by the strong and with a grinning aspect, first coupled with & then devourd, by plucking off first one limb and then another till the body was left a helpless trunk. this after grinning & kissing it with seeming fondness they devourd too; and here & there I saw one savourily picking the flesh off of his own tail; as the stench terribly annoyd us both we went into the mill, & I in my hand brought the skeleton of a body, which in the mill was Aristotles Analytics.

So the Angel said: thy phantasy has imposed upon me & thou oughtest to be ashamed.

I answerd: we impose on one another, & it is but lost time to converse with you whose works are only Analytics

Opposition is true Friendship.

PLATE 21

I have always found that Angels have the vanity to speak of themselves as the only wise; this they do with a confident insolence sprouting from systematic reasoning;

Thus Swedenborg boasts that what he writes is new; tho' it is only the Contents or Index of already publish'd books

A man carried a monkey about for a shew, & because he was a little wiser than the monkey, grew vain, and conciev'd himself as much wiser than seven men. It is so with Swedenborg; he shews the folly of churches & exposes hypocrites, till he imagines that all are religious. & himself the single [PL 22] one on earth that ever broke a net.

Now hear a plain fact: Swedenborg has not written one new truth: Now hear another: he has written all the old falshoods.

And now hear the reason. He conversed with Angels who are all religious, & conversed not with Devils who all hate religion, for he was incapable thro' his conceited notions.

Thus Swedenborgs writings are a recapitulation of all superficial opinions, and an analysis of the more sublime, but no further.

Have now another plain fact: Any man of mechanical talents may from the writings of Paracelsus or Jacob Behmen, produce ten thousand volumes of equal value with Swedenborg's: and from those of Dante or Shakespear, an infinite number.

But when he has done this, let him not say that he knows better than his master, for he only holds a candle in sunshine.

A Memorable Fancy

Once I saw a Devil in a flame of fire. who arose before an Angel that sat on a cloud. and the Devil utterd these words.

The worship of God is. Honouring his gifts in other men each according to his genius. and loving the [PL 23] greatest men best, those who envy or caluminate great men hate God, for there is no other God.

The Angel hearing this became almost blue but mastering himself he grew yellow, & at last white pink & smiling, and then replied,

Thou Idolater, is not God One? & is not he visible in Jesus Christ? and has not Jesus Christ given his sanction to the law of ten commandments and are not all other men fools, sinners, & nothings?

The Devil answer'd; bray a fool in a morter with wheat. yet shall not his folly be beaten out of him: if Jesus Christ is the greatest man, you ought to love him in the greatest degree; now hear how he has given his sanction to the law of ten commandments: did he not mock at the sabbath, and so mock the sabbaths God? murder those who were murderd because of him? turn away the law from the woman taken in adultery? steal the labor of others to support him? bear false witness when he omitted making a defence before Pilate? covet when he pray'd for his disciples, and when he bid them shake off the dust of their feet against such as refused to lodge them? I tell you, no virtue can exist without breaking these ten commandments.˙. Jesus was all virtue, and acted from im[PL 24]pulse. not from rules.

When he had so spoken: I beheld the Angel who stretched out his arms embracing the flame of fire & he was consumed and arose as Elijah.

Note. This Angel, who is now become a Devil, is my particular friend: we often read the Bible together in its infernal or diabolical sense which the world shall have if they behave well

I have also: The Bible of Hell: which the world shall have whether they will or no.

One Law for the Lion & Ox is Oppression

PLATE 25

A Song of Liberty

1. The Eternal Female groand! it was heard over all the Earth:
2. Albions coast is sick silent; the American meadows faint!
3. Shadows of Prophecy shiver along by the lakes and the rivers and mutter across the ocean? France rend down thy dungeon;
4. Golden Spain burst the barriers of old Rome;
5. Cast thy keys O Rome into the deep down falling, even to eternity down falling,

6. And weep

7. In her trembling hands she took the new born terror howling:

8. On those infinite mountains of light now barr'd out by the atlantic sea, the new born fire stood before the starry king!

9. Flag'd with grey brow'd snows and thunderous visages the jealous wings wav'd over the deep.

10. The speary hand burned aloft, unbuckled was the shield, forth went the hand of jealousy among the flaming hair, and [PL 26] hurl'd the new born wonder thro' the starry night.

11. The fire, the fire, is falling!

12. Look up! look up! O citizen of London. enlarge thy countenance; O Jew, leave counting gold! return to thy oil and wine; O African! black African! (go. winged thought widen his forehead.)

13. The fiery limbs, the flaming hair, shot like the sinking sun into the western sea.

14. Wak'd from his eternal sleep, the hoary element roaring fled away:

15. Down rushd beating his wings in vain the jealous king; his grey brow'd councellors, thunderous warriors, curl'd veterans, among helms, and shields, and chariots[,] horses, elephants: banners, castles, slings and rocks,

16. Falling, rushing, ruining! buried in the ruins, on Urthona's dens.

17. All night beneath the ruins, then their sullen flames faded emerge round the gloomy king,

18. With thunder and fire: leading his starry hosts thro' the waste wilderness [PL 27] he promulgates his ten commands, glancing his beamy eyelids over the deep in dark dismay,

19. Where the son of fire in his eastern cloud, while the morning plumes her golden breast,

20. Spurning the clouds written with curses, stamps the stony law to dust, loosing the eternal horses from the dens of night, crying

Empire is no more! and now the lion & wolf shall cease.

Chorus

Let the Priests of the Raven of dawn, no longer in deadly black, with hoarse note curse the sons of joy. Nor his accepted brethren

whom, tyrant, he calls free: lay the bound or build the roof. Nor
pale religious letchery call that virginity, that wishes but acts not!
  For every thing that lives is Holy

The Everlasting Gospel

PAGES 52–54

Was Jesus Humble or did he
Give any Proofs of Humility
Boast of high Things with Humble tone
And give with Charity a Stone
When but a Child he ran away
And left his Parents in dismay
When they had wanderd three days long
These were the words upon his tongue
No Earthly Parents I confess
I am doing my Fathers business
When the rich learned Pharisee
Came to consult him secretly
Upon his heart with Iron pen
He wrote Ye must be born again
He was too proud to take a bribe
He spoke with authority not like a Scribe
He says with most consummate Art
Follow me I am meek & lowly of heart
As that is the only way to escape
The Misers net & the Gluttons trap
What can be done with such desperate Fools
Who follow after the Heathen Schools
I was standing by when Jesus died
What I calld Humility they calld Pride
He who loves his Enemies betrays his Friends
This surely is not what Jesus intends
But the sneaking Pride of Heroic Schools
And the Scribes & Pharisees Virtuous Rules

For he acts with honest triumphant Pride
And this is the cause that Jesus died
He did not die with Christian Ease
Asking pardon of his Enemies
If he had Caiphas would forgive
Sneaking submission can always live
He had only to say that God was the devil
And the devil was God like a Christian Civil
Mild Christian regrets to the devil confess
For affronting him thrice in the Wilderness
He had soon been bloody Caesars Elf
And at last he would have been Caesar himself
Like d^r Priestly & Bacon & Newton
Poor Spiritual Knowledge is not worth a button
For thus the Gospel Sr Isaac confutes
God can only be known by his Attributes
And as for the Indwelling of the Holy Ghost
Or of Christ & his Father its all a boast
And Pride & Vanity of the imagination
That disdains to follow this Worlds Fashion
To teach doubt & Experiment
Certainly was not what Christ meant
What was he doing all that time
From twelve years old to manly prime
Was he then Idle or the Less
About his Fathers business
Or was his wisdom held in scorn
Before his wrath began to burn
In Miracles throughout the Land
That quite unnervd Caiaphas hand
If he had been Antichrist Creeping Jesus
Hed have done any thing to please us
Gone sneaking into Synagogues
And not usd the Elders & Priests like dogs
But Humble as a Lamb or Ass
Obeyd himself to Caiaphas
God wants not Man to Humble himself
This is the trick of the ancient Elf

This is the Race that Jesus ran
Humble to God Haughty to Man
Cursing the Rulers before the People
Even to the temples highest Steeple
And when he Humbled himself to God
Then descended the Cruel Rod
If thou humblest thyself thou humblest me
Thou also dwellst in Eternity
Thou art a Man God is no more
Thy own humanity learn to adore
For that is my Spirit of Life
Awake arise to Spiritual Strife
And thy Revenge abroad display
In terrors at the Last Judgment day
Gods Mercy & Long Suffering
Is but the Sinner to Judgment to bring
Thou on the Cross for them shalt pray
And take Revenge at the Last Day
Jesus replied & thunders hurld
I never will Pray for the World
Once [I] did so when I prayd in the Garden
I wishd to take with me a Bodily Pardon
Can that which was of woman born
In the absence of the Morn
When the Soul fell into Sleep
And Archangels round it weep
Shooting out against the Light
Fibres of a deadly night
Reasoning upon its own dark Fiction
In doubt which is Self Contradiction
Humility is only doubt
And does the Sun & Moon blot out
Rooting over with thorns & stems
The buried Soul & all its Gems.
This Lifes dim Windows of the Soul
Distorts the Heavens from Pole to Pole
And leads you to Believe a Lie
When you see with not thro the Eye

That was born in a night to perish in a night
When the Soul slept in the beams of Light.

PAGES 48–52

Was Jesus Chaste or did he
Give any Lessons of Chastity
The morning blushd fiery red
Mary was found in Adulterous bed
Earth groand beneath & Heaven above
Trembled at discovery of Love
Jesus was sitting in Moses Chair
They brought the trembling Woman There
Moses commands she be stoned to death
What was the sound of Jesus breath
He laid His hand on Moses Law
The Ancient Heavens in Silent Awe
Writ with Curses from Pole to Pole
All away began to roll
The Earth trembling & Naked lay
In secret bed of Mortal Clay
On Sinai felt the hand Divine
Putting back the bloody shrine
And she heard the breath of God
As she heard by Edens flood
Good & Evil are no more
Sinais trumpets cease to roar
Cease finger of God to write
The Heavens are not clean in thy Sight
Thou art Good & thou Alone
Nor may the sinner cast one stone
To be Good only is to be
A God or else a Pharisee
Thou Angel of the Presence Divine
That didst create this Body of Mine
Wherefore has thou writ these Laws
And Created Hells dark jaws

My Presence I will take from thee
A Cold Leper thou shalt be
Tho thou wast so pure & bright
That Heaven was Impure in thy Sight
Tho thy Oath turnd Heaven Pale
Tho thy Covenant built Hells Jail
Tho thou didst all to Chaos roll
With the Serpent for its soul
Still the breath Divine does move
And the breath Divine is Love
Mary Fear Not Let me see
The Seven Devils that torment thee
Hide not from my Sight thy Sin
That forgiveness thou maist win
Has no Man Condemned thee
No Man Lord! then what is he
Who shall Accuse thee. Come Ye forth
Fallen Fiends of Heavnly birth
That have forgot your Ancient love
And driven away my trembling Dove
You shall bow before her feet
You shall lick the dust for Meat
And tho you cannot Love but Hate
Shall be beggars at Loves Gate
What was thy love Let me see it
Was it love or Dark Deceit
Love too long from Me has fled.
Twas dark deceit to Earn my bread
Twas Covet or twas Custom or
Some trifle not worth caring for
That they may call a shame & Sin
Loves temple that God dwelleth in
And hide in secret hidden Shrine
The Naked Human form divine
And render that a Lawless thing
On which the Soul Expands its wing
But this O Lord this was my Sin
When first I let these Devils in

In dark pretence to Chastity
Blaspheming Love blaspheming thee
Thence Rose Secret Adulteries
And thence did Covet also rise
My sin thou hast forgiven me
Canst thou forgive my Blasphemy
Canst thou return to this dark Hell
And in my burning bosom dwell
And canst thou die that I may live
And canst thou Pity & forgive
Then Rolld the shadowy Man away
From the Limbs of Jesus to make them his prey
An Ever devo[u]ring appetite
Glittering with festering Venoms bright
Crying Crucify this cause of distress
Who dont keep the secrets of Holiness
All Mental Powers by Diseases we bind
But he heals the Deaf & the Dumb & the Blind
Whom God has afflicted for Secret Ends
He comforts & Heals & calls them Friends
But when Jesus was Crucified
Then was perfected his glittring pride
In three Nights he devourd his prey
And still he devours the Body of Clay
For dust & Clay is the Serpents meat
Which never was made for Man to Eat

PAGES 100–101

Was Jesus gentle or did he
Give any marks of Gentility
When twelve years old he ran away
And left his Parents in dismay
When after three days sorrow found
Loud as Sinai's trumpet sound
No Earthly Parents I confess
My Heavenly Fathers business

Ye understand not what I say
And angry force me to obey
Obedience is a duty then
And favour gains with God & Men
John from the Wilderness loud cried
Satan gloried in his Pride
Come said Satan come away
Ill soon see if youll obey
John for disobedience bled
But you can turn the stones to bread
Gods high king & Gods high Priest
Shall Plant their Glories in your breast
If Caiaphas you will obey
If Herod you with bloody Prey
Feed with the Sacrifice & be
Obedient fall down worship me
Thunders & lightnings broke around
And Jesus voice in thunders sound
Thus I sieze the Spiritual Prey
Ye smiters with disease make way
I come Your King & God to sieze
Is God a Smiter with disease
The God of this World raged in vain
He bound Old Satan in his Chain
And bursting forth his furious ire
Became a Chariot of fire
Throughout the land he took his course
And traced diseases to their source
He cursd the Scribe & Pharisee
Trampling down Hipocrisy
Where eer his Chariot took its way
There Gates of Death let in the day
Broke down from every Chain & Bar
And Satan in his Spiritual War
Dragd at his Chariot wheels loud howld
The God of this World louder rolld
The Chariot Wheels & louder still
His voice was heard from Zions hill

And in his hand the Scourge shone bright
He scourgd the Merchant Canaanite
From out the Temple of his Mind
And in his Body tight does bind
Satan & all his Hellish Crew
And thus with wrath he did subdue
The Serpent Bulk of Natures dross
Till he had naild it to the Cross
He took on Sin in the Virgins Womb
And put it off on the Cross & Tomb
To be Worshipd by the Church of Rome

PAGE 33

The Vision of Christ that thou dost see
Is my Visions Greatest Enemy
Thine has a great hook nose like thine
Mine has a snub nose like to mine
Thine is the friend of All Mankind
Mine speaks in parables to the Blind
Thine loves the same world that mine hates
Thy Heaven doors are my Hell Gates
Socrates taught what Melitus
Loathd as a Nations bitterest Curse
And Caiphas was in his own Mind
A benefactor to Mankind
Both read the Bible day & night
But thou readst black where I read white

II

CHANGING CONCEPTS OF RELIGION

Friedrich Daniel Ernst Schleiermacher

[1768–1834]

MATTHEW ARNOLD, at the end of the nineteenth century, described religion as "morality touched with emotion," and sought to salvage Christian truth for modern man by setting aside dogma and letting the Bible speak as literature. By substituting "The Eternal" for a plainly anthropomorphic God, Arnold set out to mediate between orthodoxy and unbelief, to provide an increasingly secular age with access to a simplified version of the traditional faith. In so doing, he was repeating a task performed at the beginning of the century by Friedrich Schleiermacher. The tradition which embraces both men is not, properly speaking, a radical one; but it is significant as an influential trend within Protestant thought as well as in the churches' encounter with the world.

Schleiermacher was, in Karl Barth's words, "*the* great theologian of the Prussian Church Union."[1] His *Reden über die Religion* reflect the secular and religious situation of their time, 1799, when Napoleon's armies were advancing across Europe and the ideas of the Enlightenment, typified by Immanuel Kant, had already begun to penetrate the churches under the banner of "rationalism." At the same time, strong currents of Pietism and orthodoxy

---

[1] Karl Barth, *Theology and Church* (New York: Harper & Row, 1962), p. 166. An excellent brief introduction to Schleiermacher's thought, written in 1926, constitutes one chapter of this collection of essays. See also Richard R. Niebuhr, *Schleiermacher on Christ and Religion* (New York: Scribner, 1964).

persisted in a social order barely begun to emerge from feudalism and yet to experience the impact of industrialization.

Schleiermacher's thought is conventional in its theological vocabulary of sin, grace, the Trinity, etc., and there is much in it of the preacher and pastor. As a philosopher, Schleiermacher is at best a minor figure *among* philosophers—but an extremely important one for the church. Like Kierkegaard in a different context, he is an enlightened son of the Pietist tradition, transforming its naïve emphases on "inwardness," "purity of heart" and the like into a psychological understanding of religion as a matter of *Gefühl* (feeling) and *Erlebnis* (inner experience). He is concerned to expound and systematize the inherited dogmas of the church, but he insists that these are derivative and in a sense lifeless unless man can have the "insights and feelings" that can make them meaningful. Hence he predicates revelation on man's ability to experience "the divine in us"; Christian doctrine is, so to speak, latently true but dependent upon man's God-consciousness to make it actually true *for us*. As he states explicitly in the following extract from the *Reden*, the concept of God as a transcendent being is at best inadequate; what counts is "immediate consciousness of the Deity as He is found in ourselves and in the world."[2] This may not be an unequivocal assertion of immanence or radical subjectivity, but it is in line with the modern thrust and it is not surprising that his influence continues to be felt within the church more than a century after his death.

---

[2] "He postulated the intuition of the infinite in the finite as the essence of religion. Thus religion was founded on aesthetic principles."—Paul Tillich, *Die religionsgeschichtliche Konstruktion in Schellings positiver Philosophie* (Breslau: 1910), p. 95n. Tillich goes on to contrast this position with that of Hegel, quoting the latter: "Religion is only through and in thought. God is not the highest feeling (*Empfindung*), He is the highest thought." (*Religionsphilosophie*, I, 62.)

The God of Feeling and Intuition[1]

Every man, a few choice souls excepted, does, to be sure, require a guide to lead and stimulate, to wake his religious sense from its first slumber, and to give it its first direction. But this you accord to all powers and functions of the human soul, and why not to this one? For your satisfaction, be it said, that here, if anywhere, this tutelage is only a passing state. Hereafter, shall each man see with his own eyes, and shall produce some contribution to the treasures of religion; otherwise, he deserves no place in its kingdom, and receives none. You are right in despising the wretched echoes who derive their religion entirely from another, or depend on a dead writing, swearing by it and proving out of it.

Every sacred writing is in itself a glorious production, a speaking monument from the heroic time of religion, but, through servile reverence, it would become merely a mausoleum, a monument that a great spirit once was there, but is now no more. Did this spirit still live and work, he would look with love, and with a feeling of equality upon his work which yet could only be a weaker impress of himself. Not every person has religion who believes in a sacred writing, but only the man who has a lively and immediate understanding of it, and who, therefore, so far as he himself is concerned, could most easily do without it.

Your very contempt for the poverty-stricken and powerless venerators of religion, in whom, from lack of nourishment, religion died before ever it came to the birth, convinces me that you have a talent for religion. The same thing appears from your regard for the persons of all true heroes of religion. That you should treat them with shallow scoffing or not acknowledge what is great or powerful in them, I would hardly ascribe to you. This regard for the persons confirms me in the thought that your contempt for the thing rests merely on a misunderstanding, and has

[1] From *On Religion: Speeches to Its Cultured Despisers.* The title above is mine, not Schleiermacher's. The text is from the chapter titled "The Nature of Religion."—Ed.

for its object only the miserable figure which religion takes in the great incapable mass, and the abuses which presumptuous leaders carry on.

I have tried, as best I could, therefore, to show you what religion really is. Have you found anything therein unworthy of you, nay, of the highest human culture? Must you not rather long all the more for that universal union with the world which is only possible through feeling, the more you are separated and isolated by definite culture and individuality? Have you not often felt this holy longing, as something unknown? Become conscious of the call of your deepest nature and follow it, I conjure you. Banish the false shame of a century which should not determine you but should be made and determined by you. Return to what lies so near to you, yes, even to you, the violent separation from which cannot fail to destroy the most beautiful part of your nature.

It appears to me, however, that many among you do not believe that I can here mean to end my present business. How can I have spoken thoroughly of the nature of religion, seeing I have not treated at all of immortality, and of God only a little in passing? Is it not incumbent upon me, most of all, to speak of these two things and to represent to you how unhappy you would be without belief in them? For are not these two things, for most pious people, the very poles and first articles of religion?

But I am not of your opinion. First of all, I do not believe I have said nothing about immortality and so little about God. Both, I believe, are in all and in everything that I have adduced as an element of religion. Had I not presupposed God and immortality I could not have said what I have said, for, only what is divine and immortal has room in which to speak of religion.

In the second place, just as little do I consider that I have the right to hold the conceptions and doctrines of God and of immortality, as they are usually understood, to be the principal things in religion. Only what in either is feeling and immediate consciousness, can belong to religion. God and immortality, however, as they are found in such doctrines, are ideas. How many among you—possibly most of you—are firmly convinced of one or other or both of those doctrines, without being on that account pious or having religion. As ideas they can have no greater value in religion than ideas generally.

But that you may not think I am afraid to speak a straightforward word on this subject, because it would be dangerous to speak, till some definition of *God* and *existence* that has stood its trial has been brought to light and has been accepted in the German Empire as good and valid; or lest you should, on the other hand, perhaps, believe that I am playing on you a pious fraud and wish, in order to be all things to all men, with seeming indifference to make light of what must be of far greater importance to me than I will confess—lest you should think these things, I shall gladly be questioned and will endeavor to make clear to you that, according to my best conviction, it really is, as I have just now maintained.

Remember in the first place that any feeling is not an emotion of piety because in it a single object as such affects us, but only insofar as in it and along with it, it affects us as revelation of God. It is, therefore, not an individual or finite thing, but God, in whom alone the particular thing is one and all, that enters our life. Nor do we stand over against the world and in it at the same time by any one faculty, but by our whole being. The divine in us, therefore, is immediately affected and called forth by the feeling. Seeing then that I have presented nothing but just this immediate and original existence of God in us through feeling, how can anyone say that I have depicted a religion without God? Is not God the highest, the only unity? Is it not God alone before whom and in whom all particular things disappear? And if you see the world as a Whole, a Universe, can you do it otherwise than in God? If not, how could you distinguish the highest existence, the original and eternal Being from a temporal and derived individual? Otherwise than by the emotions produced in us by the world we do not claim to have God in our feeling, and consequently I have not said more of Him.

If you will not admit that this is to have God, and to be conscious of Him, I can neither teach nor direct you farther. How much you may know I do not judge, for it does not at present concern me, but in respect of feeling and sentiment, you would be for me godless. Science, it is true, is extolled as giving an immediate knowledge about God, that is the source of all other knowledge; only we are not now speaking of science, but of religion. This way of knowing about God which most praise and which I also am to laud is neither the idea of God as the undivided unity and source of all that is placed by you at the head of all knowledge, nor is it the feeling of God in the heart, of which we boast ourselves. It lags far behind the demands of science, and is for piety something quite subordinate. It is an idea compounded from characteristics, from what are called attributes of God. These attributes correspond to the different ways in which the unity of the individual and the Whole, expresses itself in feeling. Hence I can only say of this idea what I have said of ideas generally, in reference to religion, that there can be much piety without it, and that it is first formed when piety is made an object of contemplation.

Yet this idea of God, as it is usually conceived, is different from the other ideas before adduced, for though it seeks to be the highest and to stand above all, God, being thought of as too like us, as a thinking and willing Person, is drawn down into the region of opposition. It therefore appears natural that the more like man God is conceived, the more easily another mode of presentation is set over against it. Hence, we have an idea of the Highest Being, not as personally thinking and willing, but exalted above all personality, as the universal, productive, connecting necessity of all thought and existence.

Nothing seems to me less fitting than for the adherents of the former view to charge with godlessness those who, in dread of this anthropomorphism, take refuge in the other, or for the adherents of this latter view to make the humanness of the idea of God a ground for charging the adherents of the former with idolatry, or for declaring their piety void.

It matters not what conceptions a man adheres to, he can still be pious. His piety, the divine in his feeling, may be better than his conception, and his desire to place the essence of piety in conception only makes him misunderstand himself. Consider how narrow is the presentation of God in the one conception, and how dead and rigid in the other. Neither corresponds to its object, and thus cannot be a proof of piety, except insofar as it rests on something in the mind, of which it has come far short. Rightly understood, both present, at least, one element of feeling, but, without feeling, neither is of any value. Many believe in and accept a God presented in conception, and yet are nothing less than pious, and in no case is this conception the germ from which their piety could ever spring, for it has no life in itself. Neither conception is any sign of a perfect or of an imperfect religion, but perfection and imperfection depend upon the degree of cultivation of the religious sense. As I know of nothing more that could bring us to an understanding on this subject of conceptions, let us now go on to consider the development of the religious sense.

As long as man's whole relation to the world has not arrived at clearness, this feeling is but a vague instinct, the world can appear to him nothing but a confused unity. Nothing of its complexity is definitely distinguishable. It is to him a chaos, uniform in its confusion, without division, order, or law. Apart from what most immediately concerns the subsistence of man, he distinguishes nothing as individual except by arbitrarily cutting it off in time and space. Here you will find but few traces of any conceptions, and you will scarcely discern to which side they incline. You will not set much value on the difference, whether a blind fate, only to be indicated by magic rites, exhibits the character of the Whole, or a being, alive indeed, but without definite characteristics, an idol, a fetich, one, or, if many, only distinguishable by the arbitrarily appointed limits of their sphere.

As we advance, the feeling becomes more conscious. Circumstances display themselves in their complexity and definiteness. The multiplicity of the heterogeneous elements and powers, by whose constant and determined strife phenomena are determined, becomes more prominent in man's consciousness of the world. In the same degree the result of the contemplation of this feeling changes. The opposite forms of the idea stand more distinctly apart. Blind fate changes into a higher necessity, in which, though unattainable and unsearchable, reason and connection rest. Similarly, the idea of a personal God becomes higher but at the same time divides and multiplies; each power and element becomes animate, and gods arise in endless number. They are now distinguishable by means of the different objects of their activity, and different inclinations and dispositions. A stronger, fairer life of the Universe in feeling you must acknowledge is here exhibited. It is most beautiful when this new-won complexity and this innate highest unity are most intimately bound together in feeling, as, for example, among the Greeks, whom you so justly revere. Both forms then unite in reflection, one being of more value for thought, the other for art, one showing more of the complexity, the other of the unity. But this stage, even without such a union, is more perfect than the former, especially if the idea of the Highest Being is placed rather in the eternal unattainable necessity than in single gods.

Let us now mount higher where opposing elements are again united, where existence, by exhibiting itself as totality, as unity in variety, as system, first deserves its name. Is not the man who perceives existence both as one and as all, who stands over against the Whole, and yet is one with it in feeling, to be accounted happier in his religion, let his feeling mirror itself in idea as it may? There as elsewhere, then, the manner in which the Deity is present to man in feeling is decisive of the worth of his religion, not the manner, always inadequate, in which it is copied in idea. Suppose there is someone arrived at this stage who rejects the idea of a personal God. I will not decide on the justice of the names you are accustomed to apply to him, whether Pantheist or Spinozist. This rejection of the idea of a personal Deity does not decide against the presence of the Deity in his feeling. The ground of such a rejection might be a humble consciousness of the limitation of personal existence, and particularly of personality joined to consciousness. He might stand as high above a worshiper of the twelve gods whom you would rightly name after Lucretius as a pious person at that stage would be above an idolater.

But we have here the old confusion, the unmistakable sign of defective culture. Those who are at the same stage, only not at the same point, are most strongly repudiated. The proper standard of religiousness, that which announces the stage to which a man has attained, is his sense for the Deity. But to which idea he will attach himself depends purely on what he requires it for, and whether his imagination chiefly inclines towards existence and nature or consciousness and thought.

You will not, I trust, consider it blasphemy or incongruity that such a matter should depend on the direction of the imagination. By imagination I do not mean anything subordinate or confused, but the highest and most original faculty in man. All else in the human mind is simply reflection upon it, and is therefore dependent on it. Imagination in this sense is the free generation of thoughts, whereby you come to a conception of the world; such a conception you cannot receive from without, nor compound from inferences. From this conception you are then impressed with the feeling of omnipotence. The subsequent translation into thought depends on whether one is willing in the consciousness of his own weakness to be lost in the mysterious obscurity, or whether, first of all, seeking definiteness of thought, he cannot think of anything except under the one form given to us, that of consciousness or self-consciousness. Recoil from the obscurity of indefinite thought is the one tendency of the imagination, recoil from the appearance of contradiction in transferring the forms of the finite to the Infinite is the other.

Now cannot the same inwardness of religion be combined with both? Would not a closer consideration show that the two ways of conceiving are not very wide apart? But the pantheistic idea is not to be thought of as death, and no effort is to be spared to surpass in thought the limits of the personal idea.

So much I have thought it necessary to say, not so much in explanation of my own position, as to prevent you from thinking that all are despisers of religion who will not accept the personality of the Highest Being as it is usually set forth. And I am quite convinced that what has been said will not make the idea of the personality of God more uncertain for anyone who truly has it; nor will anyone more easily rid himself of the almost absolute necessity to acquire it, for knowing whence this necessity comes. Among truly religious men there have never been zealots, enthusiasts, or fanatics for this idea. Even when timidity and hesitation about it is called atheism, truly pious persons will leave it alone with great tranquillity. Not to have the Deity immediately present in one's feeling has always seemed to them more irreligious. They would most unwillingly believe that anyone could in point of fact be quite without religion. They believe that only those who are quite without feeling, and whose nature has become brutish, can have no consciousness of the God that is in us and in the world, and of the divine life and operation whereby all things consist. But whosoever insists, it matters not how many excellent men he excludes, that the highest piety consists in confessing that the Highest Being thinks as a person and wills outside the world, cannot be far traveled in the region of piety. Nay, the profoundest words of the most zealous defenders of his own faith must still be strange to him.

The number who would have something from this God, that is alien to piety, is only too great. He is to give an outward guarantee of their blessedness and incite them to morality. They want to have it before their eyes. They would not have God working on man by freedom, but in the only way in which one free being can work on another, by necessity, by making himself known either by pain or by pleasure. But this cannot incite us to morality. Every external incitement is alien to morality, whether it be hope or fear. To follow it where it concerns morality is unfree, therefore unmoral. But the Highest Being, particularly when he is thought of as free, cannot wish to make freedom itself not free, and morality not moral.

This now brings me to the second point, to immortality. I cannot conceal that in the usual manner of treating this subject there is still more that seems to me inconsistent with the nature of piety. I believe I have just shown you in what way each one bears in himself an unchangeable and eternal nature. If our feeling nowhere attaches itself to the individual, but if its content is our relation to God wherein all that is individual and fleeting disappears, there can be nothing fleeting in it, but all must be eternal. In the religious life, then, we may well say we have already offered up and disposed of all that is mortal, and that we actually are enjoying immortality. But the immortality that most men imagine and their longing for it seem to me irreligious, nay, quite opposed to the spirit of piety. Dislike to the very aim of religion is the ground of their wish to be immortal. Recall how religion earnestly strives to expand the sharply cut outlines of personality. Gradually they are to be lost in the Infinite that we, becoming conscious of the Universe, may as much as possible be one with it. But men struggle against this aim. They are anxious about their personality, and do not wish to overstep the accustomed limit or to be anything else but a manifestation of it. The one opportunity that death gives them of transcending it they are very far from wishing to embrace. On the contrary, they are concerned as to how they are to carry it with them beyond this life, and their utmost endeavor is for longer sight and better limbs. But God speaks to them as it stands written, "Whosoever loses his life for my sake, the same shall keep it, and whosoever keeps it, the same shall lose it." The life that they would keep is one that cannot be kept. If their concern is with the eternity of their single person, why are they not as anxious about what it has been as about what it is to be? What does forwards avail when they cannot go backwards? They desire an immortality that is no immortality. They are not even capable of comprehending it, for who can endure the effort to conceive an endless temporal existence? Thereby they lose the immortality they could always have, and their mortal life in addition, by thoughts that distress and torture them in vain. Would they but attempt to surrender their lives from love to God! Would they but strive to annihilate their personality and to live in the One and in the All! Whosoever has learned to be more than himself knows that he loses little when he loses himself. Only the man who denying himself sinks himself in as much of the whole Universe as he can attain, and in whose soul a greater and holier longing has arisen, has a right to the hopes that death gives. With him alone it is really possible to hold further converse about the endlessness to which, through death, we infallibly soar.

This then is my view of these subjects. The usual conception of God as one single being outside of the world and behind the world is not the beginning and the end of religion. It is only one manner of expressing God, seldom entirely pure and always inadequate. Such an idea may be formed from mixed motives, from the need for such a being to console and help, and such a God may be believed in without piety, at least in my sense, and

I think in the true and right sense. If, however, this idea is formed, not arbitrarily, but somehow by the necessity of a man's way of thinking, if he needs it for the security of his piety, the imperfections of his idea will not cumber him nor contaminate his piety. Yet the true nature of religion is neither this idea nor any other, but immediate consciousness of the Deity as He is found in ourselves and in the world. Similarly the goal and the character of the religious life is not the immortality desired and believed in by many—or what their craving to be too wise about it would suggest, pretended to be believed in by many. It is not the immortality that is outside of time, behind it, or rather after it, and which still is in time. It is the immortality which we can now have in this temporal life; it is the problem in the solution of which we are forever to be engaged. In the midst of finitude to be one with the Infinite and in every moment to be eternal is the immortality of religion.

Georg W. F. Hegel

[1770–1831]

TWO YEARS YOUNGER than Schleiermacher and a fellow member of the faculty of the University of Berlin, Hegel's influence on the whole course of modern thought was vast. "Without contraries is no progression," wrote Blake. For Hegel this insight, derived from pre-Socratic philosophers such as Heraklitos, Anaximenes and Anaximander, became a central element in an all-encompassing system of philosophy. Mind and matter, soul and body, belief and understanding, subject and object, essence and substance, the individual and the state—these are all treated dialectically as parts of a historic process whereby mankind moves toward the ultimate resolution of the discrepancy between what is and what should be.

Although Hegel was later to become an apologist for the Prussian state as well as for Lutheran orthodoxy, his earliest writings and indeed the genesis of his system and method were given strong impetus by the French Revolution. Hegel was a theology student at Tübingen when the Bastille fell, and as late as 1806 he was an admirer of Napoleon. In that year he rejoiced at the French victory in the battle of Jena—at the time, he happened to be *Privatdozent* at Jena, and finished his *Phänomenologie des Geistes* the day before the great battle. Even before Waterloo, the optimism of his youth began to wane and the concept of "historical necessity" came to resolve the contradiction between individual freedom and social order in terms of the latter. But the question initially arose from an observed discrepancy between enlightened verbiage about "the dignity of man" and actual conditions of despotism and serfdom in Hegel's native Württemberg,

49

a circumstance that led young Hegel to extol the ancient Athenian city-state as he did the virtues of early Christianity.

For Hegel, Christianity had a definite place in world history, representing the "absolute religion" as a culmination and purification of earlier forms of religion, providing man with an "absolute" center and life with a final goal. He emphasized Christ as the unifying resolution of the dialectical contradiction between spirit and matter, between God and man. Implicit in his earlier writings is a sense that the gospel of Christ could point the way to freedom in the political and socio-economic order. As his thinking evolved, it took on a less theological, more clearly philosophical character. An excellent if partial summary of the outcome is given by Herbert Marcuse:

> Hegel's philosophy is in a large sense a reinterpretation of Aristotle's ontology, rescued from the distortion of metaphysical dogma and linked to the pervasive demand of modern rationalism that the world be transformed into a medium for the freely developing subject, that the world become, in short, the reality of reason.[1]

And, Marcuse adds, Hegel was the first philosopher to appropriate the Aristotelian notion of being as process. The reference to Aristotle is apt, for Hegel represents not so much the inauguration of a new line of thought as the definitive culmination of an old one.

> Hegel's system brings to a close the entire epoch in modern philosophy that had begun with Descartes and had embodied the basic ideas of modern society. Hegel was the last to interpret the world as reason, subjecting nature and history alike to the standards of thought and freedom.[2]

Hegel took the quest as far as it could go in terms of reason and cosmic process, and his system constituted a springboard for its own dialectical negation, and with it the negation of theology and of the metaphysical view of history. As Martin Buber puts it, "The Hegelian house of the universe is admired, explained and

[1] Herbert Marcuse, *Reason and Revolution* (New York: Oxford University Press, 1941), p. 42.
[2] *Ibid.*, p. 252.

imitated; but it proves uninhabitable."[3] And even more to the point:

> In Hegel's system, Messianism is secularized, that is, it is trans-
> ferred from the sphere of faith . . . to the sphere of evident con-
> viction . . . Faith in creation may be replaced by a conviction
> about evolution, faith in revelation by a conviction about increas-
> ing knowledge, but faith in salvation will not really be replaced
> by a conviction about the perfecting of the world by the idea,
> since only trust in the trustworthy is able to establish a relation
> of unconditional certainty toward the *future*.[4]

What is lacking in Hegel is the pragmatism of empirical science—yet the latter, lacking a purposive structure or concept of
process, was mechanistic. It is in large part from the encounter
between the two that modern social theory emerged. Not only
Marxism but sociology as a whole, political science, social and
individual psychology, and anthropology are all partially indebted
to this encounter for their theoretical bases, enabling them to be
not merely speculative but logically rigorous and self-critical—
and above all secular, even when dealing with matters of religion
and ethics. We need not wait for the humanism of Royce, Whitehead, Dewey and Santayana to see its effects in philosophy and
in religious studies; the reaction is already under way among the
so-called Young Hegelians, men a generation younger than Hegel
himself—Strauss and Feuerbach in particular.

For these and other thinkers, the question of the obsolescence
of Christianity or the "death of God" is the pursuit of an issue
raised by Hegel himself. A pivotal statement of the issue is his
essay "Glauben und Wissen" (1802), a radical critique of the
transcendental idealism of Kant, Fichte and Jacobi. Its rather
dense, cryptic concluding paragraph is a milestone in the transition from faith to knowledge or, as Buber puts it above, "evident
conviction," which is the dialectical product of these two opposites. Hegel distinguishes three forms that the same spiritual
content can take: feeling, as in Schleiermacher, imagination or

[3] Martin Buber, *Between Man and Man* (London: Fontana Library, 1961),
p. 173.
[4] *Ibid.*, p. 175.

figurative thought, and objective conceptual thought. Feeling and imagination are both subjective and capricious, finally only matters of whim and opinion. "God is essentially in the process of conceptual thought," which is the true province of philosophy, and it is the philosopher's task to discard those forms which belong to feeling and imagination. As Karl Löwith has said,

> The final sentences of "Glauben und Wissen" are a culmination of this exaltation of religion to the level of "'philosophical existence"; they transform the death of God into a "speculative Good Friday." The historico-empirical "feeling" that God himself is dead, this infinite grief "which forms the basis for the religion of the modern era," must be comprehended as a "component" of the "ultimate ideal," namely as a component of absolute freedom![5]

Commenting on the same passage, Carl Michalson paraphrases from the extract from the *Phänomenologie* which follows it in this volume:

> The crucifixion of God is not only the event in history, celebrated by Luther in one of his chorales, "God himself is dead." It is a productive though painful event in the dialectical process of the mind. The human mind must pass through the "Good Friday of speculation," where the abstract God is crucified, in order for it to pass on to the Easter of the Absolute Idea, where God comes to life as a concrete God.[6]

Like so much of Hegel's writing, the pages from the *Phänomenologie* given here resist summary or interpretation except in relation to his system as a whole, a task that is beyond our present scope. But even a casual reading suggests that there is support here for Altizer's thesis concerning the incarnation and crucifixion as parts of a dialectical process in which God as the Absolute empties himself into the world, thus abolishing transcendence and inaugurating a new age of the immanent Spirit. In the realm

---

[5] Karl Löwith, *From Hegel to Nietzsche* (New York: Holt, Rinehart & Winston, 1964), p. 333.
[6] Carl Michalson, *The Boundary Between Faith and Reason* (Madison, N. J.: Drew University Studies), p. 10.

of thought, this for Hegel is true history, above the empirical. According to Löwith, Hegel simultaneously transforms and vindicates the religious thought with which he began. At the same time, he raises its content above religion. In a former age, philosophy had been a handmaiden of faith; now the circumstance is not just a turning of the tables but a definitive critique in which reason absorbs the content of faith and negates its "weaker" forms. "The historical consequence of Hegel's ambiguous 'translation' was an absolute destruction of Christian philosophy and of the Christian religion."[7] Even for Kierkegaard, the "knight of faith," this now became the basis not for the defense of Christianity but for its reconstruction. For others, notably Strauss and Feuerbach, the task was seen quite differently. And for Marx, the problem of God was removed entirely from philosophy as such and deposited in the realm of ideology, as part of the ideational superstructure. In short, Hegel's secularization of religious thought opens the door to a new variety of humanism, implicitly or explicitly atheistic, and poses an indelible challenge to theism in all its manifestations.

The Good Friday of Speculation[1]

The pure concept, however, or infinity (*Unendlichkeit*), as the abyss of nothingness (*Nichts*) into which all Being sinks, must denote infinite (*unendlichen*) pain which previously was historical only in culture (*Bildung*) and as the feeling (*Gefühl*) on which the religion of today is based—the feeling: God himself is dead (which Pascal expressed, so to speak, only empirically: *la nature est telle qu'elle marque partout un Dieu perdu et dans*

---

[7] Löwith, *op. cit.*

[1] From "Glauben und Wissen, oder die Reflexions-philosophie der Subjektivität," *Kritische Journal der Philosophie*, Band II, Stück I, 1802. This journal was edited by Hegel and Schelling. The essay may also be found in G. W. F. Hegel, *Sämtliche Werke*, Jubiläumsausgabe, vol. 1 (Stuttgart: Fr. Frommer, 1927). For an alternative translation, see Ronald Gregor Smith, *Secular Christianity* (New York: Harper & Row, 1966), p. 160.—Ed.

l'homme et hors de l'homme),[2] purely as a moment of the highest
Idea, yet not as more than a moment; and so it [the pure con-
cept] must also give a philosophical existence to what happened
to be either a moral rule (*Vorschrift*) for a self-sacrifice of empirical reality (*Wesen*) or else the concept of formal abstraction,
and therefore it restores to philosophy the idea of absolute freedom, and therewith the absolute sorrow or the speculative Good
Friday which otherwise was historical precisely in the utter hardness and truth of its godlessness:—out of which hardness alone
(because what was more cheerful, careless and individual in the
dogmatic philosophies, just as in the natural religions, had to
disappear) the highest Totality in its full seriousness and from
its deepest basis, all-embracing, can and must be resurrected, and
in the clearest freedom of its form (*Gestalt*).

from *The Phenomenology of the Spirit*[1]

But this self, through its being empty, has let the content go;
this consciousness is Being merely within itself. Its own existence,
the legal recognition of the person, is an unfulfilled empty abstraction. It thus really possesses merely the thought of itself; in
other words, as it there exists and knows itself as object, it is
something unreal. Consequently, it is merely stoic independence,
the independence of thought; and this finds, by passing through
the process of skepticism, its ultimate truth in that form we called
the "unhappy self-consciousness"—the soul of despair.

This knows how the case stands with the actual claims to
validity which the abstract [legal] person puts forward, as also
with the validity of this person in pure thought [in Stoicism]. It
knows that a vindication of such validity means really being
altogether lost; it is just this loss become conscious of itself, and

---

[2] "nature is such that it bears witness everywhere to a lost God, both in man
and outside him"—*Pensées*, 130 (Lafuma ed.), trans. Martin Turnell (London: Harvill, 1962). But see the full context, in which it appears that God
is "lost" to man because of the latter's sin.—Ed.

[1] Trans. J. B. Baillie as *The Phenomenology of Mind* (London: Allen &
Unwin, 1910).—Ed.

is the surrender and relinquishment of its knowledge about itself. We see that this "unhappy consciousness" constituted the counterpart and the complement of the perfectly happy consciousness, that of comedy. All divine reality goes back into this latter type of consciousness; it means, in other words, the complete relinquishment and emptying of substance. The former, on the contrary, is conversely the tragic fate that befalls certainty of self which aims at being absolute, at being self-sufficient. It is consciousness of the loss of everything of significance in this certainty of itself, and of the loss even of this knowledge or certainty of self—the loss of substance as well as of self; it is the bitter pain which finds expression in the cruel words, "God is dead."[2]

In the condition of right or law, then, the ethical world has vanished, and its type of religion has passed away in the mood of Comedy. The "unhappy consciousness," the soul of despair, is just the knowledge of all this loss. It has lost both the worth and dignity it attached to its immediate personality [as a legal person] as well as that attaching to its personality when reflected in the medium of thought [in the case of Stoicism]. Trust in the eternal laws of the gods is likewise silenced, just as the oracles are dumb, who pretended to know what to do in particular cases. The statues set up are now corpses in stone whence the animating soul has flown, while the hymns of praise are words from which all belief has gone. The tables of the gods are bereft of spiritual food and drink, and from his games and festivals man no more receives the joyful sense of his unity with the Divine Being. The works of the muse lack the force and energy of the spirit which derived the certainty and assurance of itself just from the crushing ruin of gods and men. They are themselves now just what they are for us—beautiful fruit broken off the tree; a kindly fate has passed on those works to us, as a maiden might offer such fruit off a tree. Their actual life as they exist is no longer there, not the tree that bore them, not the earth and the elements, which constituted their substance, nor the climate that determined their constitutive character, nor the change of seasons which controlled the process of their growth. So too it is not their living world that Fate preserves and gives us with those works of ancient art, not the spring

2 From a hymn of Luther.

and summer of that ethical life in which they bloomed and ripened, but the veiled remembrance alone of all this reality. . . .

The reconciliation of the Divine Being with its other as a whole, and, specifically, with the *thought* of this other—evil—is thus presented here in a figurative way. If this reconciliation is expressed *conceptually*, by saying it consists in the fact that evil is inherently the same as what goodness is, or again that the Divine Being is the same as Nature in its entire extent, just as Nature separated from God is simply nothingness, then this must be looked at as an unspiritual mode of expression which is bound to give rise to misunderstandings. When evil is the *same* as goodness, then evil is just *not* evil nor goodness good; on the contrary, both are really done away with—evil in general, self-centered self-existence, and goodness, self-less simplicity. Since in this way they are both expressed in terms of their notion, the unity of the two is at once apparent; for self-centered self-existence is simple knowledge; and what is self-less simplicity is similarly pure self-existence centered within itself. Hence, if it must be said that good and evil in this their conception, i.e. so far as they are *not* good and evil, are the same, just as certainly it must be said that they are not the same, but absolutely different; for simple self-existence, or again pure knowledge, are equally pure negativity or *per se* absolute distinction. It is only these two propositions that make the whole complete; and when the first is asserted and asseverated, it must be met and opposed by insisting on the other with immovable obstinacy. Since both are equally right, they are both equally wrong, and their wrong consists in taking such abstract forms as "the same" and "not the same," "identity" and "nonidentity," to be something true, fixed, real, and in resting on them. Neither the one nor the other has truth; their truth is just their movement, the process in which simple sameness is abstraction and thus absolute distinction, while this again, being distinction *per se*, is distinguished from itself and so is self-identity. Precisely this is what we have in sameness of the Divine Being and Nature in general and human nature in particular: the former is Nature so far as it is not essential Being; Nature is Divine in its essential Being. But it is in Spirit that we find both abstract aspects affirmed as they truly are, viz. as canceled and preserved at once: and this way of affirming them cannot be expressed by the judgment, by the soulless word "is," the copula of the judgment. In the same way Nature is nothing outside its essential Being [God]; but this nothing itself *is* all the same; it is absolute abstraction, therefore pure thought or self-centeredness, and with its moment of opposition to spiritual unity it is the principle of Evil. The difficulty people find in these conceptions is due solely to sticking to the term "is," and forgetting the character of thought, where the moments as much *are* as they *are not*—are only the process which is Spirit. It is this spiritual unity—unity where the distinctions are merely in the form of moments, or as transcended—which became known to pictorial thinking in that atoning reconciliation spoken of above. And since this unity is the universality of self-consciousness, self-consciousness has ceased to be figurative or pictorial in its thinking; the process has turned back into it.

Spirit thus takes up its position in the third element, in universal self-consciousness: Spirit is its own community. The movement of this community being that of self-consciousness, which distinguishes itself from its figurative idea, consists in explicitly bringing out what has implicitly become established. The dead Divine Man, or Human God, is implicitly universal self-consciousness; he has to become explicitly so for this self-consciousness. Or, since this self-consciousness constitutes one side of the opposition involved in figurative thought, viz. the side of evil, which takes natural existence and individual self-existence to be the essential reality—this aspect, which is pictured as independent, and not yet as a moment, has, on account of its independence, to raise itself in and for itself to the level of spirit; it has to reveal the process of Spirit in its self.

This particular self-consciousness is Spirit in natural form, natural spirit: self has to withdraw from this natural existence and enter into itself, become self-centered; that would mean, it has to become evil. But this aspect is already *per se* evil: entering into itself consists, therefore, in persuading itself that natural existence is what is evil. By picture-thinking the world is supposed actually to become evil and be evil as an actual fact, and the atoning reconcilement of the Absolute Being is viewed as an actual existent phenomenon. By self-consciousness as such, however, this pictured truth, as regards its form, is considered to be merely a moment that is already superseded and transcended; for the self is the negative, and hence knowledge—a knowledge which is a pure act of consciousness within itself. This moment of the negative must in like manner find expression in the content. Since, that is to say, the essential Being is inherently and from the start reconciled with itself and is a spiritual unity, in which what are parts for figurative thought are sublated, are moments, what we find is that each part of figurative thought receives here the opposite significance to that which it had before. By this means each meaning finds its completion in the other, and the content is then and thereby a spiritual content. Since the specific determinateness of each is just as much its opposite, unity in otherness—spiritual reality—is achieved: just as formerly we saw the opposite meanings combined objectively (*für uns*), or in themselves, and even the abstract forms of "the same" and "not-the-same," "identity" and "nonidentity" canceled one another and were transcended.

If, then, from the point of view of figurative thought, the becoming self-centered on the part of the natural self-consciousness was actually existing evil, that process of becoming fixed in itself is in the sphere of self-consciousness, the *knowledge of evil* as something that *per se* belongs to existence. This knowledge is certainly a process of becoming evil, but merely of the *thought* of evil, and is therefore recognized as the first moment of reconciliation. For, being a return into self out of the immediacy of nature, which is specifically characterized as evil, it is a forsaking of that immediacy, and a dying to sin. It is not natural existence as such that consciousness forsakes, but natural existence that is at the same time known to be evil. The immediate process of becoming self-centered is just as much a mediate process: it presupposes itself, i.e. is its own ground and reason: the reason for self-concentrating is because nature has *per se* already done so. Because of evil man must be self-centered (*in sich gehen*); but evil is itself the state of self-concentration. This first movement is just on that account itself merely immediate, is its simple notion, because it is the same as what its ground or reason is.

The movement, or the process of passing into otherness, has therefore still to come on the scene in its own more peculiar form.

Beside this immediacy, then, the mediation of figurative thought is necessary. The knowledge of nature as the untrue existence of spirit, and this universality of self which has arisen within the life of the self—these constitute implicitly the reconciliation of spirit with itself. This implicit state is apprehended by the self-consciousness, that does not comprehend (*Begreifen*), in the form of an objective existence, and as something presented to it figuratively. Conceptual comprehension (*Begreifen*), therefore, does not mean for it a grasping (*Ergreifen*) of this conception (*Begriff*) which knows natural existence when canceled and transcended to be universal and thus reconciled with itself; but rather a grasping of the imaginative idea (*Vorstellung*) that the Divine Being is reconciled with its existence through an event— the event of God's emptying Himself of His Divine Being through His factual Incarnation and His Death. The grasping of this idea now expresses more specifically what was formerly called in figurative thinking spiritual resurrection, or the process by which God's individual self-consciousness[3] becomes the universal, becomes the religious communion. The death of the Divine Man, *qua* death, is abstract negativity, the immediate result of the process which terminates only in the universality belonging to nature. In spiritual self-consciousness death loses this natural significance; it passes into its true conception, the conception just mentioned. Death then ceases to signify what it means directly— the nonexistence of *this* individual—and becomes transfigured into the universality of the spirit, which lives in its own communion, dies there daily, and daily rises again.

That which belongs to the sphere of pictorial thought—viz., that Absolute Spirit presents the nature of spirit in its existence, *qua* individual or rather *qua* particular—is thus here transferred to self-consciousness itself, to the knowledge which maintains itself in its otherness. This self-consciousness does not therefore really die, as the particular person[4] is pictorially imagined to have really died; its particularity expires in its universality, i.e. in its

[3] The Christ.
[4] See above, note 3.

knowledge, which is essential Being reconciling itself with itself. That immediately preceding element of figurative thinking is thus here affirmed as transcended, has, in other words, returned into the self, into its notion. What was in the former merely an (objective) existent has come to assume the form of *Subject.* By that very fact the first element too, pure thought and the spirit eternal therein, are no longer away beyond the mind thinking pictorially nor beyond the self; rather the return of the whole into itself consists just in containing all moments within itself. When the death of the mediator is grasped by the self, this means the sublation of his factuality, of his particular independent existence: this particular self-existence has become universal self-consciousness.

On the other side, the universal, just because of this, is self-consciousness, and the pure or nonactual Spirit of bare thought has become actual. The death of the mediator is death not merely of his *natural* aspect, of his particular self-existence: what dies is not merely the outer encasement, which, being stripped of essential Being, is *eo ipso* dead, but also the abstraction of the Divine Being. For the mediator, as long as his death has not yet accomplished the reconciliation, is something one-sided, which takes as essential Being the simple abstract element of thought, not concrete reality. This one-sided extreme of self has not yet equal worth and value with essential Being; the self first gets this as Spirit. The death of this pictorial idea implies at the same time the death of the abstraction of Divine Being, which is not yet affirmed as a self. That death is the bitterness of feeling of the "unhappy consciousness," when it feels that God Himself is dead. This harsh utterance is the expression of inmost self-knowledge which has simply self for its content; it is the return of consciousness into the depth of darkness where Ego is nothing but bare identity with Ego, a darkness distinguishing and knowing nothing more outside it. This feeling thus means, in point of fact, the loss of the Substance and of its objective existence over against consciousness. But at the same time it is the pure subjectivity of Substance, the pure certainty of itself, which it lacked when it was object or immediacy, or pure essential Being. This knowledge is thus spiritualization, whereby Substance becomes Subject, by which its abstraction and lifelessness have expired, and Substance therefore has become real, simple, and universal self-consciousness.

In this way, then, Spirit is Spirit knowing its own self. It knows itself; that, which is for it object, exists, or, in other words, its figurative idea is the true absolute content. As we saw, the content expresses just Spirit itself. It is at the same time not merely content of self-consciousness, and not merely object *for* self-consciousness; it is also actual Spirit. It is this by the fact of its passing through the three elements of its nature: this movement through its whole self constitutes its actual reality. What moves itself, that is Spirit; it is the subject of the movement, and it is likewise the moving process itself, or the substance through which the subject passes. We saw how the notion of spirit arose when we entered the sphere of religion: it was the process of spirit certain of its self, which forgives evil, and in so doing puts aside its own simplicity and rigid unchangeableness: it was, to state it otherwise, the process, in which what is absolutely in opposition recognizes itself as the same as its opposite, and this knowledge breaks out into the "yea, yea" with which one extreme meets the other. The religious consciousness, to which the Absolute Being is revealed, beholds this notion, and does away with the distinction of its self from what it beholds; and as it is Subject, so it is also Substance; and is thus itself Spirit just because and in so far as it is this process.

This religious communion, however, is not yet fulfilled in this its self-consciousness. Its content, in general, is put before it in the form of a pictorial idea; so that this disruption still attaches even to the actual spiritual character of the communion—to its return out of its figurative thinking; just as the element of pure thought itself was also hampered with that opposition.[5] This spiritual communion is not also consciously aware what it is; it is spiritual self-consciousness, which is not object to itself as this self-consciousness, or does not develop into clear consciousness of itself. Rather, so far as it is consciousness, it has before it those picture-thoughts which were considered.

We see self-consciousness at its last turning point become in-

[5] I.e. between spiritual consciousness and objective idea.

ward to itself and attain to knowledge of its inner being, of its self-centeredness. We see it relinquish its natural existence, and reach pure negativity. But the positive significance—viz. that this negativity, or pure inwardness of knowledge, is just as much the self-identical essential Being: put otherwise, that Substance has here attained to being absolute self-consciousness—this is, for the devotional consciousness, an external other. It grasps this aspect—that the knowledge which becomes purely inward is inherently absolute simplicity, or Substance—as the pictorial idea of something which is not thus by its very conception, but as the act of satisfaction obtained from an (alien) other. . . .

Søren Aabye Kierkegaard

[1813–1855]

THE SEVENTH SON of a wealthy retired merchant, Søren Kierkegaard was born in a great mansion facing Kongens Nytorv, a
beautiful green square in central Copenhagen, just a short distance from Frederiksborg Palace and the Royal Opera House.
His father, as a boy, had been a shepherd on the lonely Jutland
heath, and had once cursed God in his loneliness; but at the age
of twelve he had been taken in charge by a well-to-do uncle and
miraculously set on the path to success in business. The family
name means "churchyard," and was bestowed on peasants who
occupied the glebe of a country church too poor to provide for a
regular pastor. The elder Kierkegaard was fifty-eight when Søren
was born, the last child of a loveless second marriage.

Søren Kierkegaard was frail of body but robust of intellect. As
a youth he was both indulged and dominated by his morose,
devout father. The religion he learned at home as a child was a
grim vision of the crucifixion, unrelieved by the usual images of
"gentle Jesus." It was a religion of sin and guilt. Despite an
inclination to write fiction, he promised his father to study theology and did so. For reasons that remain obscure,[1] he broke his
engagement to a comely young lady and resolved upon a solitary
life, sacrificing himself to religious and philosophical studies. In
his own words, he entered what he considered an "engagement
to God."[2]

The engagement lasted seventeen years and took a variety of

[1] A visit to a brothel in 1836 resulted in severe pangs of guilt. His betrothal
to Regina Olsen in 1838 was followed by his father's death. Although the
old man was eighty-two, Søren somehow construed his death as a sacrifice.
[2] Quoted in Walter Lowrie, *A Short Life of Kierkegaard* (Princeton University Press, 1942), p. 147.

forms. Between 1843 and 1844 he published *Either/Or*, *Repetition*, *The Concept of Dread* and *Fear and Trembling*, works that today are regarded as laying the groundwork of existential philosophy as well as of the psychological understanding of anxiety.[3] His education and viewpoint were by this time virtually complete. An early and enduring attraction to the dialogues of Socrates led to an appreciation for Hegel's dialectic, but as he embraced Christianity he rejected Hegel—partly for his abstracting of God and partly for his absolutizing of the state and its official religion. In the winter of 1841–1842 he spent some four months at the University of Berlin for the express purpose of hearing Schelling "demolish" Hegel, but he soon tired of Schelling's "drivel" and returned to the writing of *Either/Or*, which he had already begun. Although he was familiar with Boehme and Novalis, he rejected mysticism as a means to religious truth. For Kierkegaard, revelation and reason were the dialectical means of discovering and interpreting the truth, which transcended reason and was ultimately to be understood not as mystery but as paradox. The very center of Christian faith, for Kierkegaard, was the paradox of the incarnation.

Kierkegaard's understanding of the Bible, although shrewd, was literalistic, reflecting the ecclesiastical theology he had learned from his father and from his father's friend, Bishop Mynster, primate of the Lutheran state church of Denmark. He was apparently unaffected by Strauss' *Das Leben Jesu* (*The Life of Jesus*), although it was available to him before his first book was written. Yet his Socratic interpretation transmuted Tertullian's "*credo quia absurdam*" into a basic existentialist insight later to be found in the philosophies of Sartre and Camus. In the words of one Danish theologian, "the concept of 'the absurd' is the negative criterion of that which is higher than human reason and human knowledge"[4]—not contrary to reason

---

[3] See Karl Jaspers, *Reason and Existenz* (New York: Noonday, 1955), pp. 19–50. Jaspers' comparison of Kierkegaard and Nietzsche is very illuminating. See also Rollo May, *The Meaning of Anxiety* (New York: Ronald Press, 1950), pp. 27–45, for a detailed discussion of *The Concept of Dread*.
[4] Niels H. Søe, "Kierkegaard's Doctrine of the Paradox" in Johnson and Thulstrup, *A Kierkegaard Critique* (New York: Harper & Row, 1962), p. 209.

but beyond its reach. Among the implications of this idea is the paradox posed by Lessing: How can eternal salvation be dependent on the temporal, historical event of the life and death of Jesus? Lessing resolved the paradox by denying it; Kierkegaard sought not to resolve but to explicate and affirm it. Hence it forms a recurrent theme in his writings, first stated in the following selection from the *Philosophical Fragments* of 1844. In *On Authority and Revelation*, written two years later, he observed:

> The Christian fact has no history, for it is the paradox that God once came into existence in time. . . . whether this was eighteen hundred years ago or yesterday, one can just as well be contemporary with it.[5]

The culmination of this thrust proceeds through *Training in Christianity* (1850), which is a sustained proclamation of the contemporaneity of Christ and a call to discipleship, to *The Attack Upon "Christendom,"* a posthumous compilation of articles documenting Kierkegaard's repudiation of Bishop Mynster and the established church. Not by an explicit disavowal but by a decided shift of emphasis, the Father God of a decade earlier has now receded. The paradox that remains is that of contemporaneity alone, of loyalty to Christ. The issue is not one of transcendence versus immanence but of existence versus essence —of Christianity as a "way to be" versus Christianity as a set of opinions. Even more, it is a matter of honesty, of life and character versus pomp and pretense. To be a Christian is not helped but impeded, he wrote in the last months of his life, by "a complete inventory of churches, bells, organs, foot-warmers, hearses, etc."[6] When asked, on his deathbed, if he wanted to receive communion, he replied, "Yes, but not from a parson . . . royal functionaries are not related to Christianity."[7]

---

[5] Kierkegaard, *On Authority and Revelation* (Princeton University Press, 1955), p. 60.
[6] Quoted in Lowrie, *op. cit.*, p. 249.
[7] *Ibid.*, p. 254.

The Absolute Paradox:
A Metaphysical Crotchet

In spite of the fact that Socrates studied with all diligence to
acquire a knowledge of human nature and to understand himself,
and in spite of the fame accorded him through the centuries as
one who beyond all other men had an insight into the human
heart, he has himself admitted that the reason for his shrinking
from reflection upon the nature of such beings as Pegasus and
the Gorgons was that he, the life-long student of human nature,
had not yet been able to make up his mind whether he was a
stranger monster than Typhon, or a creature of a gentler and
simpler sort, partaking of something divine (*Phaedrus*, 229 E).
This seems to be a paradox. However, one should not think
slightingly of the paradoxical; for the paradox is the source of
the thinker's passion, and the thinker without a paradox is like
a lover without feeling: a paltry mediocrity. But the highest pitch
of every passion is always to will its own downfall; and so it is
also the supreme passion of the Reason to seek a collision, though
this collision must in one way or another prove its undoing. The
supreme paradox of all thought is the attempt to discover something that thought cannot think. This passion is at bottom present
in all thinking, even in the thinking of the individual, insofar
as in thinking he participates in something transcending himself.
But habit dulls our sensibilities, and prevents us from perceiving
it. So for example the scientists tell us that our walking is a constant falling. But a sedate and proper gentleman who walks to his
office in the morning and back again at noon, probably thinks
this to be an exaggeration, for his progress is clearly a case of
mediation; how should it occur to him that he is constantly falling
when he religiously follows his nose!

But in order to make a beginning, let us now assume a daring
proposition; let us assume that we know what man is.[1] Here we

[1] It may seem ridiculous to give this proposition a doubtful form by "assuming" it, for in this theocentric age such matters are of course known to all.
Aye, if it were only so well with us. Democritus also knew what man is,

have that criterion of the Truth, which in the whole course of Greek philosophy was either *sought*, or *doubted*, or *postulated*, or *made fruitful*. Is it not remarkable that the Greeks should have borne us this testimony? And is it not an epitome, as it were, of the significance of Greek culture, an epigram of its own writing, with which it is also better served than with the frequently voluminous disquisitions sometimes devoted to it? Thus the proposition is well worth positing, and also for another reason, since we have already explained it in the two preceding chapters; while anyone who attempts to explain Socrates differently may well beware lest he fall into the snare of the earlier or later Greek skepticism. For unless we hold fast to the Socratic doctrine of Recollection, and to his principle that every individual man is Man, Sextus Empiricus stands ready to make the transition involved in "learning" not only difficult but impossible; and Protagoras will begin where Sextus Empiricus leaves off, teaching that man is the measure of all things, in the sense that the individual man is the measure for others, but by no means in the Socratic sense that each man is his own measure, neither more nor less.

So then we know what man is, and this wisdom, which I shall be the last to hold in light esteem, may progressively become richer and more significant, and with it also the Truth. But now the Reason hesitates, just as Socrates did; for the paradoxical passion of the Reason is aroused and seeks a collision; without rightly understanding itself, it is bent upon its own downfall. This is like what happens in connection with the paradox of love. Man lives undisturbed a self-centered life, until there awakens within him the paradox of self-love, in the form of love for another, the object of his longing. (Self-love is the underlying

---

for he defines man as follows: "Man is what we all know," and then goes on to say: "for we all know what a dog, a horse, a plant is, and so forth; but none of these is a man." We do not aspire to the malice of Sextus Empiricus, nor have we his wit; for he concludes as we know, from the above definition, and quite correctly, that man is a dog; for man is what we all know, and we all know what a dog is, *ergo*—but let us not be so malicious. Nevertheless, has this question been so thoroughly cleared up in our own time that no one need feel a little uneasy about himself when he is reminded of poor Socrates and his predicament?

principle, or the principle that is made to lie under, in all love; whence if we conceive a religion of love, this religion need make but one assumption, as epigrammatic as true, and take its realization for granted: namely the condition that man loves himself, in order to command him to love his neighbor as himself.) The lover is so completely transformed by the paradox of love that he scarcely recognizes himself; so say the poets, who are the spokesmen of love, and so say also the lovers themselves, since they permit the poets merely to take the words from their lips, but not the passion from their hearts. In like manner the paradoxical passion of the Reason, while as yet a mere presentiment, retroactively affects man and his self-knowledge, so that he who thought to know himself is no longer certain whether he is a more strangely composite animal than Typhon, or if perchance his nature contains a gentler and diviner part. (σκοπῶ οὐ ταῦτα, ἀλλὰ ἐμαυτόν, εἴτε τι θηρίον ὢν τυγκάνω πολυπλοκώτερον καὶ μᾶλλον ἐπιτεθυμμένον εἴτε ἡμερώτερόν τε καὶ ἁπλούστερον ζῷον, θείας τινος καὶ ἀτύφου μοί ρας φύσει μετέχον. Phaedrus, 230 A.)

But what is this unknown something with which the Reason collides when inspired by its paradoxical passion, with the result of unsettling even man's knowledge of himself? It is the Unknown. It is not a human being, insofar as we know what man is; nor is it any other known thing. So let us call this unknown something: God. It is nothing more than a name we assign to it. The idea of demonstrating that this unknown something (God) exists could scarcely suggest itself to the Reason. For if God does not exist it would of course be impossible to prove it; and if he does exist it would be folly to attempt it. For at the very outset, in beginning my proof, I will have presupposed it, not as doubtful but as certain (a presupposition is never doubtful, for the very reason that it is a presupposition), since otherwise I would not begin, readily understanding that the whole would be impossible if he did not exist. But if when I speak of proving God's existence I mean that I propose to prove that the Unknown, which exists, is God, then I express myself unfortunately. For in that case I do not prove anything, least of all an existence, but merely develop the content of a conception. Generally speaking, it is a difficult matter to prove that anything exists; and what is still worse for the intrepid souls who undertake the venture, the difficulty is such that fame scarcely awaits those who concern themselves with it. The entire demonstration always turns into something very different from what it assumes to be, and becomes an additional development of the consequences that flow from my having assumed that the object in question exists. Thus I always reason from existence, not toward existence, whether I move in the sphere of palpable sensible fact or in the realm of thought. I do not for example prove that a stone exists, but that some existing thing is a stone. The procedure in a court of justice does not prove that a criminal exists, but that the accused, whose existence is given, is a criminal. Whether we call existence an *accessorium* or the eternal *prius*, it is never subject to demonstration. Let us take ample time for consideration. We have no such reason for haste as have those who from concern for themselves or for God or for some other thing must make haste to get its existence demonstrated. Under such circumstances there may indeed be need for haste, especially if the prover sincerely seeks to appreciate the danger that he himself, or the thing in question, may be nonexistent unless the proof is finished; and does not surreptitiously entertain the thought that it exists whether he succeeds in proving it or not.

If it were proposed to prove Napoleon's existence from Napoleon's deeds, would it not be a most curious proceeding? His existence does indeed explain his deeds, but the deeds do not prove *his* existence, unless I have already understood the word "his" so as thereby to have assumed his existence. But Napoleon is only an individual, and in so far there exists no absolute relationship between him and his deeds; some other person might have performed the same deeds. Perhaps this is the reason why I cannot pass from the deeds to existence. If I call these deeds the deeds of Napoleon the proof becomes superfluous, since I have already named him; if I ignore this, I can never prove from the deeds that they are Napoleon's, but only in a purely ideal manner that such deeds are the deeds of a great general, and so forth. But between God and his works there exists an absolute

relationship; God is not a name but a concept. Is this perhaps the
reason that his *essentia involvit existentiam?*[2] The works of God
are such that only God can perform them. Just so, but where then
are the works of God? The works from which I would deduce
his existence are not immediately given. The wisdom of God in
nature, his goodness, his wisdom in the governance of the world
—are all these manifest, perhaps, upon the very face of things?
Are we not here confronted with the most terrible temptations

---

[2] So Spinoza, who probes the depths of the God-idea in order to bring existence out of it by way of thought, but not, it should be noted, as if existence
were an accidental circumstance, but rather as if it constituted an essential
determination of content. Here lies Spinoza's profundity, but let us examine
his reasoning. In *principia philosophiae Cartesianae, pars I, propositio VII,
lemma I*, he says: *"quo res sua natura perfectior est, eo majorem existentiam
et magis necessariam involvit; et contra, quo magis necessariam existentiam
res sua natura involvit, eo perfectior."* The more perfect therefore a thing is,
the more being it has; the more being it has, the more perfect it is. This is
however a tautology, which becomes still more evident in a note, *nota II:
"quod hic non loquimur de pulchritudine et aliis perfectionibus, quas
homines ex superstitione et ignorantia perfectiones vocare voluerunt. Sed per
perfectionem intelligo tantum realitatem sive esse."* He explains *perfectio* by
realitas, esse; so that the more perfect a thing is, the more it is; but its perfection consists in having more *esse* in itself; that is to say, the more a thing
is, the more it is. So much for the tautology, but now further. What is lacking here is a distinction between factual being and ideal being. The terminology which permits us to speak of more or less of being, and consequently
of degrees of reality or being, is in itself lacking in clearness, and becomes
still more confusing when the above distinction is neglected; when, in other
words, Spinoza does indeed speak profoundly, but fails first to consider the
difficulty. In the case of factual existence it is meaningless to speak of more
or less of being. A fly, when it exists, has as much being as God; the stupid
remark I here set down has as much factual existence as Spinoza's profundity; for factual existence is subject to the dialectic of Hamlet: to be or
not to be. Factual existence is wholly indifferent to any and all variations
in essence, and everything that exists participates without petty jealousy in
being, and participates in the same degree. Ideally, to be sure, the case is
quite different. *But the moment I speak of being in the ideal sense I no
longer speak of being, but of essence.* Highest ideality has this necessity and
therefore it is. But this its being is identical with its essence; such being
does not involve it dialectically in the determinations of factual existence,
since it is; nor can it be said to have more or less of being in relation to
other things. In the old days this used to be expressed, if somewhat imper-
fectly, by saying that if God is possible, he is *eo ipso* necessary (Leibniz).
Spinoza's principle is thus quite correct and his tautology in order; but it is
also certain that he altogether evades the difficulty. For the difficulty is to lay
hold of God's factual existence, and to introduce God's ideal essence dialectically into the sphere of factual existence.

to doubt, and is it not impossible finally to dispose of all these doubts? But from such an order of things I will surely not attempt to prove God's existence; and even if I began I would never finish, and would in addition have to live constantly in suspense, lest something so terrible should suddenly happen that my bit of proof would be demolished. From what works then do I propose to derive the proof? From the works as apprehended through an ideal interpretation, i.e., such as they do not immediately reveal themselves. But in that case it is not from the works that I prove God's existence. I merely develop the ideality I have presupposed, and because of my confidence in *this* I make so bold as to defy all objections, even those that have not yet been made. In beginning my proof I presuppose the ideal interpretation, and also that I will be successful in carrying it through; but what else is this but to presuppose that God exists, so that I really begin by virtue of confidence in him?

And how does God's existence emerge from the proof? Does it follow straightway, without any breach of continuity? Or have we not here an analogy to the behavior of these toys, the little Cartesian dolls? As soon as I let go of the doll it stands on its head. As soon as I let it go—I must therefore let it go. So also with the proof for God's existence. As long as I keep my hold on the proof, i.e., continue to demonstrate, the existence does not come out, if for no other reason than that I am engaged in proving it; but when I let the proof go, the existence is there. But this act of letting go is surely also something; it is indeed a contribution of mine. Must not this also be taken into the account, this little moment, brief as it may be—it need not be long, for it is a *leap*. However brief this moment, if only an instantaneous now, this "now" must be included in the reckoning. If anyone wishes to have it ignored, I will use it to tell a little anecdote, in order to show that it really does exist. Chrysippus was experimenting with a sorites to see if he could not bring about a break in its quality, either progressively or retrogressively. But Carneades could not get it in his head when the new quality actually emerged. Then Chrysippus told him to try making a little pause in the reckoning, and so—so it would be easier to understand. Carneades replied: With the greatest pleasure, please do not hesitate on my account; you may not only pause, but even lie down to sleep, and it will help you just as little; for when you awake we will begin again where you left off. Just so; it boots as little to try to get rid of something by sleeping as to try to come into the possession of something in the same manner.

Whoever therefore attempts to demonstrate the existence of God (except in the sense of clarifying the concept, and without the *reservatio finalis* noted above, that the existence emerges from the demonstration by a leap) proves in lieu thereof something else, something which at times perhaps does not need a proof, and in any case needs none better; for the fool says in his heart that there is no God, but whoever says in his heart or to men: Wait just a little and I will prove it—what a rare man of wisdom is he![3] If in the moment of beginning his proof it is not absolutely undetermined whether God exists or not, he does not prove it; and if it is thus undetermined in the beginning he will never come to begin, partly from fear of failure, since God perhaps does not exist, and partly because he has nothing with which to begin. A project of this kind would scarcely have been undertaken by the ancients. Socrates at least, who is credited with having put forth the physicoteleological proof for God's existence, did not go about it in any such manner. He always presupposes God's existence, and under this presupposition seeks to interpenetrate nature with the idea of purpose. Had he been asked why he pursued this method, he would doubtless have explained that he lacked the courage to venture out upon so perilous a voyage of discovery without having made sure of God's existence behind him. At the word of God he casts his net as if to catch the idea of purpose; for nature herself finds many means of frightening the inquirer, and distracts him by many a digression.

The paradoxical passion of the Reason thus comes repeatedly into collision with the Unknown, which does indeed exist, but is unknown, and in so far does not exist. The Reason cannot advance beyond this point, and yet it cannot refrain in its paradoxicalness from arriving at this limit and occupying itself therewith. It will not serve to dismiss its relation to it simply by asserting that the Unknown does not exist, since this itself involves a rela-

[3] What an excellent subject for a comedy of the higher lunacy!

tionship. But what then is the Unknown, since the designation of it as God merely signifies for us that it is unknown? To say that it is the Unknown because it cannot be known, and even if it were capable of being known, it could not be expressed, does not satisfy the demands of passion, though it correctly interprets the Unknown as a limit; but a limit is precisely a torment for passion, though it also serves as an incitement. And yet the Reason can come no further, whether it risks an issue *via negationis* or *via eminentia*.

What then is the Unknown? It is the limit to which the Reason repeatedly comes, and in so far, substituting a static form of conception for the dynamic, it is the different, the absolutely different. But because it is absolutely different, there is no mark by which it could be distinguished. When qualified as absolutely different it seems on the verge of disclosure, but this is not the case; for the Reason cannot even conceive an absolute unlikeness. The Reason cannot negate itself absolutely, but uses itself for the purpose, and thus conceives only such an unlikeness within itself as it can conceive by means of itself; it cannot absolutely transcend itself, and hence conceives only such a superiority over itself as it can conceive by means of itself. Unless the Unknown (God) remains a mere limiting conception, the single idea of difference will be thrown into a state of confusion, and become many ideas of many differences. The Unknown is then in a condition of dispersion (διασπορά), and the Reason may choose at pleasure from what is at hand and the imagination may suggest (the monstrous, the ludicrous, etc.).

But it is impossible to hold fast to a difference of this nature. Every time this is done it is essentially an arbitrary act, and deepest down in the heart of piety lurks the mad caprice which knows that it has itself produced its God. If no specific determination of difference can be held fast, because there is no distinguishing mark, like and unlike finally become identified with one another, thus sharing the fate of all such dialectical opposites. The unlikeness clings to the Reason and confounds it, so that the Reason no longer knows itself and quite consistently confuses itself with the unlikeness. On this point paganism has been sufficiently prolific in fantastic inventions. As for the last-named supposition, the self-irony of the Reason, I shall attempt to delineate it merely by a stroke or two, without raising any question of its being historical. There lives an individual whose appearance is precisely like that of other men; he grows up to manhood like others, he marries, he has an occupation by which he earns his livelihood, and he makes provision for the future as befits a man. For though it may be beautiful to live like the birds of the air, it is not lawful, and may lead to the sorriest of consequences: either starvation if one has enough persistence, or dependence on the bounty of others. This man is also God. How do I know? I cannot know it, for in order to know it I would have to know God, and the nature of the difference between God and man; and this I cannot know, because the Reason has reduced it to likeness with that from which it was unlike. Thus God becomes the most terrible of deceivers, because the Reason has deceived itself. The Reason has brought God as near as possible, and yet he is as far away as ever.

Now perhaps someone will say: "You are certainly a crotcheteer, as I know very well. But you surely do not believe that I would pay any attention to such a crotchet, so strange or so ridiculous that it has doubtless never occurred to anyone, and above all so absurd that I must exclude from my consciousness everything that I have in it in order to hit upon it." And so indeed you must. But do you think yourself warranted in retaining all the presuppositions you have in your consciousness, while pretending to think about your consciousness without presuppositions? Will you deny the consistency of our exposition: that the Reason, in attempting to determine the Unknown as the unlike, at last goes astray, and confounds the unlike with the like? From this there would seem to follow the further consequence, that if man is to receive any true knowledge about the Unknown (God) he must be made to know that it is unlike him, absolutely unlike him. This knowledge the Reason cannot possibly obtain of itself; we have already seen that this would be a self-contradiction. It will therefore have to obtain this knowledge from God. But even if it obtains such knowledge it cannot understand it, and thus is quite unable to possess such knowledge. For how should the

Reason be able to understand what is absolutely different from itself? If this is not immediately evident, it will become clearer in the light of the consequences; for if God is absolutely unlike man, then man is absolutely unlike God; but how could the Reason be expected to understand this? Here we seem to be confronted with a paradox. Merely to obtain the knowledge that God is unlike him, man needs the help of God; and now he learns that God is absolutely different from himself. But if God and man are absolutely different, this cannot be accounted for on the basis of what man derives from God, for in so far they are akin. Their unlikeness must therefore be explained by what man derives from himself, or by what he has brought upon his own head. But what can this unlikeness be? Aye, what can it be but sin; since the unlikeness, the absolute unlikeness, is something that man has brought upon himself. We have expressed this in the preceding by saying that man was in Error, and had brought this upon his head by his own guilt; and we came to the conclusion, partly in jest and yet also in earnest, that it was too much to expect of man that he should find this out for himself. Now we have again arrived at the same conclusion. The connoisseur in self-knowledge was perplexed over himself to the point of bewilderment when he came to grapple in thought with the unlike; he scarcely knew any longer whether he was a stranger monster than Typhon, or if his nature partook of something divine. What then did he lack? The consciousness of sin, which he indeed could no more teach to another than another could teach it to him, but only God—if God consents to become a Teacher. But this was his purpose, as we have imagined it. In order to be man's Teacher, God proposed to make himself like the individual man, so that he might understand him fully. Thus our paradox is rendered still more appalling, or the same paradox has the double aspect which proclaims it as the Absolute Paradox; negatively by revealing the absolute unlikeness of sin, positively by proposing to do away with the absolute unlikeness in absolute likeness.

But can such a paradox be conceived? Let us not be over-hasty in replying; and since we strive merely to find the answer to a question, and not as those who run a race, it may be well to remember that success is to the accurate rather than to the swift.

The Reason will doubtless find it impossible to conceive it, could not of itself have discovered it, and when it hears it announced will not be able to understand it, sensing merely that its downfall is threatened. In so far the Reason will have much to urge against it; and yet we have on the other hand seen that the Reason, in its paradoxical passion, precisely desires its own downfall. But this is what the Paradox also desires, and thus they are at bottom linked in understanding; but this understanding is present only in the moment of passion. Consider the analogy presented by love, though it is not a perfect one. Self-love underlies love; but the paradoxical passion of self-love when at its highest pitch wills precisely its own downfall. This is also what love desires, so that these two are linked in mutual understanding in the passion of the moment, and this passion is love. Why should not the lover find this conceivable? But he who in self-love shrinks from the touch of love can neither understand it nor summon the courage to venture it, since it means his downfall. Such is then the passion of love; self-love is indeed submerged but not annihilated; it is taken captive and become love's *spolia opima*, but may again come to life, and this is love's temptation. So also with the Paradox in its relation to the Reason, only that the passion in this case has another name; or rather, we must seek to find a name for it.

Ludwig Feuerbach

[1804–1872]

LUDWIG FEUERBACH was born in Landshut, Bavaria. His childhood coincides with the period of Napoleonic influence, when the Holy Roman Empire was dissolved and Bavaria became part of the Confederation of the Rhine, a French satellite. His is the first generation of the democratic age, growing to maturity under the Metternich reaction, a period marked by uprisings in Madrid (1820), Greece (1821), St. Petersburg (1825) and Paris (1830). After a stay at Heidelberg, Feuerbach studied under Hegel at the University of Berlin from 1824 to 1828, when he became a *Privatdozent* at Erlangen. His major period as a writer is the same one during which Karl Marx, his junior by fourteen years, became a "Marxist." His chief books are *The Essence of Chrisianity* (1841), *The Philosophy of the Future* (1843) and *The Essence of Religion* (1851), a series of lectures given at Heidelberg in 1848, the year of the *Communist Manifesto* and of revolutions in France, Germany and Italy.

Friedrich Engels regarded Feuerbach as the last spokesman of the tradition of German idealism that began with Kant, recognizing in him, however, a nascent materialism unlike that of Holbach or Hobbes. As G. D. H. Cole has put it, Feuerbach "called speculation back from the pure reason to observe the actual march of events in its own right"[1]—in contrast to what might be called Hegel's "march of ideas." The historical materialism of Karl Marx is an outgrowth of this development, as reflected in Marx's *Theses on Feuerbach*, 1845.

[1] G. D. H. Cole, *A History of Socialist Thought* (New York: St. Martin's Press, 1953), Vol. I, p. 236.

Feuerbach's contribution to modern thought is largely transitional rather than seminal. Yet, says Karl Barth,

> Among the philosophers of modern times there is perhaps no other who occupied himself so exclusively with the problem of theology as did Feuerbach . . . Feuerbach, in his work—especially in all which was concerned with the Bible, the Church Fathers and particularly with Luther—showed himself to possess a theological knowledge which sets him far above the majority of modern philosophers.[2]

If Marx may be said to have used the Hegelian dialectic as the basis of social theory, Feuerbach does likewise for a theory of interpersonal relations. His philosophical concept of "anthropology" is not to be confused with the social science that bears this name; it is rather analogous to theology, and in Feuerbach's specific interpretation it borders on psychology. Three or four generations before Freud, his investigations of myth led him to the insight that religion may be understood as "the dream of waking consciousness."[3] From Wilhelm von Humboldt he took up and adumbrated the conception of dialogue that Martin Buber would later take as the cornerstone of his philosophy. "True dialectic," wrote Feuerbach, "is not a monologue of the solitary thinker within himself, it is a dialogue between *I* and *Thou*."[4] His "essence of Christianity" is precisely this dialogue: "Man with man—the unity of *I* and *Thou*—is God." This is the meaning of the incarnation, that Jesus stood in this relation, and whoever obeys his command, "Love one another as I have loved you," also enters into it. "Christ is the consciousness of our unity. Therefore, whoever loves man for the sake of man . . . is a Christian; he is Christ himself."[5]

---

[2] Karl Barth, *Theology and Church* (New York: Harper & Row, 1962), p. 217.
[3] See H. B. Acton, *The Illusion of an Epoch* (University of Toronto Press, 1955).
[4] Ludwig Feuerbach, *Die Philosophie der Zukunft* (Stuttgart: Fromann, 1922), p. 41. See also Martin Buber, *Between Man and Man* (London: Fontana, 1961), p. 46. Humboldt founded the University of Berlin in 1810. His book *The Dual Number* was published in 1827, when Feuerbach was a student there.
[5] See p. 103 of this anthology.

Feuerbach is vulnerable to criticism. His identification of the spirit of Jesus with the spirit of man leaves a vital question unanswered: What is man? "His anthropological reduction of being," says Buber, "is a reduction to *unproblematical* man."[6] Karl Barth hits the same target in saying that Feuerbach fails to take account of evil and death. Yet if Feuerbach was an ebullient child of his century, says Barth, the bourgeois church whose God he attacked was just as vulnerable. For its God was a "beautiful dream . . . suspected of being a means of deceit deliberately sustained to quench the proletarian struggle for freedom."[7]

It is important to distinguish between Feuerbach's and Marx's critiques of religion, for that "beautiful dream" did not signify the same thing to each. To Marx, religion was unredeemable, a form of "alienated human self-consciousness," an obstacle that must be superseded by a completely empirical humanism. For him, two of Feuerbach's great achievements were

> (1) to have shown that philosophy is nothing more than religion brought into thought and developed by thought, and that it is equally to be condemned as another form and mode of human alienation;
> (2) to have founded *genuine materialism* and *positive science* by making the social relationship of "man to man" the basic principle of his theory.[8]

Part of Marx's accolade is misplaced. To him, "atheism is humanism mediated to itself by the annulment of religion."[9] This may well be Feuerbach's point too, but with important qualifications. For to Feuerbach, as the following selections make clear, the essence of man is not to be discerned solely by "positive science."

---

[6] Buber, *op. cit.*, p. 181.

[7] Karl Barth, *Die Theologie und die Kirche* (Zürich: Evangelischer Verlag, 1928).

[8] Karl Marx, "Critique of Hegel's Dialectic and General Philosophy," in Erich Fromm, *Marx's Concept of Man* (New York: Ungar, 1961), p. 171. Cf. also pp. 186ff.

[9] *Ibid.*, p. 189. See also Karl Löwith, *From Hegel to Nietzsche* (New York: Holt, Rinehart & Winston, 1964), pp. 310–312, and Herbert Marcuse, *Reason and Revolution* (New York: Oxford University Press, 1941), pp. 267–273.

In his materialism New Testament doctrines are taken as hypotheses about man rather than as dogmas about God. It is a Christian materialism, a Christian atheism, asserting that it is not possible to say that God is love but it is possible to derive from the Bible a de-theologized statement that amounts to the same thing. Marx in his "post-Christian" affirmation of man simply takes for granted what Feuerbach makes clear in great detail. Hence Feuerbach remains a key figure in present-day dialogue between Marxism and Christianity, posing a critical challenge to each. His achievement is incomplete and defective; at crucial junctures he resorts to clichés and invites ridicule by *preaching* human personality as related to its environment, while operationally reducing man to an ethical abstraction. In its simplest terms, his "essence of Christianity" humanizes God and dehumanizes man by making the incarnation a mere symbol of human self-sufficiency. Yet if his conclusions are platitudinous, many of his speculations are not; they provide a basis for the more rigorous and fruitful thinking of Buber, Altizer and others.

The Mystery of the Incarnation[1]

It is the consciousness of love by which man reconciles himself with God, or rather with his own nature as represented in the moral law. The consciousness of the divine love, or what is the same thing, the contemplation of God as human, is the mystery of the Incarnation. The Incarnation is nothing else than the practical, material manifestation of the human nature of God. God did not become man for his own sake; the need, the want of man—a want which still exists in the religious sentiment—was the cause of the Incarnation. God became man out of mercy: thus he was in himself already a human God before he became an actual man; for human want, human misery, went to his heart. The Incarnation was a tear of the divine compassion, and hence

---

[1] From *The Essence of Christianity* [1841], trans. George Eliot, 1854. I have very slightly revised her translation to accord with modern usage, e.g. substituting "you" for "thou."—Ed.

it was only the visible advent of a Being having human feelings, and therefore essentially human.

If in the Incarnation we stop short at the fact of God becoming man, it certainly appears a surprising, inexplicable, marvelous event. But the incarnate God is only the apparent manifestation of deified man; for the descent of God to man is necessarily preceded by the exaltation of man to God. Man was already in God, was already God himself, before God became man, i.e., showed himself as man.[2] How otherwise could God have become man? The old maxim *ex nihilo nihil fit* is applicable here also. A king who has not the welfare of his subjects at heart, who, while seated on his throne, does not mentally live with them in their dwellings, who, in feeling, is not, as the people say, "a common man," such a king will not descend bodily from his throne to make his people happy by his personal presence. Thus, has not the subject risen to be a king before the king descends to be a subject? And if the subject feels himself honored and made happy by the personal presence of his king, does this feeling refer merely to the bodily presence, and not rather to the manifestation of the disposition, of the philanthropic nature which is the cause of the appearance? But that which in the truth of religion is the cause, takes in the consciousness of religion the form of a consequence; and so here the raising of man to God is made a consequence of the humiliation or descent of God to man. God, says religion, made himself human that he might make man divine.[3]

That which is mysterious and incomprehensible, i.e., contradictory, in the proposition "God is or becomes a man," arises only

[2] "Such descriptions as those in which the Scriptures speak of God as of a man, and ascribe to him all that is human, are very sweet and comforting—namely, that he talks with us as a friend, and of such things as men are wont to talk of with each other; that he rejoices, sorrows, and suffers, like a man, for the sake of the mystery of the future humanity of Christ."—Luther (Th. ii. p. 334).

[3] "Deus homo factus est, ut homo Deus fieret."—Augustinus (Serm. ad Pop. p. 371, c. 1). In Luther, however (Th. i. p. 334), there is a passage which indicates the true relation. When Moses called man "the image of God, the likeness of God," he meant, says Luther, obscurely to intimate that "God was to become man." Thus here the incarnation of God is clearly enough represented as a consequence of the deification of man.

from the mingling or confusion of the idea or definitions of the universal, unlimited, metaphysical being with the idea of the religious God, i.e., the conditions of the understanding with the conditions of the heart, the emotive nature; a confusion which is the greatest hindrance to the correct knowledge of religion. But, in fact, the idea of the Incarnation is nothing more than the human *form* of a God who already in his nature, in the profoundest depths of his soul, is a merciful and therefore a human God.

The form given to this truth in the doctrine of the Church is that it was not the first person of the Godhead who was incarnate, but the second, who is the representative of man in and before God; the second person being however in reality, as will be shown, the sole, true, first person in religion. And it is only apart from this distinction of persons that the God-man appears mysterious, incomprehensible, "speculative"; for, considered in connection with it, the Incarnation is a necessary, nay, a self-evident consequence. The allegation, therefore, that the Incarnation is a purely empirical fact, which could be made known only by means of a revelation in the theological sense, betrays the most crass religious materialism; for the Incarnation is a conclusion which rests on a very comprehensible premise. But it is equally perverse to attempt to deduce the Incarnation from purely speculative, i.e., metaphysical, abstract grounds; for metaphysics applies only to the first person of the Godhead, who does not become incarnate, who is not a dramatic person. Such a deduction would at the utmost be justifiable if it were meant consciously to deduce from metaphysics the negation of metaphysics.

This example clearly exhibits the distinction between the method of our philosophy and that of the old speculative philosophy. The former does not philosophize concerning the Incarnation, as a peculiar, stupendous mystery, after the manner of speculation dazzled by mystical splendor; on the contrary, it destroys the illusive supposition of a peculiar supernatural mystery; it criticizes the dogma and reduces it to its natural elements, immanent in man, to its originating principle and central point— love.

The dogma presents to us two things—God and love. God is

love: but what does that mean? Is God something besides love? a being distinct from love? Is it as if I said of an affectionate human being, he is love itself? Certainly; otherwise I must give up the name God, which expresses a special personal being, a subject in distinction from the predicate. Thus love is made something apart. God out of love sent his only-begotten Son. Here love recedes and sinks into insignificance in the dark background —God. It becomes merely a personal, though an essential, attribute; hence it receives both in theory and in feeling, both objectively and subjectively, the rank simply of a predicate, not that of a subject, of the substance; it shrinks out of observation as a collateral, an accident; at one moment it presents itself to me as something essential, at another, it vanishes again. God appears to me in another form besides that of love; in the form of omnipotence, of a severe power not bound by love; a power in which, though in a smaller degree, the devils participate.

So long as love is not exalted into a substance, into an essence, so long there lurks in the background of love a subject who even without love is something by himself, an unloving monster, a diabolical being, whose personality, separable and actually separated from love, delights in the blood of heretics and unbelievers— the phantom of religious fanaticism. Nevertheless the essential idea of the Incarnation, though enveloped in the night of the religious consciousness, is love. Love determined God to the renunciation of his divinity.[4] Not because of his Godhead as such, according to which he is the *subject* in the proposition, God is love, but because of his love, of the *predicate*, is it that he renounced his Godhead; thus love is a higher power and truth than deity. Love conquers God. It was love to which God sacrificed his divine majesty. And what sort of love was that? another than

[4] It was in this sense that the old uncompromising enthusiastic faith celebrated the Incarnation. "*Amor triumphat de Deo,*" says St. Bernard. And only in the sense of a real self-renunciation, self-negation of the Godhead, lies the reality, the *vis* of the Incarnation; although this self-negation is in itself merely a conception of the imagination, for, looked at in broad daylight, God does not negative himself in the Incarnation, but he shows himself as that which he is, as a human being. The fabrications which modern rationalistic orthodoxy and pietistic rationalism have advanced concerning the Incarnation, in opposition to the rapturous conceptions and expressions of ancient faith, do not deserve to be mentioned, still less controverted.

ours? than that to which we sacrifice life and fortune? Was it the love of himself? of himself as God? No! it was love to man. But is not love to man human love? Can I love man without loving him humanly, without loving him as he himself loves, if he truly loves? Would not love be otherwise a devilish love? The devil too loves man, but not for man's sake—for his own; thus he loves man out of egotism, to aggrandize himself, to extend his power. But God loves man for man's sake, i.e., that he may make him good, happy, blessed. Does he not then love man as the true man loves his fellow? Has love a plural? Is it not everywhere like itself? What then is the true unfalsified import of the Incarnation but absolute, pure love, without adjunct, without a distinction between divine and human love? For though there is also a self-interested love among men, still the true human love, which is alone worthy of this name, is that which impels the sacrifice of self to another. Who then is our Saviour and Redeemer? God or Love? Love; for God as God has not saved us, but Love, which transcends the difference between the divine and human personality. As God has renounced himself out of love, so we, out of love, should renounce God; for if we do not sacrifice God to love, we sacrifice love to God, and, in spite of the predicate of love, we have the God—the evil being—of religious fanaticism.

While, however, we have laid open this nucleus of truth in the Incarnation, we have at the same time exhibited the dogma in its falsity; we have reduced the apparently supernatural and super-rational mystery to a simple truth inherent in human nature: a truth which does not belong to the Christian religion alone, but which, implicitly at least, belongs more or less to every religion as such. For every religion which has any claim to the name presupposes that God is not indifferent to the beings who worship him, that therefore what is human is not alien to him, that, as an object of human veneration, he is a human God. Every prayer discloses the secret of the Incarnation, every prayer is in fact an incarnation of God. In prayer I involve God in human distress, I make him a participator in my sorrows and wants. God is not deaf to my complaints; he has compassion on me; hence he renounces his divine majesty, his exaltation above all that is finite and human; he becomes a man with man; for if he listens to me, and pities me, he is affected by my sufferings. God loves man—i.e., God suffers from man. Love does not exist without sympathy, sympathy does not exist without suffering in common. Have I any sympathy for a being without feeling? No! I feel only for that which has feeling, only for that which partakes of my nature, for that in which I feel myself, whose sufferings I myself suffer. Sympathy presupposes a like nature. The Incarnation, Providence, prayer, are the expression of this identity of nature in God and man.[5]

It is true that theology, which is preoccupied with the metaphysical attributes of eternity, unconditionedness, unchangeableness, and the like abstractions, which express the nature of the understanding—theology denies the possibility that God should suffer, but in so doing it denies the truth of religion.[6] For religion—the religious man in the act of devotion believes in a real sympathy of the Divine Being in his sufferings and wants, believes that the will of God can be determined by the fervor of prayer, i.e., by the force of feeling, believes in a real, present fulfillment of his desire, wrought by prayer. The truly religious man unhesitatingly assigns his own feelings to God; God is to him a heart susceptible to all that is human. The heart can betake itself only to the heart; feeling can appeal only to feeling; it finds consolation in itself, in its own nature alone.

The notion that the fulfillment of prayer has been determined from eternity, that it was originally included in the plan of creation, is the empty, absurd fiction of a mechanical mode of thought, which is in absolute contradiction with the nature of religion. "We need," says Lavater somewhere, and quite correctly according to the religious sentiment, "an arbitrary God." Besides, even according to this fiction, God is just as much a being deter-

---

[5] "Nos scimus affici Deum misericordia nostri et non solum respicere lacrymas nostras, sed etiam numerare stillulas, sicut scriptum in Psalmo LVI. Filius Dei vere afficitur sensu miseriarum nostrarum."—Melancthonis et aliorum (Declam. Th. iii. p. 286, p. 450).

[6] St. Bernard resorts to a charmingly sophistical play of words:—"Impassibilis est Deus, sed non incompassibilis, cui proprium est misereri semper et parcere."—(Sup. Cant. Sermo 26) As if compassion were not suffering—the suffering of love, it is true, the suffering of the heart. But what does suffer if not your sympathizing heart? No love, no suffering. The material, the source of suffering, is the universal heart, the common bond of all beings.

mined by man, as in the real, present fulfillment consequent on the power of prayer; the only difference is, that the contradiction with the unchangeableness and unconditionedness of God—that which constitutes the difficulty—is thrown back into the deceptive distance of the past or of eternity. Whether God decides on the fulfillment of my prayer now, on the immediate occasion of my offering it, or whether he did decide on it long ago, is fundamentally the same thing.

It is the greatest inconsequence to reject the idea of a God who can be determined by prayer, that is, by the force of feeling, as an unworthy anthropomorphic idea. If we once believe in a being who is an object of veneration, an object of prayer, an object of affection, who is providential, who takes care of man—in a Providence, which is not conceivable without love—in a being, therefore, who is loving, whose motive of action is love, we also believe in a being who has, if not an anatomical, yet a psychical human heart. The religious mind, as has been said, places everything in God, excepting that alone which it despises. The Christians certainly gave their God no attributes which contradicted their own moral ideas, but they gave him without hesitation, and of necessity, the emotions of love, of compassion. And the love which the religious mind places in God is not an illusory, imaginary love, but a real, true love. God is loved and loves again; the divine love is only human love made objective, affirming itself. In God love is absorbed in itself as its own ultimate truth.

It may be objected to the import here assigned to the Incarnation, that the Christian Incarnation is altogether peculiar, that at least it is different (which is quite true in certain respects, as will hereafter be apparent) from the incarnations of the heathen deities, whether Greek or Indian. These latter are mere products of men or deified men; but in Christianity is given the idea of the true God; here the union of the divine nature with the human is first significant and "speculative." Jupiter transforms himself into a bull; the heathen incarnations are mere fancies. In paganism there is no more in the nature of God than in his incarnate manifestation; in Christianity, on the contrary, it is God, a separate, superhuman being, who appears as man. But this objection is refuted by the remark already made, that even the premise of the Christian Incarnation contains the human nature. God loves man; moreover God has a Son; God is a father; the relations of humanity are not excluded from God; the human is not remote from God, not unknown to him. Thus here also there is nothing more in the nature of God than in the incarnate manifestation of God. In the Incarnation religion only confesses what in reflection on itself, as theology, it will not admit; namely, that God is an altogether human being. The Incarnation, the mystery of the "God-man," is therefore no mysterious composition of contraries, no synthetic fact, as it is regarded by the speculative religious philosophy, which has a particular delight in contradiction; it is an analytic fact—a human word with a human meaning. If there be a contradiction here, it lies before the Incarnation and out of it; in the union of providence, of love, with deity; for if this love is a real love, it is not essentially different from our love—there are only our limitations to be abstracted from it; and thus the Incarnation is only the strongest, deepest, most palpable, open-hearted expression of this providence, this love. Love knows not how to make its object happier than by rejoicing it with its personal presence, by letting itself be seen. To see the invisible benefactor face to face is the most ardent desire of love. To see is a divine act. Happiness lies in the mere sight of the beloved one. The glance is the certainty of love. And the Incarnation has no other significance, no other effect, than the indubitable certitude of the love of God to man. Love remains, but the Incarnation upon the earth passes away; the appearance was limited by time and place, accessible to few, but the essence, the nature which was manifested, is eternal and universal. We can no longer believe in the manifestation for its own sake, but only for the sake of the thing manifested; for to us there remains no immediate presence but that of love.

The clearest, most irrefragable proof that man in religion contemplates himself as the object of the Divine Being, as the end of the divine activity, that thus in religion he has relation only to his own nature, only to himself—the clearest, most irrefragable proof of this is the love of God to man, the basis and central point of religion. God, for the sake of man, empties himself of his Godhead, lays aside his Godhead. Herein lies the elevating influence of the Incarnation; the highest, the perfect being humiliates, lowers himself for the sake of man. Hence in God I learn to estimate my own nature; I have value in the sight of God; the divine significance of my nature is become evident to me. How can the worth of man be more strongly expressed than when God, for man's sake, becomes a man, when man is the end, the object of the divine love? The love of God to man is an essential condition of the Divine Being: God is a God who loves me—who loves man in general. Here lies the emphasis, the fundamental feeling of religion. The love of God makes me loving; the love of God to man is the cause of man's love to God; the divine love causes, awakens human love. "We love God because he first loved us." What, then, is it that I love in God? Love: love to man. But when I love and worship the love with which God loves man, do I not love man; is not my love of God, though indirectly, love of man? If God loves man, is not man, then, the very substance of God? That which I love, is it not my inmost being? Have I a heart when I do not love? No! love only is the heart of man. But what is love without the thing loved? Thus what I love is my heart, the substance of my being, my nature. Why does man grieve, why does he lose pleasure in life when he has lost the beloved object? Why? Because with the beloved object he has lost his heart, the activity of his affections, the principle of life. Thus if God loves man, man is the heart of God—the welfare of man his deepest anxiety. If man, then, is the object of God, is not man, in God, an object to himself? Is not the content of the divine nature the human nature? If God is love, is not the essential content of this love man? Is not the love of God to man—the basis and central point of religion—the love of man to himself made an object, contemplated as the highest objective truth, as the highest being to man? Is not then the proposition "God loves man" an orientalism (religion is essentially Oriental), which in plain speech means, the highest is the love of man?

The truth to which, by means of analysis, we have here reduced the mystery of the Incarnation has also been recognized even in the religious consciousness. Thus Luther, for example, says, "He who can truly conceive such a thing (namely, the incarnation of God) in his heart, should, for the sake of the flesh and blood which sits at the right hand of God, bear love to all flesh and blood here upon the earth, and never more be able to be angry with any man. The gentle manhood of Christ our God should at a glance fill all hearts with joy, so that never more could an angry, unfriendly thought come therein—yea, every man ought, out of great joy, to be tender to his fellow-man for the sake of that our flesh and blood. This is a fact which should move us to great joy and blissful hope that we are thus honored above all creatures, even above the angels, so that we can with truth boast, My own flesh and blood sits at the right hand of God and reigns over all. Such honor has no creature, not even an angel. This ought to be a furnace that should melt us all into one heart, and should create such a fervor in us men that we should heartily love each other." But that which in the truth of religion is the essence of the fable, the chief thing, is to the religious conscious-ness only the moral of the fable, a collateral thing.

The Mystery of the Christian Christ

The fundamental dogmas of Christianity are realized wishes of the heart; the essence of Christianity is the essence of human feeling. It is pleasanter to be passive than to act, to be redeemed and made free by another than to free oneself; pleasanter to make one's salvation dependent on a person than on the force of one's own spontaneity; pleasanter to set before oneself an object of love than an object of effort; pleasanter to know oneself beloved by God than merely to have that simple, natural self-love which is innate in all beings; pleasanter to see oneself imaged in the love-beaming eyes of another personal being than to look into the concave mirror of self or into the cold depths of the ocean of Nature; pleasanter, in short, to allow oneself to be acted on by one's own feeling, as by another, but yet fundamentally identical being, than to regulate oneself by reason. Feeling is the oblique case of the *ego*, the *ego* in the accusative. The *ego* of Fichte is destitute of feeling, because the accusative is the same as the nominative, because it is indeclinable. But feeling or senti-

ment is the *ego* acted on by itself, and by itself as another being
—the passive *ego*. Feeling changes the active in man into the
passive, and the passive into the active. To feeling, that which
thinks is the thing thought, and the thing thought is that which
thinks. Feeling is the dream of Nature; and there is nothing more
blissful, nothing more profound than dreaming. But what is
dreaming? The reversing of the waking consciousness. In dreaming, the active is the passive, the passive the active; in dreaming,
I take the spontaneous action of my own mind for an action upon
me from without, my emotions for events, my conceptions and
sensations for true existences apart from myself. I suffer what I
also perform. Dreaming is a double refraction of the rays of light;
hence its indescribable charm. It is the same *ego*, the same being
in dreaming as in waking; the only distinction is, that in waking,
the *ego* acts on itself; whereas in dreaming it is acted on by itself
as by another being. "I think myself" is a passionless, rationalistic
position; "I am thought by God," and think myself only as thought
by God, is a position pregnant with feeling, religious. Feeling is
a dream with the eyes open, religion the dream of waking consciousness; dreaming is the key to the mysteries of religion.

The highest law of feeling is the immediate unity of will and
deed, of wishing and reality. This law is fulfilled by the Redeemer. As external miracles, in opposition to natural activity,
realize immediately the physical wants and wishes of man, so the
Redeemer, the Mediator, the God-man, in opposition to the moral
spontaneity of the natural or rationalistic man, satisfies immediately the inward moral wants and wishes, since he dispenses man
on his own side from any intermediate activity. What you wish
is already effected. You desire to win, to deserve happiness.
Morality is the condition, the means of happiness. But you cannot
fulfill this condition; that is, in truth, you need not. What you
seek to do has already been done. You have only to be passive,
you need only believe, only enjoy. You desire to make God favor-
able to you, to appease his anger, to be at peace with your conscience. But this peace exists already; this peace is the Mediator,
the God-man. He is your appeased conscience; he is the fulfillment of the law, and therewith the fulfillment of your own wish
and effort.

Therefore it is no longer the law, but the fulfiller of the law, who is the model, the guiding thread, the rule of your life. He who fulfills the law annuls the law. The law has authority, has validity, only in relation to him who violates it. But he who perfectly fulfills the law says to it: What you will I spontaneously will, and what you command I enforce by deeds; my life is the true, the living law. The fulfiller of the law, therefore, necessarily steps into the place of the law; moreover he becomes a new law, one whose yoke is light and easy. For in place of the merely imperative law, he presents himself as an example, as an object of love, of admiration and emulation, and thus becomes the Saviour from sin. The law does not give me the power to fulfill the law; no! it is hard and merciless; it only commands, without troubling itself whether I can fulfill it, or how I am to fulfill it; it leaves me to myself, without counsel or aid. But he who presents himself to me as an example lights up my path, takes me by the hand, and imparts to me his own strength. The law lends no power of resisting sin, but example works miracles. The law is dead; but example animates, inspires, carries men involuntarily along with it. The law speaks only to the understanding, and sets itself directly in opposition to the instincts; example, on the contrary, appeals to a powerful instinct immediately connected with the activity of the senses, that of involuntary imitation. Example operates on the feelings and imagination. In short, example has magical, i.e., sense-affecting powers; for the magical or involuntary force of attraction is an essential property, as of matter in general, so in particular of that which affects the senses. . . .

That the idea of miraculous power is one with the idea of the intermediate being, at once divine and human, has historical proof in the fact that the miracles of the Old Testament, the delivery of the law, providence—all the elements which constitute the essence of religion—were in the later Judaism attributed to the Logos. In Philo, however, this Logos still hovers in the air between heaven and 'earth, now as abstract, now as concrete; that is, Philo vacillates between himself as a philosopher and himself as a religious Israelite—between the positive element of religion and the metaphysical idea of deity; but in such a way that even the abstract element is with him more or less invested with imaginative forms. In Christianity this Logos first attained perfect consistency, i.e., religion now concentrated itself exclusively on that element, that object, which is the basis of its essential difference. The Logos is the personified essence of religion. Hence the definition of God as the essence of feeling has its complete truth only in the Logos.

God as God is feeling as yet shut up, hidden; only Christ is the unclosed, open feeling or heart. In Christ feeling is first perfectly certain of itself, and assured beyond doubt of the truth and divinity of its own nature; for Christ denies nothing to feeling; he fulfills all its prayers. In God the soul is still silent as to what affects it most closely—it only sighs; but in Christ it speaks out fully; here it has no longer any reserves. To him who only sighs, wishes are still attended with disquietude; he complains that what he wishes is not, rather than openly, positively declares what he wishes; he is still in doubt whether his wishes have the force of law. But in Christ all anxiety of the soul vanishes; he is the sighing soul passed into a song of triumph over its complete satisfaction; he is the joyful certainty of feeling that its wishes hidden in God have truth and reality, the actual victory over death, over all the powers of the world and Nature, the resurrection no longer merely hoped for, but already accomplished; he is the heart released from all oppressive limits, from all sufferings—the soul in perfect blessedness, the Godhead made visible.

. . . Christ is God known personally; Christ, therefore, is the blessed certainty that God is what the soul desires and needs him to be. God, as the object of prayer, is indeed already a human being, since he sympathizes with human misery, grants human wishes; but still he is not yet an object to the religious consciousness as a real man. Hence, only in Christ is the last wish of religion realized, the mystery of religious feeling solved—solved, however, in the language of imagery proper to religion, for what God is in essence, that Christ is in actual appearance. So far the Christian religion may justly be called the absolute religion. That God, who in himself is nothing else than the nature of man, should also have a real existence as such, should be as man an object to the consciousness—this is the goal of religion; and this the Christian religion has attained in the incarnation of God, which is by no means a transitory act, for Christ remains man even after his ascension—man in heart and man in form, only that his body is no longer an earthly one, liable to suffering.

The incarnations of the Deity with the Orientals—the Hindus, for example—have no such intense meaning as the Christian incarnation; just because they happen often they become indifferent, they lose their value. The manhood of God is his personality; the proposition that God is a personal being means: God is a human being, God is a man. Personality is an abstraction, which has reality only in an actual man.[1] The idea which lies at the foundation of the incarnations of God is therefore infinitely better conveyed by one incarnation, one personality. Where God appears in several persons successively, these personalities are evanescent. What is required is a permanent, an exclusive personality. Where there are many incarnations, room is given for innumerable others; the imagination is not restrained; and even those incarnations which are already real pass into the category of the merely possible and conceivable, into the category of fancies or of mere appearances. But where one personality is exclusively believed in and contemplated, this at once impresses with the power of a historical personality; imagination is done away with, the freedom to imagine others is renounced. This one personality presses on me the belief in its reality. The characteristic of real personality is precisely exclusiveness—the Leibnitzian principle of distinction, namely, that no one existence is exactly like another. The tone, the emphasis, with which the one personality is expressed produces such an effect on the feelings that it presents itself immediately as a real one, and is converted from an object of the imagination into an object of historical knowledge. . . .

[1] This exhibits clearly the untruthfulness and vanity of the modern speculations concerning the personality of God. If you are not ashamed of a personal God, do not be ashamed of a corporeal God. An abstract colorless personality, a personality without flesh and blood, is an empty shade.

It is superficial to say that Christianity is not the religion of one personal God, but of three personalities. These three personalities have certainly an existence in dogma; but even there the personality of the Holy Spirit is only an arbitrary decision which is contradicted by impersonal definitions; as, for example, that the Holy Spirit is the gift of the Father and Son.[2] Already the very "procession" of the Holy Ghost presents an evil prognostic for his personality, for a personal being is produced only by generation, not by an indefinite emanation or by *spiratio*. And even the Father, as the representative of the rigorous idea of the Godhead, is a personal being only according to opinion and assertion, not according to his definitions; he is an abstract idea, a purely rationalistic being. Only Christ is the plastic personality. To personality belongs form; form is the reality of personality. Christ alone is the personal God; he is the real God of Christians, a truth which cannot be too often repeated.[3] In him alone is concentrated the Christian religion, the essence of religion in general. He alone meets the longing for a personal God; he alone is an existence identical with the nature of feeling; on him alone are heaped all the joys of the imagination, and all the sufferings of the heart; in him alone are feeling and imagination exhausted. Christ is the blending in one of feeling and imagination.

Christianity is distinguished from other religions by this, that

[2] This was excellently shown by Faustus Socinus. See his Defens. Animadv. in Assert. Theol. Coll. Posnan. de trino et uno Deo. Irenopoli, 1656, c. 11.
[3] Let the reader examine, with reference to this, the writings of the Christian orthodox theologians against the heterodox; for example, against the Socinians. Modern theologians, indeed, agree with the latter, as is well known, in pronouncing the divinity of Christ as accepted by the Church to be unbiblical; but it is undeniably the characteristic principle of Christianity, and even if it does not stand in the Bible in the form which is given to it by dogma, it is nevertheless a necessary consequence of what is found in the Bible. A being who is the fulness of the Godhead bodily, who is omniscient (John xvi. 30) and almighty (raises the dead, works miracles), who is before all things, both in time and rank, who has life in himself (though an imparted life) like as the Father has life in himself,—what, if we follow out the consequences, can such a being be, but God? "Christ is one with the Father in will;"—but unity of will presupposes unity of nature. "Christ is the ambassador, the representative of God;"—but God can only be represented by a divine being. I can only choose as my representative one in whom I find the same or similar qualities as in myself; otherwise I belie myself.

in other religions the heart and imagination are divided, in Christianity they coincide. Here the imagination does not wander, left to itself; it follows the leadings of the heart; it describes a circle, whose center is feeling. Imagination is here limited by the wants of the heart, it only realizes the wishes of feeling, it has reference only to the one thing needful; in brief, it has, at least generally, a practical, concentric tendency, not a vagrant, merely poetic one. The miracles of Christianity—no product of free, spontaneous activity, but conceived in the bosom of yearning, necessitous feeling—place us immediately on the ground of common, real life; they act on the emotional man with irresistible force, because they have the necessity of feeling on their side. The power of imagination is here at the same time the power of the heart— imagination is only the victorious, triumphant heart. With the Orientals, with the Greeks, imagination, untroubled by the wants of the heart, reveled in the enjoyment of earthly splendor and glory; in Christianity, it descended from the palace of the gods into the abode of poverty, where only want rules—it humbled itself under the sway of the heart. But the more it limited itself in extent, the more intense became its strength. The wantonness of the Olympian gods could not maintain itself before the rigorous necessity of the heart; but imagination is omnipotent when it has a bond of union with the heart. And this bond between the freedom of the imagination and the necessity of the heart is Christ. All things are subject to Christ; he is the Lord of the world, who does with it what he will; but this unlimited power over Nature is itself again subject to the power of the heart— Christ commands raging Nature to be still, but only that he may hear the sighs of the needy.

The Contradiction of Faith and Love

The essence of religion, its latent nature, is the *identity* of the divine being with the human; but the form of religion, or its apparent, conscious nature, is the *distinction* between them. God is the human being; but he presents himself to the religious consciousness as a distinct being. Now, that which reveals the basis, the hidden essence of religion, is Love; that which constitutes its conscious form is Faith. Love identifies man with God and God with man, consequently it identifies man with man; faith separates God from man, consequently it separates man from man, for God is nothing else than the idea of the species invested with a mystical form—the separation of God from man is therefore the separation of man from man, the unloosening of the social bond. By faith religion places itself in contradiction with morality, with reason, with the unsophisticated sense of truth in man; by love it opposes itself again to this contradiction. Faith isolates God, it makes him a particular, distinct being; love universalizes, it makes God a common being, the love of whom is one with the love of man. Faith produces in man an inward disunion, a disunion with himself, and by consequence an outward disunion also; but love heals the wounds which are made by faith in the heart of man. Faith makes belief in its God a law; love is freedom—it condemns not even the atheist, because it is itself atheistic, itself denies, if not theoretically, at least practically, the existence of a particular, individual God, opposed to man. Love has God in itself; faith has God out of itself, it estranges God from man, it makes him an external object.

. . . Faith is essentially intolerant; essentially, because with faith is always associated the illusion that its cause is the cause of God, its honor his honor. The God of faith is nothing else than the objective nature of faith—faith become an object to itself. Hence in the religious consciousness also the cause of faith and the cause of God are identified. God himself is interested; the interest of faith is the nearest interest of God. . . .

Faith is the opposite of love. Love recognizes virtue even in sin, truth in error. It is only since the power of faith has been supplanted by the power of the natural unity of mankind, the power of reason, of humanity, that truth has been seen even in polytheism, in idolatry generally—or at least that there has been any attempt to explain on positive grounds what faith, in its bigotry, derives only from the devil. Hence love is reconcilable with reason alone, not with faith; for as reason, so also love is free, universal, in its nature; whereas faith is narrow-hearted, limited. Only where reason rules, does universal love rule; reason is itself nothing else than universal love. It was faith, not love, not reason, which invented Hell. To love, Hell is a horror; to reason, an absurdity. It would be a pitiable mistake to regard Hell as a mere aberration of faith, a false faith. Hell stands already in the Bible. Faith is everywhere like itself; at least positive religious faith, faith in the sense in which it is here taken, and must be taken unless we would mix with it the elements of reason, of culture—a mixture which indeed renders the character of faith unrecognizable.

Thus if faith does not contradict Christianity, neither do those dispositions which result from faith, neither do the actions which result from those dispositions. Faith condemns, anathematizes; all the actions, all the dispositions, which contradict love, humanity, reason, accord with faith. All the horrors of Christian religious history, which our believers aver not to be due to Christianity, have truly arisen out of Christianity, because they have arisen out of faith. This repudiation of them is indeed a necessary consequence of faith; for faith claims for itself only what is good, everything bad it casts on the shoulders of unbelief, or of misbelief, or of men in general. . . .

Faith necessarily passes into hatred, hatred into persecution, where the power of faith meets with no contradiction, where it does not find itself in collision with a power foreign to faith, the power of love, of humanity, of the sense of justice. Faith left to itself necessarily exalts itself above the laws of natural morality. The doctrine of faith is the doctrine of duty towards God—the highest duty of faith. By how much God is higher than man, by so much higher are duties to God than duties toward man; and duties toward God necessarily come into collision with common human duties. God is not only believed in, conceived as the universal being, the Father of men, as Love—such faith is the faith of love—he is also represented as a personal being, a being by himself. And so far as God is regarded as separate from man, as an individual being, so far are duties to God separated from duties to man—faith is, in the religious sentiment, separated from morality, from love.[1] Let it not be replied that faith in God is faith in love, in goodness itself; and that thus faith is itself an expression of a morally good disposition. In the idea of personality, ethical definitions vanish; they are only collateral things, mere accidents. The chief thing is the subject, the divine *Ego*. Love to God himself, since it is love to a personal being, is not a moral but a personal love. Innumerable devout hymns breathe nothing but love to the Lord; but in this love there appears no spark of an exalted moral idea or disposition.

. . . But although the deeds opposed to love which mark Christian religious history are in accordance with Christianity, and its antagonists are therefore right in imputing to it the horrible actions resulting from dogmatic creeds, those deeds nevertheless at the same time contradict Christianity, because Christianity is not only a religion of faith, but of love also—pledges us not only to faith, but to love. Uncharitable actions, hatred of heretics, at once accord and clash with Christianity? How is that possible? Perfectly. Christianity sanctions both the actions that spring out of love, and the actions that spring from faith without love. If Christianity had made love only its law, its adherents would be right—the horrors of Christian religious history could not be imputed to it; if it had made faith only its law, the reproaches of its antagonists would be unconditionally, unrestrictedly true. But Christianity has not made love free; it has not raised itself to the height of accepting love as absolute. And it has not given this freedom, nay, cannot give it, because it is a religion—and hence subjects love to the dominion of faith. Love is only the exoteric, faith the esoteric doctrine of Christianity; love is only the *morality*, faith the *religion* of the Christian religion.

---

[1] Faith, it is true, is not "without good works," nay, according to Luther's declaration, it is as impossible to separate faith from works as to separate heat and light from fire. Nevertheless, and this is the main point, good works do not belong to the article of justification before God, i.e., men are justified and "saved without works, through faith alone." Faith is thus expressly distinguished from good works; faith alone avails before God, not good works; faith alone is the cause of salvation, not virtue; thus faith alone has substantial significance, virtue only accidental; i.e., faith alone has religious significance, divine authority—and not morality. It is well known that many have gone so far as to maintain that good works are not necessary, but are even "injurious, obstructive to salvation." Quite correctly.

God is love. This is the sublimest dictum of Christianity. But the contradiction of faith and love is contained in the very proposition. Love is only a predicate, God the subject. What, then, is this subject in distinction from love? And I must necessarily ask this question, make this distinction. The necessity of the distinction would be done away with only if it were said conversely: Love is God, love is the absolute being. Thus love would take the position of the substance. In the proposition "God is love," the subject is the darkness in which faith shrouds itself; the predicate is the light, which first illuminates the intrinsically dark subject. In the predicate I affirm love, in the subject faith. Love does not alone fill my soul: I leave a place open for my uncharitableness by thinking of God as a subject in distinction from the predicate. It is therefore inevitable that at one moment I lose the thought of love, at another the thought of God, that at one moment I sacrifice the personality of God to the divinity of love, at another the divinity of love to the personality of God. The history of Christianity has given sufficient proof of this contradiction. Catholicism, especially, has celebrated Love as the essential deity with so much enthusiasm that to it the personality of God has been entirely lost in this love. But at the same time it has sacrificed love to the majesty of faith. Faith clings to the self-subsistence of God; love does away with it. "God is love" means, God is nothing by himself: he who loves, gives up his egoistical independence; he makes what he loves indispensable, essential to his existence. But while Self is being sunk in the depths of love, the idea of the Person rises up again and disturbs the harmony of the divine and human nature which had been established by love. Faith advances with its pretensions, and allows only just so much to Love as belongs to a predicate in the ordinary sense. It does not permit love freely to unfold itself; it makes love the abstract, and itself the concrete, the fact, the basis. The love of faith is only a rhetorical figure, a poetical fiction of faith— faith in ecstasy. If faith comes to itself, Love is fled.

. . . Christian love is already signalized as a particular, limited love, by the very epithet "Christian." But love is in its nature universal. So long as Christian love does not renounce its qualification of Christian, does not make love, simply, its highest law, so long is it a love which is injurious to the sense of truth, for the very office of love is to abolish the distinction between Christianity and so-called heathenism—so long is it a love which by its particularity is in contradiction with the nature of love, an abnormal, loveless love, which has therefore long been justly an object of sarcasm. True love is sufficient to itself; it needs no special title, no authority. Love is the universal law of intelligence and Nature—it is nothing else than the realization of the unity of the species through the medium of moral sentiment. To found this love on the name of a person is only possible by the association of superstitious ideas, either of a religious or speculative character. For with superstition is always associated particularism, and with particularism, fanaticism. Love can only be founded on the unity of the species, the unity of intelligence—on the nature of mankind; then only is it a well-grounded love, safe in its principle, guaranteed, free, for it is fed by the original source of love, out of which the love of Christ himself arose. The love of Christ was itself a derived love. He loved us not out of himself, by virtue of his own authority, but by virtue of our common human nature. A love which is based on his person is a particular, exclusive love, which extends only so far as the acknowledgment of this person extends, a love which does not rest on the proper ground of love. Are we to love each other because Christ loved us? Such love would be an affected, imitative love. Can we truly love each other only if we love Christ? Is Christ the cause of love? Is he not rather the apostle of love? Is not the ground of his love the unity of human nature? Shall I love Christ more than mankind? Is not such love a chimerical love? Can I step beyond the idea of the species? Can I love anything higher than humanity? What ennobled Christ was love; whatever qualities he had, he held in fealty to love; he was not the proprietor of love, as he is represented to be in all superstitious conceptions. The idea of love is an independent idea; I do not first deduce it from the life of Christ; on the contrary, I revere that life only because I find it accordant with the law, the idea of love.

This is already proved historically by the fact that the idea of love was by no means first introduced into the consciousness of mankind with and by Christianity—is by no means peculiarly Christian. The horrors of the Roman Empire present themselves with striking significance in company with the appearance of this idea. The empire of policy which united men after a manner corresponding with its own idea was coming to its necessary end. Political unity is a unity of force. The despotism of Rome must turn in upon itself, destroy itself. But it was precisely through this catastrophe of political existence that man released himself entirely from the heart-stifling toils of politics. In the place of Rome appeared the idea of humanity; to the idea of dominion succeeded the idea of love. Even the Jews, by imbibing the principle of humanity contained in Greek culture, had by this time mollified their malignant religious separatism. Philo celebrates love as the highest virtue. The extinction of national differences lay in the idea of humanity itself. Thinking minds had very early overstepped the civil and political separation of man from man. Aristotle distinguishes the man from the slave, and places the slave, as a man, on a level with his master, uniting them in friendship. Epictetus, the slave, was a Stoic; Antoninus, the emperor, was a Stoic also: thus did philosophy unite men. The Stoics taught[2] that man was not born for his own sake, but for the sake of others, i.e., for love: a principle which implies infinitely more than the celebrated dictum of the Emperor Antoninus, which enjoined the love of enemies. The practical principle of the Stoics is so far the principle of love. The world is to them one city, men its citizens. Seneca, in the sublimest sayings, extols love, clemency, humanity, especially toward slaves. Thus political rigor and patriotic narrowness were on the wane.

Christianity was a peculiar manifestation of these human tendencies—a popular, consequently a religious, and certainly a most intense manifestation of this new principle of love. That which elsewhere made itself apparent in the process of culture, expressed itself here as religious feeling, as a matter of faith. Christianity thus reduced a general unity to a particular one, it made love collateral to faith; and by this means it placed itself in contradiction with universal love. The unity was not referred

[2] The Peripatetics also; who founded love, even that towards all men, not on a particular, religious, but a natural principle.

to its true origin. National differences indeed disappeared; but in their place difference of faith, the opposition of Christian and un-Christian, more vehement than a national antagonism, and also more malignant, made its appearance in history.

All love founded on a special historical phenomenon contradicts, as has been said, the nature of love, which endures no limits, which triumphs over all particularity. Man is to be loved for man's sake. Man is an object of love because he is an end in himself, because he is a rational and loving being. This is the law of the species, the law of the intelligence. Love should be immediate, undetermined by anything else than its object—nay, only as such is it love. But if I interpose between my fellow man and myself the idea of an individuality, in whom the idea of the species is supposed to be already realized, I annihilate the very soul of love, I disturb the unity by the idea of a third external to us; for in that case my fellow man is an object of love to me only on account of his resemblance or relation to this model, not for his own sake. Here all the contradictions reappear which we have in the personality of God, where the idea of the personality by itself, without regard to the qualities which render it worthy of love and reverence, fixes itself in the consciousness and feelings. Love is the subjective reality of the species, as reason is its objective reality. In love, in reason, the need of an intermediate person disappears. Christ is nothing but an image, under which the unity of the species has impressed itself on the popular consciousness. Christ loved men: he wished to bless and unite them all without distinction of sex, age, rank, or nationality. Christ is the love of mankind to itself embodied in an image—in accordance with the nature of religion as we have developed it—or contemplated as a person, but a person who (we mean, of course, as a religious object) has only the significance of an image, who is only ideal. For this reason love is pronounced to be the characteristic mark of the disciples. But love, as has been said, is nothing else than the active proof, the realization of the unity of the race, through the medium of the moral disposition. The species is not an abstraction; it exists in feeling, in the moral sentiment, in the energy of love. It is the species which infuses love into me. A loving heart is the heart of the species throbbing in the individual. Thus Christ, as the consciousness of love, is the consciousness of the species. We are all one in Christ. Christ is the consciousness of our identity. He therefore who loves man for the sake of man, who rises to the love of the species, to universal love, adequate to the nature of the species,[3] he is a Christian, is Christ himself. He does what Christ did, what made Christ Christ. Thus, where there arises the consciousness of the species as a species, the idea of humanity as a whole, Christ disappears, without, however, his true nature disappearing; for he was the substitute for the consciousness of the species, the image under which it was made present to the people, and became the law of the popular life.

God As Man's Highest Self

God is man's highest feeling of self, freed from all contrarieties or disagreeables. God is the highest being; therefore, to feel God is the highest feeling. But is not the highest feeling also the highest feeling of self? So long as I have not had the feeling of the highest, so long I have not exhausted my capacity of feeling, so long I do not yet fully know the nature of feeling. What, then, is an object to me in my feeling of the highest being? Nothing else than the highest nature of my power of feeling. So much as a man can feel, so much is (his) God. But the highest degree of the power of feeling is also the highest degree of the feeling of self. In the feeling of the *low* I feel myself lowered, in the feeling of the *high* I feel myself exalted. The feeling of self and feeling are inseparable, otherwise feeling would not belong to myself. Thus God, as an object of feeling, or what is the same thing, the feeling of God, is nothing else than man's highest feeling of self. But God is the freest, or rather the absolutely only free being; thus God is man's highest feeling of freedom. How could you

---

[3] Active love is and must of course always be particular and limited, i.e., directed to one's neighbor. But it is yet in its nature universal, since it loves man for man's sake, in the name of the race. Christian love, on the contrary, is in its nature exclusive.

be conscious of the highest being as freedom, or freedom as the highest being, if you did not feel yourself free? But when do you feel yourself free? When you feel God. To feel God is to feel oneself free. For example, you feel desire, passion, the conditions of time and place, as limits. What you feel as a limit you struggle against, you break loose from, you deny. The consciousness of a limit, as such, is already an anathema, a sentence of condemnation pronounced on this limit, for it is an oppressive, disagreeable, negative consciousness. Only the feeling of the good, of the positive, is itself good and positive—is joy. Joy alone is feeling in its element, its paradise, because it is unrestricted activity. The sense of pain in an organ is nothing else than the sense of a disturbed, obstructed, thwarted activity; in a word, the sense of something abnormal, anomalous. Hence you strive to escape from the sense of limitation into unlimited feeling. By means of the will, or the imagination, you negative limits, and thus obtain the feeling of freedom. This feeling of freedom is God. God is exalted above desire and passion, above the limits of space and time. But this exaltation is your own exaltation above that which appears to you as a limit. Does not this exaltation of the divine being exalt you? How could it do so, if it were external to you? No; God is an exalted being only for him who himself has exalted thoughts and feelings. Hence the exaltation of the divine being varies according to that which different men or nations perceive as a limitation to the feeling of self, and which they consequently negative or eliminate from their ideal.

Ernest Renan

[1823–1892]

BEST KNOWN for his immensely popular *La Vie de Jésus*, the first critical biography of Jesus (as contrasted with Strauss' study of the documents), Ernest Renan may best be understood biographically, but not so much for an understanding of the man as of his era, for Renan's life is paradigmatic of what is "modern" in nineteenth-century religious thought.

His ancestors were Breton peasants, and his grandparents had supported the Revolution. Renan's father, a seaman, died when the boy was five; for the next four years he remained with his mother, who ran a grocery store in Tréguier, until the priests of the local *collège ecclésiastique*, who were good customers of hers, took him in charge. It was virtually the only way a poor boy could hope to receive an education. Thus for a dozen years spanning puberty and adolescence, he was nurtured in the bosom of the church. He was precocious and brilliant, and he was also free to correspond with his sister Henriette, a teacher, who had lost her faith by the time Renan was eighteen or nineteen. Thus he had someone in whom to confide his own doubts, and in 1842 he wrote to her that only Pascal and the Bible kept him a Christian. As he approached the series of steps that led into the Catholic priesthood, he was assailed by "terrible doubts." He had come to feel that God was hidden from him; not for a long time had he felt that God was an "active presence" in his life.

He had already received the tonsure and was soon due to be ordained a subdeacon. In May 1845 he wrote an *Essai psychologique sur Jésus-Christ*, which was not published till 1921, and in this work he was able to see clearly the gulf that had opened between his thought and that of the church. He had hoped for a personal revelation to restore his faith in time for him to be ordained, but it had not come. What he discovered instead was that, in the words of a recent biographer, "he no longer believed in the immortality of the soul or in the existence of God, although he retained a belief in the workings of a hidden God. Neither did he believe in the divinity of Christ. He did believe in the 'eminent personality of Jesus,' which, he says, sustained him in his struggle with theology."[1]

It was without rancor that he left the seminary of Saint-Sulpice, and for at least the following year he continued to attend mass and confession. When he enrolled in the pension Crouzet, a secular institution, in the fall of 1845, it was with a sense of pride that he had sacrificed a priestly career to the "intellectual Christ" within himself. Soon thereafter he became close friends with a young chemist, Marcelin Berthelot, from whom he acquired a smattering of scientific knowledge as readily as he had earlier mastered Hebrew. At Crouzet, he rapidly established his academic qualifications and in 1847 won the Volney prize in linguistics.

Renan was twenty-five when the bourgeois monarchy of King Louis-Philippe was overthrown. In June 1848 the workers of Paris rose against the Second Republic and were ruthlessly suppressed. Renan was greatly stirred by these events and his thinking took an apocalyptic turn, as his soul-searching, his scholarly pursuits and the course of political events all seemed to be converging on the possible advent of a radical innovation in religion. It was in such an atmosphere that he wrote two articles on D. F. Strauss and the rationalist historians of the origins of Christianity —a rehearsal for his later multivolume *Histoire des Origines du Christianisme*, of which *La Vie de Jésus* was the first volume. And it was then also that he wrote his ambitious *L'Avenir de Science*, which Wardman describes as follows:

> Promethean, Christian and Faustian elements go to make up what is in short a humanistic version of the story of the Fall and redemption of man. . . . The work as a whole expresses Renan's messianic hope that the intellectuals would take over from the

[1] H. W. Wardman, *Ernest Renan: A Critical Biography* (London: Athlone Press, 1964), p. 19.

Revolution of 1848 and lead the way, with the help of a new Napoleon, towards the age of synthesis. . . . Of all Renan's philosophical writings it is the least disciplined and mature, but it is also the most intellectually alive and the most generous.[2]

The philosophy of Hegel inevitably looms behind this work, which may be regarded as a religious parallel to the dialectical materialism of Marx and Engels which emerged from the very same historical context. With some justification it can be called a messianic humanism. It is visionary rather than positivistic, and it veers toward an authoritarianism predicated on a paradoxical faith in "the goodness of the hidden God, in whom he believed so far as he had faith in himself and mankind."[3] There are echoes of Blake and pre-echoes of Nietzsche here as well as resonances from Hegel, and these become even clearer in the *Histoire*, which sees in Christianity itself a dialectic of both love and hate, which it is the task of "science"—dispassionate humanistic studies—to transcend and transvalue. There is also a Nietzschean sense of class distinction as between the intellectual and the people, and this leads to an élitist view of history; but Renan's condescension is compassionate, not scornful. As a dabbler in politics, Renan too often conformed to the *status quo* after 1848, and this may be one reason why, except for a couple of chapters, he withheld publication of *L'Avenir de Science* until 1890. But beneath the somewhat florid style and despite the youthful romanticism, the exuberance of the seminary-trained scholar only recently plunged into a most secular environment, there is both matter-of-factness and what Tillich was later to call "ultimate concern." Matter-of-factness above all in his acceptance of the unpromising future of popular religious consciousness; ultimate concern in a more pervasive sense, perhaps most manifested in his conception of scholarship as the pursuit of moral and intellectual perfection. Renan's humanism, finally, unlike that of Strauss, is not facile and banal even when it seems so. As the following extract attests, when it is truly humane it also evinces the persistence of "God-consciousness," even if it is of a God who no longer exists. Even at its most serene, it embodies an inability to shrug off or patch

[2] *Ibid.*, p. 49.
[3] *Ibid.*, p. 210.

up the crisis of faith to which experience led him and in which it left him.

The Future of Religion in an Age of Science[1]

Religion is the word under which has been resumed, up to the present, the life of the mind. Take the Christian of the first ages; religion is his whole spiritual life. Not a thought, not a feeling which is not attached to it: material life is almost entirely absorbed in this great movement of idealism. *Sive manducatis, sive bibitis*, says St. Paul. What a superb system of life, all ideal, all divine and really worthy of the children of God. There is no exclusion there, the chain is not felt; for, although the limit is narrow our wants do not go beyond it. The law, severe as it is, is entirely the expression of man. In the Middle Ages this great equation still existed. The fairs, the meetings for business or pleasure are religious fêtes; the scenic representations are mysteries; voyages are pilgrimages; wars are crusades. Take, on the contrary, a Christian, even the most severe, in the time of Louis XIV, Montausier, Arnauld, Beauvilliers, you will find two divisions in his life: the religious portion, which, although the principal, is not sufficiently strong to assimilate itself with the rest; the profane portion, to which one must accord some value. Then, but not before, the ascetics began to preach renunciation. The first Christian had no need to renounce anything, for his life was complete; his law was adequate to his wants. Afterward, religion, not being able to provide for everything, cursed what escaped it. I am sure that Beauvilliers took a very delicate pleasure in the tragedies of Racine, and perhaps even in the comedies of Molière; and yet it is certain that in going to see them he did not consider that he was performing a religious act, perhaps he even thought that he was sinning. This separation was a matter of necessity. At that epoch religion was received as a letter closed and sealed,

[1] From *The Future of Science* [1849], English translation Boston, 1891.—Ed.

which was not to be opened, but which one was bound to receive and transmit, and yet, human life always opening up, it was necessary that new wants should overcome all scruples, and that, not being able to find a place in religion, they should take up a position opposite to it. Hence a system of life both colorless and indifferent. Religion is respected but people guard against its *invasions*; they give it its share, to it which is only something on condition of being everything. Hence these petty theories concerning the separation of the two powers, of the respective rights of reason and faith.

The result must be that religion, being isolated, cut off from the heart of humanity, no longer receiving anything from the general circulation, like a limb which is bound, must wither and become an appendage of secondary importance, while on the contrary profane life, in which all the actual and living feelings, all discoveries, all new ideas, are concentrated, must become the master portion. Without doubt the great men of the eighteenth century were more religious than they thought; what they banished under the name of religion was clerical despotism, superstition, narrow forms. The reaction, however, carried them too far; the religious color was almost entirely wanting in that century. The philosophers placed themselves without knowing it in the position of their adversaries, and, under the empire of the association of obstinate ideas, appeared to suppose that the secularization of existence would bring about the elimination of all religious habits. I think, like the Catholics, that our society founded upon a supposititious pact, and our atheistical law, are temporary anomalies, and that until we can speak of "*our holy constitution*" stability will not be conquered. Now, the return to religion can be nothing else than the return to the great unity of life, to the religion of the intellect without exclusion and without limit. The sage has no need of praying at certain hours, for his whole life is a prayer. If religion is to have a distinct place in life it must absorb life altogether. The most rigorous asceticism is alone consistent. Only superficial-minded or weak-hearted people, once Christianity is admitted, can take any interest in life, in science, in poetry, in the things of this world. The mystics look with pity upon this weakness, and they are right. The true philosophical religion would not reduce this great tree, which has its roots in the soul of man, to a few branches, it would only be a manner of spending one's whole life in seeing beneath everything the ideal and divine sense, and in sanctifying one's whole life by the purity of the soul and the elevation of the heart.

Religion, as I understand it, is far removed from what the philosophers call *natural religion*, a kind of petty theology without poetry, without action upon humanity. All the attempts made in this direction have been and will remain fruitless. Theodicy has no meaning regarded as an individual science. Is there any man of sense who can hope to make discoveries in such an order of speculations? True theodicy is the science of things, physics, physiology, history looked upon in a religious light. Religion is to know and to love the truth of things. A proposition is only of value in so far as it is understood and felt. What signifies this sealed formula, this unknown tongue, this $a \times b$ theology, which you present to humanity saying, "This will preserve your soul for life eternal: eat and you shall be healed"—a pill which you must not bite on pain of feeling a cruel bitterness? Well! what matters it to me if I do not taste it? Give me a leaden bullet to swallow, that will have the same effect. What to me are stereotyped phrases devoid of sense, like the formulas of the alchemist and the magicians which operate of themselves *ex opere operato*, as the theologians say? Black and scholastic doctors occupied only with your Incarnation and your real Presence, the time has come when you shall worship the father, not on this mountain nor in Jerusalem, but in spirit and in truth.

M. Proudhon is certainly a distinguished philosopher of great intelligence. But I cannot pardon him his airs of atheism and irreligion. It is to commit suicide to write such phrases as this: "Man is destined to live without religion. A number of symptoms show that society, by an internal work constantly tends to shake off this envelope henceforward useless." That if you practice the worship of what is noble and true, if the sanctity of morality speaks to your heart, if all beauty, all truth, all goodness leads you to the threshold of a holy life, to intelligence; that if, arrived there, you refuse to speak, you wrap yourself up, you purposely mix up your thought and your language in order to say nothing limited in presence of the infinite, how do you dare to speak of atheism? That if your faculties, resounding simultaneously, have never uttered that grand and unique rite, which we call God, I have nothing more to say, you are devoid of the essential and characteristic element of our nature.

Humanity is only converted when it falls in love with the divine charm of beauty. Now beauty in the moral order is religion. This is why a religion dead and outstripped is still more efficacious than all the institutions which are purely profane; this is why Christianity is still more creative, comforts more suffering, acts more vigorously upon humanity than all the principles acquired in modern times. The men of the future will not be mean disputatious reasoners, insulters, men of party, intriguers, without ideal. They will be noble, they will be amiable, they will be poetic. I, inflexible critic, I shall not be suspected of flattery for a man who searches the Trinity in all things and who believes, God pardon me, in the efficacy of the name of Jehovah; well! I prefer Pierre Leroux, mistaken as he is, to these pretended philosophers who would recast humanity in the narrow mold of their scholastic ideas and triumph with politics over the divine instincts of the human heart.

The word God having taken possession of the respect of humanity, this word having a long prescription in its favor and having been employed in beautiful poems, it would perplex humanity to suppress it. Although it is not very univocal, as the scholastics say, it corresponds to an idea sufficiently clear: the *summum* and the *ultimum*, the limit where the mind stops in the scale of the infinite. Suppose even that we philosophers should prefer another word, "reason," for example, in addition that these words are too abstract and do not sufficiently express real existence, there would be a great inconvenience to deprive us thus of all the poetic sources of the past and to separate us by our language from the simple who adore so well after their fashion. Tell the simple to live by aspiration after truth and beauty; these words would have no meaning for them. Tell them to love God, not to offend God; they will understand you perfectly. God, providence, soul, good old words, rather heavy, but expressive and respectable, which science will explain but will never replace with advantage. What is God for humanity if not the transcendent epitome of its suprasensitive wants, *the category of the ideal,* that is to say the form under which we conceive the ideal, as time and space are categories, that is to say forms under which we conceive bodies? Everything reduces itself to this fact of human nature; man in presence of the divine is no longer himself, he clings to a celestial charm, he lays aside his paltry personality, is carried away and absorbed. What is that if it is not to adore?

If one views the matter as regards substance and asks oneself: This God does He or does He not exist?—Oh, God would I reply, it is He who is and all the rest which appears to be. If "to be" has any meaning, it is assuredly applied to the ideal. What, you would admit that matter exists, because your hands and your eyes say so, and you would doubt of the divine being which all your nature proclaims from the first? What is the meaning of this phrase "Matter is"? what would remain of it in the hands of a strict analysis? I do not know and to tell the truth I consider the question senseless; for one must confine oneself to simple notions. Beyond is the gulf. Reason only attains a certain mean region; above and below it loses itself as a sound which by dint of becoming sharp or flat ceases to be a sound or at least to be perceived. I like, for my own part, to compare the object of reason to those foaming or frothy substances where the substance is hardly anything and which only exist thanks to their effervescence. If one pursues too closely the substantial foundation nothing remains but the bare unity; as mathematical formulas too closely pressed render all identity fundamental and only mean something on the condition of not being too simplified. Every intellectual act, like every equation, reduces itself at bottom to $A = A$. Now, with this limit, there is no more knowledge, there is no more intellectual work. Science commences only with details. In order that there should be any effort of the mind a superfices is necessary, something variable, diverse, otherwise one loses oneself in the infinite One. The One only exists and is perceptible when developing itself in diversity, that is to say in phenomena. Beyond, it is repose, it is death. Knowledge is the infinite poured into a finite mold. The knot alone has any value. The faces of the unity are alone an object of science.

There is not a word in the philosophical language which may not give rise to great errors if one takes it in its substantial and vulgar sense, instead of using it to design classes of phenomena. Realism and abstraction touch each other; Christianity may have been turn about with good reason accused of realism and of abstraction. Phenomenalism alone is genuine. I hope that no one will ever accuse me of being materialist and yet I regard the hypothesis of two substances joined together to form man as one of the most clumsy inventions made by philosophy. The words "body" and "soul" remain perfectly distinct insofar as they represent the orders of irreducible phenomena; but to make this diversity, entirely phenomenal, synonymous to an ontological distinction, is to fall into a ponderous realism and to imitate the ancient hypotheses of physical sciences, which suppose as many causes as different effects, and explain by those real and substantial fluids facts in which a more advanced science sees nothing but various orders of phenomena. Of a truth it is much more absurd to say in a spirit of exclusion: "Man is a body"; the truth is that there is a unique substance, which is neither body nor soul, but which reveals itself by two orders of phenomena, which are the body and the soul, that these two words have no meaning except in their opposition, and that this opposition exists only in acts. The spiritualist is not him who believes in two substances coarsely united; it is he who is persuaded that the acts of the mind alone have a transcendental value. Man is; he is matter, that is to say expanded, tangible, endowed with physical properties; he is mind, that is to say thinking, feeling, adoring. The mind is the goal as the goal of the plant is the flower; without roots, without leaves, there are no flowers.

The most simple act of intelligence comprehends the perception of God; for it comprehends the perception of being and the perception of the infinite. The infinite exists in all our faculties and constitutes, it is true, the distinctive feature of humanity, the unique category of pure reason which distinguishes man from the animal. This element may become effaced in the vulgar acts of intelligence; but as it is to be found indubitably in the acts of the mind, this is a reason to conclude that it is to be found in all those acts; for that which exists in one degree exists in all the others; and besides the infinite shows itself much more energetically in the acts of primitive humanity, in that life vague and without conscience, in that spontaneous state, in that native enthusiasm, in those temples and pyramids than in our age of polished reflection and analytical view. This is the God of whom we have an innate idea and who does not require demonstration. Against this God atheism is impossible; because people affirm Him while denying Him. Everywhere man has outpaced nature; everywhere, beyond the visible, he has supposed the invisible. This is the only feature which is truly universal, the identical foundation upon which divers instincts have embroidered infinite varieties, from the multiple forces of savages to Jehovah, from Jehovah to the Indian Oum. To look for a universal consent on the part of humanity to anything else but this psychological fact is to misuse terms. Humanity has always believed in something beyond the finite, this something, it is suitable to call God. Therefore all humanity has believed in God. Very well. But do not, misusing a definition of words, pretend that humanity has believed in such and such a God, in a moral and personal God formed by anthropomorphic analogy. That God is so little innate that the half of humanity has not believed in Him and that it has required ages to formulate this system in a complete manner, in ordering man to love God. It is not that I entirely blame the method of anthropomorphic psychology. God being the ideal of every one, it is right that every one should fashion Him after his manner and on his own model. One must not therefore fear to employ all the goodness and beauty that can be imagined. But it is contrary to all criticism to pretend to erect such a method into a scientific method and to raise, out of an ideal construction, a discussion on the qualities of a being. Let us say that the supreme being is eminently possessed of all that is perfection; let us say that he has in him something analogous, to intelligence, to liberty; but do not let us say that he is intelligent that he is free: this would be trying to limit the infinite, to give a name to the ineffable (192).

One is accustomed to consider monotheism as a definitive and absolute conquest, beyond which there can be no ulterior progress. In my eyes monotheism is, like polytheism, only an age in

the relgion of humanity. This word, besides, is far from designat-
ing a doctrine absolutely identical. Our monotheism is only a
system like another, inferring it is true very advanced notions.
It is the Jewish system, it is Jehovah. Neither the ancient polytheism, which also contained a great portion of truth; nor India,
so learned in its conception of God, understood things in this
manner. The deva of India is a superior being to man, by no
means our God. Although the Jewish system has entered into
our intellectual habits it should not make us forget all that was
profound and poetic in other systems. No doubt, if the ancients
had understood by God what we ourselves understand, polytheism
would have been a contradiction of terms. But their terminology
in this matter reposed upon notions quite different from ours
respecting the government of the world. They had not yet arrived
at the conception of unity of government in the universe. The
Greek worship representing at bottom of the worship of human
nature and the beauty of things, and that without any orthodox
pretension, without any dogmatic organization, is only a poetical
form of universal religion perhaps not far removed from that to
which philosophy will return (193). This is so true that where
the moderns have wished to make some trials of natural worship
they have been obliged to approach it. The great moral superiority
of Christianity makes us too easily forget the breadth, the toleration, the respect for all that was natural which existed in Grecian
mythologism. The origin of the severe manner in which we have
judged it lies in the ridiculous way in which mythology has been
presented to us. One imagines a religious body obliged to enter
our conceptions by force. A religion which has a God for thieves,
another for drunkards, appears to us the height of absurdity.
Now, as humanity has never lost its common sense, we must
admit that until we can conceive these fables naturally we do
not possess the key to the enigma. Polytheism only appears
absurd to us because we do not understand it. Humanity is never
absurd. The religions which do not pretend to repose upon a
revelation, so inferior as machines of action to religions organized
dogmatically, are, in one sense, more philosophical, or rather they
only differ from truly philosophical religion by a more or less
symbolical expression. These religions are, at bottom, only the

State, the family, art and morality elevated to a high and poetic expression. They do not divide life in two; they have no sacred and profane. They know nothing of mystery, renouncement and sacrifice since they accept and sanctify nature at first sight. These were bonds, but bonds of flowers. There lies the secret of their feebleness in the work of humanity; they are not strong but also less dangerous. They do not possess that prodigious psychological subtlety, that spirit of limit, of intolerance, of *particularism*, if I dare say so, that force of abstraction, veritable vampire which has gone on absorbing all that is gentle and mild in humanity ever since it was given to the wan image of the crucified One to fascinate the human conscience. It sucked everything even to the last drop out of poor humanity: juice and force, blood and life, nature and art, family, people, country; everything went down, and on the ruins of an exhausted world there remained but the phantom of the Me, tottering and distrustful.

Up to the present, men as far as religion is concerned have been divided into two categories: religious men believing in a positive dogma, and irreligious men holding themselves aloof from all revealed belief. This is insupportable. Henceforth they must be classed thus: religious persons taking a serious view of life and the sanctity of things; frivolous men, without faith, without seriousness, without morality. All those who adore something are brothers, or certainly not such great enemies as those who adore simply pleasure and interest. It is indubitable that I resemble more a Catholic or a Buddhist than a skeptical laugher, and my intimate sympathies are a proof of this. I love one, I detest the other. I can even call myself a Christian, in this sense that I admit being indebted to Christianity for most of the elements of my faith, just as M. Cousin might have called himself Platonician or Cartesian without accepting all the inheritance of Plato or Descartes, and above all without feeling himself obliged to regard them as prophets. Do not say that I am twisting words when I thus arrogate to myself a name the acceptation of which I have greatly altered. No doubt if one understands by religion a number of imposed dogmas and external practices, then I admit that I am not religious; but I also maintain that humanity is not essentially so and will not always be so in that sense. What is a part of humanity, and will consequently be as eternal as itself, is the religious want, the religious faculty, to which up to the present the great ensembles of doctrine and ceremonies have corresponded but which will be sufficiently satisfied with the pure worship of good and beautiful things. We have therefore the right to speak of religion, since we have the analogy, if not the thing itself; since the want which was formerly satisfied by positive religions is now satisfied by something equivalent which has the right of being called by the same name. If people absolutely persist in taking this moral in a more restricted sense, we will not dispute over a free definition, we will merely remark that religion thus understood is not essential and that it will disappear from humanity, leaving vacant a place which will be filled up by something analogous.

A great deal has been said within the last few years of a religious revival, and I willingly admit that this revival has generally shown itself in the form of a return to Catholicism. This is as it should be. Humanity feeling the imperious want of a religion will always cling to that which it finds already made. It is not to Catholicism, as Catholicism, that this century has returned but to Catholicism as a religion. It must also be admitted that Catholicism with its harsh and absolute forms, its rigorous rules and its perfect centralization, must please a nation which saw in it the most perfect model of its own government. France, which finds it quite natural that a law emanating from Paris should become at once applicable to the Breton peasant, to the Alsatian workman, to the nomad shepherd of the Landes, must also find it quite natural that there should be at Rome an *infallible being* who regulates the belief of the world. This is very convenient. Delivered from the care of making one's creed and even of understanding it one can, after that, attend in full security to one's affairs, saying, "That does not concern me; tell me what I must believe; I believe it." Strange contradiction, for, formulas having no value except the *sense* they contain, it is of no advantage to say, "I trust to the Pope; he knows what to believe and I believe as he does." People believe that faith is like a talisman which saves by its own virtue; that they will be saved if they believe some unintelligible proposition, without taking the trouble to understand it; they do not feel that these things are only of value according to the good which they do the soul, by their personal application to the believer.

If a return toward Catholicism has taken place it is therefore in no way because progress in the way of criticism has brought it back, it is because the want of a religion has been more sharply felt and because Catholicism alone was ready at hand. Catholicism, for the immense majority of those who profess it, is no longer Catholicism; it is religion. It is repugnant to pass one's life like the brute, to be born, to contract marriage, to die without any religious ceremony consecrating these holy acts. Catholicism is there to satisfy this want; then let us have Catholicism. People do not examine matters more closely; they do not enter into details of dogmas, they pity those who undertake so sterile a task; they are heretics a hundred times over without being aware of it. What has made the fortune of Catholicism in our days is that it is little known. It is only seen through certain imposing externals, one only takes into consideration what is elevated and moral in its dogmas; one does not enter into the brushwood. What is more, one bravely rejects or complacently explains those dogmas which are too openly opposed to modern ideas. If one were obliged to accept as an article of faith every text of Scripture and every decree of the Council of Trent, it would be a different matter; one would be surprised to find oneself incredulous. Those who have been led by peculiar circumstances to wage a death struggle on this ground have reasons for not being accommodating.

David Friedrich Strauss

[1808–1874]

D. F. STRAUSS was twenty-four when he arrived in Berlin, eager to study under Hegel, who died within a couple of months. Strauss had recently begun a massive critical study, *Das Leben Jesu*, which was published three years later. Highly controversial and internationally influential in its time, it appeared in an English translation by the novelist George Eliot a decade later. Applying Hegel's philosophy of religion to the New Testament documents, albeit under the influence of Schleiermacher, Strauss takes a direction quite the opposite of Hegel's; instead of moving from image to concept, Strauss reduces the religious imagination to the level of myth. His detailed exegesis of the New Testament as myth dealt a devastating blow to orthodox Christian doctrine and provoked a vigorous counterattack. The upshot of Strauss' new theology was that, through Jesus, mankind is the incarnation of God. This view, rooted in Hegel's kenotic understanding of the incarnation, was later to issue in a sharp break with even liberal Protestantism. In his last years, Strauss abandoned the Hegelian philosophy, pronounced Christianity obsolete and called for a "new faith" in which "God" is superseded by "cosmos," and an ethic rooted in the teachings of Jesus is infused with an optimism based on "the spirit of scientific progress" to form a new, positivistic humanism.

There is something very dated about the extract from *Der alte und der neue Glaube* that follows. It is not very profound, and much of what it says we have by now heard again and again. We can sympathize with Nietzsche's rollicking contempt for Strauss' pompous sentimentality, and indeed we can take these pages as partial documentation of Nietzsche's parable of the madman. What is absent from these pages is even more incriminating. Along with his divagations on the "new" religion and ethics, Strauss calls for a cultural renovation and betrays a smug Prussian arrogance in his choice of "great poets and musicians" to augment the spirit of Jesus and the spirit of science. All the more ironic is the spectacle of this self-styled "humanist" snubbing the irenic Renan and rebuffing the latter's conciliatory gestures during the Franco-Prussian War, at the very time that Strauss was writing this book, which was published in 1872.

Yet when all this is said, "Are We Still Christians?" and the basis on which the question was asked are of historic importance as part of the secularizing process. Strauss remains a key figure in the "quest of the historical Jesus," an antecedent of Bultmann's demythologizing inquiry and, perhaps above all, a representative voice for a later generation of churchless millions whose exodus to a shallow, sentimental "new faith" he tacitly describes. However we otherwise assess Strauss' importance, the "self-dissolution of Protestant theology" that he achieved had, unlike that of, say, Tom Paine, "an effect both enormous and liberating."[1]

Are We Still Christians?[1]

Let us now bethink ourselves what it was that we really set out to discover. We had quite given up the ecclesiastical conception of Jesus as the Saviour and Son of God, and had found Schleiermacher's "God in Christ" to be a mere phrase. But we asked whether as a historical personage he might not have been one on whom our religious life still continues to be dependent, on whom more than to any other great man it must look for moral perfection. This question we are now in a position to answer.

---

[1] Karl Löwith, *From Hegel to Nietzsche* (New York: Holt, Rinehart & Winston, 1964), p. 335. See also Johann Friedrich Overbeck, *Die Christlichkeit der Theologie* (1873), pp. 110f.
[1] From *The Old Faith and the New* [1872], English translation, 1873.

To begin with, we shall be obliged to state that our authentic information respecting Jesus is far too scanty for this purpose. The evangelists have overlaid the picture of his life with so thick a coat of supernatural coloring, have confused it by so many cross lights of contradictory doctrine, that the natural colors cannot now be restored. If one may not with impunity walk among palms, still less so among gods. He who has once been deified has irretrievably lost his manhood. It is an idle notion that by any kind of operation we could restore a natural and harmonious picture of a life and a human being from sources of information which, like the Gospels, have been adapted to suit a supernatural being, and distorted, moreover, by parties whose conceptions and interests conflicted with each other's. To check these, we ought to possess information concerning the same life, compiled from a purely natural and common-sense point of view; and in this case we are not in possession of such. However grandiloquently the most recent delineators of the life of Jesus may have come forward, and pretended to be enabled by our actual sources of information to depict a human development, a natural germination and growth of insight, a gradual expansion of Jesus' horizon, their essays have been shown to be apologetic artifices, devoid of all historical value, from the absence of all proof in the record (with the exception of that vague phrase in Luke's history of the Infancy) and by the necessity of most gratuitously transposing the various accounts.

But not only does the manner of Jesus' development remain enveloped in impenetrable obscurity; it is by no means very apparent into what he developed, and ultimately became. To mention only one more fact, after all we have said, we cannot even be certain whether at the last he did not lose his faith in himself and his mission. If he spoke the famous words on the cross, "My God, my God, why hast thou forsaken me?" then he did. It is possible, and I myself have pointed out the possibility, of the exclamation only being attributed to him in order that a psalm, considered by the earliest Christianity as the program of the Messianic agony, might at its very commencement be applicable to him; but it certainly is equally probable that he may really have uttered the significant words. If he rose afterward, i.e., if he was the incarnate suffering deity, then it is nowise prejudicial to him; then it only marks the lowest degree of this agony, is the cry of anguish wrung from weak mortality, which is compensated for by the strength of his divine nature as immediately manifested in his resuscitation. If, however, he is regarded as purely a human hero, the words, if he uttered them, give rise to grave misgivings. If so, then he had not calculated upon his death, then he had to the very end nursed the illusion respecting the angelic hosts, and at last, as still they came not, as they suffered him to hang languishing to death on the cross and to perish, then he had died with blasted hope and broken heart. And however much, even then, we should commiserate him on account of the excellence of his heart and his aspirations, however much we might deprecate the punishment awarded him as cruel and unjust, nevertheless we could not fail to acknowledge that so enthusiastic an expectation but receives its deserts when it is mocked by miscarriage.

As we have said, nothing is firmly established, save the objection that so many and such essential facts in the life of Jesus are *not* firmly established that we neither are clearly cognizant of his aims, nor the mode and degree in which he hoped for their realization. Perhaps these things may be ascertained; but the necessity of first ascertaining them, and the prospect of at best only attaining probability as the result of far-reaching critical investigations, instead of the intuitive assurance of faith, gives a rather discouraging aspect to the matter. Above all, I must have a distinct, definite conception of him in whom I am to believe, whom I am to imitate as an exemplar of moral excellence. A being of which I can only catch fitful glimpses, which remains obscure to me in essential respects, may, it is true, interest me as a problem for scientific investigation, but it must remain ineffectual as regards practical influence on my life. But a being with distinct features, capable of affording a definite conception, is only to be found in the Christ of faith, of legend, and there, of course, only by the votary who is willing to take into the bargain all the impossibilities, all the contradictions contained in the picture: the Jesus of history, of science, is only a problem; but a problem cannot be an object of worship, or a pattern by which to shape our lives.

And among the things which, comparatively speaking, we still know most positively of Jesus, there is unfortunately something which we must mention as the second and decisive reason why, if science is to assert her rights in his case, he, as the religious leader, must come to be daily more and more estranged from mankind, as mankind has developed under the influence of the civilizing momenta of modern times.

Whether he designed his kingdom for Jews, or Gentiles as well; whether he attached much or little importance to the Mosaic law and the services of the Temple; whether he assigned to himself and his disciples a greater or less amount of actual authority; whether he foresaw his death, or was surprised by it—either there is no historical basis to be found anywhere in the Gospels, or Jesus expected promptly to reappear enthroned on the clouds of heaven, in order to inaugurate the kingdom of the Messiah as foretold by him. Now, if he was the Son of God, or otherwise a being of supernatural dignity, all we have to say is that the event did not occur, and that therefore he who predicted it could not have been a divinity. But if he was not such—if he was a mere man, and yet nourished such an expectation—then there is no help for it: according to our conceptions he was an enthusiast. The word has long since ceased to be a term of opprobrium and obloquy, as it was in the last century. We know there have been noble enthusiasts—enthusiasts of genius; the influence of an enthusiast can rouse, exalt, and occasion prolonged historic effects; but we shall not be desirous to choose him as the guide of our life. He will be sure to mislead us, if we do not subject his influence to the control of our reason.

But this latter precaution was neglected by Christendom during the Middle Ages. Not only did it suffer itself to be seduced by Christ's utter disdain for the world; it even outdid him. He at least continued to abide in the world, were it only to convince men of its worthlessness; if hermits and monks at a later period shunned all intercourse with it, they indeed outstripped him, but only on the path along which he led them himself. As concerned

renunciation of worldly goods, indeed, they were at no loss for
a subterfuge: the individual, it was true, could own nothing, but
the community, the monastery, the church, and its heads, so much
the more. Thus, too, the precept of turning the other cheek to the
smiter has always found its corrective in the sound common sense
of mankind; some personages of especial sanctity excepted, the
pious Middle Ages were as contentious and bellicose as any other
era in the history of the world. Its sturdy goodmen and housewives, moreover, took good thought for the morrow, in spite of
the precept of their Saviour; but the performance of their worldly
duties weighed on the conscience of these excellent people; at
least, made them appear low and common in their own eyes. For
had not Jesus told the wealthy youth, that if he would be perfect
he must sell all his possessions and give the price to the poor?
And at another time he had likewise said that all, indeed, could
not receive this saying, but that there were those who had made
themselves eunuchs for the sake of God's kingdom.

The Reformation first went to work on a systematic principle,
in order to place this ascetic, fanatical side of Christianity under
the due control of reason. Luther's dicta concerning the value of
the performance of duty in all the relations of life, whether matri-
monial, domestic, or civil—on the useful activity of housewives,
mothers, maid or manservants, as compared with the profitless
macerations, senseless babble, and dronelike laziness of monks
and nuns—are inspired by a thoroughly healthy humanity. But
this was supposed to militate against the degeneracy of the Catholic Church, not against Christianity itself. The earth continued
a vale of tears; man's gaze was still to remain fixed on the celestial
glories to come. "If heaven is our home," asked Calvin, "what is
the earth but a place of exile? Only because God has placed us
in this world, and appointed us our functions therein, must it also
be our endeavor to fulfil the same; it is solely the divine commandment which imparts a true value to our earthly vocations,
which are in themselves devoid of such." This is clearly a miserable compromise: if our earthly occupations are valueless in themselves, this value cannot be imparted to them from without; but
if they do possess such value, it can consist in nothing but the

moral relations which are implied by them. Man's earthly existence bears its own law, its rule of guidance, its aims and ends
included in itself.

But, we are told, he whom you call an enthusiast was at the
same time he who, not to mention many other moral precepts of
the highest value, first implanted in mankind, both by precept
and example, the principles of charity, of compassion—nay, of
the love of foes, and fraternal feelings for all men; and even he
who should only profess these principles professes thereby his
belief in Christ and in Christianity. They certainly remain its fairest attribute, we reply, and are the highest glory of its founder;
but they neither exclusively appertain to him, nor are they
annulled without him.

Five centuries before the Christian era Buddhism had already
inculcated gentleness and compassion, not only toward men, but
toward all living creatures. Among the Jews themselves, the
Rabbi Hillel had already taught, a generation before Christ, that
the commandment of loving one's neighbor as one's self constituted the very essence of the law. To assist even our enemies was
a maxim of the Stoics in Jesus' time. And but one generation
later, although without doubt independently of him, and strictly
in keeping with the principles of the Stoic school, Epictetus
called all men brothers, inasmuch as all were the children of
God. The recognition of this truth is so obviously involved in the
development of humanity, that it must inevitably occur at certain
stages of the process, and not to one individual alone. At that
very time this perception had been brought home to the nobler
minds of Greece and Rome by the abolition of barriers between
nation and nation in the Roman Empire, to the Jews by their dis-
persal into all lands. In exile among the Gentiles, a close band
of fellowship, a readiness to help and support each other, was
developed and organized, and rendered still more intimate by
the additional element of Christian faith in the recent manifestation and speedy return of the Messiah. The two centuries of
oppression and persecution which Christianity had still to pass
through—a time to which on the whole it owes all that is best

in its development—were a continuous training in those very virtues.

It must be admitted that compatriots and fellow believers were the first to benefit by this active charity. Jesus himself, it is true, had proposed to his disciples the example of their heavenly Father, who caused the sun to shine equally on the evil and the good, and sent his rain upon the just and the unjust. Nevertheless, he had prohibited his disciples, on their first mission, from suffering the sunshine and fertilizing rain of his saving doctrine to fall also on Gentiles and Samaritans; thus, at least, we are informed by Matthew the Evangelist. No wonder that the Christian Church yielded more and more to the temptation of limiting its charity to the circle of the faithful—nay, even within the confines of this circle, to the professors of the pretended true Christianity, i.e., the members of that Church which each respectively considered orthodox. Christianity as such never rose above crusades and persecutions of heretics; it has never even attained to tolerance, which yet is merely the negative side of universal benevolence. Their assiduity in works of philanthropy, their zeal and ability in the organization of charitable labors and institutions, are qualities of the "unco gude" among us, the glory of which shall not be diminished, excepting insofar as they diminish it themselves, by the *arrière pensée* of hierarchy or proselytism. Christianity indeed emphasized the idea of humanity; but the task of elaborating it into a pure and complete form, of stating it as a principle, was reserved for the philosophico-secular civilization of the skeptical eighteenth century. The belief that Christ died for all men is not only a transcendental ground for the love of all mankind, the true reason of which lies much closer at hand; it also runs the danger of confining this love to those who believe in the atonement, at least to those who do not wittingly disbelieve it.

The same holds good of all the other Christian precepts; Christianity did not bring them to the world, nor will they disappear from the world along with it. We shall retain all that was really achieved by Christianity as we have retained what was accomplished by Greece and Rome, without the form of religion in which that kernel ripened as in its husk. Thus only shall we succeed in discarding at the same time the narrowness and the partiality which throughout adhered to the doctrines of Christianity.

But why, we shall perhaps be asked, separate what after all might be capable of union? In its present development Christianity is not likely to circumscribe our philanthropy, rather to vivify it; and such quickening will be by no means amiss in this age of materialistic interests, of unfettered egotism. Why not, then, in this case also, try to come up to the precept, "This ought ye to have done, and not to have left the other undone?"

Because, we answer, this absolutely will not do. Why it will not do has been sufficiently elucidated in the foregoing pages; we cannot make a prop of our action out of a faith which we no longer possess, a community from whose persuasions and temper we are estranged. We will make a trial of it, but it shall be the last. The old creed was our starting-point, and as step by step we traced its development and transformation, we found that in none of its forms was it any longer acceptable by us. Let us now, to conclude, take it in its latest, mildest, most modern and at the same time concrete form, as it reveals itself in worship; let us assist in thought at the Christian festivals in a Protestant church, the minister of which is versed in the scientific modes of thought, and see whether we can still be sincerely and naturally edified thereby. How will this man—or we, if we put ourselves in his place—set to work, and what must the chain of his reasoning necessarily be, even if he does not care to give formal expression to everything?

At Christmas he will tell himself, and perhaps also hint to the intelligent among his audience, that the miraculous birth and the virgin mother are utterly out of the question. Further, that the whole story as to the journey of Jesus' parents to Bethlehem because of the tax imposed under Cyrenius is an awkward fiction, as the tax was not imposed until Jesus had already reached boyhood. That the child presumably came quite peaceably into the world in the bosom of its Nazarene family. That the shepherds vanish with the manger, and the angels with the shepherds. That with this child not peace alone came on earth, but enough and to spare of warfare and contention. In short, that although on that day we certainly celebrate the birthday of a remarkable personage, destined to great influence on the history of mankind, we nevertheless only celebrate that of one worker among many in the cause of human progress.

Such a minister would again have to make a clearance at the Epiphany, i.e., to eliminate the gospel narrative as a Messianic myth. He would remind himself, and if he were courageous enough, his congregation also, how the errant star was none other than that star which, according to the narrative in Numbers, the heathen seer Balaam had foretold should come out of Jacob, only, however, using it as an emblem of a triumphant Jewish king; how the wise men of the East had only been invented to suit the star, while their gifts were modeled after a passage of the pseudo-Isaiah, where, of the light which had risen over Jerusalem—i.e., the light of divine favor again vouchsafed to the Jews at the end of their exile—it is said, that the Gentiles shall come to this light, and all they from Sheba shall bring gold and incense. The infant Jesus, this clergyman must admit, had undoubtedly at that time lain as unheeded by the wide world—and moreover, not in Bethlehem, but probably in Nazareth—as children of plain citizens usually do.

As at Christmas the virgin's son, so on Good Friday our clergyman would have to set aside the sacrificial death—the idea of the Redeemer altogether. The more honestly he should do this, the more would he offend the staunch believers; the more discreetly, the less satisfied would be the more advanced among his audience, who, in fact, would be justified in accusing him of equivocation, should he still wish to hold fast by the conception of salvation and a Saviour in any non-natural sense.

His task would become more critical still as regards Easter. In this case it is hardly possible to call the thing by its correct name in a Christian Church, and if this be not done, then all speech concerning it is mere phrase.

Lastly, on Ascension Day it becomes difficult to refrain from satire. To speak of this event as one of actual occurrence is simply to affront educated people at this time of day. Therefore it must be treated symbolically; as has already been done with the resurrection, and must likewise be done with the miracles, the healing of the sick, the raising from the dead, the casting out of devils—themes which repeatedly furnish texts for sermons on ordinary Sundays, and which all admit of a moral application. But why take such a roundabout way? Why beat the bush after things for which we have no use, in order at last to reach some desired point, which we might have attained in much simpler and at the same time more decided fashion by going straight at it?

On all these festivals, as well as on ordinary Sundays, our clergyman begins his discourse with prayer, not only to God but to Christ as well, after which he reads verses or sections from Holy Writ as a text. Very well; but now, as to the first point, whence does he derive the right of praying to a mere man? For as such he regards Christ. Habit alone makes us overlook the enormity of such a usage, which has been imported from quite another standpoint; or is the fact to be looked at in the light of rhetorical licence, as it may be allowable to address a mountain, a river? Then it must be objected that the church, where everything is and should be seriously treated, is not the place for such a licence. But as regards the texts of Scripture—has the minister arrived at an understanding with his audience as to what they possess in the so-called Holy Scripture? Has he told them the men of the Reformation have conquered for us the right of free inquiry in Scripture, but modern science has conquered for itself that of free inquiry *about* Scripture? And has he clearly shown them what this implies? That reason which institutes inquiries about Scripture—i.e., not in order to comprehend its contents, but also to ascertain its origin, the measure of its credibility and its worth—necessarily stands above Scripture? That Scripture has ceased, therefore, to be the highest source of religious knowledge? We can count the theologians who have hitherto honestly spoken out on this point. Progress, it is pretended, has taken place in gradual ascent along easy ground, from the standpoint of the reformers to the liberal theology of our time, while the fact of the displacement of Scripture as a supreme authority involves a step higher and more dangerous even than that other one which had to be scaled from the Catholic standpoint by the Reformers.

But let us still for a moment remain in our modern Protestant church, and assist at the administration of the sacraments. Deducting all mere formalism, we here get the impression that the rite of baptism might not have been without a sufficient meaning at a time when it was necessary to gather in the new Messianic community from the world of Jew and Gentile, and to unite it by a common consecration. Today, in the midst of a Christian world, there is no longer any meaning in this; but as the later ecclesiastical relation of baptism to original sin and the devil is even more out of the question, baptisms in the modern church, in the service of which we are mentally participating, must necessarily appear as a ceremony without any real significance, nay, with a meaning which is repugnant to us. We will leave it to the Jews to stamp their infant sons as something special by a permanent physical mark; we would not have even a transient one, for we would not have our children something special, we would only have them men, and to be men we will bring them up.

As baptism, along with its relations to the world of Jew and Gentile, and further, to original sin and the devil, has lost its real meaning, thus also has it fared with the Lord's Supper in regard to the atonement, nothing remaining now but the repulsive Oriental metaphor of drinking the blood and eating of the body of a man. In the next place, the imbecile and yet fateful quarrels about it, as to whether the thing should not be taken literally—whether it were not the actual flesh and blood—are painful to remember. We might be well pleased by a fraternal feast of humanity, with a common draught from a single cup; but blood would be the very last beverage we should dream of putting into the latter.

On the altar of our modern Protestant church, insofar as it stands on Lutheran ground, we shall find the image of the crucified Christ, the so-called crucifix. This old chief symbol of Christianity the Catholic church, as is known, is extravagantly fond of placing up and down the countryside; the Protestant church, insofar as it did not put it on one side with other images, has, at least, with a kind of shame, removed it to the interior of churches and houses, besides allowing the empty cross to stand on cemeteries, steeples, and the like. It was possibly on his Italian journey, or in some other Catholic country, that Goethe, vexed by its obtrusiveness, took the dislike which impelled him, in the notorious verse of his Venetian epigram, to put the cross side by side with garlic and vermin. Nothing but the mere form of this sign—the stiff little piece of wood placed crosswise on another little piece of wood, as he expresses it in the "West-Eastern Divan"—was unpleasant to him, and it would certainly have cheered him had he known that in this he agreed with that staunch Elizabeth Charlotte, Princess of the Palatinate and Duchess of Orleans, who likewise confessed "to not at all liking to see the cross," because its form did not please her. Perhaps even half-unconsciously in her case, and certainly in Goethe's, there was something over and above the mere form, over and above a simple æsthetic dislike, which repelled him in the cross. It was "the image of sorrow on the tree," which, according to the passage referred to in the "Divan," ought not to be "made a god." The crucifix is, on the one hand, the visible and tangible pledge of the remission of sins to the faithful; on the other, however, the deification of sorrow generally; it is humanity in its saddest plight, broken and shattered in all its limbs, so to speak, and in a certain sense rejoicing thereat; it is the most one-sided, rigid embodiment of Christian world-renunciation and passiveness. In a symbol of this kind, mankind rejoicing in life and action can now no longer find the expression of its religious consciousness; and the continued regard accorded it in the modern Protestant Church is, after all, but one more of those compromises and untruths which make it a thing of such feeble vitality.

And now, I think we have reached the end. And the result? Our answer to the question with which we have headed this section of our account? Shall I still give a distinct statement, and place the sum of all we have said in round numbers under the account? Most unnecessary, I should say; but I would not, on any consideration, appear to shirk even the most unpalatable word. My conviction, therefore, is, if we would not evade difficulties or put forced constructions upon them, if we would have our yea yea, and our nay nay—in short, if we would speak as honest, upright men, we must acknowledge we are no longer Christians.

III

THE
NEW ATHEISMS

Friedrich Nietzsche

[1844–1900]

BORN IN THE SAXON VILLAGE of Röcken, Nietzsche was six years old and an only child when his father died. His father was a Lutheran pastor, as were both grandfathers, and the Nietzsche household was very pious. It was not till the age of twenty, in his first term at the University of Bonn, that he reacted against his Christian upbringing. Here and at Leipzig he plunged into the study of philology and became enraptured with Greek mythology; and it was at Leipzig that he discovered the philosophy of Arthur Schopenhauer, met the composer Richard Wagner and became an ardent Prussian nationalist. A brilliant student, he was only twenty-four when he was offered a professorship in classical philology at the University of Basel. His academic career was twice interrupted, in 1867 and 1870, by military service, for which he volunteered. The first time, he was thrown from a horse while in artillery training and received a severe injury to his chest, resulting in a medical discharge. The second time, he was an ambulance attendant in the Franco-Prussian War. He contracted diphtheria and did not wait until he had completely recovered before returning to Basel. Constantly in poor health, he had to abandon his university post a few years later. His most productive years, 1879–1888, were spent in a lonely search for health at various places in Germany, Switzerland, Italy and the French Riviera. He drove himself ruthlessly. After an attack of apoplexy in January 1889, he became psychotic and his career as a philosopher came to an abrupt end.

It is important to note that there is no evidence of mental illness during Nietzsche's active life; its sudden onset crippled a brilliant mind and thwarted a heroic will. It is tempting, too, to dismiss him as a "madman," for many of his opinions are repugnant. He was a merciless polemicist, a passionate egotist and the exponent of a Byronic anarchism of the élite; he had nothing but contempt for the masses, whom he called "bungled and botched." Bertrand Russell goes so far as to say that much of his thought bears the imprint of megalomania. For Nietzsche, "the whole importance of the period from 1789 to 1815 is summed up in Napoleon," and the emergence of one such "great man" justifies the suffering of millions.[1]

When all this has been said, however, Nietzsche's hectic, aphoristic philosophy is too full of challenging insights to be scorned. Whatever political opinions anyone may attach to it, Nietzsche's concept of the will to power offers a vital perspective on human nature. The fundamental drive in man, he says, is not for pleasure, repose, adaptation or equilibrium, but for the realization of one's potentialities. The values open to man are not predetermined, not inherited from the past or conferred by God; they are completely the subject of autonomous choice and decision. Man's ultimate responsibility is to himself, and his task is to become fully himself, to become free, to remove all restrictions and to discover whatever values he can live with that will enhance and fulfill his power of becoming.

Belief, for Nietzsche, signifies submission to power. The task of self-realization necessitates the "transvaluation" of this submission into a seizure of power:

> When a man arrives at the fundamental conviction that he *requires* to be commanded, he becomes "a believer." Reversely, one could imagine a delight and a power of self-determining, and a *freedom* of will, whereby a spirit could bid farewell to every belief . . . and to dance even on the verge of abysses.[2]

All values, indeed, must be called into question. Fixed opinions, faith—these are tokens of weakness, crutches for those unready to stand on their own feet. His point here is that power tran-

[1] Bertrand Russell, *A History of Western Philosophy* (New York: Simon and Schuster, 1945), p. 762.
[2] Friedrich Nietzsche, *The Joyful Wisdom* (New York: Ungar, 1960), p. 287.

scends truth; throughout history, man has displayed a "longing for certainty" based on weakness.

> Most people in old Europe, as it seems to me, still need Christianity at present, and on that account it still finds belief. For such is man: a theological dogma might be refuted to him a thousand times,—provided, however, that he had need of it, he would again and again accept it as "true."[3]

To speak of power and weakness in this fashion is to transfer values from an ethical to a psychological context. The pious believer in a set of beliefs that thwart his potentialities cannot merely rest content in those beliefs; instincts that are repressed for the sake of an ideal do not disappear but turn inward. Tranquillity, complacency, passivity run against the grain of human nature; the hidden result of one's dammed-up resentment against a slave morality is the enslavement of others—and this is a charge he hurls most passionately at Christianity.

In his assertion of the death of God, Nietzsche proclaimed a historic event both triumphant and fearsome. As Erich Heller reminds us, "He never said that there was no God, but that the Eternal had been vanquished by Time and the Immortal suffered death at the hands of mortals."[4] A more prosaic way of stating the case is to say that, as a profound classical scholar, Nietzsche was well aware of the evolution of thought from the mythopoetic to the rational and scientific. There was a time when it was not possible for man to "create" God; God was, however, inexorably present to the kind of perceptions man then had—a fact borne out by the structure of language.[5] Later it becomes possible to separate the concept of God from the reality, to attach attributes, to analyze and reason about this concept and the reality it represents. In the nineteenth century, Nietzsche saw the culmination

[3] *Ibid.*, p. 285.
[4] Erich Heller, "The Importance of Nietzsche" in *Encounter*, April 1964, p. 60.
[5] See Bruno Snell, *The Discovery of the Mind* (Cambridge: Harvard University Press, 1953). Snell notes, for example, a multiplicity of verbs in Homeric Greek that distinguish various kinds of seeing, but only later does a single verb emerge to denote seeing as such, to be modified by adverbs. The later form reflects a refinement in the direction of analytical thought that was impossible for the Homeric vocabulary.

of this process. The evolution of consciousness had overtaken and annulled the reality of God, rendering the concept obsolete and by the same token necessitating a further step in the process—not a new version of God, but the creation of a new being, the Superman. Man's transvaluation of all values through the will to power must, Nietzsche believed, lead to just such a fulfillment, a heroic self-transcendence based on unfettered self-knowledge activated by the will. God dies in order that man may live, but in order to live man must now become God.

The God whom modern man has killed is the very God that Christianity is predicated on. Hence it is above all the values of Christianity that are to be reexamined and transvalued, including not only religion and morals but its understanding of the nature of man.

If God is dead, said Dostoevsky, "everything is permitted." For a few generations, perhaps, Christian morality may continue on its own momentum, but eventually, says Nietzsche, "All purely moral demands without their religious basis must needs end in nihilism." The task that he announced but left unfinished is not to formulate a new basis for moral demands, but to transcend morality itself. The selections that follow comprise Nietzsche's autopsy on God, Christian man and the civilization he produced, together with Nietzsche's vision of the "free spirit" to whom he assigned the task of becoming the Superman. It may well be asked whether, despite the prejudicial terminology, Nietzsche represents not merely a repudiation of the old Christianity but the harbinger of a radically *new* Christianity. For the impact of his critique will be seen later, especially in Tillich and Altizer.

The Death of God[1]

The Madman.—Have you ever heard of the madman who on a bright morning lighted a lantern and ran to the market place calling out unceasingly: "I seek God! I seek God!" As there were

[1] From *The Joyful Wisdom* (*La Gaya Scienza*), trans. Thomas Common. *Complete Works*, Vol. 10, ed. Oscar Levy (Edinburgh: T. N. Foulis, 1910). —Ed.

many people standing about who did not believe in God, he caused a great deal of amusement. Why! Is he lost? said one. Has he strayed away like a child? said another. Or does he keep himself hidden? Is he afraid of us? Has he taken a sea voyage? Has he emigrated?—the people cried out laughingly, all in a hubbub. The insane man jumped into their midst and transfixed them with his glances. "Where is God gone?" he called out. "I mean to tell you! *We have killed him,* you and I! We are all his murderers! But how have we done it? How were we able to drink up the sea? Who gave us the sponge to wipe away the whole horizon? What did we do when we loosened this earth from its sun? Whither does it now move? Whither do we move? Away from all suns? Do we not dash on unceasingly? Backwards, sideways, forwards, in all directions? Is there still an above and below? Do we not stray, as through infinite nothingness? Does not empty space breathe upon us? Has it not become colder? Does not night come on continually, darker and darker? Shall we not have to light lanterns in the morning? Do we not hear the noise of the gravediggers who are burying God? Do we not smell the divine putrefaction? For even Gods putrefy! God is dead! God remains dead! And we have killed him! How shall we console ourselves, the most murderous of all murderers? The holiest and the mightiest that the world has hitherto possessed, has bled to death under our knife—who will wipe the blood from us? With what water could we cleanse ourselves? What lustrums, what sacred games shall we have to devise? Is not the magnitude of this deed too great for us? Shall we not ourselves have to become Gods, merely to seem worthy of it? There never was a greater event—and on account of it, all who are born after us belong to a higher history than any history hitherto!" Here the madman was silent and looked again at his hearers; they also were silent and looked at him in surprise. At last he threw his lantern on the ground, so that it broke in pieces and was extinguished. "I come too early," he then said, "I am not yet at the right time. This prodigious event is still on its way, and is traveling—it has not yet reached men's ears. Lightning and thunder need time, the light of the stars needs time, deeds need time, even after they are done, to be seen and heard. This deed is as yet further from them than the furthest star—*and yet they have done it!*" It is further stated that the madman made his way into different churches on the same day, and there intoned his *Requiem aeternam deo.* When led out and called to account, he always gave the reply: "What are these churches now, if they are not the tombs and monuments of God?"

The Religious Mood[1]

45

The human soul and its limits, the range of man's inner experiences hitherto attained, the heights, depths and distances of these experiences, the entire history of the soul *up to the present time,* and its still unexhausted possibilities: this is the preordained hunting domain for a born psychologist and lover of a "big hunt." But how often must he say despairingly to himself: "A single individual! alas, only a single individual! And this great forest, this virgin forest!" So he would like to have some hundreds of hunting assistants, and fine trained hounds, which he could send into the history of the human soul, to drive *his* game together. In vain: again and again he experiences, profoundly and bitterly, how difficult it is to find assistants and dogs for all the things that directly excite his curiosity. The evil of sending scholars into new and dangerous hunting domains, where courage, sagacity, and subtlety in every sense are required, is that they are no longer serviceable just when the "*big hunt,*" and also the great danger commences—it is precisely then that they lose their keen eye and nose. In order, for instance, to divine and determine what sort of history the problem of *knowledge and conscience* has hitherto had in the souls of *homines religiosi,* a person would perhaps himself have to possess as profound, as bruised, as immense an experience as the intellectual conscience of Pascal; and

[1] From *Beyond Good and Evil: Prelude to a Philosophy of the Future,* trans. Helen Zimmermann. *Complete Works,* Vol. 10.—Ed.

then he would still require that widespread heaven of clear, wicked spirituality, which, from above, would be able to oversee, arrange, and effectively formulize this mass of dangerous and painful experiences. But who could do me this service! And who would have time to wait for such servants! They evidently appear too rarely, they are so improbable at all times! Eventually one must do everything *oneself* in order to know something; which means that one has *much* to do! But a curiosity like mine is once for all the most agreeable of vices—pardon me! I mean to say that the love of truth has its reward in heaven, and already upon earth.

46

Faith, such as early Christianity desired, and not infrequently achieved in the midst of a skeptical and southernly free-spirited world, which had centuries of struggle between philosophical schools behind it and in it, counting besides the education in tolerance which the *imperium Romanum* gave—this faith is *not* that sincere, austere slave faith by which perhaps a Luther or a Cromwell, or some other northern barbarian of the spirit remained attached to his God and Christianity; it is much rather the faith of Pascal, which resembles in a terrible manner a continuous suicide of reason—a tough, long-lived, wormlike reason, which is not to be slain at once and with a single blow. The Christian faith, from the beginning, is sacrifice: the sacrifice of all freedom, all pride, all self-confidence of spirit; it is at the same time subjection, self-derision, and self-mutilation. There is cruelty and religious Phœnicianism in this faith, which is adapted to a tender, many-sided, and very fastidious conscience; it takes for granted that the subjection of the spirit is indescribably *painful*, that all the past and all the habits of such a spirit resist the *absurdissimum*, in the form of which "faith" comes to it. Modern men, with their obtuseness as regards all Christian nomenclature, have no longer the sense for the terribly superlative conception which was implied to an antique taste by the paradox of the formula "God on the Cross." Hitherto there had never and nowhere been such boldness in inversion, nor anything at once so dreadful, questioning, and questionable as this formula: it promised a transvaluation of all ancient values. It was the Orient, the *profound* Orient, it was the Oriental slave who thus took revenge on Rome and its noble, light-minded toleration, on the Roman "Catholicism" of nonfaith; and it was always, not the faith, but the freedom from the faith, the half-stoical and smiling indifference to the seriousness of the faith, which made the slaves indignant at their masters and revolt against them. "Enlightenment" causes revolt: for the slave desires the unconditioned, he understands nothing but the tyrannous, even in morals; he loves as he hates, without *nuance*, to the very depths, to the point of pain, to the point of sickness—his many *hidden* sufferings make him revolt against the noble taste which seems to *deny* suffering. The skepticism with regard to suffering, fundamentally only an attitude of aristocratic morality, was not the least of the causes, also, of the last great slave-insurrection which began with the French Revolution.

47

Wherever the religious neurosis has appeared on the earth so far, we find it connected with three dangerous prescriptions as to regimen: solitude, fasting, and sexual abstinence—but without it being possible to determine with certainty which is cause and which is effect, or *if* any relation at all of cause and effect exists there. This latter doubt is justified by the fact that one of the most regular symptoms among savage as well as among civilized peoples is the most sudden and excessive sensuality; which then with equal suddenness transforms into penitential paroxysms, world-renunciation, and will-renunciation—both symptoms perhaps explainable as disguised epilepsy? But nowhere is it *more* obligatory to put aside explanations; around no other type has there grown such a mass of absurdity and superstition, no other type seems to have been more interesting to men and even to philosophers—perhaps it is time to become just a little indifferent here, to learn caution, or, better still, to look away, *to go away.*

Yet in the background of the most recent philosophy, that of Schopenhauer, we find almost as the problem in itself, this terrible note of interrogation of the religious crisis and awakening. How is the negation of will *possible*? how is the saint possible? That seems to have been the very question with which Schopenhauer made a start and became a philosopher. And thus it was a genuine Schopenhauerian consequence that his most convinced adherent (perhaps also his last, as far as Germany is concerned), namely, Richard Wagner, should bring his own life work to an end just here, and should finally put that terrible and eternal type upon the stage as Kundry, *type vécu*, and as it loved and lived, at the very time that the mad-doctors in almost all European countries had an opportunity to study the type close at hand, wherever the religious neurosis—or as I call it, "the religious mood"—made its latest epidemical outbreak and display as the "Salvation Army." If it be a question, however, as to what has been so extremely interesting to men of all sorts in all ages, and even to philosophers, in the whole phenomenon of the saint, it is undoubtedly the appearance of the miraculous therein—namely, the immediate *succession of opposites*, of states of the soul regarded as morally antithetical: it was believed here to be self-evident that a "bad man" was all at once turned into a "saint," a good man. The hitherto existing psychology was wrecked at this point; is it not possible it may have happened principally because psychology had placed itself under the dominion of morals, because it *believed* in oppositions of moral values, and saw, read, and *interpreted* these oppositions into the text and facts of the case? What? "Miracle" only an error of interpretation? A lack of philology?

48

It seems that the Latin races are far more deeply attached to their Catholicism than we Northerners are to Christianity generally, and that consequently unbelief in Catholic countries means something quite different from what it does among Protestants—namely, a sort of revolt against the spirit of the race, while with us it is rather a return to the spirit (or nonspirit) of the race. We Northerners undoubtedly derive our origin from barbarous races, even as regards our talents for religion—we have *poor* talents for it. One may make an exception in the case of the Celts, who have therefore furnished also the best soil for the Christian infection in the north: the Christian ideal blossomed forth in France as much as ever the pale sun of the north would allow it. How strangely pious for our taste are still these later French skeptics, whenever there is any Celtic blood in their origin! How Catholic, how un-German does Auguste Comte's Sociology seem to us, with the Roman logic of its instincts! How Jesuitical, that amiable and shrewd cicerone of Port-Royal, Sainte-Beuve, in spite of all his hostility to Jesuits! And even Ernest Renan: how inaccessible to us Northerners does the language of such a Renan appear, in whom every instant the merest touch of religious thrill throws his refinedly voluptuous and comfortably couching soul off its balance! Let us repeat after him these fine sentences—and what wickedness and haughtiness is immediately aroused by way of an-swer in our probably less beautiful but harder souls, that is to say, in our more German souls! *"Disons donc hardiment que la religion est un produit de l'homme normal, que l'homme est le plus dans le vrai quand il est le plus religieux et le plus assuré d'une destinée infinie. . . . C'est quand il est bon qu'il veut que la virtu corresponde à un ordre éternel, c'est quand il contemple les choses d'une manière désintéressée qu'il trouve la mort ré-voltante et absurde. Comment ne pas supposer que c'est dans ces moments-là, que l'homme voit le mieux?"*[1] These sentences are so extremely *antipodal* to my ears and habits of thought, that in my first impulse of rage on finding them, I wrote on the margin, *"la niaiserie religieuse par excellence!"*—until in my later rage I even took a fancy to them, these sentences with their truth abso-lutely'inverted! It is so nice and such a distinction to have one's own antipodes!

[1] "Therefore let us say boldly that religion is a product of normal man, that man is at his truest when he is most religious and most assured of an infinite destiny. . . . It is when he is good that he wants virtue to correspond with an eternal order, it is when he contemplates things in a disinterested way that he finds death revolting and absurd. How can we not suppose that it is in those moments that man sees best?"—ED.

49

That which is so astonishing in the religious life of the ancient Greeks is the irrestrainable stream of *gratitude* which it pours forth—it is a very superior kind of man who takes *such* an attitude toward nature and life. Later on, when the populace got the upper hand in Greece, *fear* became rampant also in religion; and Christianity was preparing itself.

50

The passion for God: there are churlish, honest-hearted, and importunate kinds of it, like that of Luther—the whole of Protestantism lacks the southern *delicatezza*. There is an Oriental exaltation of the mind in it, like that of an undeservedly favored or elevated slave, as in the case of St. Augustine, for instance, who lacks in an offensive manner all nobility in bearing and desires. There is a feminine tenderness and sensuality in it, which modestly and unconsciously longs for a *unio mystica et physica*, as in the case of Madame de Guyon. In many cases it appears, curiously enough, as the disguise of a girl's or youth's puberty; here and there even as the hysteria of an old maid, also as her last ambition. The Church has frequently canonized the woman in such a case.

51

The mightiest men have hitherto always bowed reverently before the saint, as the enigma of self-subjugation and utter voluntary privation—why did they thus bow? They divined in him —and as it were behind the questionableness of his frail and wretched appearance—the superior force which wished to test itself by such a subjugation; the strength of will, in which they recognized their own strength and love of power, and knew how to honor it: they honored something in themselves when they honored the saint. In addition to this, the contemplation of the saint suggested to them a suspicion: such an enormity of self-negation and anti-naturalness will not have been coveted for nothing—they have said, inquiringly. There is perhaps a reason for it, some very great danger, about which the ascetic might wish to be more accurately informed through his secret interlocutors and visitors? In a word, the mighty ones of the world learned to have a new fear before him, they divined a new power, a strange, still unconquered enemy: it was the "Will to Power" which obliged them to halt before the saint. They had to question him.

52

In the Jewish "Old Testament," the book of divine justice, there are men, things, and sayings on such an immense scale, that Greek and Indian literature has nothing to compare with it. One stands with fear and reverence before those stupendous remains of what man was formerly, and one has sad thoughts about old Asia and its little out-pushed peninsula Europe, which would like, by all means, to figure before Asia as the "Progress of Mankind." To be sure, he who is himself only a slender, tame house animal, and knows only the wants of a house animal (like our cultured people of today, including the Christians of "cultured" Christianity), need neither be amazed nor even sad amid those ruins—the taste for the Old Testament is a touchstone with respect to "great" and "small": perhaps he will find that the New Testament, the book of grace, still appeals more to his heart (there is much of the odor of the genuine, tender, stupid beadsman and petty soul in it). To have bound up this New Testament (a kind of *rococo* of taste in every respect) along with the Old Testament into one book, as the "Bible," as "The Book in Itself," is perhaps the greatest audacity and "sin against the Spirit" which literary Europe has upon its conscience.

53

Why Atheism nowadays? "The father" in God is thoroughly refuted; equally so "the judge," "the rewarder." Also his "free will": he does not hear—and even if he did, he would not know how to help. The worst is that he seems incapable of communicating himself clearly; is he uncertain? This is what I have made out (by questioning, and listening at a variety of conversations) to be the cause of the decline of European theism; it appears to me that though the religious instinct is in vigorous growth, it rejects the theistic satisfaction with profound distrust.

54

What does all modern philosophy mainly do? Since Descartes —and indeed more in defiance of him than on the basis of his procedure—an *attentat* has been made on the part of all philosophers on the old conception of the soul, under the guise of a criticism of the subject and predicate conception—that is to say, an *attentat* on the fundamental presupposition of Christian doctrine. Modern philosophy, as epistemological skepticism, is secretly or openly *anti-Christian*, although (for keener ears, be it said) by no means anti-religious. Formerly, in effect, one believed in "the soul" as one believed in grammar and the grammatical subject: one said, "I" is the condition, "think" is the predicate and is conditioned—to think is an activity for which one *must* suppose a subject as cause. The attempt was then made, with marvelous tenacity and subtlety, to see if one could not get out of this net—to see if the opposite was not perhaps true: "think" the condition, and "I" the conditioned; "I," therefore, only a synthesis which has been *made* by thinking itself. Kant really wished to prove that, starting from the subject, the subject could not be proved—nor the object either: the possibility of an *apparent existence* of the subject, and therefore of "the soul," may not always have been strange to him—the thought which once had an immense power on earth as the Vedanta philosophy.

55

There is a great ladder of religious cruelty, with many rounds; but three of these are the most important. Once on a time men sacrificed human beings to their God, and perhaps just those they loved the best—to this category belong the firstling sacrifices of all primitive religions, and also the sacrifice of the Emperor Tiberius in the Mithra-Grotto on the Island of Capri, that most terrible of all Roman anachronisms. Then, during the moral epoch of mankind, they sacrificed to their God the strongest instincts they possessed, their "nature"; *this* festal joy shines in the cruel glances of ascetics and "antinatural" fanatics. Finally, what still remained to be sacrificed? Was it not necessary in the end for men to sacrifice everything comforting, holy, healing, all hope, all faith in hidden harmonies, in future blessedness and justice? Was it not necessary to sacrifice God himself, and out of cruelty to themselves to worship stone, stupidity, gravity, fate, nothingness? To sacrifice God for nothingness—this paradoxical mystery of the ultimate cruelty has been reserved for the rising generation; we all know something thereof already.

56

Whoever, like myself, prompted by some enigmatical desire, has long endeavored to go to the bottom of the question of pessimism and free it from the half-Christian, half-German narrowness and stupidity in which it has finally presented itself to this century, namely, in the form of Schopenhauer's philosophy; whoever, with an Asiatic and super-Asiatic eye, has actually looked inside, and into the most world-renouncing of all possible modes of thought—beyond good and evil, and no longer like Buddha and Schopenhauer, under the dominion and delusion of morality—whoever has done this, has perhaps just thereby, without really desiring it, opened his eyes to behold the opposite ideal: the ideal of the most world-approving, exuberant and vivacious man, who has not only learned to compromise and arrange with that which was and is, but wishes to have it again *as it was and is*, for all eternity, insatiably calling out *da capo*, not only to himself, but to the whole piece and play; and not only to the play, but actually to him who requires the play— and makes it necessary; because he always requires himself anew—and makes himself necessary. What? And this would not be—*circulus vitiosus deus?*

57

The distance, and as it were the space around man, grows with the strength of his intellectual vision and insight: his world becomes profounder; new stars, new enigmas, and notions are ever coming into view. Perhaps everything on which the intellectual eye has exercised its acuteness and profundity has just been an occasion for its exercise, something of a game, something for children and childish minds. Perhaps the most solemn conceptions that have caused the most fighting and suffering, the conceptions "God" and "sin," will one day seem to us of no more importance than a child's plaything or a child's pain seems to an old man; and perhaps another plaything and another pain will then be necessary once more for "the old man"—always childish enough, an eternal child!

58

Has it been observed to what extent outward idleness, or semi-idleness, is necessary to a real religious life (alike for its favourite microscopic labor of self-examination, and for its soft placidity called "prayer," the state of perpetual readiness for the "coming of God"), I mean the idleness with a good conscience, the idleness of olden times and of blood, to which the aristocratic sentiment that work is *dishonoring*—that it vulgarizes body and soul—is not quite unfamiliar? And that consequently the modern, noisy, time-engrossing, conceited, foolishly proud laboriousness educates and prepares for "unbelief" more than anything else? Amongst these, for instance, who are at present living apart from religion in Germany, I find "free-thinkers" of diversified species and origin, but above all a majority of those in whom laboriousness from generation to generation has dissolved the religious instincts; so that they no longer know what purpose religions serve, and only note their existence in the world with a kind of dull astonishment. They feel themselves already fully occupied, these good people, be it by their business or by their pleasures, not to mention the "Fatherland," and the newspapers, and their "family duties"; it seems that they have no time

whatever left for religion; and above all, it is not obvious to them
whether it is a question of a new business or a new pleasure—for
it is impossible, they say to themselves, that people should go to
church merely to spoil their tempers. They are by no means
enemies of religious customs; should certain circumstances, State
affairs perhaps, require their participation in such customs, they
do what is required, as so many things are done—with a patient
and unassuming seriousness, and without much curiosity or dis-
comfort; they live too much apart and outside to feel even the
necessity for a *for* or *against* in such matters. Among those indifferent persons may be reckoned nowadays the majority of German Protestants of the middle classes, especially in the great
laborious centers of trade and commerce; also the majority of
laborious scholars, and the entire University personnel (with the
exception of the theologians, whose existence and possibility there
always gives psychologists new and more subtle puzzles to solve).
On the part of pious, or merely churchgoing people, there is
seldom any idea of *how much* goodwill, one might say arbitrary
will, is now necessary for a German scholar to take the problem
of religion seriously; his whole profession (and as I have said,
his whole workmanlike laboriousness, to which he is compelled
by his modern conscience) inclines him to a lofty and almost
charitable serenity as regards religion, with which is occasionally
mingled a slight disdain for the "uncleanliness" of spirit which
he takes for granted wherever any one still professes to belong
to the Church. It is only with the help of history (*not* through
his own personal experience, therefore) that the scholar succeeds
in bringing himself to a respectful seriousness, and to a certain
timid deference in presence of religions; but even when his sentiments have reached the stage of gratitude toward them, he has
not personally advanced one step nearer to that which still maintains itself as Church or as piety; perhaps even the contrary. The
practical indifference to religious matters in the midst of which
he has been born and brought up usually sublimates itself in his
case into circumspection and cleanliness, which shuns contact
with religious men and things; and it may be just the depth of
his tolerance and humanity which prompts him to avoid the deli-

cate trouble which tolerance itself brings with it. Every age has its own divine type of naïveté, for the discovery of which other ages may envy it: and how much naïveté—adorable, childlike, and boundlessly foolish naïveté—is involved in this belief of the scholar in his superiority, in the good conscience of his tolerance, in the unsuspecting, simple certainty with which his instinct treats the religious man as a lower and less valuable type, beyond, before, and *above* which he himself has developed—he, the little arrogant dwarf and mob-man, the sedulously alert, head-and-hand drudge of "ideas," of "modern ideas"!

59

Whoever has seen deeply into the world has doubtless divined what wisdom there is in the fact that men are superficial. It is their preservative instinct which teaches them to be flighty, lightsome, and false. Here and there one finds a passionate and exaggerated adoration of "pure forms" in philosophers as well as in artists: it is not to be doubted that whoever has *need* of the cult of the superficial to that extent, has at one time or another made an unlucky dive *beneath* it. Perhaps there is even an order of rank with respect to those burnt children, the born artists who find the enjoyment of life only in trying to *falsify* its image (as if taking wearisome revenge on it); one might guess to what degree life has disgusted them by the extent to which they wish to see its image falsified, attenuated, ultrified, and deified—one might reckon the *homines religiosi* amongst the artists, as their *highest* rank. It is the profound, suspicious fear of an incurable pessimism which compels whole centuries to fasten their teeth into a religious interpretation of existence: the fear of the instinct which divines that truth might be attained *too soon*, before man has become strong enough, hard enough, artist enough . . . Piety, the "Life in God," regarded in this light, would appear as the most elaborate and ultimate product of the *fear* of truth, as artist-adoration and artist-intoxication in presence of the most logical of all falsifications, as the will to the inversion of truth, to untruth at any price. Perhaps there has hitherto been no more effective means of beautifying man than piety; by means of it man can become so artful, so superficial, so iridescent, and so good, that his appearance no longer offends.

60

To love mankind *for God's sake*—this has so far been the noblest and remotest sentiment to which mankind has attained. That love to mankind, without any redeeming intention in the background, is only an *additional* folly and brutishness, that the inclination to this love has first to get its proportion, its delicacy, its grain of salt and sprinkling of ambergris from a higher inclination—whoever first perceived and "experienced" this, however his tongue may have stammered as it attempted to express such a delicate matter, let him for all time be holy and respected, as the man who has so far flown highest and gone astray in the finest fashion!

61

The philosopher, as *we* free spirits understand him—as the man of the greatest responsibility, who has the conscience for the general development of mankind—will use religion for his disciplining and educating work, just as he will use the contemporary political and economic conditions. The selecting and disciplining influence—destructive, as well as creative and fashioning—which can be exercised by means of religion is manifold and varied, according to the sort of people placed under its spell and protection. For those who are strong and independent, destined and trained to command, in whom the judgment and skill of a ruling race is incorporated, religion is an additional means for overcoming resistance in the exercise of authority—as a bond which binds rulers and subjects in common, betraying and surrendering to the former the conscience of the latter, their inmost heart, which would fain escape obedience. And in the case of the unique natures of noble origin, if by virtue of superior spirituality they should incline to a more retired and contemplative life, reserving to themselves only the more refined forms of government (over chosen disciples or members of an order), religion itself may be used as a means for obtaining peace from the noise and trouble of managing *grosser* affairs, and for securing immunity from the *unavoidable* filth of all political agitation. The Brahmins, for instance, understood this fact. With the help of a religious organization, they secured to themselves the power of nominating kings for the people, while their sentiments prompted them to keep apart and outside, as men with a higher and super-regal mission. At the same time religion gives inducement and opportunity to some of the subjects to qualify themselves for future ruling and commanding: the slowly ascending ranks and classes, in which, through fortunate marriage customs, volitional power and delight in self-control are on the increase. To them religion offers sufficient incentives and temptations to aspire to higher intellectuality, and to experience the sentiments of authoritative self-control, of silence, and of solitude. Asceticism and Puritanism are almost indispensable means of educating and ennobling a race which seeks to rise above its hereditary baseness and work itself upward to future supremacy. And finally, to ordinary men, to the majority of the people, who exist for service and general utility, and are only so far entitled to exist, religion gives invaluable contentedness with their lot and condition, peace of heart, ennoblement of obedience, additional social happiness and sympathy, with something of transfiguration and embellishment, something of justification of all the commonplaceness, all the meanness, all the semi-animal poverty of their souls. Religion, together with the religious significance of life, sheds sunshine over such perpetually harassed men, and makes even their own aspect endurable to them; it operates upon them as the Epicurean philosophy usually operates upon sufferers of a higher order, in a refreshing and refining manner, almost *turning* suffering *to account*, and in the end even hallowing and vindicating it. There is perhaps nothing so admirable in Christianity and Buddhism as their art of teaching even the lowest to elevate themselves by piety to a seemingly higher order of things, and thereby to retain their satisfaction with the actual world in which they find it difficult enough to live—this very difficulty being necessary.

62

To be sure—to make also the bad counter-reckoning against such religions, and to bring to light their secret dangers—the cost is always excessive and terrible when religions do *not* operate as an educational and disciplinary medium in the hands of the philosopher, but rule voluntarily and *paramountly*, when they wish to be the final end, and not a means along with other means. Among men, as among all other animals, there is a surplus of defective, diseased, degenerating, infirm, and necessarily suffering individuals; the successful cases, among men also, are always the exception; and in view of the fact that man is *the animal not yet properly adapted to his environment*, the rare exception. But worse still. The higher the type a man represents, the greater is the improbability that he will *succeed*; the accidental, the law of irrationality in the general constitution of mankind, manifests itself most terribly in its destructive effect on the higher orders of men, the conditions of whose lives are delicate, diverse, and difficult to determine. What, then, is the attitude of the two greatest religions above mentioned to the *surplus* of failures in life? They endeavor to preserve and keep alive whatever can be preserved; in fact, as the religions *for sufferers*, they take the part of these upon principle; they are always in favor of those who suffer from life as from a disease, and they would fain treat every other experience of life as false and impossible. However highly we may esteem this indulgent and preservative care (inasmuch as in applying to others, it has applied, and applies also to the highest and usually the most suffering type of man), the hitherto *paramount* religions—to give a general appreciation of them—are among the principal causes which have kept the type of "man" upon a lower level—they have preserved too much *that which should have perished*. One has to thank them for invaluable services; and who is sufficiently rich in gratitude not to feel poor at the contemplation of all that the "spiritual men" of Christianity have done for Europe hitherto! But when they had given comfort to the sufferers, courage to the oppressed and despairing, a staff and support to the helpless, and when they had allured from society into convents and spiritual penitentiaries the brokenhearted and distracted, what else had they to do in order to work systematically in that fashion, and with a good conscience, for the preservation of all the sick and suffering, which means, in deed and in truth, to work for *the deterioration of the European race?* To *reverse* all estimates of value—*that* is what they had to do! And to shatter the strong, to spoil great hopes, to cast suspicion on the delight in beauty, to break down everything autonomous, manly, conquering, and imperious—all instincts which are natural to the highest and most successful type of "man"—into uncertainty, distress of conscience, and self-destruction; forsooth, to invert all love of the earthly and of supremacy over the earth, into hatred of the earth and earthly things—*that* is the task the Church imposed on itself, and was obliged to impose, until, according to its standard of value, "unworldliness," "unsensuousness," and "higher man" fused into one sentiment. If one could observe the strangely painful, equally coarse and refined comedy of European Christianity with the derisive and impartial eye of an Epicurean god, I should think one would never cease marveling and laughing; does it not actually seem that some single will has ruled over Europe for eighteen centuries in order to make a *sublime abortion* of man? He, however, who, with opposite requirements (no longer Epicurean) and with some divine hammer in his hand, could approach this almost voluntary degeneration and stunting of mankind, as exemplified in the European Christian (Pascal, for instance), would he not have to cry aloud with rage, pity, and horror: "Oh, you bunglers, presumptuous pitiful bunglers, what have you done! Was that a work for your hands? How you have hacked and botched my finest stone! What have *you* presumed to do!"—I should say that Christianity has hitherto been the most portentous of presumptions. Men, not great enough, nor hard enough, to be entitled as artists to take part in fashioning *man*; men, not sufficiently strong and far-sighted to *allow*, with sublime self-constraint, the obvious law of the thousandfold failures and perishings to prevail; men, not sufficiently noble to see the radically different grades of rank and intervals of rank that separate man from man: *such* men, with their "equality before God," have hitherto swayed the destiny of Europe; until at last a dwarfed, almost ludicrous species has been produced, a gregarious animal, something obliging, sickly, mediocre, the European of the present day.

The Antichrist[1]

With a little freedom in the use of words, one might actually call Jesus a "free spirit"[2]—he cares nothing for what is established: the word *killeth*,[3] whatever is established *killeth*. The idea of "life" as an *experience*, as he alone conceives it, stands opposed to his mind to every sort of word, formula, law, belief and dogma. He speaks only of inner things: "life" or "truth" or "light" is his word for the innermost—in his sight everything else, the whole of reality, all nature, even language, has significance only as sign, as allegory. Here it is of paramount importance to be led into no error by the temptations lying in Christian, or rather *ecclesiastical* prejudices: such a symbolism par excellence stands outside all religion, all notions of worship, all history, all natural science, all worldly experience, all knowledge, all politics, all psychology, all books, all art—his "wisdom" is precisely a pure *ignorance*[4] of all such things. He has never heard of *culture*; he doesn't have to make war on it—he doesn't even deny it. . . . The same thing may be said of the *state*, of the whole bourgeois social order, of labor, of war—he has no ground for denying "the world," for he knows nothing of the ecclesiastical concept of "the world". . . . *Denial* is precisely the thing that is impossible to him. In the same way he lacks argumentative capacity, and has no belief that an article of faith, a "truth," may be established by proofs (*his* proofs are inner "lights," subjective sensations of happiness and self-approval, simple "proofs of power"). Such a doctrine *cannot* contradict: it doesn't know that other doctrines exist, or *can* exist, and is wholly incapable of imagining anything

[1] From *The Antichrist*, trans. H. L. Mencken (New York: Knopf, 1920).
—Ed.
[2] Nietzsche's name for one accepting his own philosophy.
[3] That is, the strict letter of the law—the chief target of Jesus's early preaching.
[4] A reference to the "pure ignorance" (*reine Thorheit*) of Parsifal.

opposed to it. . . . If anything of the sort is ever encountered, it laments the "blindness" with sincere sympathy—for it alone has "light"—but it does not offer objections. . . .

33

In the whole psychology of the "Gospels" the concepts of guilt and punishment are lacking, and so is that of reward. "Sin," which means anything that puts a distance between God and man, is abolished—*this is precisely the "glad tidings."* Eternal bliss is not merely promised, nor is it bound up with conditions: it is conceived as the *only* reality—what remains consists merely of signs useful in speaking of it.

The *results* of such a point of view project themselves into a new *way of life*, the special evangelical way of life. It is not a "belief" that marks off the Christian; he is distinguished by a different mode of action; he acts *differently*. He offers no resistance, either by word or in his heart, to those who stand against him. He draws no distinction between strangers and countrymen, Jews and Gentiles ("neighbor," of course, means fellow-believer, Jew). He is angry with no one, and he despises no one. He neither appeals to the courts of justice nor heeds their mandates ("Swear not at all"[5]). He never under any circumstances divorces his wife, even when he has proofs of her infidelity. And under all of this is one principle; all of it arises from one instinct.

The life of the Saviour was simply a carrying out of this way of life—and so was his death. . . . He no longer needed any formula or ritual in his relations with God—not even prayer. He had rejected the whole of the Jewish doctrine of repentance and atonement; he *knew* that it was only by a *way* of life that one could feel one's self "divine," "blessed," "evangelical," a "child of God." *Not* by "repentance," *not* by "prayer and forgiveness" is the way to God: *only the Gospel way* leads to God—it is *itself* "God"! What the Gospels *abolished* was the Judaism in the concepts of "sin," "forgiveness of sin," "faith," "salvation through faith"—the whole *ecclesiastical* dogma of the Jews was denied by the "glad tidings."

[5] Matthew v, 34.

The deep instinct which prompts the Christian how to *live* so, that he will feel that he is "in heaven" and is "immortal," despite many reasons for feeling that he is *not* "in heaven": this is the only psychological reality in "salvation." A new way of life, *not* a new faith. . . .

34

If I understand anything at all about this great symbolist, it is this: that he regarded only *subjective* realities as realities, as "truths"—that he saw everything else, everything natural, temporal, spatial and historical, merely as signs, as materials for parables. The concept of "the Son of God" does not connote a concrete person in history, an isolated and definite individual, but an "eternal" fact, a psychological symbol set free from the concept of time. The same thing is true, and in the highest sense, of the *God* of this typical symbolist, of the "kingdom of God," and of the "sonship of God." Nothing could be more un-Christian than the *crude ecclesiastical* notions of God as a *person*, of a "kingdom of God" that is to come, of a "kingdom of heaven" beyond, and of a "son of God" as the *second person* of the Trinity. All this—if I may be forgiven the phrase—is like thrusting one's fist into the eye (and what an eye!) of the Gospels: a disrespect for symbols amounting to *world-historical cynicism*. . . . But it is nevertheless obvious enough what is meant by the symbols "Father" and "Son"—not, of course, to everyone: the word "Son" expresses *entrance* into the feeling that there is a general transformation of all things (beatitude), and "Father" expresses *that feeling itself*—the sensation of eternity and of perfection. I am ashamed to remind you of what the church has made of this symbolism: has it not set an Amphitryon story[6] at the threshold of the Christian "faith"? And a dogma of "immaculate conception" for good measure? . . . *And thereby it has robbed conception of its immaculateness*—

The "kingdom of heaven" is a state of the heart—not something to come "beyond the world" or "after death." The whole

---

[6] Amphitryon was the son of Alcaeus, King of Tiryns. His wife was Alcmene. During his absence she was visited by Zeus, and bore Heracles.

idea of natural death is *absent* from the Gospels: death is not a bridge, not a passing; it is absent because it belongs to a quite different, a merely apparent world, useful only as a symbol. The "hour of death" is *not* a Christian idea—"hours," time, the physical life and its crises have no existence for the bearer of "glad tidings." . . . The "kingdom of God" is not something that men wait for: it had no yesterday and no day after tomorrow, it is not going to come at a "millennium"—it is an experience of the heart, it is everywhere and it is nowhere. . . .

35

This "bearer of glad tidings" died as he lived and *taught—not* to "save mankind," but to show mankind how to live. It was a *way of life* that he bequeathed to man: his demeanor before the judges, before the officers, before his accusers—his demeanor on the *cross*. He does not resist; he does not defend his rights; he makes no effort to ward off the most extreme penalty—more, *he invites it.* . . . And he prays, suffers and loves *with* those, *in* those, who do him evil. . . . *Not* to defend one's self, *not* to show anger, *not* to lay blames. . . . On the contrary, to submit even to the Evil One—to *love* him. . . .

36

We free spirits—we are the first to have the necessary prerequisite to understanding what nineteen centuries have misunderstood—that instinct and passion for integrity which makes war upon the "holy lie" even more than upon all other lies. . . . Mankind was unspeakably far from our benevolent and cautious neutrality, from that discipline of the spirit which alone makes possible the solution of such strange and subtle things: what men always sought, with shameless egoism, was their *own* advantage therein; they created the *church* out of denial of the Gospels. . . .

Whoever sought for signs of an ironical divinity's hand in the great drama of existence would find no small indication thereof in the *stupendous question mark* that is called Christianity. That mankind should be on its knees before the very antithesis of what was the origin, the meaning and the *law* of the Gospels—that in the concept of the "church" the very things should be pronounced holy that the "bearer of glad tidings" regards as *beneath* him and *behind* him—it would be impossible to surpass this as a grand example of *world-historical irony*—

37

Our age is proud of its historical sense: how, then, could it delude itself into believing that the *crude fable of the wonder-worker and Saviour* constituted the beginnings of Christianity— and that everything spiritual and symbolical in it only came later? Quite to the contrary, the whole history of Christianity—from the death on the cross onward—is the history of a progressively clumsier misunderstanding of an *original* symbolism. With every extension of Christianity among larger and ruder masses, ever less capable of grasping the principles that gave birth to it, the need arose to make it more and more *vulgar* and *barbarous*—it absorbed the teachings and rites of all the *subterranean* cults of the *imperium Romanum*, and the absurdities engendered by all sorts of sickly reasoning. It was the fate of Christianity that its faith had to become as sickly, as low and as vulgar as the needs were sickly, low and vulgar to which it had to administer. A *sickly barbarism* finally lifts itself to power as the church—the church, that incarnation of deadly hostility to all honesty, to all loftiness of soul, to all discipline of the spirit, to all spontaneous and kindly humanity. *Christian* values—*noble* values: it is only we, we *free* spirits, who have reestablished this greatest of all antitheses in values! . . .

38

I cannot, at this place, avoid a sigh. There are days when I am visited by a feeling blacker than the blackest melancholy— *contempt of man.* Let me leave no doubt as to *what* I despise, *whom* I despise: it is the man of today, the man with whom I am unhappily contemporaneous. The man of today—I am suffocated by his foul breath! . . . Toward the past, like all who understand, I am full of tolerance, which is to say, *generous* self-control: with gloomy caution I pass through whole millenniums of this madhouse of a world, call it "Christianity," "Christian faith" or the "Christian church," as you will—I take care not to hold mankind responsible for its lunacies. But my feeling changes and breaks out irresistibly the moment I enter modern times, *our* times. Our age *knows better*. . . . What was formerly merely sickly now becomes indecent—it is indecent to be a Christian today. *And here my disgust begins.* I look about me: not a word survives of what was once called "truth"; we can no longer bear to hear a priest pronounce the word. Even a man who makes the most modest pretensions to integrity *must* know that a theologian, a priest, a pope of today not only errs when he speaks, but actually *lies*—and that he no longer escapes blame for his lie through "innocence" or "ignorance." The priest knows, as every one knows, that there is no longer any "God," or any "sinner," or any "Saviour"—that "free will" and the "moral order of the world" are lies: serious reflection, the profound self-conquest of the spirit, *allow* no man to pretend that he does *not* know it. . . . *All* the ideas of the church are now recognized for what they are—as the worst counterfeits in existence, invented to debase nature and all natural values; the priest himself is seen as he actually is—as the most dangerous form of parasite, as the venomous spider of creation. . . . We know, our *conscience* now knows—just *what* the real value of all those sinister inventions of priest and church has been and *what ends they have served*, with their debasement of humanity to a state of self-pollution, the very sight of which excites loathing—the concepts "the other world," "the last judgment," "the immortality of the soul," the "soul" itself: they are all merely so many instruments of torture, systems of cruelty, whereby the priest becomes master and remains master. . . . Every one knows this, *but nevertheless things remain as before*. What has become of the last trace of decent feeling, of self-respect, when our statesmen, otherwise an unconventional class of men and thoroughly anti-Christian in their acts, now call themselves Christians and go to the communion table? . . .

A prince at the head of his armies, magnificent as the expression of the egoism and arrogance of his people—and yet acknowledging, *without* any shame, that he is a Christian! . . . Whom, then, does Christianity deny? *What* does it call "the world"? To be a *soldier*, to be a judge, to be a patriot; to defend one's self; to be careful of one's honor; to desire one's own advantage; to be *proud* . . . every act of every day, every instinct, every valuation that shows itself in a *deed*, is now anti-Christian: what a *monster of falsehood* the modern man must be to call himself nevertheless, and *without* shame, a Christian!—

62

With this I come to a conclusion and pronounce my judgment. I *condemn* Christianity; I bring against the Christian church the most terrible of all the accusations that an accuser has ever had in his mouth. It is, to me, the greatest of all imaginable corruptions; it seeks to work the ultimate corruption, the worst possible corruption. The Christian church has left nothing untouched by its depravity; it has turned every value into worthlessness, and every truth into a lie, and every integrity into baseness of soul. Let anyone dare to speak to me of its "humanitarian" blessings! Its deepest necessities range it against any effort to abolish distress; it lives by distress; it *creates* distress to make *itself* immortal. . . . For example, the worm of sin: it was the church that first enriched mankind with this misery!—The "equality of souls before God"—this fraud, this *pretext* for the *rancunes* of all the base-minded—this explosive concept, ending in revolution, the modern idea, and the notion of overthrowing the whole social order—this is *Christian* dynamite. . . . The "humanitarian" blessings of Christianity forsooth! To breed out of *humanitas* a self-contradiction, an art of self-pollution, a will to lie at any price, an aversion and contempt for all good and honest instincts! All this, to me, is the "humanitarianism" of Christianity! Parasitism as the *only* practice of the church; with its anemic and "holy" ideals, sucking all the blood, all the love, all the hope out of life; the beyond as the will to deny all reality; the cross as the distinguishing mark of the most subterranean conspiracy ever heard

of,—against health, beauty, well-being, intellect, *kindness* of soul
—*against life itself*. . . .

This eternal accusation against Christianity I shall write upon
all walls, wherever walls are to be found—I have letters that even
the blind will be able to see. . . . I call Christianity the one great
curse, the one great intrinsic depravity, the one great instinct of
revenge, for which no means are venomous enough, or secret,
subterranean and *small* enough—I call it the one immortal blem-
ish upon the human race. . . .

And mankind reckons *time* from the *dies nefastus* when this
fatality befell—from the *first* day of Christianity! *Why not rather
from its last? From today?* The transvaluation of all values! . . .

The Will to Power[1]

This is my fundamental objection to all philosophical and moral
cosmologies and theologies, to all wherefores and highest values
that have appeared in philosophies and philosophic religions
hitherto. A kind of means is misunderstood as the object itself:
conversely life and its growth of power were debased to a means.

If we wished to postulate an adequate object of life it would
not necessarily be related in any way with the category of conscious life; it would require rather to explain conscious life as a
mere means to itself. . . .

The "denial of life" regarded as the object of life, the object
of evolution! Existence—a piece of tremendous stupidity! Any
such mad interpretation is only the outcome of life's being measured by the factors of consciousness (pleasure and pain, good
and evil). Here the means are made to stand against the end—
the "unholy," absurd, and, above all, disagreeable means: how
can the end be any use when it requires such means? But where
the fault lies is here—instead of looking for the end which would
explain the necessity of such means, we posited an end from the
start which actually excludes such means, i.e. we made a desidera-

[1] From *The Will to Power*, trans. A. M. Ludovici. *Complete Works*. Vol.
15—ED.

tum in regard to certain means (especially pleasurable, rational, and virtuous) into a rule, and then only did we decide what end would be desirable. . . .

Where the fundamental fault lies is in the fact that, instead of regarding consciousness as an instrument and an isolated phenomenon of life in general, we made it a standard, the highest value in life: it is the faulty standpoint of *a parte ad totum*, and that is why all philosophers are instinctively seeking at the present day for a collective consciousness, a thing that lives and wills consciously with all that happens, a "Spirit," a "God." But they must be told that it is precisely thus that life is converted into a monster; that a "God" and a general sensorium would necessarily be something on whose account the whole of existence would have to be condemned. . . . Our greatest relief came when we eliminated the general consciousness which postulates ends and means—in this way we ceased from being necessarily pessimists. . . . Our greatest indictment of life was the existence of God.

708

Concerning the value of "Becoming." If the movement of the world really tended to reach a final state, that state would already have been reached. The only fundamental fact, however, is that it does not tend to reach a final state: and every philosophy and scientific hypothesis (e.g. materialism) according to which such a final state is necessary is refuted by this fundamental fact.

I should like to have a concept of the world which does justice to this fact. Becoming ought to be explained without having recourse to such final designs. Becoming must appear justified at every instant (or it must defy all valuation: which has unity as its end); the present must not under any circumstances be justified by a future, nor must the past be justified for the sake of the present. "Necessity" must not be interpreted in the form of a prevailing and ruling collective force or as a prime motor; and still less as the necessary cause of some valuable result. But to this end it is necessary to deny a collective consciousness for Becoming, a "God," in order that life may not be veiled under the shadow of a being who feels and knows as we do and yet *wills* nothing: "God" is useless if he wants nothing; and if he does want something, this presupposes a general sum of suffering and irrationality which lowers the general value of Becoming. Fortunately any such general power is lacking (a suffering God overlooking everything, a general sensorium and ubiquitous Spirit, would be the greatest indictment of existence).

Strictly speaking, nothing of the nature of Being must be allowed to remain, because in that case Becoming loses its value and gets to be sheer and superfluous nonsense.

The next question, then, is: How did the illusion Being originate (why was it obliged to originate)?

Likewise: How was it that all valuations based upon the hypothesis that there was such a thing as Being came to be depreciated?

But in this way we have recognized that this hypothesis concerning Being is the source of all the calumny that has been directed against the world (the "Better world," the "True world," the "World Beyond," the "Thing-in-itself").

(1) Becoming has no final state, it does not tend toward stability.

(2) Becoming is not a state of appearance; the world of Being is probably only appearance.

(3) Becoming is of precisely the same value at every instant; the sum of its value always remains equal: expressed otherwise, it has no value; for that according to which it might be measured, and in regard to which the word value might have some sense, is entirely lacking. The collective value of the world defies valuation; for this reason philosophical pessimism belongs to the order of farces.

1035

The more modern man has exercised his idealising power in regard to a *God* mostly by *moralizing the latter* ever more and more—what does that mean? Nothing good, a diminution in man's strength.

As a matter of fact, the reverse would be possible, and indications of this are not wanting. God imagined as emancipation from morality, comprising the whole of the abundant assembly of Life's contrasts, and *saving* and *justifying* them in a divine agony. God as the beyond, the superior elevation, to the wretched *cul-de-sac* morality of "Good and Evil."

1036

A humanitarian God cannot be *demonstrated* from the world that is known to us: so much are you driven and forced to conclude today. But what conclusion do you draw from this? "He cannot be demonstrated to *us*": the skepticism of knowledge. You all *fear* the conclusion: "From the world that is known to us quite a different God would be *demonstrable*, such a one as would certainly not be humanitarian"—and, in a word, you cling fast to your God, and invent a world for Him which *is unknown to us.*

1037

Let us banish the highest good from our concept of God: it is unworthy of a God. Let us likewise banish the highest wisdom: it is the vanity of philosophers who have perpetrated the absurdity of a God who is a monster of wisdom; the idea was to make Him as like them as possible. No! God *as the highest power* —that is sufficient! Everything follows from that, even—"the world"!

1038

And how many new Gods are not still possible! I, myself, in whom the religious—that is to say, the god-*creating*—instinct occasionally becomes active at the most inappropriate moments: how very differently the divine has revealed itself every time to me! . . . So many strange things have passed before me in those timeless moments, which fall into a man's life as if they came from the moon, and in which he absolutely no longer knows how old he is or how young he still may be! . . . I would not doubt that there are several kinds of gods. . . . Some are not wanting which one could not possibly imagine without a certain halcyonic calm and levity. . . . Light feet perhaps belong to the concept "God." Is it necessary to explain that a *God* knows how to hold Himself preferably outside all Philistine and rationalist circles? Also (between ourselves) beyond good and evil? His outlook is a *free* one—as Goethe would say. And to invoke the authority of Zarathustra, which cannot be too highly appreciated in this regard: Zarathustra goes as far as to confess, "I would only believe in a God who knew how to *dance*. . . ."

1052

The two types: Dionysus and Christ on the Cross. We should ascertain whether the typically *religious* man is a decadent phenomenon (the great innovators are one and all morbid and epileptic); but do not let us forget to include that type of the religious man who is *pagan*. Is the pagan cult not a form of gratitude for, and affirmation of, Life? Ought not its most representative type to be an apology and deification of Life? The type of a well-constituted and ecstatically overflowing spirit! The type of a spirit which absorbs the contradictions and problems of existence, and which *solves* them!

At this point I set up the *Dionysus* of the Greeks: the religious affirmation of Life, of the whole of Life, not of denied and partial Life (it is typical that in this cult the sexual act awakens ideas of depth, mystery, and reverence).

Dionysus *versus* "Christ"; here you have the contrast. It is *not* a difference in regard to the martyrdom—but the latter has a different meaning. Life itself—Life's eternal fruitfulness and recurrence caused anguish, destruction, and the will to annihilation. In the other case, the suffering of the "Christ as the Innocent One" stands as an objection against Life, it is the formula of Life's condemnation. Readers will guess that the problem concerns the meaning of suffering; whether a Christian or a tragic meaning be given to it. In the first case it is the road to a holy mode of existence; in the second case *existence itself is regarded as sufficiently holy* to justify an enormous amount of suffering. The tragic man says yea even to the most excruciating suffering: he is sufficiently strong, rich, and capable of deifying, to be able to do this; the Christian denies even the happy lots on earth: he is weak, poor, and disinherited enough to suffer from life in any form. God on the Cross is a curse upon Life, a signpost directing people to deliver themselves from it; Dionysus cut into pieces is a *promise* of Life: it will be forever born anew, and rise afresh from destruction.

1059

1. The thought of eternal recurrence: its first principles, which must necessarily be true if it were true. What its result is.

2. It is the most *oppressive* thought: its probable results, provided it be not prevented, that is to say, provided all values be not transvalued.

3. The means of *enduring it*: the transvaluation of all values. Pleasure no longer to be found in certainty, but in uncertainty; no longer "cause and effect," but continual creativeness; no longer the will to self-preservation, but to power; no longer the modest expression "it is all *only* subjective," but "it is all *our* work! let us be proud of it."

1060

In order to endure the thought of recurrence, freedom from morality is necessary; new means against the fact *pain* (pain regarded as the instrument, as the father of pleasure; there is no accretive consciousness of pain); pleasure derived from all kinds of uncertainty and tentativeness, as a counterpoise to extreme fatalism; suppression of the concept "necessity"; suppression of the "will"; suppression of "absolute knowledge."

Greatest elevation of man's *consciousness of strength*, as that which creates superman.

1061

The two extremes of thought—the materialistic and the platonic—are reconciled in *eternal recurrence*: both are regarded as ideals.

1062

If the universe had a goal, that goal would have been reached by now. If any sort of unforeseen final state existed, that state also would have been reached. If it were capable of any halting or stability of any "being," it would only have possessed this capability of becoming stable for one instant in its development; and again becoming would have been at an end for ages, and with it all thinking and all "spirit." The fact of "intellects" being in a *state of development*, proves that the universe can have no goal, no final state, and is incapable of being. But the old habit of thinking of some purpose in regard to all phenomena, and of thinking of a directing and creating deity in regard to the universe, is so powerful, that the thinker has to go to great pains in order to avoid thinking of the very aimlessness of the world as intended. The idea that the universe intentionally evades a goal, and even knows artificial means wherewith it prevents itself from falling into a circular movement, must occur to all those who would fain attribute to the universe the capacity of eternally regenerating itself—that is to say, they would fain impose upon a finite, definite force which is invariable in quantity, like the universe, the miraculous gift of renewing its forms and its conditions *for all eternity*. Although the universe is no longer a God, it must still be capable of the divine power of creating and transforming; it must forbid itself to relapse into any one of its previous forms; it must not only have the intention, but also the means, of avoiding any sort of repetition; every second of its existence, even, it must control every single one of its movements, with the view of avoiding goals, final states, and repetitions—and all the other results of such an unpardonable and insane method of thought and desire. All this is nothing more than the old religious mode of thought and desire, which, in spite of all, longs to believe that in some way or other the universe resembles the old, beloved, infinite, and infinitely creative God—that in some way or other "the old God still lives"—that longing of Spinoza's which is expressed in the words *"deus sive natura"* (what he really felt was *"natura sive deus"*). Which, then, is the proposition and belief in which the decisive change, the present *preponderance* of the scientific spirit over the religious and god-fancying spirit, is best formulated? Ought it not to be: the universe, as force, must not be thought of as unlimited, because it cannot be thought of in this way—we forbid ourselves the concept *infinite* force, because it is *incompatible* with the idea of force? Whence it follows that the universe lacks the power of eternal renewal.

Sigmund Freud

[1856–1939]

As a child in Freiberg, Sigmund Freud had a Slovak nursemaid who took him regularly to each of the five Catholic churches of that small Saxon city. When she scolded him, it was with threats of hellfire. The boy's father was religious to the extent that he read the Torah at home and occasionally took him to synagogue; and when Freud married, his wife was an Orthodox Jew. As a youth, he read Strauss and Feuerbach, but later denied that they had any influence on him. His biographer insists that Freud "went through his life from beginning to end as a *natural atheist*,"[1] and his correspondence with the Protestant minister Oskar Pfister[2] makes it clear that Freud was both hostile to religion as he knew it from childhood and remarkably incurious about serious theology.

Freud considered law as a possible career before studying medicine, and it was as a medical practitioner that he came to develop his distinctive theories of psychoanalysis. His first work was in the field of hysteria, and his first original contribution was in the interpretation of dreams and other forms of nonrational mental activity. In later years he advanced a number of ideas about the nature of the self, love, sexuality, pleasure and death that purported to be nothing but principles derived from the empirical practice of psychoanalysis, but that nonetheless belong to the domain of philosophy. As Erich Fromm has pointed out,

[1] Ernest Jones, *The Life and Work of Sigmund Freud* (New York: Basic Books, 1957), Vol. 3, p. 351. See also Ludwig Binswanger, *Sigmund Freud: Reminiscences of a Friendship* (New York: Grune & Stratton, 1957), pp. 74f, pp. 81f.

[2] See Sigmund Freud, *Psychoanalysis and Faith* (New York: Basic Books, 1963).

much of Freud's ostensibly scientific outlook is conditioned by
unexamined assumptions about the nature of man.[3] He unwit-
tingly retraced Feuerbach's steps when, in *Totem and Taboo* and
subsequent books and articles, he set out to explore both primitive and Judaeo-Christian myths. But if he covered the same
ground, he did so in a different way and carried the process
farther. Where Feuerbach sought to dethrone theology in favor
of what he called "anthropology," Freud set out to "transform
metaphysics into metapsychology."[4] In a letter to Pfister, he wrote
in 1909 that "the general lines of religious thinking are laid down
in advance in the family. God is equivalent to father, the Ma-
donna is the mother, and the patient himself is no other than
Christ."[5]

The scientific compilation and study of primitive myth, ritual
and folklore was in its infancy when Freud was born. *Totem and
Taboo* owes most of its substance to the work of J. G. Frazer,
Robertson Smith and other scholars of anthropology who not
only recorded but established parallels between the myths of
various cultures. It became possible, for example, to see the pattern of "death and resurrection" as a mythical expression of man's
experience of winter and spring, planting and harvesting. Jesus
Christ is not the only figure in this pattern; there are also Attis,
Marsyas, Adonis, Osiris, Dionysos and others. The most obvious
example of Freud's attempt at "metapsychology" on such a basis
is his theory of the Oedipus complex, which finds in a particular
Greek myth an archetypal pattern of motivation and behavior
transcending its time and place, and affording insight into present-day relationships. In *Totem and Taboo*, Freud suggests that
the doctrine of original sin is a reworking of a hypothetical myth
of the "murder" of God the Father, necessitating an expiatory
human sacrifice, and that the human Jesus by his voluntary self-
sacrifice displaces the murdered deity as God the Son. Anthro-
pologically, this process reflects guilt and conflict and their

[3] See Erich Fromm, *Sigmund Freud's Mission* (New York: Harper & Row,
1959), pp. 95–120.
[4] Jones, *op. cit.*, p. 353.
[5] Freud, *op. cit.*, p. 22. Note the ethical neutrality of the symbolism, in contrast with Feuerbach's "whoever loves man for the sake of man . . . is Christ
himself." This is characteristic of Freud's metapsychology.

resolution within a patriarchal agrarian culture. Metapsychologically, it is far from clear what conclusions Freud would draw here, but it is at least obvious from his remarks elsewhere that Christ represents man in his struggle for autonomy, for freedom from the heteronomous Father God.[6]

Freud's colleague C. G. Jung was to develop a theory of the psychology of religion based on studies of mythical archetypes, occult phenomena and the like.[7] Freud's own further encounter with religion was much simpler, and it is summed up in the following selection. It is at bottom a repudiation of religion in the name of humanistic ethics. Fromm has summarized this point: "If the validity of ethical norms rests upon their being God's commands, the future of ethics stands or falls with the belief in God."[8] Freud's concern is not to condemn religion *because* it is an illusion. But by showing the psychological immaturity fostered by belief in an all-powerful Heavenly Father, he seeks to alert modern man to the dangerous moral consequences of such belief. Ethics, he recognizes, historically evolved in conjunction with religion—just as, in the life of the individual, the child first learns moral behavior not by reason but by parental authority. Hence for Freud, continued dependence on the authority of God is a barrier to man's maturity; it is "neurotic" and "infantile."

In none of his writings does Freud show any acquaintance with contemporary theology. Pfister remonstrated with him on the appearance of *The Future of an Illusion*, calling his attention to the writings of Schweitzer, Eucken and Brunstäd. In his reply Freud politely ignored these remarks. It is clear that he was content to concern himself with the "opiate of the masses" rather than the elixir of the theologians.[9] There is a great deal of naïveté in his plea for reason and free inquiry as sources of human values.

[6] See Sigmund Freud, *Totem and Taboo* (New York: Moffat, Yard, 1918), pp. 253ff. Also, Theodor H. Gaster, ed., *The New Golden Bough* (Great Meadows, N.J.: Phillips, 1959), pp. 297f.

[7] See the section concerned with Martin Buber in this anthology, pp. 202–228.

[8] Erich Fromm, *Psychoanalysis and Religion* (New Haven: Yale, 1950), p. 13.

[9] *Psychoanalysis and Faith*, pp. 114f. See also Oskar Pfister, "Die Illusion einer Zukunft" in *Imago Jahrbuch* (Vienna), 1928.

As Gregory Zilboorg has shown, Freud was reluctant to honor his debt to a specifically biblical seedbed of ethics, yet "Freud always viewed St. Paul in a perspective of greatness and creative power. . . . He said openly that he wanted his Eros to be used in the sense of St. Paul's *caritas*."[10] In effect, psychoanalysis bids to supplant religion in the modern world. In Freud's own dispensation it rests ambiguously on Christian ethical values reduced to matters of opinion. For the future of both Christianity and psychoanalysis, however, the dialogue between them has barely begun. Freud's essay offers a challenge, both in what it says and in what it leaves unsaid.

The Future of an Illusion [1]

Religious ideas are teachings and assertions about facts and conditions of external (or internal) reality which tell one something one has not discovered for oneself and which lay claim to one's belief. Since they give us information about what is most important and interesting to us in life, they are particularly highly prized. Anyone who knows nothing of them is very ignorant; and anyone who has added them to his knowledge may consider himself much the richer.

. . . When we ask on what their claim to be believed is founded, we are met with three answers, which harmonize remarkably badly with one another. Firstly, these teachings deserve to be believed because they were already believed by our primal ancestors; secondly, we possess proofs which have been handed down to us from those same primeval times; and thirdly, it is forbidden to raise the question of their authentication at all. In former days anything so presumptuous was visited with the severest penalties, and even today society looks askance at any attempt to raise the question again.

[10] Gregory Zilboorg, *Freud and Religion* (Westminster: Newman, 1958), p. 41. See also Norman O. Brown, *Life Against Death* (New York: Vintage, 1959), p. 49; and page 7 of this anthology.
[1] Abridged from *The Future of an Illusion* (London: The Hogarth Press, 1928).—Ed.

This third point is bound to rouse our strongest suspicions. After all, a prohibition like this can only be for one reason—that society is very well aware of the insecurity of the claim it makes on behalf of its religious doctrines. Otherwise it would certainly be very ready to put the necessary data at the disposal of anyone who wanted to arrive at conviction. This being so, it is with a feeling of mistrust which it is hard to allay that we pass on to an examination of the other two grounds of proof. We ought to believe because our forefathers believed. But these ancestors of ours were far more ignorant than we are. They believed in things we could not possibly accept today; and the possibility occurs to us that the doctrines of religion may belong to that class too. The proofs they have left us are set down in writings which themselves bear every mark of untrustworthiness. They are full of contradictions, revisions and falsifications, and where they speak of factual confirmations they are themselves unconfirmed. It does not help much to have it asserted that their wording, or even their content only, originates from divine revelation; for this assertion is itself one of the doctrines whose authenticity is under examination, and no proposition can be a proof of itself.

Thus we arrive at the singular conclusion that of all the information provided by our cultural assets it is precisely the elements which might be of the greatest importance to us and which have the task of solving the riddles of the universe and of reconciling us to the sufferings of life—it is precisely those elements that are the least well authenticated of any. We should not be able to bring ourselves to accept anything of so little concern to us as the fact that whales bear young instead of laying eggs, if it were not capable of better proof than this.

. . . I am reminded of one of my children who was distinguished at an early age by a peculiarly marked matter-of-factness. When the children were being told a fairy story and were listening to it with rapt attention, he would come up and ask: "Is that a true story?" When he was told it was not, he would turn away with a look of disdain. We may expect that people will soon behave in the same way toward the fairy tales of religion, in spite of the advocacy of "As if."

But at present they still behave quite differently; and in past times religious ideas, in spite of their incontrovertible lack of authentication, have exercised the strongest possible influence on mankind. This is a fresh psychological problem. We must ask where the inner force of those doctrines lies and to what it is that they owe their efficacy, independent as it is of recognition by reason.

I think we have prepared the way sufficiently for an answer to both these questions. It will be found if we turn our attention to the psychical origin of religious ideas. These, which are given out as teachings, are not precipitates of experience or end-results of thinking: they are illusions, fulfillments of the oldest, strongest and most urgent wishes of mankind. The secret of their strength lies in the strength of those wishes. As we already know, the terrifying impression of helplessness in childhood aroused the need for protection—for protection through love—which was provided by the father; and the recognition that this helplessness lasts throughout life made it necessary to cling to the existence of a father, but this time a more powerful one. Thus the benevolent rule of a divine Providence allays our fear of the dangers of life; the establishment of a moral world-order ensures the fulfillment of the demands of justice, which have so often remained unfulfilled in human civilization; and the prolongation of earthly existence in a future life provides the local and temporal framework in which these wish fulfillments shall take place. Answers to the riddles that tempt the curiosity of man, such as how the universe began or what the relation is between body and mind, are developed in conformity with the underlying assumptions of this system. It is an enormous relief to the individual psyche if the conflicts of its childhood arising from the father complex—conflicts which it has never wholly overcome—are removed from it and brought to a solution which is universally accepted.

When I say that these things are all illusions, I must define the meaning of the word. An illusion is not the same thing as an error; nor is it necessarily an error. Aristotle's belief that vermin are developed out of dung (a belief to which ignorant people still cling) was an error; so was the belief of a former generation of doctors that *tabes dorsalis* is the result of sexual excess. It would be incorrect to call these errors illusions. On the other hand, it was an illusion of Columbus' that he had discovered a new sea route to the Indies. The part played by his wish in this error is very clear. One may describe as an illusion the assertion made by certain nationalists that the Indo-Germanic race is the only one capable of civilization; or the belief, which was only destroyed by psychoanalysis, that children are creatures without sexuality. What is characteristic of illusions is that they are derived from human wishes. In this respect they come near to psychiatric delusions. But they differ from them, too, apart from the more complicated structure of delusions. In the case of delusions, we emphasize as essential their being in contradiction with reality. Illusions need not necessarily be false—that is to say, unrealizable or in contradiction to reality. For instance, a middle-class girl may have the illusion that a prince will come and marry her. This is possible; and a few such cases have occurred. That the Messiah will come and found a golden age is much less likely. Whether one classifies this belief as an illusion or as something analogous to a delusion will depend on one's personal attitude. Examples of illusions which have proved true are not easy to find, but the illusion of the alchemists that all metals can be turned into gold might be one of them. The wish to have a great deal of gold, as much gold as possible, has, it is true, been a good deal damped by our present-day knowledge of the determinants of wealth, but chemistry no longer regards the transmutation of metals into gold as impossible. Thus we call a belief an illusion when a wish-fulfillment is a prominent factor in its motivation, and in doing so we disregard its relations to reality, just as the illusion itself sets no store by verification.

Having thus taken our bearings, let us return once more to the question of religious doctrines. We can now repeat that all of them are illusions and insusceptible of proof. No one can be compelled to think them true, to believe in them. Some of them are so improbable, so incompatible with everything we have laboriously discovered about the reality of the world, that we may compare them—if we pay proper regard to the psychological differences—to delusions. Of the reality value of most of them we cannot judge; just as they cannot be proved, so they cannot be refuted. We still know too little to make a critical approach to them. The riddles of the universe reveal themselves only slowly to our investigation; there are many questions to which science today can give no answer. But scientific work is the only road which can lead us to a knowledge of reality outside ourselves. It is once again merely an illusion to expect anything from intuition and introspection; they can give us nothing but particulars about our own mental life, which are hard to interpret, never any information about the questions which religious doctrine finds it so easy to answer. It would be insolent to let one's own arbitrary will step into the breach and, according to one's personal estimate, declare this or that part of the religious system to be less or more acceptable. Such questions are too momentous for that; they might be called too sacred.

At this point one must expect to meet with an objection. "Well then, if even obdurate skeptics admit that the assertions of religion cannot be refuted by reason, why should I not believe in them, since they have so much on their side—tradition, the agreement of mankind, and all the consolations they offer?" Why not, indeed? Just as no one can be forced to believe, so no one can be forced to disbelieve. But do not let us be satisfied with deceiving ourselves that arguments like these take us along the road of correct thinking. If ever there was a case of a lame excuse we have it here. Ignorance is ignorance; no right to believe anything can be derived from it. In other matters no sensible person will behave so irresponsibly or rest content with such feeble grounds for his opinions and for the line he takes. It is only in the highest and most sacred things that he allows himself to do so. In reality these are only attempts at pretending to oneself or to other people that one is still firmly attached to religion, when one has long since cut oneself loose from it. Where questions of religion are concerned, people are guilty of every possible sort of dishonesty and intellectual misdemeanour. Philosophers stretch the meaning of words until they retain scarcely anything of their original sense. They give the name of "God" to some vague abstraction which they have created for themselves; having done so they can pose before all the world as deists, as believers in God, and they can even boast that they have recognized a higher, purer concept of God, notwithstanding that their God is now nothing more than an insubstantial shadow and no longer the mighty personality of religious doctrines. Critics persist in describing as "deeply religious" anyone who admits to a sense of man's insignificance or impotence in the face of the universe, although what constitutes the essence of the religious attitude is not this feeling but only the next step after it, the reaction to it which seeks a remedy for it. The man who goes no further, but humbly acquiesces in the small part which human beings play in the great world—such a man is, on the contrary, irreligious in the truest sense of the word.

To assess the truth value of religious doctrines does not lie within the scope of the present enquiry. It is enough for us that we have recognized them as being, in their psychological nature, illusions. But we do not have to conceal the fact that this discovery also strongly influences our attitude to the question which must appear to many to be the most important of all. We know approximately at what periods and by what kind of men religious doctrines were created. If in addition we discover the motives which led to this, our attitude to the problem of religion will undergo a marked displacement. We shall tell ourselves that it would be very nice if there were a God who created the world and was a benevolent Providence, and if there were a moral order in the universe and an afterlife; but it is a very striking fact that all this is exactly as we are bound to wish it to be. And it would be more remarkable still if our wretched, ignorant and downtrodden ancestors had succeeded in solving all these difficult riddles of the universe.

Religion has clearly performed great services for human civilization. It has contributed much toward the taming of the asocial instincts. But not enough. It has ruled human society for many thousands of years and has had time to show what it can achieve. If it had succeeded in making the majority of mankind happy, in comforting them, in reconciling them to life and in making them into vehicles of civilization, no one would dream of attempting to alter the existing conditions. But what do we see instead?

We see that an appallingly large number of people are dissatisfied with civilization and unhappy in it, and feel it as a yoke which must be shaken off; and that these people either do everything in their power to change that civilization, or else go so far in their hostility to it that they will have nothing to do with civilization or with a restriction of instinct. At this point it will be objected against us that this state of affairs is due to the very fact that religion has lost a part of its influence over human masses precisely because of the deplorable effect of the advances of science. We will note this admission and the reason given for it, and we shall make use of it later for our own purposes; but the objection itself has no force.

It is doubtful whether men were in general happier at a time when religious doctrines held unrestricted sway; more moral they certainly were not. They have always known how to externalize the precepts of religion and thus to nullify their intentions. The priests, whose duty it was to ensure obedience to religion, met them halfway in this. God's kindness must lay a restraining hand on His justice. One sinned, and then one made a sacrifice or did penance and then one was free to sin once more. Russian introspectiveness has reached the pitch of concluding that sin is indispensable for the enjoyment of all the blessings of divine grace, so that, at bottom, sin is pleasing to God. It is no secret that the priests could only keep the masses submissive to religion by making such large concessions as these to the instinctual nature of man. Thus it was agreed: God alone is strong and good, man is weak and sinful. In every age immorality has found no less support in religion than morality has. If the achievements of religion in respect to man's happiness, susceptibility to culture and moral control are no better than this, the question cannot but arise whether we are not overrating its necessity for mankind, and whether we do wisely in basing our cultural demands upon it.

Let us consider the unmistakable situation as it is today. We have heard the admission that religion no longer has the same influence on people that it used to. (We are here concerned with European Christian civilization.) And this is not because its promises have grown less but because people find them less credible. Let us admit that the reason—though perhaps not the only reason—for this change is the increase of the scientific spirit in the higher strata of human society. Criticism has whittled away the evidential value of religious documents, natural science has shown up the errors in them, and comparative research has been struck by the fatal resemblance between the religious ideas which we revere and the mental products of primitive peoples and times.

The scientific spirit brings about a particular attitude toward worldly matters; before religious matters it pauses for a little, hesitates, and finally there too crosses the threshold. In this process there is no stopping; the greater the number of men to whom the treasures of knowledge become accessible, the more widespread is the falling away from religious belief—at first only from its obsolete and objectionable trappings, but later from its fundamental postulates as well. . . .

Civilization has little to fear from educated people and brain-workers. In them the replacement of religious motives for civilized behavior by other, secular motives would proceed unobtrusively; moreover, such people are to a large extent themselves vehicles of civilization. But it is another matter with the great mass of the uneducated and oppressed, who have every reason for being enemies of civilization. So long as they do not discover that people no longer believe in God, all is well. But they will discover it, infallibly, even if this piece of writing of mine is not published. And they are ready to accept the results of scientific thinking, but without the change having taken place in them which scientific thinking brings about in people. Is there not a danger here that the hostility of these masses to civilization will throw itself against the weak spot that they have found in their taskmistress? If the sole reason why you must not kill your neighbor is because God has forbidden it and will severely punish you for it in this or the next life—then, when you learn that there is no God and that you need not fear His punishment, you will certainly kill your neighbor without hesitation, and you can only be prevented from doing so by mundane force. Thus either these dangerous masses must be held down most severely and kept most carefully away from any chance of intellectual awakening, or else the relationship between civilization and religion must undergo a fundamental revision.

. . . I know how difficult it is to avoid illusions; perhaps the hopes I have confessed to are of an illusory nature, too. But I hold fast to one distinction. Apart from the fact that no penalty is imposed for not sharing them, my illusions are not, like religious ones, incapable of correction. They have not the character of a delusion. If experience should show—not to me, but to others after me, who think as I do—that we have been mistaken, we will give up our expectations. Take my attempt for what it is. A psychologist who does not deceive himself about the difficulty of finding one's bearings in this world, makes an endeavor to assess the development of man, in the light of the small portion of knowledge he has gained through a study of the mental processes of individuals during their development from child to adult. In so doing, the idea forces itself upon him that religion is comparable to a childhood neurosis, and he is optimistic enough to suppose that mankind will surmount this neurotic phase, just as so many children grow out of their similar neurosis. These discoveries derived from individual psychology may be insufficient, their application to the human race unjustified, and his optimism unfounded. I grant you all these uncertainties. But often one cannot refrain from saying what one thinks, and one excuses oneself on the ground that one is not giving it out for more than it is worth.

And there are two points that I must dwell on a little longer. Firstly, the weakness of my position does not imply any strengthening of yours. I think you are defending a lost cause. We may insist as often as we like that man's intellect is powerless in comparison with his instinctual life, and we may be right in this. Nevertheless, there is something peculiar about this weakness. The voice of the intellect is a soft one, but it does not rest till it has gained a hearing. Finally, after a countless succession of rebuffs, it succeeds. This is one of the few points on which one may be optimistic about the future of mankind, but it is in itself a point of no small importance. And from it one can derive yet other hopes. The primacy of the intellect lies, it is true, in a distant, distant future, but probably not in an *infinitely* distant one. It will presumably set itself the same aims as those whose realization you expect from your God (of course within human limits—so far as external reality, 'Aνάγκη, allows it), namely the love of man and the decrease of suffering. This being so, we may tell ourselves that our antagonism is only a temporary one and not irreconcilable. We desire the same things, but you are more impatient, more exacting, and—why should I not say it?—more self-seeking than I and those on my side. You would have the state of bliss begin directly after death; you expect the impossible from it and you will not surrender the claims of the individual. Our God, Λόγος,[2] will fulfill whichever of these wishes nature outside us allows, but he will do it very gradually, only in the unforeseeable future, and for a new generation of men. He promises no compensation for us, who suffer grievously from life. On the way to this distant goal your religious doctrines will have to be discarded, no matter whether the first attempts fail, or whether the first substitutes prove to be untenable. You know why: in the long run nothing can withstand reason and experience, and the contradiction which religion offers to both is all too palpable. Even purified religious ideas cannot escape this fate, so long as they try to preserve anything of the consolation of religion. No doubt if they confine themselves to a belief in a higher spiritual being, whose qualities are indefinable and whose purposes cannot be discerned, they will be proof against the challenge of science; but then they will also lose their hold on human interest.

And secondly: observe the difference between your attitude to illusions and mine. You have to defend the religious illusion with all your might. If it becomes discredited—and indeed the threat to it is great enough—then your world collapses. There is nothing left for you but to despair of everything, of civilization and the future of mankind. From that bondage I am, we are, free. Since

[2] The twin gods Λόγος [*Logos:* Reason] and 'Aνάγκη [*Anagke:* Necessity] of the Dutch writer Multatuli. [Cf. an Editor's footnote to "The Economic Problem of Masochism" (1924c), *Standard Ed., 19,* 168.]

we are prepared to renounce a good part of our infantile wishes, we can bear it if a few of our expectations turn out to be illusions.

Education freed from the burden of religious doctrines will not, it may be, effect much change in men's psychological nature. Our god Λόγος is perhaps not a very almighty one, and he may only be able to fulfill a small part of what his predecessors have promised. If we have to acknowledge this we shall accept it with resignation. We shall not on that account lose our interest in the world and in life, for we have one sure support which you lack. We believe that it is possible for scientific work to gain some knowledge about the reality of the world, by means of which we can increase our power and in accordance with which we can arrange our life. If this belief is an illusion, then we are in the same position as you. But science has given us evidence by its numerous and important successes that it is no illusion. Science has many open enemies, and many more secret ones, among those who cannot forgive her for having weakened religious faith and for threatening to overthrow it. She is reproached for the smallness of the amount she has taught us and for the incomparably greater field she has left in obscurity. But, in this, people forget how young she is, how difficult her beginnings were and how infinitesimally small is the period of time since the human intellect has been strong enough for the tasks she sets. Are we not all at fault, in basing our judgments on periods of time that are too short? We should make the geologists our pattern. People complain of the unreliability of science—how she announces as a law today what the next generation recognizes as an error and replaces by a new law whose accepted validity lasts no longer. But this is unjust and in part untrue. The transformations of scientific opinion are developments, advances, not revolutions. A law which was held at first to be universally valid proves to be a special case of a more comprehensive uniformity, or is limited by another law, not discovered till later; a rough approximation to the truth is replaced by a more carefully adapted one, which in turn awaits further perfectioning. There are various fields where we have not yet surmounted a phase of research in which we make trial with hypotheses that soon have to be rejected as inadequate; but in other fields we already possess an assured and almost unalterable core of knowledge. Finally, an attempt has been made to discredit scientific endeavor in a radical way, on the ground that, being bound to the conditions of our own organization, it can yield nothing else than subjective results, whilst the real nature of things outside ourselves remains inaccessible. But this is to disregard several factors which are of decisive importance for the understanding of scientific work. In the first place, our organization—that is, our mental apparatus— has been developed precisely in the attempt to explore the external world, and it must therefore have realized in its structure some degree of expediency; in the second place, it is itself a constituent part of the world which we set out to investigate, and it readily admits of such an investigation; thirdly, the task of science is fully covered if we limit it to showing how the world must appear to us in consequence of the particular character of our organization; fourthly, the ultimate findings of science, precisely because of the way in which they are acquired, are determined not only by our organization but by the things which have affected that organization; finally, the problem of the nature of the world without regard to our percipient mental apparatus is an empty abstraction, devoid of practical interest.

No, our science is no illusion. But an illusion it would be to suppose that what science cannot give us we can get elsewhere.

IV

THE GOD
BEYOND GOD

John Middleton Murry

[1889–1957]

As MUCH AS Nietzsche and Freud, Middleton Murry was a thoroughly secular man in a clearly modern world. A child of working-class parents, he was baptized in the Church of England and received conventional religious instruction, but virtually as a matter of course he had left this behind by the time he finished his secondary schooling on scholarship. Although he was later to be known as a foremost Keats scholar, his first major literary work was *Dostoevsky: A Critical Study* (1916), perhaps the first book in English to interpret Dostoevsky as an existentialist. He read intensively in Rousseau and Nietzsche before turning to Keats.

Murry was a force in the world of literature. He was closely associated with D. H. Lawrence. With Aldous Huxley as his assistant, he brilliantly edited *The Athenaeum* from 1919 to 1921, publishing such writers as Lawrence, T. S. Eliot, Valéry, Proust, Gide and Santayana. During the 1930s and after, he became engrossed in social concerns; he was wartime editor of *Peace News*, and his last major book was *The Free Society* (1948).

Murry was in his forties before he joined the church. Even then and later when he briefly considered being ordained a priest, his Christianity was unorthodox. Yet his biographer could say of him, referring to an earlier time, "Jesus was a great deal more real to him than anybody he had known in the flesh,"[1] and that "the question to which Murry related poetry was the one real question, the same yesterday, today and tomorrow: 'What shall I do to be saved?' "[2] What intrigued him in Dostoevsky was that he pushed

[1] F. A. Lea, *John Middleton Murry* (New York: Oxford University Press, 1963), p. 137.
[2] *Ibid.*, p. 126.

skepticism to its paralyzing limit, only to find himself seeking "the sudden revelation of a new consciousness, when all eternity shall be gathered into a moment, when there shall be no more division between the body and the soul . . ."[3]

In his thirties, Murry knew no more about contemporary theology than did Freud, and indeed he had some acquaintance with the latter's writings before religious questions forced themselves upon him. Like others of his generation, World War I opened an abyss for him that drew him to Dostoevsky and Nietzsche; and the crisis was made indelibly personal when his wife contracted tuberculosis, from which she died in 1923. Her illness and death found Murry spiritually empty and alone. In search of a meaning for his own life, he studied Ludwig Wittgenstein, Meister Eckhart and others. One result was his highly original study *The Life of Jesus* (1926), which deserves to rank with those of Strauss and Renan, although it surpasses both in psychological insight. Another, more closely related to his own crisis of faith, was *God* (1929).

Possibly Murry knew of Freud's notion of "metapsychology," although he does not refer to it, and it may be that "metabiology" is entirely his own coinage. The term explains itself in the following selection. It is unfortunate that Murry never again took up this concept. It is even more unfortunate that Murry never entered into the currents of discourse represented by Buber and Tillich. Yet for just this reason his thought is of extraordinary interest, for in a very individual and untheological way it mirrors their confrontation with the crisis of modern man. Common influences are at work, to be sure, especially Eckhart and Nietzsche; but in Murry they occur in dialogue with such pragmatic terms as "significant variation" and "value," which give his thought a more secular orientation. Apparently Murry bypassed Schelling on his way to Eckhart: hence his particular stress on "organic growth" rather than logical "dialectic"—hence, too, the implication throughout of *life* rather than *being*. By steering clear of metaphysical categories he is thus able to speak of Jesus as "the new man" in a way that directly answers Nietzsche's call for a super-

[3] John Middleton Murry, *Dostoevsky: A Critical Study* (London: Jonathan Cape, 1916), p. 241.

man. As Murry says elsewhere, echoing Nietzsche, "If we deny God, as we must, then we must bear his burden." He then goes on to say, "In him, a new man emerged; he must emerge, henceforward, in us."[4]

Murry regarded *God* as a post-Christian work, yet later became a Christian and a church member and also retreated from the language of *God* into an acceptance of orthodox theological terms. But the contribution remains, and it is clearer now that it is precisely a contribution to the new Christianity, whether we accept it or not, by a transvaluation that goes beyond natural theology while retaining a core of Christian meaning. And despite Murry's claim that it is "naturalistic," it is not so in any reductionist sense if we follow his meaning carefully.

Biology and Metabiology[1]

God, as we have explained, is the means by which man seeks to make the universe a unity which he can assimilate, or to which he can assimilate himself, which comes to the same thing. The assertion of the existence of God is the assertion that the universe is not a chaos; it may be incomprehensible, but it is not a chaos. The continuous projection into God of man's own highest achievements, or more strictly the achievements which were precious to men most deeply concerned that the universe should not be a chaos, was the necessary means of asserting an ultimate unity. For among all the things for which God was responsible in the mind of any God discoverer, he was certainly responsible for the God discoverer himself. What he was God must be. God might be many things besides; but he must be that. God was thus the ever growing repository of painfully achieved human perfections. He grew with man, and he helped man to grow.

The deification of an actual man was the necessary consumma-

[4] John Middleton Murry, *God: An Introduction to the Science of Metabiology* (London: Jonathan Cape, 1929), p. 233.
[1] From *God: An Introduction to the Science of Metabiology* (London: Jonathan Cape, 1929).—Ed.

tion of the process of God creation. Not any man could thus have been deified; only a great man, and a new man, and a man moreover whose greatness and newness should be perpetually evident. Christianity, as we have said, is more than the man Jesus; but without him it would be only a vaguely remembered philosophy. The new man who spoke words that testify his newness to all who have ears to hear them; the new man who was killed for his newness—this was the deity. Newness and the impotence of death against it manifest in a single man, and this man God.

What had happened was this. Jesus had enriched God with his living self; his followers enriched God with his death and agony. Thereafter, there was little indeed that God could not contain. God was comprehensive at last; the pain of the world in travail of the future was now in him. He was a true God, now. He would not cease to be a true God, even when men ceased to believe in him. He could only cease to be a true God, when men were prepared to do for themselves what he had done for them. They must make the universe a unity; they must bear the burden of their own newness, without hope of reward; they must take responsibility for themselves.

The unity of the real universe, of which struggling and suffering man is a part; the necessity that man must struggle and suffer and struggle again; and the truth that only by admitting, in his depths, this unity and this necessity he could find his own unity—these perceptions were the great new values with which Christianity enriched the conception of God. They were all manifest in the pure phenomenon of Jesus. Christianity blazed it and them across the heavens.

To find a place in the unity of the universe for the emergent variation of the new man, and for the biological disaster which overtook him; to accept Jesus as a significant variation, and to refuse the despair which his fate appeared to impose—this was the effort and achievement of Christianity. That it necessitated paradox and could ultimately be secured only by Faith may seem to modern minds to invalidate it. But that is because modern minds do not think so well as they believe themselves to do. If they thought more deeply they would find that paradox is inevitable in any complete description of the real, and that Faith is inevitable also if we refuse to believe that the real is a chaos; Faith, indeed, is that refusal. The modern mind will not recognize its own faith; it prefers to leave it hidden and obscurely septic. That is certainly no reason why it should refuse attention to a system which from the beginning has sought to keep the nature of its own faith keen and clear before its eyes. It is obviously no *reason*; but it probably is the unconscious motive for the determined disregard of Christianity which now prevails.

In short, we believe that men today, and among them some of the most genuinely enlightened, are unconsciously afraid of Christianity. It is a mystery into which they are obscurely warned from penetrating. It is strange, alien, and forbidding. It is a grim and grisly relic of the Dark Ages; a fearful survival. Spells and enchantment lurk within it, and if a man were to venture himself within the cavern door, who knows what might happen to him?

Who knows indeed? For he might learn something about himself which he does not want to know. He might learn, for instance, that it is man's duty to know what he veritably is instead of indulging some vain conceit of himself. He might learn, again, that a chaotic universe necessitates a chaotic man. Worst of all, he might learn that there *is* salvation and there *is* damnation, and that these tremendous words express not idle and superstitious fancies, but verities of human life which lie open to the knowledge of any man with the courage to look at the facts of his own experience.

2

Christianity is the form taken by the greatest effort of the world organism to maintain its own achieved and emergent values. In so describing it we have been compelled to use the word "value" freely; but always the word has been used in the sense of our own definition, that "value" is a quality attached, by any given individual, to certain organic variations which he desires to perpetuate. When many individuals desire to perpetuate the same variations, there is a class of values.

The real values of mankind are simply the variations which maintain themselves. My values are simply the variations which

I resolve to maintain. When, therefore, I say that Christianity is the greatest effort of the world organism to maintain its own achieved and emergent values, I am saying that the variations to which I respond are, in the main, those which Christianity strove to perpetuate; and, further, I am saying that there is a whole great class of people (Christian or otherwise) which responds to these variations as I myself respond to them.

We call the variations which Christianity has sought to maintain in existence significant variations. There are for ourselves other significant variations which Christianity has not sought to maintain. The effort required to bring these new variations into organic unity with those which it maintained was at a given point in history too great for Christianity. Christianity, after all, is simply the succession of Christian men and woman. Of these a few elected to make the effort to reconcile the new variations with the old. This effort is called the Reformation; but far fewer of the reformers than is generally supposed by Protestant historians really embodied an effort of the organism to advance. Most of them were retrogressive and reversionary. Most of those who separated themselves from the Catholic Church did not understand from what they were separating themselves: they did not themselves incorporate the significant variation of Catholicism. They were rudimentary Christians, not superior ones, as they believed themselves to be. Luther and Calvin were rudimentary; Melancthon and Zwingli might reasonably claim to mark an advance. So might Erasmus; but he did not leave the Church.

Ever since that time, the problem has been growing more and more acute. The problem is to reconcile the significant variations maintained by Christianity with the no less significant variations embodied in men who in pursuit of order in the universe had found it more and more necessary to restrict the category of the supernatural. Somehow a new unity had to be achieved. Conscious man was divided by the pull of a new and mighty variation making its imperative organic claim upon him. Such stresses resolve themselves, it is true, but the place where they resolve themselves is man. The variations which are destined to maintain themselves, maintain themselves; but they maintain themselves through man. To know that there is Destiny is to know oneself the battleground where it is decided.

3

To know that the variation, if it is significant, will maintain itself, and that, if it does not maintain itself, it is not significant, does not absolve man from the struggle. Far from it, it teaches him that the struggle is inevitable and right. There is a reason for it. His effort to maintain the significant variation, his will to let himself become the mortal instrument by which the conflicting variations struggling within him may attain a new embodiment—this is his loyalty to life. The struggle is not his struggle; if it were, he could not endure it, nor would he be required to endure it.

It is a wholly natural process. That, for long centuries, the supernatural category was invoked to describe it, was due simply to the nonexistence of any other category which could contain the facts. Just as the simple recognition of the fact that Jesus was a new man compelled men to describe him as God incarnate, so the simple recognition of the fact that, by the contemplation of the fact of Jesus, "a new man" emerged within the individual after conflict, and chaos, and despair compelled men to describe the new "birth" as the reclamation of a soul by God. The dynamic of life cannot be described in merely rational terms. In Jesus a new man *was* born into the world; in those who recognized him for what he was, whether during his life or in the long years of Christianity after his death, something happened, automatically by the sheer fact of that recognition, which could only be described as a rebirth. These were facts, not vain imaginations; scientific facts, because all facts are scientific, but incapable of recognition by science until a science should arise that resolutely set itself to include them.

Such a science begins to emerge in this book. It does not claim to explain these facts, because science explains nothing. It does with them precisely what science, when it is not self-deceived, is conscious of doing to its facts: it gives the simplest and most economic description of them. It does this by observing, what has not been previously observed with the same comprehensiveness, that the so-called spiritual is absolutely continuous with the biological. There is no dividing line between them. In the so-called spiritual order life proceeds by precisely the same kind of process as in the biological. There is organic variation, and response to variation; when the responses to variation are conflicting, there is inward struggle which, if maintained, produces first stasis, and then resolution into newness. A new variation has emerged.

The intellectual consciousness is a means of the process; but it does not at any point control it. Take intellectual self-consciousness to the extreme conceivable pitch, still the process is hidden from it. Not that it happens in the unconscious, for there is no such place. It happens in and to the organism as a whole of which the intellectual consciousness is only a particular modality. The intellectual consciousness is simply a means of response to variation.

Response to variation is, like variation itself, always organic. We speak of the will. But the will is really appearance. A man's awareness of his will is merely his consciousness of organic response at work in him. The will to maintain a significant variation is *inevitably* aroused in man when he attains the knowledge that a variation is significant. There is deliberate tautology here; for the knowledge that a variation is significant is a mere description of the fact of complete organic response to a variation. When we say we know that such a variation is significant, we are simply saying that we are aware of ourselves as organically responding to it. What we call the will is already at work in the organic response.

It is so incredibly simple that it will probably appear simply incredible. I cannot really recognize that Jesus was a significant variation without willing, almost literally, to absorb him into myself. I cannot really recognize that Plato was a significant variation, without willing, almost literally, to absorb him into myself. This absorption is what we have called organic assimilation on the metabiological plane. The organic assimilation is, in reality, the knowledge of significant variation *in act*. The two are inseparable, a single organic process separated only for the purpose of discourse. And this organic process includes and subsumes all the most abstract processes of mind. Thus, the will to maintain a significant variation is only a description from one particular angle of a process which can be as truly described as the self-maintenance of a variation. Simply, the organic process, being metabiological, involves the exercise of will. Equally, it demands the exercise of intellect and emotion. The three traditionally separable aspects of man's metabiological unity are inevitably involved in the self-maintenance of the metabiological variation, which is "value."

4

The effort of man is not merely to maintain the significant metabiological variation, but also to achieve metabiological unity. This achievement of metabiological unity is the condition of really maintaining metabiological variations. In other words, the variations which he organically assimilates must become organic unity in himself. That, on the pure biological plane, would be a tautology; on that plane no organic assimilation without organic unity is possible. On the metabiological plane organic unity is not so automatically assured. For variation may be intellectually assimilated, or it may be emotionally assimilated, or it may be assimilated quite unconsciously by moral habit, or physical disposition. And intellect, emotion, moral habit and physical disposition may perfectly well be discordant with one another; indeed, they almost invariably are. To resolve them into organic and metabiological unity is not an easy matter.

For the moment, to simplify matters, we leave out the purely biological element, to consider the metabiological situation. The various responses to variation are not reconciled: those which have been aroused through intellect, through emotion, through moral habit are at war with one another. This conflict is the great metabiological crisis in the life of man; on its solution depends the decision how much of significant variation shall be perpetuated through him. By the comprehensiveness of the elements involved in the metabiological crisis, and the comprehensiveness of the solution, the importance of his part in the organic evolution of the whole is determined. He is become a focus of the life process. Shall he revert, or shall he be new? Shall he repeat a pattern, or become a new form? Shall he become a new combination of significant variations, or shall he be an old one? How can he maintain all significant variations? Obviously, he cannot maintain them all; he cannot perpetuate all values. But since, by definition, value attaches only to those variations which do maintain themselves, he is not required to perpetuate them all. Some values are doomed to die; variations which have maintained themselves over long periods become at last rudimentary. The resolution of the metabiological crisis demands as much the rejection of dying values as a new incorporation of living ones. The individual, in his period of metabiological crisis, which lasts in a less acute form for the whole of his period of metabiological activity, is the battleground of variations which seek to maintain themselves in and through him. The significance of his own metabiological life depends on the significance of the variations which he embodies and transmits. That will be judged not in his lifetime, or by the minds of men. Life itself will ultimately pronounce upon him: He became a significant variation, or he reverted. In a long sequence of the metabiological crises of posterity he will maintain himself, or he will be rejected.

To strive to become oneself significant variation, by embodying significant variations in a new creative whole, is, we believe, the modern equivalent of doing "the will of God." It is easy to say: You cannot do the will of God except you believe in his existence. But a childish argument of that kind can be ignored by those who have realized that God himself is nothing but a means of perpetuating the variations which are called values. To perpetuate the living value, and let die the dying one in ourselves, is to do the will of God; and not the least of the dying values is the belief that God exists. It is the will of God that God should die, and we are doing what we can to obey it. Of course, it is open to any lover of confusion to say that the organic process which we here describe is God. It is not. The only verdict that can be accepted on what is, or what is not, God, is the verdict of the Catholic Church; and there is no doubt about that. That the organic process is mysterious, thrilling, satisfying; that it awakens in those who discern it a response of the same kind as the Christian once received from his contemplation of the manifold God of Orthodoxy; that every essential element in the great whole of Catholic Christianity has its equivalent somewhere in the system outlined here—all this is true. But nonetheless a God cannot be extracted from it without an equivocation of which an honest mind should be ashamed. Here simply is reality. It is a reality to which man responds, and which responds to man.

It is perfectly true that the nearest historical approximation to the system here developed is Orthodox Christianity. That is necessary. They were created to meet the same fundamental need, and in somewhat the same fashion. Both are based on a determination to recognize the reality of the man Jesus, of the mystical experience, and of all "values." Two systems which arise out of the same basic recognitions must needs be like one another. At the same time, they are utterly different. The fluxing agent in either system is of a different kind. In the Christian system, Jesus is God, the object of mystical experience is God, and all values are God. God is the medium where they meet and merge. In this system the reality of organic evolution is the medium. Jesus is a supremely significant variation—a new man; the object of mystical experience is the underlying unity of biological life; and values of all kinds are organic variations which maintain themselves. The scheme is wholly natural; but with a genuine and thoroughgoing Naturalism. It replaces the old comprehensive Christian bisection of the Universe into natural and supernatural, by an equally comprehensive unification of the Universe into a continuity of biological and metabiological. In it, conscious Science and conscious Religion become absolutely identical.

When we cease to hypostatize values, the need and the possibility of what is ordinarily known as Religion disappears. Values, in order to be real, do not have to be eternal: if they are eternal, they necessarily cease to be real. The notion that the reality of values depends on their eternity is a fallacy congenital to the logical intellect, which is, by the laws of its operation, forced to separate the universal from the particular. That separation is false to reality. So long as we believe that the operations of the logical intellect alone bring us to reality, this separation of the universal from the particular, of the value from the variation, is inescapable. And inescapable ultimately, if the universe is not to be divided forever, is God to unite it again. A thoroughgoing intellectualism, which refuses finally to accept an irrational and contradictory universe, is bound to end in God, and in Faith. It is strange that this is not clearly recognized.

At one end or the other of the process the intellect must abnegate. The choice is simple and clear. Either it must abnegate at the end or at the beginning. At the end it must abnegate in obedience to the deep and primary organic demand that the Universe which it has riven in twain, and cannot join together, must be one. If it becomes truly conscious of the nature and origin of the demand it is forced to obey, it will be ashamed of this ultimate capitulation, and will recognize, gladly and with good will, that the true moment for capitulation was the beginning. The universal ought never to have been separated from the particular, nor the value from the variation. That the operation of intellect depends upon and demands the separation is no reason for allowing it to endure. But not to allow the separation to endure does not mean that the operations of the intellect should cease. They should be allowed absolute freedom as before; only it should never for one moment be forgotten that they are leading away from the ultimate reality and not toward it. Reality is the pure phenomenon, and there is no other. In other words, we must recognize clearly that the logical intellect is only a partial and peculiar faculty of the organic and integral human being. The organic and integral human being is active in the response to the pure phenomenon.

This, on the logical or intellectual side, is the beginning of wisdom. Once we have reintegrated the universal into the particular, the value into the variation, and determined that it shall remain embodied there, we are safeguarded against the abuse of intellect. We can use it fully, without danger of becoming its slaves. Of all its services in clearing the way for us to reach the sequence of pure phenomena which is history and reality, we may avail ourselves without stint; but we shall always be mindful to restore the continuity of process which it seeks to separate and make static. The unity of the universe is biological, not logical.

To contemplate the richness and variety of the universal process not as a march of dialectic, but as an actual growth of the same kind as the growth of a flower or a child; to apprehend it immediately as real and organic; to watch in the human history which most nearly concerns us the total organism slowly and inevitably responding to the significant variation which is value; to see the rise and fall of Gods, and to know them as always organic to the process which for a time they subserve, to which inevitably they become rudimentary; to follow the slow change in the faculties and potentialities of men as more and more new variations maintain themselves in him by his response to them; to understand how marvelously the great achievements endure, so that not one of them is lost, and how the everlasting newness of life makes its inevitable way into the unknown against the vast inertia that lurks forever throughout the whole—to know reality after this fashion is to be freed finally from the need of God. There is no place for him in the universe; there is no place for him in the unity of man. There is nothing for him to do.

To this universe we do not need to be reconciled. To know it is to be reconciled to it, and to be reconciled within ourselves. Its unity is the condition of our own unity; and these unities are one.

Martin Buber

[1878–1965]

ALTHOUGH BORN IN VIENNA, Martin Buber grew up in the home
of his grandfather, Solomon Buber, one of the last scholars of
the Haskalah (Jewish Enlightenment). At Berlin and Vienna he
studied art history and philosophy, receiving his Ph.D. in 1904.
During the following two decades he absorbed the philosophy
of Kant and Goethe, became steeped in existentialism and under-
took a decisive study of Hasidism, the beliefs of a Jewish mystical sect that flourished in eastern Europe from the late eighteenth
century. His best-known book is *I and Thou* (1923), which ex-
pounds a philosophy of dialogue rooted in Feuerbach's concept
of interpersonal relation but worked out in great detail. Integral
to the personalism of I-Thou is a sociopolitical perspective that
emphasizes cooperatives like the *kibbutzim* of Palestine, where
Buber and his Christian wife went to live after Hitler's rise to
power.

Long identified with the Zionist movement and numbered
among the leading Jewish thinkers of his day, Buber considered
Jesus his "great brother,"[1] and like Jesus he felt no obligation to
observe the law of the Torah—for, as Arthur Cohen has said,
"he refuses to acknowledge that the Word of God transmits more
than the person of God."[2]

For Buber, says Maurice Friedman, the assertion "God is dead"
signifies modern man's loss of the capacity "to experience a reality
absolutely independent of himself."[3] Buber has preferred to speak

[1] Martin Buber, *Two Types of Faith* (London: Routledge, 1951), p. 12.
[2] Arthur A. Cohen, *The Natural and the Supernatural Jew* (New York:
Pantheon, 1962), p. 171.
[3] Maurice Friedman, *Martin Buber: The Life of Dialogue* (University of
Chicago Press, 1955), p. 155.

of the "eclipse" rather than the "death" of God, and regards this as an expression of modern man's experience of alienation. Authentic existence, for Buber, means wholeness—whether in encounter between persons or in the social ownership of industry—and the trend of modern life is toward the impersonal, toward fragmentation and manipulation. To quote Cohen, "The living God cannot be perceived other than by the whole man. The recovery of God requires the revived spontaneity, self-awareness and openness of man before the world."[4]

It is from these assumptions that Buber, in the following selection, examines several contemporary viewpoints that are predicated on the "death of God." In so doing, Buber helps us to understand the nature of the God that "died" for Heidegger, Jung and Sartre and, by implication, to achieve a new stance toward the living God of the I-Thou relation. In the Feuerbachian way that we have already noted, Buber's dialogical understanding of God as "presence" is humanistic rather than theistic. God does not initiate but responds to human initiatives. As Friedman says, "Each man lets God into the world through hallowing the everyday."[5] That is to say, what is holy is what is made whole; God is incarnated whenever this occurs, and this is the very nature of redemption. Buber, who translated the Hebrew Bible into modern German, identifies this God with that of Moses and Abraham as well as with that of the Baal Shem Tov. He does not enter into dialogue with Christian theology on this point, but there are obvious resonances between a philosophy that sees I-Thou as a "primary word" implying redemption, and a gospel such as that of John, which speaks of "word made flesh" "in the beginning." Further, despite obvious differences, the reader will find Buber's "primary word" illuminating for Altizer's concept of the "kenotic Word," for each implies that which is unnamably sacred, each implies a relation of love—and it is these that are unaccounted for in the perspectives of Sartre, Heidegger and Jung that are here under review.

[4] Cohen, *loc. cit.*
[5] Friedman, *op. cit.*, p. 282.

Religion and Modern Thinking[1]

I shall speak of the relation of modern thought to religion. By this I do not mean the attempts to think from the standpoint of religious reality, or to create an understanding between it and philosophy based on mutual tolerance. My subject shall rather be modern thought only insofar as it undertakes to give a verdict as to whether or under what conditions or within what limits the character of a living human reality can be ascribed to religion. We find a judgment of this sort in the ontological sense, on the one hand, in the so-called existentialism of Sartre and Heidegger, and in the psychological sense, on the other, in Jung's theory of the collective unconscious. Basic to both positions is the assumption that the outcome of the crisis in which religion has entered depends essentially upon the judgments which are made by modern ontological or psychological thought. It is this assumption that we must examine.

In naming Heidegger and Sartre together, I by no means imply that they have the same attitude toward religion. On the contrary, in this respect as in so many others they are without doubt radically dissimilar, and accordingly the reply to the one must be entirely different from the reply to the other.

Sartre proclaims his atheism; he says, "The atheistic existentialism, which I represent. . . ."[2] Among the representatives of this position he has, to be sure, included Heidegger; but Heidegger has refused to allow himself to be thus classified. We must therefore deal with Sartre by himself. He clearly wishes his atheism to be understood as a logical consequence of his existential philosophy. We undoubtedly have here before us an atheism which is basically different from any materialistic one. That it follows, however, from an existential conception of the

---

[1] From *Eclipse of God* (New York: Harper & Row, 1952).—Ed.

[2] *L'existentialisme est un humanisme* (1946), p. 21. All the quotations in this essay except one (see note 55) are translated directly and literally from the French or German original. For the context in translation cf. *Existentialism*, translated by Bernard Frechtman (1947), p. 18.

world, that is, from one which proceeds from the reality of human existence, cannot be substantiated.

Sartre accepts Nietzsche's cry, or better shout, "God is dead!" as a valid statement of fact. Our generation appears to him as specifically the one which has outlived God. He says once[3]— although elsewhere he most emphatically asserts, as one who knows, "*Dieu n'existe pas*"[4]—that the fact that God is dead does not mean that he does not exist nor even that he no longer exists. In place of these interpretations he presents another which is singular enough. "He is dead," he says, "he spoke to us and now is silent, all that we touch now is his corpse."[5] I shall not deal here with the shockingly trivial concluding sentence. But let us turn to that which precedes it: "He spoke to us and now he is silent." Let us try to take it seriously, that is, let us ignore what Sartre really meant by it, namely, that man in earlier times believed that he heard God and now is no longer capable of so believing. Let us ask whether it may not be literally true that God formerly spoke to us and is now silent, and whether this is not to be understood as the Hebrew Bible understands it, namely, that the living God is not only a self-revealing but also a self-concealing God.[6] Let us realize what it means to live in the age of such a concealment, such a divine silence, and we shall perhaps understand its implication for our existence as something entirely different from that which Sartre desires to teach us.

What Sartre desires to teach us, he says to us clearly enough.[7] "This silence of the transcendent, combined with the perseverance of the religious need in modern man, that is the great concern today as yesterday. It is the problem which torments Nietzsche, Heidegger, Jaspers." In other words, existentialism must take courage, it must give up once for all the search for God, it must "forget" God.[8] After a century-long crisis of faith as well as of knowledge, man must finally recover the creative

[3] *Situations* I (1947), p. 153, Section "*Un nouveau mystique*" of 1943.
[4] *L'existentialisme*, pp. 33f. Cf. *Existentialism*, pp. 27f.
[5] *Situations* I, *loc. cit.*
[6] Isaiah 45:15.
[7] *Situations* I, *loc. cit.*
[8] *Ibid.*, p. 154.

freedom which he once falsely ascribed to God. He must recognize himself as the being through whose appearance the world exists. For, says Sartre, "there is no universe other than a human universe, the universe of human subjectivity."[9] The sentence that I have just quoted sounds like the thesis of a resurrected idealism.

The problem that "torments" the existentialist thinker of our age, insofar as he does not, like Sartre, dismiss it out of hand, lies deeper than Sartre thinks. It focuses finally in the question of whether the perseverance of the "religious need" does not indicate something inherent in human existence. Does existence really mean, as Sartre thinks, existing "for oneself" encapsuled in one's own subjectivity? Or does it not essentially mean standing *over against* the x—not an x for which a certain quantity could be substituted, but rather the X itself, the undefinable and unfathomable? "God," says Sartre, "is the quintessence of the Other."[10] But the Other for Sartre is he who "looks at" me, who makes me into an object, as I make him.[11] The idea of God, moreover, he also understands as that of an inescapable witness, and if that is so, "What need have we of God? The Other is enough, no matter what other."[12] But what if God is not the quintessence of the Other, but rather its absoluteness? And what if it is not primarily the reciprocal relation of subject and object which exists between me and the other, but rather the reciprocal relation of I and Thou? Each empirical other does not, of course, remain my Thou; he becomes an It, an object for me as I for him. It is not so, however, with that absolute Other, the Absolute over against me, that undefinable and unfathomable X that I call "God." God can never become an object for me; I can attain no other relation to Him than that of the I to its eternal Thou, that of the Thou to its eternal I. But if man is no longer able to attain this relation, if God is silent toward him and he toward God, then something has taken place, not in human subjectivity but in Being itself. It would be worthier not to explain

[9] *L'existentialisme*, p. 93. Cf. *Existentialism*, p. 60.
[10] *Situations* I, p. 237, Section *"Aller et retour,"* probably of 1942.
[11] *L'être et le néant* (1943), Section *"L'existence d'autrui."*
[12] *Situations* I, *loc. cit.*

it to oneself in sensational and incompetent sayings, such as that of the "death" of God, but to endure it as it is and at the same time to move existentially toward a new happening, toward that event in which the word between heaven and earth will again be heard. Thus the perseverance of the "religious need," to which Sartre objects and which he thinks contradicts the silence of the transcendent, instead points directly to the situation in which man becomes aware of this silence as such.

Still more questionable is Sartre's demand, reminiscent of Ludwig Feuerbach, that man should recover for himself the creative freedom which he ascribed to God and that he should affirm himself as the being through whom a world exists.[13] That ordering of known phenomena which we call the world is, indeed, the composite work of a thousand human generations, but it has come into being through the fact that manifold being, which is not our work, meets us, who are, likewise, together with our subjectivity, not our work. Nor is this meeting, out of which arises the whole of the phenomena which we order into the "world," our work. All that being is *established*, we are established, our meeting with it is established, and in this way the becoming of a world, which takes place through us, is established. This establishment of a universe, including ourselves and our works, is the fundamental reality of existence which is accessible to us as living beings. Contrasted with this reality, the demand that man recover his creative freedom appears as a demagogic phrase. That "creative freedom" which really belongs to us, our participation in creation, is established, as we ourselves. It is a question of using this freedom properly, that is, in a manner worthy of the fact that it is a freedom which is given to us, nothing less and nothing more. He who sets in the place of it the postulate of the "recovery of freedom" turns aside from true human existence, which means being sent and being commissioned.

Sartre has started from the "silence" of God without asking himself what part our not hearing and our not having heard has played in that silence. From the silence he has concluded that God does not exist, at any rate not for us, for a god whose object

[13] *Situations* I, p. 334, Section *"La liberté cartésienne."*

I am without his being mine does not concern me.[14] This conclusion is possible for Sartre because he holds the subject-object relation to be the primary and exclusive relation between two beings. He does not see the original and decisive relation between I and Thou, compared with which the subject-object relation is only a classifying elaboration. Now, however, Sartre goes further: One "must draw the consequences."[15] God is silent, that is, nothing is said to one that is unconditional or unconditionally binding. "There is no sign in the world."[16] Since, therefore, no universal morality can tell us what to do, since all possibility of discovering absolute values has disappeared with God, and since man, to whom henceforth "all is permitted,"[17] is at last free, is indeed freedom itself, it is for him to determine values. "If I have done away with God the father (*si j'ai supprimé Dieu le père*)," Sartre says literally, "someone is needed to invent values (*pour inventer les valeurs*). . . . Life has no meaning *a priori* . . . it is up to you to give it a meaning, and value is nothing else than this meaning which you choose."[18] That is almost exactly what Nietzsche said, and it has not become any truer since then. One can believe in and accept a meaning or value, one can set it as a guiding light over one's life if one has discovered it, not if one has invented it. It can be for me an illuminating meaning, a direction-giving value only if it has been revealed to me in my meeting with Being, not if I have freely chosen it for myself from among the existing possibilities and perhaps have in addition decided with some fellow creatures: This shall be valid from now on. The thesis reminds me of that curious concept of Georges Sorel, the social myth, the classic example of which is the general strike. This avowedly unrealizable myth shall show the workers the direction in which they shall be active, but it can function naturally only so long as they do not read Sorel and learn that it is just a myth.

[14] *L'être et le néant*, pp. 286f., 341.
[15] *L'existentialisme*, pp. 33ff. Cf. *Existentialism*, pp. 25ff.
[16] *Ibid.*, p. 47. Cf. *Existentialism*, p. 33.
[17] *Ibid.*, p. 36. Cf. *Existentialism*, p. 27.
[18] *Ibid.*, p. 89. Cf. *Existentialism*, p. 58.

More important than these arguments of a remarkable psychological observer and highly gifted literary man, for whom genuine ontological considerations are always intermingled with entirely different matters, is that argument which Heidegger, who undoubtedly belongs to the historical rank of philosophers in the proper sense of the term, brings forward concerning the problem of religion in our time. These thoughts, it is true, are first explicitly expressed in the writings of his second period, from about 1943 on, but we already find indications of them earlier.

Like Sartre, Heidegger also starts from Nietzsche's saying "God is dead," which he has interpreted at length.[19] It is evident to him that Nietzsche wanted in this saying to dispense with not only God but also the absolute in all its forms, therefore, in truth, not only religion but also metaphysics. Heidegger believes that he can erect at the point of this extremest negation a new position which will be a pure ontological thinking. It is the teaching of being as attaining its illumination in or through man. In this teaching the doctrine of Parmenides which posits being as the original absolute which is prior to and above form is curiously interwoven with the Hegelian theory of the original principle which attains self-consciousness in the human spirit.

It has been possible for Heidegger to erect this new position despite the "death of God" because being for him is bound to and attains its illumination through the destiny and history of man, without its becoming thereby a function of human subjectivity. But by this it is already indicated that, to use an image that Heidegger himself avoids, God can rise from the dead. This means that the unfolding of the new ontological thought can prepare for a turning-point in which the divine, or as Heidegger, in agreement with the poet Hölderlin, prefers to say, the holy, will appear in new and still unanticipated forms. This thinking is consequently, as Heidegger repeatedly emphasizes, not atheism, for it "decides neither positively nor negatively about the possibility of God's existing."[20] Rather "through its adequate conception of existence" it makes it possible for the first time legiti-

[19] *Holzwege* (1950), pp. 193ff., Section *"Nietzsches Wort 'Gott ist tot.'"*
[20] *Vom Wesen des Grundes* (1929), p. 28.

mately to ask "what is the ontological state of the relation of
existence to the divine."

Heidegger not only protests against our regarding this view as
atheism but also against our regarding it as an indifferentism
which must deteriorate into nihilism.[21] He by no means wants to
teach an indifference toward the religious question. The single
need of this hour is, to him, much more the thinking through
of the basic religious concepts, the cogitative clarification of the
meaning of words such as God or the Holy. "Must we not first be
able," he asks, "to understand and hear these words with the
greatest care if we, as men, that is as existing beings, are to experience a relation of God to man?" But this in his opinion would
belong to a new thinking of being through man. According to
Heidegger's conception, to be sure, it is not for man to decide
whether and how the divine will reappear.[22] Such an appearance,
he explains, will take place only through the fate of being itself.
Since, however, he has stated as the presupposition for this appearance that "beforehand and in long preparation being itself
is clarified and is experienced in its truth,"[23] there can be no
doubt as to what part is to be ascribed here to human thought
about truth in the determination of "whether and how the day
of the holy will dawn." It is indeed precisely in human thought
about truth that being becomes illuminated. Heidegger usually
conceives of this still uncertain sunrise of the holy as the clear
background before which "an appearance of God and the gods
can begin anew."

Once in interpreting Hölderlin, who had called our time an
indigent one, he explains this as "the time of the gods who have
fled *and* of the God who is coming."[24] It is indigent because it
stands in a double lack: "in the no longer of the departed gods
and the not yet of the Coming One." As the denominating Word

---

[21] *Platons Lehre von der Wahrheit. Mit einem Brief über den Humanismus*
(1947), pp. 102f.
[22] *Ibid.*, p. 75.
[23] *Ibid.*, pp. 85f.
[24] *Erläuterungen zu Hölderlins Dichtungen* (1944), 2nd ed. (1951), p. 44,
Section "*Hölderlin und das Wesen der Dichtung*" of 1936. For an English
translation of "*Hölderlin und das Wesen der Dichtung*" cf. Martin Heidegger, *Existence and Being* (1949), "*Hölderlin and the Essence of Poetry.*"

is wanting that could tell "who He Himself is who dwells in the holy,"[25] so is God Himself wanting. This is "the age in which God is absent";[26] the Word and God are absent together. The Word is not absent because God is absent, and God is not absent because the Word is absent. Both are absent together and appear together because of the nearness of man to being, which is at times, historically, illuminated in him. Thus, admonishes Heidegger, man living in this hour should not strive to make a God for himself, nor call any longer on an accustomed God.

Heidegger warns in this way against "religion" in general, but in particular against the prophetic principle in the Judaeo-Christian tradition. "The 'prophets' of these religions," he says, "do not begin by foretelling the word of the Holy. They announce immediately the God upon whom the certainty of salvation in a supernatural blessedness reckons."[27] Incidentally, I have never in our time encountered on a high philosophical plane such a far-reaching misunderstanding of the prophets of Israel. The prophets of Israel have never announced a God upon whom their hearers' striving for security reckoned. They have always aimed to shatter all security and to proclaim in the opened abyss of the final insecurity the unwished-for God who demands that His human creatures become real, they become human, and confounds all who imagine that they can take refuge in the certainty that the temple of God is in their midst. This is the God of the historical demand as the prophets of Israel beheld Him. The primal reality of these prophecies does not allow itself to be tossed into the attic of "religions": it is as living and actual in this historical hour as ever.

This is not the place for a critical discussion of Heidegger's theory of being. I shall only confess that for me a concept of being that means anything other than the inherent fact of all existing being, namely, that it exists, remains insurmountably empty. That is, unless I have recourse to religion and see in it a philosophical characterization of the Godhead similar to that of some Christian scholastics and mystics who contemplate, or think

[25] *Ibid.*, p. 26.
[26] *Ibid.*, p. 27.
[27] *Ibid.*, p. 108, Section *"Andenken"* of 1943.

that they contemplate, the Godhead as it is in itself, thus as prior
to creation. It should also be noted, however, that one of them,
and the greatest of them all, Meister Eckhart, follows in Plato's
footsteps by placing above the *esse est Deus*, as the higher truth,
the sentence, "*Est enim (Deus) super esse et ens.*" Compare this
with Heidegger's statement: "'Being'—that is not God and it is
not a ground of the world. Being is more than all that exists and
is, nonetheless, nearer than any existing thing, be it . . . an angel
or God. Being is the nearest thing."[28] If by the last sentence,
however, something other is meant than that I myself am, and
not indeed as the subject of a *cogito*, but as my total person,
then the concept of being loses for me the character of genuine
conceivability that obviously it eminently possesses for Heidegger.

I shall, however, limit myself to his theses about the divine.
These theses, out of the extremest consciousness of self-drawn
boundaries, are only concerned with the "appearance" of the
divine. They are concerned in particular with those presuppositions of future reappearances which pertain to human thought,
human thought, that is, about being. The most surprising and
questionable thing about these theses to me is the fact that they
designate it or him, the possible reappearance of whom is their
subject, as the divine or God. In all tongues since men first found
names for the eternally nameless, those who have been named by
this word have been transcendent beings. They have been beings
who by their nature were not given to us as knowable objects,
yet beings whom we nonetheless became aware of as entering
into relation with us. They stepped into relation with us, form-
changing, form-preserving, formless, and allowed us to enter into
relation with them. Being turned toward us, descended to us,
showed itself to us, spoke to us in the immanence. The Coming
One came of his own will out of the mystery of his withdrawn-
ness; we did not cause him to come.

That has always distinguished religion from magic; for he
whom man imagined that he had conjured up could not, even if
he yet figured as god, be believed in any longer as god. He had
become for man a bundle of powers of which man's mysterious
knowledge and might could dispose. He who conjured was no

[28] *Platons Lehre*, p. 76.

longer addressed nor was any answer any longer awakened in him, and even though he recited a prayer, he no longer prayed. And indeed, as Heidegger once said in interpreting the words of Hölderlin, who understood poetry as the combined work of the inspiring gods and the men inspired by them, not only does man need god, but also "the heavenly need the mortal."[29] God needs man independent—man has divined that from of old—as partner in dialogue, as comrade in work, as one who loves Him; God needs His creature thus or wills to need him thus.

In no sphere or time in the history of the relations between the divine and the human, however, has that proved true which Heidegger further asserts, namely, that "neither men nor the gods can ever of themselves bring about the direct relation to the holy." Always, again and again, men are accosted by One who of Himself disconcerts and enraptures them, and, although overcome, the worshipper prays of himself to Him. God does not let Himself be conjured, but He also will not compel. He is of Himself, and He allows that which exists to be of itself. Both of these facts distinguish divine from demonic powers. It may not be, indeed, unimportant to God whether man gives himself or denies himself to Him. Through this giving or denying, man, the whole man with the decision of his whole being, may have an immeasurable part in the actual revelation or hiddenness of the divine. But there is no place between heaven and earth for an influence of concept-clarifying thought. He whose appearance can be effected or co-effected through such a modern magical influence clearly has only the name in common with Him whom we men, basically in agreement despite all the differences in our religious teachings, address as God. To talk of a reappearance of this conjured god of thought is inadmissable.

It is not that Heidegger is not somewhat aware of what is at stake here. Once in 1936, again in a Hölderlin interpretation, he came remarkably close to the essential reality to which I have just pointed. Hölderlin says of us humans,

> Since we exist as talk
> And can hear from one another.

[29] *Erläuterungen*, p. 66, Section *"Wie wenn am Feiertage"* of 1941.

Heidegger explains this thus, "The gods can only enter the Word if they themselves address us and place their demand upon us. The Word that names the gods is always an answer to this demand."[30] That is a testimony to that which I call the dialogical principle, to the dialogical relation between a divine and a human spontaneity.

But since then we have not heard the like from Heidegger. In fact, if we set next to each other all of his later statements about the divine, it appears to us as if pregnant seeds have been destroyed by a force which has passed over them. Heidegger no longer shows himself as concerned with that which there is in common between the great God-impressions of mankind and the "Coming One." Rather he summons all of the power of his thoughts and words in order to distinguish him, the "Coming One," from all that has been. To one who observes the way in which Heidegger now speaks of the historical, there can be no doubt that it is current history which has pulled up those seeds and planted in their place a belief in the entirely new. How this has gradually come about can be clearly seen if one compares with one another the occasional utterances of different stages, e.g., the Rectoral address of May, 1933, with a manifesto to the students of November 3 of the same year. In the first, Heidegger praises in general terms "the glory and the greatness" of the successful "insurrection" ("*Aufbruch*").[31] In the second, the sinister leading personality of the then current history is proclaimed as "the present and future German reality and its law."[32] Here history no longer stands, as in all believing times, under divine judgment, but it itself, the unappealable, assigns to the Coming One his way.

Heidegger, of course, understands by history something other than a list of dated events. "History," he said in 1939, "is rare."[33] And he explained: "History exists only when the essence of truth is originally decided." But it is just his hour which he believes to be history, the very same hour whose problematics in its most

---

[30] *Erläuterungen*, p. 37.

[31] *Die Selbstbehauptung der deutschen Universität*, p. 22.

[32] *Freiburger Studentenzeitung* of Nov. 3, 1933.

[33] *Erläuterungen*, p. 73.

inhuman manifestation led him astray. He has allied his thought, the thought of being,[34] in which he takes part and to which he ascribes the power to make ready for the rise of the holy, to that hour which he has affirmed as history. He has bound his thought to his hour as no other philosopher has done. Can he, the existential thinker, despite all this, existentially wrestle, in opposition to the hour, for a freedom devoted to the eternal and gain it? Or must he succumb to the fate of the hour, and with it also to a "holy" to which no human holiness, no hallowed standing fast of man in the face of historical delusion, responsibly answers? The questions that I ask are not rhetorical; they are true questions.

Of the two who have taken up Nietzsche's expression of the death of God, one, Sartre, has brought it and himself *ad absurdum* through his postulate of the free invention of meaning and value. The other, Heidegger, creates a concept of a rebirth of God out of the thought of truth which falls into the enticing nets of historical time. The path of this existentialism seems to vanish.

2

In contrast to Heidegger and Sartre, Jung, the leading psychologist of our day, has made religion in its historical and biographical forms the subject of comprehensive observations. He is not to be blamed for including among these observations an abundance of phenomena which I must characterize as pseudo-religious. I characterize them so because they do not bear witness to an essential personal relation to One who is experienced or believed in as being absolutely over against one. Jung properly explains he does not wish to overstep the self-drawn boundaries of psychology. This psychology offers no criterion for a qualitative distinction between the two realms, the religious and the pseudo-religious, even as little as, say, sociology as Max Weber understood it enabled him to make a distinction in kind between the charisma of Moses and that of Hitler. What Jung is to be criticized for instead is that he oversteps with sovereign license the boundaries of psychology in its most essential point. For the

[34] It should be noticed that the term "thought" ("*das Denken*") in the late writings of Heidegger is used in essence to describe his own thought.

most part, however, he does not note it and still less account for it.

There is certainly no lack in Jung of exact psychological statements concerning religious subjects. Many times these are even accompanied by explicit emphasis on the limited validity of the statement. An example is when revelation, as "the disclosure of the depths of the human soul,"[35] is termed "to begin with a psychological mode . . . from which, of course, nothing is to be concluded about what it may otherwise be." Occasionally, moreover, he declares on principle that "any statement about the transcendent" shall "be avoided," for such a statement is "always only a ridiculous presumption of the human mind which is unconscious of its boundaries."[36] If God is called a state of the soul, that is "only a statement about the knowable and not about the unknowable, about which [here the formula which has just been cited is repeated word for word] simply nothing is to be concluded." Such sentences express the legitimate position of psychology, which is authorized, like every science, to make objectively based assertions so long as in doing so it takes care not to overstep its boundaries.

They have already been overstepped if it is said of religion that it is "a living relation to psychical events which do not depend upon consciousness but instead take place on the other side of it in the darkness of the psychical hinterland."[37] This definition of religion is stated without qualification. Nor will it tolerate any. For if religion is a relation to psychic events, which cannot mean anything other than to events of one's own soul, then it is implied by this that it is not a relation to a Being or Reality which, no matter how fully it may from time to time descend to the human soul, always remains transcendent to it. More precisely, it is not the relation of an I to a Thou. This is, however, the way in which

---

[35] *Psychologie und Religion* (1942), p. 133. This passage is not in the English edition.

[36] Wilhelm-Jung, *Das Geheimnis der goldenen Blüte* (1929), p. 73. Cf. Wilhelm-Jung, *The Secret of the Golden Flower*, translated by Cary F. Baynes (1935), p. 135.

[37] Jung-Kerényi, *Einführung in das Wesen der Mythologie* (1941), p. 109. Cf. C. G. Jung and K. Kerényi, *Essays on a Science of Mythology* (1949), p. 102.

the unmistakably religious of all ages have understood their religion even if they longed most intensely to let their I be mystically absorbed into that Thou.

But religion is for all that only a matter of the human relation to God, not of God Himself. Consequently, it is more important for us to hear what Jung thinks of God Himself. He conceives of Him in general as an "autonomous psychic content."[38] This means he conceives of God not as a Being or Reality to which a psychical content corresponds, but rather as this content itself. If this is not so, he adds, "then God is indeed not real, for then He nowhere impinges upon our lives." According to this all that which is not an autonomous psychical content but instead produces or co-produces in us a psychical content is to be understood as not impinging upon our life and hence as also not real.

Despite this Jung also recognizes a "reciprocal and indispensable relation between man and God."[39] Jung immediately observes, to be sure, that God is "for our psychology . . . a function of the unconscious." However, this thesis is by no means intended to be valid only inside the boundaries of psychology, for it is opposed to the "orthodox conception" according to which God "exists for Himself," which means psychologically "that one is unaware of the fact that the action arises from one's own inner self."

It is thus unequivocally declared here that what the believer ascribes to God has its origin in his own soul. How this assertion is to be reconciled with Jung's assurance that he means by all this "approximately the same thing Kant meant when he called the thing in itself a 'purely negative, borderline concept' "[40] is to me incomprehensible. Kant has explained that the things in themselves are not to be recognized through any categories because they are not phenomena, but are only to be conceived of as an unknown something. However, that that phenomenon, for exam-

---

[38] *Die Beziehungen zwischen dem Ich und dem Unbewussten* (1928), p. 205. Cf. *Two Essays on Analytical Psychology*, translated by H. G. and C. F. Baynes (1928), "The Relation between the Ego and the Unconscious," p. 267.

[39] *Psychologische Typen* (1921), p. 340. Cf. *Psychological Types*, translated by H. G. Baynes (1923), pp. 300f.

[40] *Geheimnis*, p. 73. Cf. *The Secret of the Golden Flower*, p. 135.

ple, which I call the tree before my window originates not in my meeting with an unknown something but in my own inner self Kant simply did not mean.

In contradiction to his assertion that he wishes to avoid every statement about the transcendent, Jung identifies himself with a view "according to which God does not exist 'absolutely,' that is, independent of the human subject and beyond all human conditions."[41] This means, in effect, that the possibility is not left open that God—who, if the singular and exclusive word "God" is not to lose all meaning, cannot be limited to a single mode of existence as if it were only a question of one among many gods— exists independent of as well as related to the human subject. It is instead made clear that He does *not* exist apart from man. This is indeed a statement about the transcendent. It is a statement about what it is not and just through this about what it is. Jung's statements about the "relativity" of the divine are not psychological but metaphysical assertions, however vigorously he emphasizes "his contentment with the psychically experienceable and rejection of the metaphysical."[42]

Jung could cite in opposition to this a statement he once made. "Metaphysical statements are expressions of the soul, and consequently they are psychological."[43] However, all statements, if they are considered not according to the meaning and intention of their contents but according to the process of their psychic origin, could be described as "expressions of the soul." If, consequently, that sentence is to be taken seriously, the boundaries of psychology are forthwith abolished. These are the same boundaries that Jung says in still another place that psychology must guard against "overstepping through metaphysical statements or other professions of faith."[44] In the greatest possible contradiction to this, psychology becomes here the only admissable metaphysic. It is supposed to remain at the same time an empirical science. But it cannot be both at once.

[41] *Typen*, p. 340. Cf. *Psychological Types*, p. 300.
[42] *Geheimnis*, p. 73. Cf. *The Secret of the Golden Flower*, p. 135.
[43] Evans-Wentz, *Das tobetanische Totenbuch "Bardo Thödol"* (1936), p. 18.
[44] *Psychologie und Alchemie* (1944), p. 28. *Psychology and Alchemy*, translated by R. F. C. Hull (1952).

Jung also supplies the idea of the soul which belongs to this conception. "It is the soul," he says, "that produces the metaphysical expression out of inborn divine creative power; it 'sets' the distinctions between metaphysical essences. It is not only the condition for metaphysical reality, it is that reality itself."[45] The term "sets" is not chosen without reason; what is here set forth is in fact a translation of post-Kantian idealism into psychology.[46] But that which has its place within metaphysical thinking when it is a product of philosophical reflection such as Fichte's I, can demand no such place when it is applied to the concrete individual soul or, more precisely, to the psychic in an existing human person. Nor can Jung indeed mean anything other than this. According to his explanation, even the collective unconscious, the sphere of the archetypes, can enter ever again into experience only through the individual psyche, which has inherited these "typical attitudinal figures."[47]

The real soul has without question producing powers in which primal energies of the human race have individually concentrated. "Inborn divine creative powers" seems to me, to be sure, an all too lofty and all too imprecise designation for them. This soul, however, can never legitimately make an assertion, even a metaphysical one, out of its own creative power. It can make an assertion only out of a binding real relationship to a truth which it articulates. The insight into this truth cogitatively grows in this soul out of what happens to it and what is given it to experience. Anything other than this is no real assertion but merely literary phraseology or questionable combination.

The real individual soul can never be regarded as "the metaphysically real." Its essential life, whether it admits it or not, consists of real meetings with other realities, be they other real souls or whatever else. Otherwise, one would be obliged to conceive of souls as Leibnizian monads. The ideal consequences of this conception, in particular God's eternal interference, Jung

---

[45] *Totenbuch*, p. 19.
[46] There is no expression similar to this to be found in the philosophers of the preceding century who, like Fries and Beneke, wished to base metaphysics on psychology.
[47] Cf. "*Der Geist der Psychologie*" (*Eranos-Jahrbuch*, 1946), pp. 46ff.

would undoubtedly be most unwilling to draw. Or the empirical real realm of individual souls, that province given over to psychology, should indeed be overstepped and a collective being called "soul" or "the soul," which only reveals itself in the individual soul and is thus transcendent, admitted. Such a metaphysical "setting" would then necessitate an adequate philosophical determining and foundation such as, to my knowledge, we nowhere find in Jung, even in the lecture on the spirit of psychology which specifically deals with the conception of the soul.

The decisive significance which this indistinct conception of the soul has for Jung's essential attitude toward religion becomes evident in the following two sentences which have a common subject. "Modern consciousness, in contrast to the nineteenth century, turns with its most intimate and intense expectations to the soul." "Modern consciousness abhors faith and also as a result the religions that are founded on it."[48] Despite his early protest that one can find in his teaching no "barbs . . . against faith or trust in higher powers,"[49] it is evident to any careful reader[50] that Jung identifies himself with the modern consciousness that "abhors" faith. According to Jung, this modern consciousness now turns itself with its "most intimate and intense expectations" to the soul. This cannot mean anything other than that it will have nothing more to do with the God believed in by religions, who is to be sure present to the soul, who reveals Himself to it, communicates with it, but remains transcendent to it in His being. Modern consciousness turns instead toward the soul as the only sphere which man can expect to harbour a divine. In short, although the new psychology protests that it is "no world-view but a science,"[51] it no longer contents itself with the role of an inter-

---

[48] *Seelenprobleme der Gegenwart* (1931), p. 417. Cf. *Modern Man in Search of a Soul*, translated by W. F. Dell and C. F. Baynes (1933), p. 239.
[49] *Geheimnis*, p. 73. Cf. *The Secret of the Golden Flower*, p. 135.
[50] Cf. especially the second part of the sentence cited above from "*Seelenprobleme*" p. 417: "Modern consciousness . . . wishes to *know*, i.e., to have primal experience" with the sentence contained in the same book (p. 83): "We moderns are directed to experience again the spirit, i.e. to make primal experience." Cf. *Modern Man*, p. 140.
[51] *Ibid.*, p. 327. Cf. *Modern Man*, pp. 217f.

preter of religion. It proclaims the new religion, the only one which can still be true, the religion of pure psychic immanence.

Jung speaks once, and with right, of Freud's inability to understand religious experience.[52] He himself concludes his wanderings through the grounds and abysses of religious experience, in which he has accomplished astounding feats, far outstripping all previous psychology, with the discovery that that which experiences the religious, the soul, experiences simply itself. Mystics of all ages, upon whom in fact Jung also rests his position, have proclaimed something similar; yet there are two distinctions which must be kept in mind. First, they meant by the soul which has this experience only that soul which has detached itself from all earthly bustle, from the contradictoriness of creaturely existence, and is therefore capable of apprehending the divine which is above contradictions and of letting the divine work in it. Second, they understood the experience as the oneness and becoming one of the soul with the self-contained God who, in order to enter into the reality of the world, "is born" ever again in the soul.

In the place of that detachment of the whole man from the bustle of life, Jung sets the process of "individuation," determined by a detachment of the *consciousness*. In the place of that becoming one with the Self-contained, he sets the "Self," which is also, as is well known, an originally mystical concept. In Jung, however, it is no longer a genuinely mystical concept but is transformed instead into a Gnostic one. Jung himself expresses this turning toward the Gnostic. The statement quoted above that modern consciousness turns itself to the soul is followed by the explication, "and this . . . in the Gnostic sense." We have here, if only in the form of a mere allusion, the mature expression of a tendency characteristic of Jung from the beginning of his intellectual life. In a very early writing, which was printed but was not sold to the public, it appears in direct religious language as the profession of an eminent Gnostic god, in whom good and evil are bound together and, so to speak, balance each other. This union of opposites in an all-embracing total form runs since

[52] *Ibid.*, p. 77. Cf. *Modern Man*, p. 135.

then throughout Jung's thought. It is also of essential significance
for our consideration of his teaching of individuation and the
self.

Jung has given a most precise expression to that which is in
question here in one of his mandala-analyses. Mandalas, as Jung
has found them, not only in different religious cultures, especially
those of the Orient and of the early Christian Middle Ages, but
also in the drawings of neurotics and the mentally disturbed,
are circular symbolic images. He understands them as representations, arising in the collective unconscious, of a wholeness and
completeness which is as such a unification of opposites. They
are supposed to be "unifying symbols" which include the feminine as well as the masculine, evil as well as good, in their
self-contained unity. Their center, the seat of the Godhead according to Jung's interpretation, is in general, he says, especially
accentuated.

There are supposed to exist, however, a few ancient mandalas
and many modern ones in whose center "no trace of divinity is
to be found."[53] The symbol which takes its place in the modern
images is understood by the creators of these mandalas, according to Jung, as "a center within themselves." "The place of the
deity," Jung explains, "appears to be taken by the wholeness of
man." This central wholeness, which symbolizes the divine, Jung,
in agreement with ancient Indian teaching, calls the self. This
does not mean, says Jung, that the self takes the place of the
Godhead in these images in which the unconscious of modern
man expresses itself. One would grasp Jung's idea better if one
said that from now on the Godhead no longer takes the place of
the human self as it did in mankind up till now. Man now draws
back the projection of his self on a God outside of him without
thereby wishing to deify himself (as Jung here emphasizes, in
contrast to another passage, in which, as we shall see, deification
is clearly stated as a goal). Man does not deny a transcendent
God; he simply dispenses with Him. He no longer knows the
Unrecognizable; he no longer needs to pretend to know Him. In
His place he knows the soul or rather the self. It is indeed not
a god that "modern consciousness" abhors, but faith. Whatever

[53] *Religion*, pp. 145ff. Cf. *Psychology and Religion*, pp. 97ff.

may be the case concerning God, the important thing for the man of modern consciousness is to stand in no further relation of faith to Him.

This man of "modern consciousness" is not, to be sure, to be identified with the human race that is living to-day. "Mankind," says Jung, "is still in the main in a psychological state of infancy —a level which cannot be leaped over."[54] This is illustrated by the Paulinian overcoming of the law which falls only to those persons who know to set the soul in the place of conscience. This is something very few are capable of doing.

What does this mean? By conscience one understands of old, whether one ascribes to it a divine or a social origin or simply regards it as belonging to man as man, that court within the soul which concerns itself with the distinction between the right and the wrong in that which has been done and is to be done and proceeds against that which has been determined as wrong. This is not, of course, simply a question of upholding a traditional law, whether of divine or social origin. Each one who knows himself, for example, as called to a work which he has not done, each one who has not fulfilled a task which he knows to be his own, each who did not remain faithful to his vocation which he had become certain of—each such person knows what it means to say that "his conscience smites him." And in Jung himself we find an excellent explication of that which we call "vocation." "Who has vocation (*Bestimmung*) hears the voice (*Stimme*) of the inner man."[55] By this Jung means, it is true, a voice which brings near to us just that which appears to be evil and to which, in his opinion, it is necessary to succumb "in part."[56] I think, however, that he who has vocation hears at times an inner voice of an entirely different kind. This is just the voice of conscience, which compares that which he is with that which he was called to become. In clear distinction from Jung, moreover, I hold that

---

[54] *Beziehungen*, pp. 203ff. Cf. *Two Essays on Analytical Psychology*, p. 267.
[55] *The Integration of the Personality*, translated by S. M. Dell (1940), "The Development of Personality," pp. 291f. Cf. *Wirklichkeit der Seele* (1934), Lecture "*Vom Werden der Persönlichkeit*" of 1932, pp. 197ff.
[56] *Wirklichkeit der Seele*, pp. 208f. Cf. *The Integration of Personality*, pp. 302f.

each man in some measure has been called to something, which, to be sure, he in general successfully avoids.

But now, once again, what does it mean to set the soul in the place of the direction-giving and direction-preserving, the litigating and judging conscience? In the context of Jung's thought it cannot be understood in any other way than "in the Gnostic sense." The soul which is integrated in the Self as the unification in an all-encompassing wholeness of the opposites, especially of the opposites good and evil, dispenses with the conscience as the court which distinguishes and decides between the right and the wrong. It itself arbitrates an adjustment between the principles or effects the preservation of accord between them or their balancing out or whatever one may call it. This "way," which Jung certainly correctly qualifies as "narrow as a knife-edge,"[57] has not been described and obviously is not suitable to description. The question about it leads to the question about the positive function of evil.

Jung speaks somewhat more clearly in another place of the condition necessary for "the birth of the 'pneumatic man.'"[58] It is "liberation from those desires, ambitions and passions, which imprison us in the visible world," through "intelligent fulfilment of instinctive demands"; for "he who lives his instincts can also separate himself from them." The Taoist book that Jung interprets in this way does not contain this teaching; it is well known to us from certain Gnostic circles.[59]

The "process of development proper to the psyche" which Jung calls individuation leads through the integration in the consciousness of the personal and above all the collective, or archetypal, contents of the unconscious to the realization of a "new complete form" which, as has been said, he calls the self. Here a pause for clarification is necessary. Jung wishes to see the self understood as "both that or those others and the I" and individuation as a process which "does not exclude, but rather includes the world."[60] It is necessary to grasp exactly in what sense this holds

[57] *Beziehungen*, p. 205. Cf. *Two Essays*, p. 267.
[58] *Geheimnis*, p. 61. Cf. *The Secret*, p. 80.
[59] Cf. *Religion*, 139ff.; *Psychology and Religion*, pp. 94ff.
[60] "*Der Geist der Psychologie*," p. 477.

good and in what it does not. In the personality structure which arises out of the "relatively rare occurrence"[61] of the development discussed by Jung, "the others" are indeed included. However, they are included only as contents of the individual soul that shall, just as an individual soul, attain its perfection through individuation.

The actual other who meets me meets me in such a way that my soul comes in contact with his as with something that it is not and that it cannot become. My soul does not and cannot include the other, and yet can nonetheless approach the other in this most real contact. This other, what is more, is and remains over against the self, no matter what completeness the self may attain, as the other. So the self, even if it has integrated all of its unconscious elements, remains this single self, confined within itself. All beings existing over against me who become "included" in my self are possessed by it in this inclusion as an It. Only then when, having become aware of the unincludable otherness of a being, I renounce all claim to incorporating it in any way within me or making it a part of my soul, does it truly become Thou for me. This holds good for God as for man.

This is certainly not a way which leads to the goal which Jung calls the self; but it is just as little a way to the removal of self. It simply leads to a genuine contact with the existing being who meets me, to full and direct reciprocity with him. It leads from the soul which places reality in itself to the soul which enters reality.

Jung thinks that his concept of the self is also found in Meister Eckhart. This is an error. Eckhart's teaching about the soul is based on the certainty of his belief that the soul is, to be sure, like God in freedom, but that it is created while He is uncreated.[62] This essential distinction underlies all that Eckhart has to say of the relationship and nearness between God and the soul.

Jung conceives of the self which is the goal of the process of

---

[61] *Ibid.*, p. 474.
[62] "Since God alone is free and uncreated, he is like the soul in being free—but not in uncreatedness, for the soul is created." Sermon 13, Raymond Blakney, *Meister Eckhart, A Modern Translation* (1941), p. 159. For original cf. *Predigten*, ed. Quint, pp. 13f.

individuation as the "bridal unification of opposite halves"[63] in the soul. This means above all, as has been said, the "integration of evil,"[64] without which there can be no wholeness in the sense of this teaching. Individuation thereby realizes the complete archetype of the self, in contrast to which it is divided in the Christian symbolic into Christ and the Antichrist, representing its light and its dark aspects. In the self the two aspects are united. The self is thus a pure totality and as such "indistinguishable from a divine image"; self-realization is indeed to be described as "the incarnation of God." This god who unites good and evil in himself, whose opposites-nature also expresses itself in his male-femaleness,[65] is a Gnostic figure, which probably is to be traced back ultimately to the ancient Iranian divinity Zurvan (not mentioned, so far as I know, among Jung's numerous references to the history of religions) as that out of which the light god and his dark counterpart arose.

From the standpoint of this basic Gnostic view Jung recasts the Jewish and Christian conception of God. In the Old Testament the Satan, the "Hinderer," is only a serving element of God. God allows Himself to be represented by Satan, particularly for the purpose of "temptation," that is, in order to actualize man's uttermost power of decision through affliction and despair. Out of this God of the Old Testament Jung makes a demiurge who is himself half Satanic. This god then for the sake of his "guilt," the miscarried creation of the world (I now quote literally from Jung's speech of 1940,[66] the like of which is nowhere to be found in the Gnostic literature to which he refers), "must be subject to ritual killing." By this Jung means the crucifixion of Christ. The Trinity, moreover, is enlarged to a Quaternity in which the autonomous devil is included as "the fourth."[67]

These, to be sure, are all, as Jung emphasizes, "projections of

---

[63] *"Über das Selbst"* (*Eranos-Jahrbuch*, 1948), p. 315. Cf. *Psychologie und Alchemie*, p. 61.
[64] *Symbolik des Geistes* (1948), p. 385.
[65] *Ibid.*, p. 410.
[66] *"Das Wandlungssymbol in der Messe"* (*Eranos-Jahrbuch*, 1940–1941), pp. 153f.
[67] *Symbolik*, p. 439. Cf. *Religion*, pp. 108ff.; *"Zur Psychologie der Trinitätsidee"* (*Eranos-Jahrbuch*, 1940–1941), pp. 51ff.; *Alchemie*, p. 212.

psychic events," "human spiritual products to which one may not arrogate any metaphysical validity."[68] The self seems to him the prototype of all monotheistic systems, which are here unmasked as hidden Gnosis. But, on the other hand, he sees it at the same time as the *imago Dei in homine*. The soul must indeed, he says once in a formulation which so far as I know is without analogy in his other statements, have within it something which corresponds to the being of God.[69] In any case, the self, the bridal unification of good and evil, is elevated by him to the throne of the world as the new "Incarnation." "If we should like to know," he says, "what happens in the case in which the idea of God is no longer projected as an autonomous essence, then this is the answer of the unconscious soul: the unconscious creates the idea of a deified or divine man."[70] This figure, which embraces Christ and Satan within himself,[71] is the final form of that Gnostic god, descended to earth as the realization of the "identity of God and man,"[72] which Jung once professed. He has remained faithful to this god, repeatedly intimating its prospective appearance.[73]

Jung's psychology of religion is to be understood as the announcement of that god as the Coming One. To Nietzsche's saying, "All the gods are dead, now we desire that the superman live!" Heidegger, in a note otherwise foreign to him, adds this warning: "Man can never set himself in the place of God because the essence of man does not reach to God's sphere of being. On the contrary, indeed, in proportion with this impossibility, something far more uncanny may happen, the nature of which we have still hardly begun to consider. The place which, metaphysically speaking, belongs to God is the place in which the production and preservation as created being of that which exists is effected. This place of God can remain empty. Instead of it another, that is, a metaphysically corresponding place can appear, which is neither identical with God's sphere of being nor with that of man, but which, on the other hand, man can, in an

---

[68] *Symbolik*, p. 417.
[69] *Alchemie*, pp. 22f.
[70] *Religion*, pp. 172f. Cf. *Psychology and Religion*, p. 106.
[71] *Symbolik*, p. 409. Cf. "*Selbst*," p. 304.
[72] *Religion*, p. 111. Cf. *Psychology and Religion*, p. 74.
[73] Cf. especially *Religion*, pp. 175f. (*Psychology and Religion*, pp. 107ff.)

eminent relation, attain. The superman does not and never will step into the place of God; the place rather in which the will to the superman arrives is another sphere in another foundation of existing things in another being."[74] The words compel one to listen with attention. One must judge whether that which is said or intimated in them does not hold true to-day and here.

[74] *Holzwege*, p. 235. A comparison is to be recommended with Jung's expression "The interregnum is full of danger" in its context (*Psychologie und Religion*, p. 158), which means almost the opposite. (The passage is not in *Psychology and Religion*, which differs from the German edition.)

Paul Tillich

[1886–1965]

THE SON of a district superintendent of the Prussian Church Union, Paul Tillich grew up in the small town of Schönfliess, not far from Berlin. His easy-going Rhenish mother died when he was quite young. His father was a stern authority figure but sent him to public schools, where he shared his fellow students' antagonism to the privileged class to which he himself belonged. His most congenial companions as a young man were artists, actors, journalists and writers whom he met in Berlin, where he attended a humanistic *Gymnasium*.

Always of a strongly theoretical bent, Tillich says: "I was about eight when I first wrestled with the idea of the Infinite."[1] Many currents shaped his philosophical development—Schlegel's German edition of Shakespeare, postexpressionist painting, Rilke, Schleiermacher. As a student at Tübingen, he discovered by chance a bargain-priced set of Schelling's complete works, which he bought and read several times.

He received his Ph.D. from Breslau in 1911, was ordained a minister of the Evangelical Lutheran Church in 1912 and after two years as a pastor became an army chaplain, serving on the Western Front throughout the First World War.

What first struck him at the front was "that the nation was split into classes, and that the industrial masses considered the Church as an unquestioned ally of the ruling groups."[2] His grandmother had erected barricades in the revolution of 1848, and when that of 1918 came, he "began to understand such issues as

[1] Paul Tillich, *On the Boundary* (New York: Scribner, 1966), p. 30.
[2] Tillich, "Autobiographical Reflections" in Kegley and Bretall, eds., *The Theology of Paul Tillich* (New York: Macmillan, 1952), p. 12.

the political background of the war, the interrelation of capitalism and imperialism, the crisis of bourgeois society and the schism between classes."[3] He joined the Social Democratic Party and became active in the religious socialist group at the University of Berlin, where he lectured from 1919 to 1924 on the relation of religion to politics, art, philosophy, depth psychology and sociology.

It was in the "abyss" of the war that he read Nietzsche, who had a profound impact on his thinking. Because Nietzsche's vitalism "is, at least partly, historically rooted in Schelling's thought, I could readily accept it."[4] It was the revolution of 1918 that deflected him from developing his philosophy along Nietzschean lines and turned him toward "a sociologically based and politically oriented philosophy of history."[5] A common enthusiasm for Nietzsche, Schelling and Kierkegaard drew him to Heidegger when both men were at Marburg in 1925.

> His interpretation of human existence implies and develops, however unintentionally, a doctrine of man that is one of human freedom and finitude. It is so closely related to the Christian interpretation of human existence that one is forced to describe it as "theonomous philosophy" in spite of Heidegger's emphatic atheism.[6]

Tillich's relation to the church was deep-rooted, so much so that he would have become a Catholic if the Confessing Church had not emerged to oppose Hitler. Yet he distinguished between the "manifest" and the "latent" church; he was no apologist for the former. Dismissed from his post as soon as Hitler came to power, Tillich found refuge in the United States. On the advice of his American benefactor, Reinhold Niebuhr, he kept out of politics here, although till his death he held to his belief in religious socialism.

Increasingly, however, Tillich focused his "theology of culture"

[3] *On the Boundary*, pp. 32f.
[4] *Ibid.*, p. 54.
[5] *Ibid.*
[6] *Ibid.*, p. 57.

on existential philosophy, depth psychology and other secular disciplines in which he saw, as in Heidegger, a "dimension of depth" or a confrontation with "ultimate reality." He professed to despise orthodoxy as "intellectual pharisaism," but his monumental *Systematic Theology* represents in large part a vindication of classical Christian doctrines through philosophical reinterpretation. That is, it reflects a commitment to deal with each of the traditional categories instead of scrapping them for a new framework; but his achievement was to extract from each doctrine, or infuse it with, philosophical content relevant to the experience of modern man. This he called a method of "correlation," whereby he hoped to show, as in the following selections, that the "ground of being" or "ultimate reality" revealed in the biblical image of God in fact transcends the image itself. "Theism" is only a form. In an earlier age it had validity; it yielded meaning. Now it is obsolete; the same meaning must be carried by new symbols. Yet in his choice of symbols, and in the seriousness with which he takes such viewpoints as Heidegger's, there is an unresolved ambiguity. His bridge between "emphatic atheism" and "theonomous philosophy" carries a two-way traffic. In the final analysis, perhaps, the burden of the Infinite is only metaphysical ballast, and the elaborate theological system only a safeguard for an existential humanism like Buber's. "There is a correspondence," he wrote, "between reality and the human spirit which is probably expressed most adequately in the concept of 'meaning.' It led Hegel to speak of the unity of objective and subjective spirit in an Absolute Spirit."[7] It led Tillich to speak of the same thing as "ultimate reality," and to redeem the abstractness of this concept by identifying it with the love revealed in Jesus. "Love one another as I have loved you" thus becomes "ultimate concern"; that which transcends the human personality is precisely the "ground of being" that validates human existence from within, that which confers integrity. If this is indeed humanism, however, it is by no means a sellout to empirical naturalism. For, taking the love that Jesus "means" as a fulcrum of faith, it indicates *what* is ultimate and unconditional. Tillich does not supply this faith;

[7] *Ibid.*, p. 83.

he does, however, show its psychological and social dynamics to those who find it for themselves.

Theism Transcended[1]

The courage to take meaninglessness into itself presupposes a relation to the ground of being which we have called "absolute faith." It is without a *special* content, yet it is not without content. The content of absolute faith is the "God above God." Absolute faith and its consequence, the courage that takes the radical doubt, the doubt about God, into itself, transcends the theistic idea of God.

Theism can mean the unspecified affirmation of God. Theism in this sense does not say what it means if it uses the name of God. Because of the traditional and psychological connotations of the word "God" such an empty theism can produce a reverent mood if it speaks of God. Politicians, dictators, and other people who wish to use rhetoric to make an impression on their audience like to use the word "God" in this sense. It produces the feeling in their listeners that the speaker is serious and morally trustworthy. This is especially successful if they can brand their foes as atheistic. On a higher level people without a definite religious commitment like to call themselves theistic, not for special purposes but because they cannot stand a world without God, whatever this God may be. They need some of the connotations of the word "God" and they are afraid of what they call atheism. On the highest level of this kind of theism the name of God is used as a poetic or practical symbol, expressing a profound emotional state or the highest ethical idea. It is a theism which stands on the boundary line between the second type of theism and what we call "theism transcended." But it is still too indefinite to cross this boundary line. The atheistic negation of this whole type of theism is as vague as the theism itself. It may produce an irreverent mood and angry reaction of those who take their theistic

[1] From *The Courage to Be* (New Haven: Yale, 1952).—Ed.

affirmation seriously. It may even be felt as justified against the rhetorical-political abuse of the name "God," but it is ultimately as irrelevant as the theism which it negates. It cannot reach the state of despair any more than the theism against which it fights can reach the state of faith.

Theism can have another meaning, quite contrary to the first one: it can be the name of what we have called the divine-human encounter. In this case it points to those elements in the Jewish-Christian tradition which emphasize the person-to-person relationship with God. Theism in this sense emphasizes the personalistic passages in the Bible and the Protestant creeds, the personalistic image of God, the word as the tool of creation and revelation, the ethical and social character of the kingdom of God, the personal nature of human faith and divine forgiveness, the historical vision of the universe, the idea of a divine purpose, the infinite distance between creator and creature, the absolute separation between God and the world, the conflict between holy God and sinful man, the person-to-person character of prayer and practical devotion. Theism in this sense is the nonmystical side of biblical religion and historical Christianity. Atheism from the point of view of this theism is the human attempt to escape the divine-human encounter. It is an existential—not a theoretical—problem.

Theism has a third meaning, a strictly theological one. Theological theism is, like every theology, dependent on the religious substance which it conceptualizes. It is dependent on theism in the first sense insofar as it tries to prove the necessity of affirming God in some way; it usually develops the so-called arguments for the "existence" of God. But it is more dependent on theism in the second sense insofar as it tries to establish a doctrine of God which transforms the person-to-person encounter with God into a doctrine about two persons who may or may not meet but who have a reality independent of each other.

Now theism in the first sense must be transcended because it is irrelevant, and theism in the second sense must be transcended because it is one-sided. But theism in the third sense must be transcended because it is wrong. It is bad theology. This can be shown by a more penetrating analysis. The God of theological theism is a being beside others and as such a part of the whole of reality. He certainly is considered its most important part, but as a part and therefore as subjected to the structure of the whole. He is supposed to be beyond the ontological elements and categories which constitute reality. But every statement subjects him to them. He is seen as a self which has a world, as an ego which is related to a thou, as a cause which is separated from its effect, as having a definite space and an endless time. He is a being, not being-itself. As such he is bound to the subject-object structure of reality; he is an object for us as subjects. At the same time we are objects for him as a subject. And this is decisive for the necessity of transcending theological theism. For God as a subject makes me into an object which is nothing more than an object. He deprives me of my subjectivity because he is all-powerful and all-knowing. I revolt and try to make *him* into an object, but the revolt fails and becomes desperate. God appears as the invincible tyrant, the being in contrast with whom all other beings are without freedom and subjectivity. He is equated with the recent tyrants who with the help of terror try to transform everything into a mere object, a thing among things, a cog in the machine they control. He becomes the model of everything against which Existentialism revolted. This is the God Nietzsche said had to be killed because nobody can tolerate being made into a mere object of absolute knowledge and absolute control. This is the deepest root of atheism. It is an atheism which is justified as the reaction against theological theism and its disturbing implications. It is also the deepest root of the Existentialist despair and the widespread anxiety of meaninglessness in our period.

Theism in all its forms is transcended in the experience we have called absolute faith. It is the accepting of the acceptance without somebody or something that accepts. It is the power of being-itself that accepts and gives the courage to be. This is the highest point to which our analysis has brought us. It cannot be described in the way the God of all forms of theism can be described. It cannot be described in mystical terms either. It transcends both mysticism and personal encounter, as it transcends both the courage to be as a part and the courage to be as oneself.

THE GOD ABOVE GOD AND
THE COURAGE TO BE

The ultimate source of the courage to be is the "God above God"; this is the result of our demand to transcend theism. Only if the God of theism is transcended can the anxiety of doubt and meaninglessness be taken into the courage to be. The God above God is the object of all mystical longing, but mysticism also must be transcended in order to reach him. Mysticism does not take seriously the concrete and the doubt concerning the concrete. It plunges directly into the ground of being and meaning, and leaves the concrete, the world of finite values and meanings, behind. Therefore it does not solve the problem of meaninglessness. In terms of the present religious situation this means that Eastern mysticism is not the solution of the problems of Western Existentialism, although many people attempt this solution. The God above the God of theism is not the devaluation of the meanings which doubt has thrown into the abyss of meaninglessness; he is their potential restitution. Nevertheless absolute faith agrees with the faith implied in mysticism in that both transcend the theistic objectivation of a God who is a being. For mysticism such a God is not more real than any finite being, for the courage to be such a God has disappeared in the abyss of meaninglessness with every other value and meaning.

The God above the God of theism is present, although hidden, in every divine-human encounter. Biblical religion as well as Protestant theology is aware of the paradoxical character of this encounter. They are aware that if God encounters man God is neither object nor subject and is therefore above the scheme into which theism has forced him. They are aware that personalism with respect to God is balanced by a transpersonal presence of the divine. They are aware that forgiveness can be accepted only if the power of acceptance is effective in man—biblically speaking, if the power of grace is effective in man. They are aware of the paradoxical character of every prayer, of speaking to somebody to whom you cannot speak because he is not "somebody," of asking somebody of whom you cannot ask anything because he gives or gives not before you ask, of saying "thou" to somebody who is nearer to the I than the I is to itself. Each of these paradoxes drives the religious consciousness toward a God above the God of theism.

The courage to be which is rooted in the experience of the God above the God of theism unites and transcends the courage to be as a part and the courage to be as oneself. It avoids both the loss of oneself by participation and the loss of one's world by individualization. The acceptance of the God above the God of theism makes us a part of that which is not also a part but is the ground of the whole. Therefore our self is not lost in a larger whole, which submerges it in the life of a limited group. If the self participates in the power of being-itself it receives itself back. For the power of being acts through the power of the individual selves. It does not swallow them as every limited whole, every collectivism, and every conformism does. This is why the Church, which stands for the power of being-itself or for the God who transcends the God of the religions, claims to be the mediator of the courage to be. A church which is based on the authority of the God of theism cannot make such a claim. It inescapably develops into a collectivist or semicollectivist system itself.

But a church which raises itself in its message and its devotion to the God above the God of theism without sacrificing its concrete symbols can mediate a courage which takes doubt and meaninglessness into itself. It is the Church under the Cross which alone can do this, the Church which preaches the Crucified who cried to God who remained his God after the God of confidence had left him in the darkness of doubt and meaninglessness. To be as a part in such a church is to receive a courage to be in which one cannot lose one's self and in which one receives one's world.

Absolute faith, or the state of being grasped by the God beyond God, is not a state which appears beside other states of the mind. It never is something separated and definite, an event which could be isolated and described. It is always a movement in, with, and under other states of the mind. It is the situation on the boundary of man's possibilities. It *is* this boundary. Therefore it is both the courage of despair and the courage in and above every courage. It is not a place where one can live, it is without the safety of words and concepts, it is without a name, a church, a cult, a theology. But it is moving in the depth of all of them. It is the power of being, in which they participate and of which they are fragmentary expressions.

One can become aware of it in the anxiety of fate and death when the traditional symbols that enable men to stand the vicissitudes of fate and the horror of death have lost their power. When "providence" has become a superstition and "immortality" something imaginary that which once was the power in these symbols can still be present and create the courage to be in spite of the experience of a chaotic world and a finite existence. The Stoic courage returns but not as the faith in universal reason. It returns as the absolute faith which says Yes to being without seeing anything concrete which could conquer the nonbeing in fate and death.

And one can become aware of the God above the God of theism in the anxiety of guilt and condemnation when the traditional symbols that enable men to withstand the anxiety of guilt and condemnation have lost their power. When "divine judgment" is interpreted as a psychological complex and forgiveness as a remnant of the "father image," what once was the power in those symbols can still be present and create the courage to be in spite of the experience of an infinite gap between what we are and what we ought to be. The Lutheran courage returns but not supported by the faith in a judging and forgiving God. It returns in terms of the absolute faith which says Yes although there is no special power that conquers guilt. The courage to take the anxiety of meaninglessness upon oneself is the boundary line up to which the courage to be can go. Beyond it is mere nonbeing. Within it all forms of courage are reestablished in the power of the God above the God of theism. *The courage to be is rooted in the God who appears when God has disappeared in the anxiety of doubt.*

Ontology and the Question of God[1]

It is a remarkable fact that for many centuries leading theologians and philosophers were almost equally divided between those who attacked and those who defended the arguments for the existence of God. Neither group prevailed over the other in a final way. This situation admits only one explanation: the one group did not attack what the other group defended. They were not divided by a conflict over the same matter. They fought over different matters which they expressed in the same terms. Those who attacked the arguments for the existence of God criticized their argumentative form; those who defended them accepted their implicit meaning.

There can be little doubt that the arguments are a failure insofar as they claim to be arguments. Both the concept of existence and the method of arguing to a conclusion are inadequate for the idea of God. However it is defined, the "existence of God" contradicts the idea of a creative ground of essence and existence. The ground of being cannot be found within the totality of beings, nor can the ground of essence and existence participate in the tensions and disruptions characteristic of the transition from essence to existence. The scholastics were right when they asserted that in God there is no difference between essence and existence. But they perverted their insight when in spite of this assertion they spoke of the existence of God and tried to argue in favor of it. Actually they did not mean "existence." They meant the reality, the validity, the truth of the idea of God, an idea which did not carry the connotation of some*thing* or some*one* who might or might not exist. Yet this is the way in which the idea of God is understood today in scholarly as well as in popular discussions about the "existence of God." It would be a great victory for Christian apologetics if the words "God" and "existence" were very definitely separated except in the paradox of God becoming manifest under the conditions of existence, that is,

[1] From *Systematic Theology*, I (University of Chicago Press, 1951).—Ed.

in the christological paradox. God does not exist. He is being-itself beyond essence and existence. Therefore, to argue that God exists is to deny him.

The method of arguing through a conclusion also contradicts the idea of God. Every argument derives conclusions from something that is given about something that is sought. In arguments for the existence of God the world is given and God is sought. Some characteristics of the world make the conclusion "God" necessary. God is derived from the world. This does not mean that God is dependent on the world. Thomas Aquinas is correct when he rejects such an interpretation and asserts that what is first in itself may be last for our knowledge. But, if we derive God from the world, he cannot be that which transcends the world infinitely. He is the "missing link," discovered by correct conclusions. He is the uniting force between the *res cogitans* and the *res extensa* (Descartes), or the end of the causal regression in answer to the question "Where from?" (Thomas Aquinas), or the teleological intelligence directing the meaningful processes of reality—if not identical with these processes (Whitehead). In each of these cases God is "world," a missing part of that from which he is derived in terms of conclusions. This contradicts the idea of God as thoroughly as does the concept of existence. The arguments for the existence of God neither are arguments nor are they proof of the existence of God. They are expressions of the *question* of God which is implied in human finitude. This question is their truth; every answer they give is untrue. This is the sense in which theology must deal with these arguments, which are the solid body of any natural theology. It must deprive them of their argumentative character, and it must eliminate the combination of the words "existence" and "God." If this is accomplished, natural theology becomes the elaboration of the question of God; it ceases to be the answer to this question. The following interpretations are to be understood in this sense. The arguments for the existence of God analyze the human situation in such a way that the question of God appears possible and necessary.

The question of God is possible because an awareness of God is present in the question of God. This awareness precedes the question. It is not the result of the argument but its presuppposition. This certainly means that the "argument" is no argument at all. The so-called ontological argument points to the ontological structure of finitude. It shows that an awareness of the infinite is included in man's awareness of finitude. Man knows that he is finite, that he is excluded from an infinity which nevertheless belongs to him. He is aware of his potential infinity while being aware of his actual finitude. If he were what he essentially is, if his potentiality were identical with his actuality, the question of the infinite would not arise. Mythologically speaking, Adam before the fall was in an essential, though untested and undecided, unity with God. But this is not man's situation, nor is it the situation of anything that exists. Man must ask about the infinite from which he is estranged, although it belongs to him; he must ask about that which gives him the courage to take his anxiety upon himself. And he can ask this double question because the awareness of his potential infinity is included in his awareness of his finitude.

The ontological argument in its various forms gives a description of the way in which potential infinity is present in actual finitude. As far as the description goes, that is, as far as it is analysis and not argument, it is valid. The presence within finitude of an element which transcends it is experienced both theoretically and practically. The theoretical side has been elaborated by Augustine, the practical side by Kant, and behind both of them stands Plato. Neither side has constructed an argument for the reality of God, but all elaborations have shown the presence of something unconditional within the self and the world. Unless such an element were present, the question of God never could have been asked, nor could an answer, even the answer of revelation, have been received.

The unconditional element appears in the theoretical (receiving) functions of reason as *verum ipsum*, the true-itself as the norm of all approximations to truth. The unconditional element appears in the practical (shaping) functions of reason as *bonum ipsum*, the good-itself as the norm of all approximations to goodness. Both are manifestations of *esse ipsum*, being-itself as the ground and abyss of everything that is.

Augustine, in his refutation of skepticism, has shown that the skeptic acknowledges and emphasizes the absolute element in truth in his denial of the possibility of a true judgment. He becomes a skeptic precisely because he strives for an absoluteness from which he is excluded. *Veritas ipsa* is acknowledged and sought for by no one more passionately than by the skeptic. Kant has shown in an analogous way that relativism with respect to ethical content presupposes an absolute respect for ethical form, the categorical imperative, and an acknowledgment of the unconditional validity of the ethical command. *Bonum ipsum* is independent of any judgment about the *bona*. Up to this point Augustine and Kant cannot be refuted, for they do not argue; they point to the unconditional element in every encounter with reality. But both Augustine and Kant go beyond this safe analysis. They derive from it a concept of God which is more than *esse ipsum, verum ipsum*, and *bonum ipsum*, more than an analytical dimension in the structure of reality. Augustine simply identifies *verum ipsum* with the God of the church, and Kant tries to derive a lawgiver and a guarantor of the coordination between morality and happiness from the unconditional character of the ethical command. In both cases the starting point is right, but the conclusion is wrong. The experience of an unconditional element in man's encounter with reality is used for the establishment of an unconditional being (a contradiction in terms) within reality.

The Anselmian statement that God is a necessary thought and that therefore this idea must have objective as well as subjective reality is valid insofar as thinking, by its very nature, implies an unconditional element which transcends subjectivity and objectivity, that is, a point of identity which makes the idea of truth possible. However, the statement is not valid if this unconditional element is understood as a highest being called God. The existence of such a highest being is not implied in the idea of truth.

The same must be said of the many forms of the moral argument. They are valid insofar as they are ontological analyses (not arguments) in moral disguise, that is, ontological analyses of the unconditional element in the moral imperative. The concept of the moral world order which often has been used in this connection tries to express the unconditional character of the moral command in the face of the processes of nature and history which seem to contradict it. It points to the foundation of the moral principles in the ground of being, in being-itself. But no "divine coordinator" can be derived in this way. The ontological basis of the moral principles and their unconditional character cannot be used for the establishment of a highest being. *Bonum ipsum* does not imply the existence of a highest being.

The limits of the ontological argument are obvious. But nothing is more important for philosophy and theology than the truth it contains, the acknowledgment of the unconditional element in the structure of reason and reality. The idea of a theonomous culture, and with it the possibility of a philosophy of religion, is dependent on this insight. A philosophy of religion which does not begin with something unconditional never reaches God. Modern secularism is rooted largely in the fact that the unconditional element in the structure of reason and reality no longer was seen and that therefore the idea of God was imposed on the mind as a "strange body." This produced first heteronomous subjection and then autonomous rejection. The destruction of the ontological *argument* is not dangerous. What is dangerous is the destruction of an approach which elaborates the possibility of the question of God. This approach is the meaning and truth of the ontological argument.

God as Man's Ultimate Concern[1]

"God" is the answer to the question implied in man's finitude; he is the name for that which concerns man ultimately. This does not mean that first there is a being called God and then the demand that man should be ultimately concerned about him. It means that whatever concerns a man ultimately becomes god for him, and, conversely, it means that a man can be concerned ultimately only about that which is god for him. The phrase "being ultimately concerned" points to a tension in human experience. On the one hand, it is impossible to be concerned about

[1] From *Systematic Theology*, I (University of Chicago Press, 1951).—Ed.

something which cannot be encountered concretely, be it in the realm of reality or in the realm of imagination. Universals can become matters of ultimate concern only through their power of representing concrete experiences. The more concrete a thing is, the more the possible concern about it. The completely concrete being, the individual person, is the object of the most radical concern—the concern of love. On the other hand, ultimate concern must transcend every preliminary finite and concrete concern. It must transcend the whole realm of finitude in order to be the answer to the question implied in finitude. But in transcending the finite the religious concern loses the concreteness of a being-to-being relationship. It tends to become not only absolute but also abstract, provoking reactions from the concrete element. This is the inescapable inner tension in the idea of God. The conflict between the concreteness and the ultimacy of the religious concern is actual wherever God is experienced and this experience is expressed, from primitive prayer to the most elaborate theological system. It is the key to understanding the dynamics of the history of religion, and it is the basic problem of every doctrine of God, from the earliest priestly wisdom to the most refined discussions of the trinitarian dogma.

A phenomenological description of the meaning of "God" in every religion, including the Christian, offers the following definition of the meaning of the term "god." Gods are beings who transcend the realm of ordinary experience in power and meaning, with whom men have relations which surpass ordinary relations in intensity and significance. A discussion of each element of this basic description will give a full phenomenological picture of the meaning of "god," and this will be the tool with which an interpretation of the nature and the development of the phenomena which are called "religious" may be fashioned.

Gods are "beings." They are experienced, named, and defined in concrete intuitive (*anschaulich*) terms through the exhaustive use of all the ontological elements and categories of finitude. Gods are substances, caused and causing, active and passive, remembering and anticipating, arising and disappearing in time and space. Even though they are called "highest beings," they are limited in power and significance. They are limited by other gods or by the resistance of other beings and principles, for example, matter and fate. The values they represent limit and sometimes annihilate each other. The gods are open to error, compassion, anger, hostility, anxiety. They are images of human nature or subhuman powers raised to a superhuman realm. This fact, which theologians must face in all its implications, is the basis of all theories of "projection" which say that the gods are simply imaginary projections of elements of finitude, natural and human elements. What these theories disregard is that projection always is projection *on* something—a wall, a screen, another being, another realm. Obviously, it is absurd to class that on which the projection is realized with the projection itself. A screen is not projected; it receives the projection. The realm against which the divine images are projected is not itself a projection. It is the experienced ultimacy of being and meaning. It is the realm of ultimate concern.

Therefore, not only do the images of the gods bear all the characteristics of finitude—this makes them images and gives them concreteness—but they also have characteristics in which categorical finitude is radically transcended. Their identity as finite substances is negated by all kinds of substantial transmutations and expansions, in spite of the sameness of their names. Their temporal limitations are overcome; they are called "immortals" in spite of the fact that their appearance and disappearance are presupposed. Their spatial definiteness is negated when they act as multi- or omnipresent, yet they have a special dwelling place with which they are intimately connected. Their subordination to the chain of causes and effects is denied, for overwhelming or absolute power is attributed to them in spite of their dependence on other divine powers and on the influence finite beings have on them. In concrete cases they demonstrate omniscience and perfection in spite of the struggles and betrayals going on among the gods themselves. They transcend their own finitude in power of being and in the embodiment of meaning. The tendency toward ultimacy continuously fights against the tendency toward concreteness.

The history of religion is full of human attempts to participate in divine power and to use it for human purposes. This is the point at which the magic world-view enters religious practice and offers technical tools for an effective use of divine power. Magic itself is a theory and practice concerning the relation of finite beings to each other; it assumes that there are direct, physically unmediated sympathies and influences between beings on the "psychic" level, that is, on the level which comprises the vital, the subconscious, and the emotional. Insofar as the gods are beings, magic relations in both directions are possible—from man to the gods and from the gods to man—and they are the basis for human participation in divine power.

Nonmagical, personalistic world-views lead to a person-to-person relationship to divine power, which is appropriated through prayer, that is, through an appeal to the personal center of the divine being. The god answers in a free decision. He might or he might not use his power to fulfill the content of the prayer. In any case, he remains free, and attempts to force him to act in a particular way are considered magic. Seen in this context, every prayer of supplication illustrates the tension between the concrete element and the ultimate element in the idea of God. Theologians have suggested that this type of prayer should be replaced by thanksgiving in order to avoid magic connotations (Ritschl). But actual religious life reacts violently against such a demand. Men continue to use the power of their god by asking his favors. They demand a concrete god, a god with whom man can deal.

A third way of trying to use the divine power is through a mystical participation in it which is neither magical nor personalistic. Its main characteristic is the devaluation of the divine beings and their power over against the ultimate power, the abyss of being-itself. The Hindu doctrine that the gods tremble when a saint exercises radical asceticism is another illustration of the tension between the gods as beings with a higher, though limited, power and the ultimate power which they express and conceal at the same time. The conflict between the Brahma power and the god Brahman as an object of a concrete relation with man points to the same tension within the structure of man's ultimate concern which was noted above.

The gods are superior not only in power but also in meaning.

They embody the true and the good. They embody concrete values, and as gods they claim absoluteness for them. The imperialism of the gods which follows from this situation is the basis of all other imperialisms. Imperialism is never the expression of will to power as such. It always is a struggle for the absolute victory of a special value or system of values, represented by a special god or hierarchy of gods. The ultimacy of the religious concern drives toward universality in value and in meaning; the concreteness of the religious concern drives toward particular meanings and values. The tension is insoluble. The coordination of all concrete values removes the ultimacy of the religious concern. The subordination of concrete values to any one of them produces anti-imperialistic reactions on the part of the others. The drowning of all concrete values in an abyss of meaning and value evokes antimystical reactions on the part of the concrete element in man's ultimate concern. The conflict between these elements is present in every act of creedal confession, in every missionary task, in every claim to possess final revelation. It is the nature of the gods which creates these conflicts, and it is man's ultimate concern which is mirrored in the nature of the gods.

We have discussed the meaning of "god" in terms of man's relation to the divine, and we have taken this relationship into the phenomenological description of the nature of the gods. This underlines the fact that the gods are not objects within the context of the universe. They are expressions of the ultimate concern which transcends the cleavage between subjectivity and objectivity. It remains to be emphasized that an ultimate concern is not "subjective." Ultimacy stands against everything which can be derived from mere subjectivity, nor can the unconditional be found within the entire catalogue of finite objects which are conditioned by each other.

If the word "existential" points to a participation which transcends both subjectivity and objectivity, then man's relation to the gods is rightly called "existential." Man cannot speak of the gods in detachment. The moment he tries to do so, he has lost the god and has established just one more object within the world of objects. Man can speak of the gods only on the basis of his relation to them. This relation oscillates between the concreteness of a give-and-take attitude, in which the divine beings easily become objects and tools for human purposes, and the absoluteness of a total surrender on the side of man. The absolute element of man's ultimate concern demands absolute intensity, infinite passion (Kierkegaard), in the religious relation. The concrete element drives men toward an unlimited amount of relative action and emotion in the cult in which the ultimate concern is embodied and actualized, and also outside it. The Catholic system of relativities represents the concrete element most fully, while Protestant radicalism predominantly emphasizes the absolute element. The tension in the nature of the gods, which is the tension in the structure of man's ultimate concern (and which, in the last analysis, is the tension in the human situation), determines the religions of mankind in all their major aspects.

Rudolf Bultmann

[b. 1884]

BORN IN WIEFELSTEDE, on the coastal plains of northern Germany, Bultmann has led a secluded academic life. At Marburg he studied under Johannes Weiss, a pioneer of form criticism, a method of biblical study that seeks to interpret scripture in the context of the life and culture of those who wrote and compiled it. In 1912, not long after his graduation, Bultmann became a lecturer there. After four years at Breslau and one at Giessen, he returned to Marburg as professor of New Testament, a post he held from 1921 to 1951.

Bultmann's scholarship has been twofold. First of all, he has carried forward the task of demythologizing bequeathed to him by Weiss. Secondly, he has sought to utilize elements of the existential philosophy of Martin Heidegger, his colleague at Marburg for five years, to articulate a theology derived from the New Testament. In contrast to the freely humanistic type of demythologizing done by Strauss, Feuerbach, Renau and Murry, that of Weiss and Bultmann is a meticulous enterprise of determining the exact structure and function of the New Testament myths. It is, so to speak, an inquiry into the roots of Christian doctrine that does not result simply in a record of the life of Jesus but rather distinguishes several layers—such as the message of Jesus and the somewhat different message of the earliest churches. These studies involve linguistic subtlety as well as sensitivity to the whole matrix of thought and behavior in which Jesus, Paul, John and others flourished. In a word, what exactly did the earliest Christians believe, what did their beliefs mean *to them*—and what is the relationship between the *form* and the *content* of these beliefs? Only by answering such questions can the demythologizer arrive at an accurate picture of the *kerygma*, or real message, of the New Testament. Thus, for example, Bultmann finds that the motif of the resurrection of Jesus from the dead does not signify a dead man coming to life, but it *does* have profound symbolic significance for the earliest Christians—a significance that modern man can appropriate to himself without believing the myth of the resuscitation of Jesus' corpse. The Gospels are studied not as historical records but as theological documents from another era that express that era's experience of something that happened then, but also of a kernel of truth that remains valid for today.

Having arrived, provisionally, at such a kernel of truth, the next question is: What does this mean for human existence in the twentieth century? To complete the task of demythologizing, the *kerygma* has to be translated from mythical language into contemporary terms, and the terms used by Bultmann are those of Heidegger. The result is a viewpoint not vastly different from that of Tillich, particularly in its reconception of God and Christ. For Bultmann, the crucifixion and resurrection of Jesus are together an "eschatological event," a symbol like that of Tillich's Christ as "the new being," which refers to the way in which present-day man can achieve rebirth into "authentic existence." "In every moment," says Bultmann, "slumbers the possibility of being the eschatological moment. You must awaken to it."[1] That is the present-day meaning of "The kingdom of God is at hand." Bultmann and Tillich both express the presence of God in human existence as "the unconditional in the conditioned," although their exact terminology otherwise often diverges. Both may also be said to engage in a process of correlating theological and existential concepts, but of the two, Bultmann is more selective in the theological concepts he wishes to extricate from the New Testament. His commitment to traditional structures is thus more elastic than Tillich's.

As editor of an important biblical monograph series and co-

---

[1] Rudolf Bultmann, *The Presence of Eternity* (New York: Harper & Row, 1957), p. 155. Cf. his statement in this anthology, "It then remains to keep oneself open at any time for the *encounter with God in the world, in time,*" p. 263.

editor of *Theologische Rundschau*, Bultmann has long been involved in on-going discussions of these issues with other theologians. The following selection affords an excellent view of the range and scope of what Bultmann regards as the "transformations" of God. He reveals here a stubborn insistence on the incarnation, the presence of the divine among men. For Bultmann, the God who has "died" is only a mythical image, and his "death" is a transformation requiring new interpretations of the fundamental kerygmatic meaning that the New Testament holds. The chief virtue of his essay is its deployment of some of the leading discussants of this question. For a more extended and focused exposition of Bultmann's concept of demythologizing, see his essay "New Testament and Mythology," in Hans Werner Bartsch, ed., *Kerygma and Myth* (New York: Harper & Row, 1961).

The Idea of God and Modern Man[1]

At the beginning of 1963 there appeared the book of the Anglican bishop John A. T. Robinson, *Honest to God* (honest to and about God).[2] In both England and Germany (as well as in America) it has provoked a debate that was in part heated. Articles appeared in the Hamburg newspaper *Die Zeit*, with captions "Is God a metaphor?" "Is our image of God dated?" "Is faith in God finished?"—questions that were evoked by Robinson's book. Some theologians who expressed their opinions rightly observed that the ideas advanced by Robinson are not new in contemporary theology. Now Robinson had not made this claim at all. He calls repeatedly on Paul Tillich, Dietrich Bonhoeffer and others.[3] But in the process of assimilating their

[1] "Der Gottesgedanke und der moderne Mensch," *Zeitschrift für Theologie und Kirche* (Tübingen: J. C. B. Mohr), 60, 1963, trans. Robert W. Funk. —Ed.

[2] London: SCM Press; Philadelphia: Westminster Press, 1963. [The English title appears in the article; the parenthetical phrase, now redundant, translated it into German.—Ed.]

[3] Professor Bultmann's modesty prevents him from mentioning that Robinson also calls frequently on him.—Tr.

thoughts, he sees that they add up to the following sum, so to speak: *a revolution is necessary.* For, since the traditional ecclesiastical image of God is no longer credible to contemporary man, *a new image of God* is required; the old one is obsolete.

It is comprehensible that for many readers—especially for readers among the laity to whom the book is directed—this thesis is frightening. With the disposal of the old image of God, is not faith in God and thereby also God himself finished? That this question forces itself upon men today is not signalized by Robinson's book alone. As early as 1961 there appeared the book *The Death of God*,[4] by the American theologian Gabriel Vahanian, which is a peculiar and theologically more independent parallel to Robinson's book. The title of Vahanian's book takes up the famous pronouncement of Nietzsche: "God is dead."

The note *"God is dead"* was struck almost a hundred years before Nietzsche by Jean Paul in his *Siebenkäs*, which appeared in 1796–1797, and there in a ghastly vision: "Discourse of the dead Christ from atop the cosmos: there is no God."[5] This discourse is not a philosophical discussion of atheism. The import of the vision consists rather in showing that atheism is nihilism (in this respect also a precursor of Nietzsche): "The whole universe is burst asunder by the hand of atheism and fragmented into innumerable quick-silver particles of I's, which twinkle, roll about, wander, flee together and from each other without unity and stability. No one is so very much alone in the universe as the one who denies God . . . Alas, if every I is its own father and creator, why can it not also be its own angel of destruction?"

Nietzsche permits the "madman" to proclaim the message of the death of God in his work *Die fröhliche Wissenschaft* (1882).

[4] G. Vahanian, *The Death of God. The Culture of Our Post-Christian Era*, New York: George Braziller, 1961. By the same author, "Beyond the Death of God: The Need of Cultural Revolution," *Dialog* I, 4, 1962, pp. 18–21.

[5] G. Bornkamm has reprinted the speech as an appendix to the second volume of his collected essays: *Studien zu Antike und Urchristentum. Gesammelte Aufsätze* II (Beiträge zur evangelischen Theologie, Band 28, Munich, 1959), pp. 245–250. Hegel had also said that God is dead, namely, the God of church dogmatics. On this point cf. W. Anz, "Tod und Unsterblichkeit" (in: *Einsichten. Festschrift für G. Krüger*, Frankfurt, 1962, pp. 11–35), p. 25. The "atheism" of Hegel, however, is not nihilism in the sense of Jean Paul and Nietzsche.

Martin Heidegger says in his essay "Nietzsches Wort 'Gott ist tot' "[6]: "Nietzsche's word names the destiny of two thousand years of Western history." This remarkable assertion rests on the conviction that Western history has been determined for two thousand years by Greek metaphysics, through which in the last analysis the secularization of the world, brought to completion in modern times, has been established. We may here suspend judgment with respect to the correctness of this assertion. Explicit atheism, in any case, is a phenomenon of the modern period, and Gerhard Ebeling has rightly said that this atheism is a counter-movement against Christianity.[7] It is also clear that the death of God for Nietzsche means the death of the Christian God. "But," Heidegger adds, "it is not less certain and is to be borne in mind in advance that the names of God and the Christian God are used by Nietzsche to designate the supersensory world generally. God is the name for the realm of ideas and ideals."[8]

The "madman" calls it out in a figure: "What did we do when we unchained this earth from its sun?", and he continues: "Where is it moving to now? Where are we moving to? Away from all suns? Do we not stumble all the time? Backwards, sidewards, forward, in every direction? Is there an above and a below any more? Are we not wandering as through an endless nothingness?" The consequence of the death of God is therefore *nihilism*, as Jean Paul had pictured it.

We must guard against viewing atheism merely or even basically as a consequence of natural science and its world-view. To be sure, modern natural science has found the hypothesis "God" unnecessary, according to the well-known dictum of La Place, and the atheism of natural science has without doubt been widely influential, leading even to absurdity in Russia, where as the result of space flight it is given out that there was no trace of God in the space above the earth. Nevertheless, even when there are natural scientists today who again hold the hypothesis "God"

[6] M. Heidegger, *Holzwege* (Frankfurt, 1950), pp. 103–247. Cf. also K. Löwith, "Nietzsches antichristliche Bergpredigt," *Heidelberger Jahrbücher*, 6, 1962, pp. 39–50.
[7] G. Ebeling, *The Nature of Faith* (London, 1961), pp. 80f.; *Word and Faith* (London, 1963), pp. 135f., 343.
[8] Heidegger, *Holzwege*, p. 199.

to be possible and appropriate, atheism is not thereby contradicted. For it has far deeper roots.

Atheism, as Jean Paul and Nietzsche understood it, is indeed nihilism, and this is not necessarily a consequence of the way in which natural science understands the world. In this respect the loss of the supernatural can be and was replaced in the eighteenth and nineteenth centuries by the belief in progress and its accompanying optimism. The atheism of the natural sciences is a methodological procedure insofar as it subjects the world to an objectivizing way of viewing things. It must necessarily disregard God, because God, as the supersensory, cannot be the object of an objectivizing way of seeing.[9]

Atheism which ends in nihilism is rather the consequence of the *secularization of the world*, of which the objectivizing way of viewing nature is only a partial symptom. Secularization can be characterized simply as the world being conceived by man as an object[10] and thus delivered over to technology as its object.[11] This secularization takes place in every sphere of life, in morality, in law, in politics. For the relation of man to a transcendental power has been abandoned in all spheres of life. Heidegger calls this epoch in which the world has become an object the epoch *of subjectity*,[12] i.e. the era in which the world conceived as object is subjected to the planning of man as subject, a planning which is controlled by the values which man himself establishes.

And religion? One must first of all reflect that *Christianity itself*

---

[9] Cf. Ebeling, *The Nature of Faith*, pp. 81f.

[10] Cf. Heidegger, *Holzwege*, p. 236.

[11] Cf. D. Bonhoeffer, *Letters and Papers from Prison*, ed. E. Bethge, tr. R. H. Fuller (New York, 1962), p. 195: "Man has learned to cope with all questions of importance without recourse to God as a working hypothesis." (*Widerstand und Ergebung. Briefe und Aufzeichnungen aus der Haft*, ed. E. Bethge, Munich, ⁶1955, p. 215.) Further on the process of secularization, cf. Ebeling, *Word and Faith*, pp. 128ff.; R. G. Smith, "A Theological Perspective of the Secular," *The Christian Scholar*, 43, 1960, pp. 11–24, 18f.

[12] Heidegger, *Holzwege*, p. 237. *Subjectity*, of course, is to be distinguished from *subjectivity*. The latter refers to the subjective mode of the individual in his judgments (e.g. judgments of taste); the former refers to the disposition of an entire epoch to the world and history, a disposition which has achieved the status of self-evidentness. [The reader will perhaps excuse the neologism subjectity, which represents *Subjektität*; the form is drawn by analogy: *Subjektität – Subjektivität* / subjectity-subjectivity.—Tr.]

was a decisive factor in the development of the secularization of the world in that it de-divinized the world.[13] The Christian faith, by de-divinizing the world, allowed it to appear in its pure world- liness. It disclosed and evoked the *freedom* of man from the world, freedom from all powers which can encounter man from out of the world.[14] It is the freedom of which Luther said: "A Christian is a free master over all things and subject to no one." This consciousness of freedom is the presupposition of the secu- larization of the world; the latter follows, however, only when the continuation of Luther's remark is forgotten: "A Christian is a servant in the service of all things and subject to every one," or, to put it differently, when it is forgotten that *freedom from the world is at the same time *responsibility for* the world.[15] This forgetfulness increases the more man becomes conscious of the possibility, in pure objectivizing thought, of dominating the world through science and technology, of making it serve his purposes, evaluations and plans.

This process uses, so to speak, the role which *reason* plays in life. Freedom from the world is at the same time responsibility for the world; that means, the world is delivered over to the rea- son of man.[16] For in order to be able to act responsibly, to come to decisions as they are required again and again, man must

---

[13] Cf. Ebeling, *Word and Faith*, pp. 135f., 344; *The Nature of Faith*, pp. 80f. Further, especially F. Gogarten, *Verhängnis und Hoffnung der Neuzeit* (Stuttgart: 1953); R. G. Smith, "A Theological Perspective," p. 21.

[14] Cf. Gogarten, *Verhängnis und Hoffnung*, p. 8: (the most remarkable thing transpires in secularization) "that the autonomy of man gains the radical sense which it has in the modern world only through the perceptions and experiences disclosed in the Christian faith." *Ibid.*, p. 12: Secularization is the "legitimate consequence" of the Christian faith, and insofar as it "is grounded in the Christian faith," it "makes the world the world (*Verwelt- lichung der Welt*)." Cf. *ibid.*, pp. 93ff.

[15] On the interdependence of freedom from the world and responsibility for the world, cf. Gogarten, pp. 19, 24ff. Vahanian makes the same point, *Death of God*, p. 61: "Biblical thought considers the world as man's sphere of action and preeminence. Man's responsibility to God and his involvement in the world emerge as polar elements attesting to the original goodness of creation." It is significant that both Gogarten and Vahanian make the dis- tinction between a legitimate secularization (secularity) and a degenerate secularism (secularism). Cf. Gogarten, pp. 129ff.; Vahanian, pp. 60ff. Cf. R. G. Smith, "A Theological Perspective," p. 21.

[16] Cf. Gogarten, p. 88.

recognize the causal connection of events in the world, must gain insight into causes and effects, and arrive at judgments about what serves the purpose and what does not. It is to this end that he has his reason. Indeed, in the power of his reason he grasps the laws under which man's actions universally stand, i.e. the moral laws, whose force alone keeps the human community sound and whole. Thus, according to the myth of Protagoras in Plato,[17] Zeus sent reverence and justice to the earth by Hermes in order that political community might be possible. But rational judgments and plans, without which human work and community are not possible, are threatened by the danger that they will be placed in the service of self-seeking and that the authority of the moral laws will thereby wane.

The more reason is conscious of itself, the more the laws which regulate the community will no longer be simply derived from tradition, but will be understood as the moral laws which reason sanctions. And thus heteronomy turns into *autonomy*. Autonomy is equivocal. In the genuine sense autonomy means self-legislation in the sense that the individual affirms the moral law as that in which he himself comes to win his authenticity.[18] But the recognition that the rational man is a lawgiver in this sense turns into the delusion that the individual as subject arbitrarily determines what is good and evil, as was the case already in the "Greek Enlightenment" among the Sophists. And so today autonomy is unfortunately often spoken of as a self-legislation of the individual that understands itself to be free of obligations which transcend the individual level, and that determines value and valuelessness of itself. The outcome is nihilism.[19]

---

[17] Plato, *Protagoras* 322a–322c.
[18] Cf. Kant, *Critique of Practical Reason*, Part First, Book II, Chapter II, V: "In this manner the moral law leads through the conception of the *summum bonum*, as the object and final end of pure practical reason, to religion, that is, to the recognition of all duties as divine commands, not as sanctions, that is to say, arbitrary ordinances of a foreign will and contingent in themselves, but as essential laws of every free will in itself, which, however, must be regarded as commands of the supreme being, . . ." (*Kant's Critique of Practical Reason*, tr. T. K. Abbott [London: Longmans, 1923], p. 226).
[19] On autonomy cf. also R. G. Smith, "A Theological Perspective," p. 18. Ebeling puts it very well in *Word and Faith*, pp. 113f.: "But now, to the reality that concerns modern man there belongs . . . the discovery of the au-

Religion was also drawn into the wake of "subjectity." This is simply given with the fact that Christianity appears as a particular example of religion and is classified within the continuity of the history of religions (which, of course, is possible in any case). If in this context Christianity is acknowledged as the highest religion, then the capitulation to subjectity becomes evident at just that point. For the judgment about lower and higher religions can only be a judgment of the subject which evaluates. It is by no means the case that religion necessarily disappears in subjectity. The Western world, which has been a "Christian" world for centuries, today is in general not anti-Christian, but a-Christian, partly in the sense that Christianity appears to it to be antiquated and the questions to which Christianity proposes to give answers have become for it irrelevant; but partly in the sense that the questions as such remain living issues for it, but now modern man himself gives the answers. Thus there arise ideologies, which assert that they are able to reveal the meaning of the world and history;[20] or doctrines of salvation are propagated, often from exotic religions, the choice among which is left to the subjectivity of the individual; or again—especially in the U.S.A.—the biblical hope of a millennium is secularized, that is, converted into optimism which seeks to renew the world through the "social gospel."[21] But above all, there arises a *religiosity* to which men flee, so to speak, from the claims as well as from the bitterness or tediousness of profane everyday life.

"In the last analysis, religiosity is an expression of sublimated loneliness."[22] The pressing problem for man in a world which has been cut loose from ties to the beyond is to find himself, to become certain of his own being. For with the loss of reference to the transcendent, man's certainty of knowledge concerning

---

tonomy of the reason and accordingly the inescapable duty to make use of the autonomous reason—not, be it noted, to make autonomous use of the reason; for it is not man himself but reason which, rightly understood, is autonomous, whereas to confuse the autonomy of the reason with the autonomy of man results precisely in a new heteronomy of the reason . . . ."
[20] Cf. R. G. Smith, "A Theological Perspective," p. 19.
[21] Cf. Vahanian, pp. 28ff.
[22] Vahanian, p. 4. Cf. also R. G. Smith, "A Theological Perspective," pp. 20f.; *The New Man* (London, 1956), pp. 62f.

himself has also been lost.[23] The question of God does not therefore die away; but the form of the question suggests "that the
deity is a missing link in man's unsuccessful attempts to grasp
the meaning of his self and of the world."[24]

The question by no means completely dies away in decided
atheism either, where atheism draws back from the abyss of
nihilism and, even though it does not risk entertaining the ideas
of the transcendent God and his revelation, would still like to
speak in some way of the divine as somehow immanent to the
world, whether it be as the world's creative ground or as the
spiritual life which lives and evolves in the world.[25] Indeed,
one can say that such "atheism" stands nearer the Christian understanding of faith than some institutional Christians who understand the transcendence of God as a Beyond which has nothing
to do with the world.[26]

Religiosity abandons precisely that—at least according to the
Christian faith—upon which genuine religion is based: the relation of man to the transcendent God as that which stands over
against. Religiosity is conceived from the point of view of the
subjectivity of man. In this sense Karl Barth once fought against
Schleiermacher and the theology of experience inaugurated by
him, in which religion is understood as a province of the human
spirit, as the feeling of absolute dependence. To what extent
Barth's criticism of Schleiermacher was justified I leave open.[27]

---

[23] Cf. Vahanian, p. 183. Further, Bonhoeffer, *Widerstand und Ergebung*,
p. 258: "Man (*scil.* who is threatened by today's organization) is thrown
back upon himself. He is ready to cope with everything, but not with himself. He is able to insure himself against everything, but not against man.
In the last analysis, however, everything depends on man." (Cf. *Letters and
Papers From Prison*, p. 236.) Further, R. G. Smith, "A Theological Perspective," p. 12.

[24] Vahanian, p. 78.

[25] Cf., for example, what Robinson, pp. 127–29, says about Julian Huxley
and Albert Camus.

[26] It is therefore understandable when Robinson, p. 127, produces a variation on Paul's formulation in I Cor. 9:20f.: "I am prepared to be an agnostic
with the agnostic, even an atheist with the atheists." Likewise, cf. R. G.
Smith, *The New Man*, p. 109, on Feuerbach.

[27] On this point cf. Chr. Senft, *Wahrhaftigkeit und Wahrheit. Die Theologie
des 19. Jahrhunderts zwischen Orthodoxie und Aufklärung* (*Beitrage zur
Historischen Theologie* 22), Tübingen, 1956, pp. 1–46.

In any case, it was justified to the extent that the relation to God was reduced to feeling. Vahanian takes up this battle against religiosity from the standpoint of the Christian faith with renewed vigor, as did Bonhoeffer before him. And they are followed by John A. T. Robinson.

Gone is *the relation of man to the transcendent* as that which stands over against man and the world and is not at their disposal, which is manifested only through encounter, only as gift, and cannot be reached by turning away from the world in a religious flight into a beyond. Now the word *transcendence* is ambiguous. It can be said that rational thought transcends all unmethodical and random thought. Reason is transcendent with respect to primitive-innocent opinions as well as arbitrary individual judgments and evaluations. But reason remains in the sphere of subjectity, while religion, particularly the Christian faith, abandons this sphere.[28] The Christian faith speaks of a *revelation* which it understands to mean God's act as an event which is not visible to the objectivizing thought of reason, an event which as revelation does not communicate doctrines, but concerns the existence of man[29] and teaches him, or better, authorizes him to understand himself as sustained by the transcendent power of God.[30]

In this theologians like Tillich, Bonhoeffer, Ebeling, Vahanian,

---

[28] I disregard here that and to what extent it can be said that the existential life (e.g. in personal relationships) transcends the sphere of subjectity.

[29] Here I disregard the paradox, which involves the revelatory event being at once a historical as well as an eschatological event, both with respect to its origin, Jesus Christ, and with respect to his constantly renewed presence in the church's proclamation.

[30] If one is persuaded that every man is basically moved by the question of God and that therefore the Christian proclamation may reckon with a pre-understanding, then one can ask whether this pre-understanding is not also concealed precisely in religiosity. Now H. G. Gadamer, in his book *Wahrheit und Methode* (Tübingen, 1960), which is of greatest significance for theologians, has contested (in the context of the hermeneutical problem, pp. 313f.) that one can speak of a pre-understanding for the understanding of the biblical texts, namely, a pre-understanding that is given with the question of God that drives human existence. I am of the opinion that the pre-understanding is given precisely in that experience which Gadamer designates as the "authentic experience," namely, the experience in which "man becomes conscious of his finiteness" (339f.). This experience is certainly not always realized, but it surely persists as an ever-present possibility.

R. G. Smith and Robinson are one. But they are also agreed that *the transcendent* is to be sought and can be found not above or beyond the world, but *in the midst of this world.*[31] Allow me to quote some sentences of Bonhoeffer: "The 'beyond' of God is not the beyond of our cognitive faculties. Epistemological transcendence has nothing to do with the transcendence of God. God is transcendent in the midst of our life." "The transcendent is not the infinitely remote, but the nearest at hand."[32] The "death of God," according to Vahanian, takes place precisely in that the transcendent presence of God is lost if transcendence is conceived as purely otherworldly—just as in religiosity.[33] Or, to quote another formulation of Vahanian: "Religious authority does not entail the eradication of personal autonomy for the sake of blind assent to a system of beliefs claiming the sanction of absolute or divine authority. But religious authority . . . symbolizes a synthesis of subjective truth and objective reality . . . Faith is an attempt to reconcile subject and object, subjective truth and objective reality, without overwhelming either one of the terms."[34]

Faith permits the world to be the world, indeed, it gives back to the world its authentic worldliness; faith "recognizes the hidden unconditional ground even in the most autonomous of human pursuits. It needs to welcome those pursuits not for the hope that they may be violently 'baptized' into Christ, but for their own

[31] For R. G. Smith cf. "A Theological Perspective," p. 15; *The New Man,* pp. 65–70, and especially 94–112: "This-Worldly Transcendence." Ebeling, *The Nature of Faith,* pp. 16of.

[32] *Widerstand und Ergebung,* pp. 182, 255 (cf. *Letters and Papers From Prison,* pp. 166, 233). On Bonhoeffer cf. especially R. G. Smith, *The New Man,* pp. 96–106; Ebeling, "The Non-religious Interpretation of Biblical Concepts," in *Word and Faith,* pp. 98–161.

[33] Vahanian, p. 44.

[34] Vahanian, pp. 164f. Cf. p. 11: "Now, as then, today and always, the Christian problem is to correlate the truth of Christianity with the empirical truths men live by, without confusing them: man cannot live by one or the other kind of truth alone." P. 169: "On the contrary, even as the meaning of existence lies outside existence, in the dialectical relatedness implied by the polarity between Creator and creature, so also the meaning of history lies above and beyond history." The formulation of Tillich, quoted also by Vahanian, is in substantial agreement: "Theology moves back and forth between two poles, the eternal truth of its foundation and the temporal situation in which the eternal truth must be received"—*Systematic Theology,* I (Chicago University Press, 1951), p. 3.

sake."[35] Dietrich Bonhoeffer formulates the discernment of faithful relation to the world very pointedly: "And we cannot be honest without recognizing that we must live in the world—'etsi deus non daretur.' And this is just what we do recognize—before God! God himself drives us to this recognition."[36] This is precisely what Robinson designates as the necessary revolution: the God above the world having become the God beyond the world, today it is a question of finding God in the midst of the world, in the present. The contrast between here and beyond, and thus the contrast between naturalism and supernaturalism, must be overcome. God must be recognized as the Unconditional in the conditional.

It is surprising how such theological perceptions are also taken up by sociologists. Eckart Schleth says in his book *Der profane Weltchrist:* "The unity of Christian and world is found in the 'nevertheless' of the believer for the world, in his imperceptible eschatological existence here and now, in his freedom from the world, in the world and for the world." Further: "Life in faith, the character of which is to be permanently in process of fulfillment, is life in the 'ultimate reality,' which is always here and now and identical with everyday things."[37]

The relation of faith and worldliness is a dialectical relationship, as R. G. Smith especially has emphasized.[38] I will try to make the meaning of this dialectical relation clear by means of an analogy. The loving look into an eye which is loved and loving is fundamentally different from the objectivizing look with which an ophthalmologist examines the eye of a patient. But when the doctor who has to treat the diseased eye is also the one who loves, the two ways of seeing stand in a dialectical relationship; he has to examine the eye of the other in an objectivizing way precisely

---

[35] R. G. Smith, *The New Man*, p. 69.

[36] *Widerstand und Ergebung*, p. 241 (cf. *Letters and Papers From Prison*, p. 219).

[37] E. Schleth, *Der profane Weltchrist. Neubau der Lebensform für den Industriemenschen* (Munich, 1957), pp. 114, 159. Cf. p. 8: The author is of the opinion "that the church as 'eschatological phenomenon' occurs where Christians without reservation take the profane world seriously, because only in the 'solidarity of faith and unfaith' can the new creation in Christ be recognized and the world served by it."

[38] *The New Man*, pp. 106f., also pp. 58–70; "A Theological Perspective," p. 22.

in his love. The objectivizing way of seeing enters into the service of those who love. Robinson endeavors, following Tillich, to make clear the relation between faith and worldliness in the dialectical relation between engagement with the world and withdrawal from the world. To this dialectic corresponds the dialectic in the relation of man to God, namely, as the relation between personal freedom and utter dependence, between ultimacy and intimacy.[39]

He who has understood the dialectic of the relationship between worldliness and faith in relation to the transcendent God also sees that the recognition of God as the nearest at hand, as he who is in the midst of worldly life, *does not imply pantheism.*[40] For the dialectic is missing in pantheism, and it avoids the paradox that is given to man to conquer, the paradox of grasping the unconditional in the conditional in every now: that means, not in a theory, but in existential comportment, in the conscious or unconscious decisions of life.

The contrast can be made clear by saying that faith in the transcendent presence of God can be expressed in the phrase "transformations of God." Ernst Barlach chose this phrase in order to say that the paradox of the presence of God in the world takes shape in ever new form, just as he himself wished to give expression to the suprareal and infinite in his works in ever new forms.

Ernst Troeltsch once also spoke of the "transformations of God," as he sought to hold on to the idea of God in his philosophy of history in view of the "pluralism of reality and its movement" and vis-à-vis the changes in the knowledge of truth and in the ideals.[41] These changes depend upon an "inner life-movement of the All or the Divinity," upon a "life-process of the Absolute," a "becoming of the divine Spirit."

Troeltsch saw the problem, but he sought to solve it not on the basis of the historicness (*Geschichtlichkeit*) of human existence, but from a standpoint which views history from the outside and

[39] Robinson, pp. 100, 130f.
[40] R. G. Smith, "A Theological Perspective," p. 16, also emphasizes this point.
[41] E. Troeltsch, *Der Historismus und seine Probleme*, 1922. The formulations in question, to which reference is made above, are collected by Gogarten, *Verhängnis und Hoffnung der Neuzeit*, pp. 112–114.

speculatively postulates a transcendent deity, which has its life beyond my specific historicness.[42]

Hans Jonas represents the opposite extreme in his essay "Immortality and the Modern Temper,"[43] to the extent that he projects, so to speak, the historicness of man into God himself and speaks of the destiny of the deity for which man is responsible.[44] We men are experiments of eternity, as it were, and God's own destiny is at stake in our decisions, in the universe which he has left to itself. God's being at the mercy of the world does not mean his immanence in the sense of pantheism. Rather, there is the paradox that the deity has chosen a destiny which consists in the continuous elevation out of immanence into transcendence, for which we men are responsible. In such a process, in the succession of surrender and deliverance, the deity becomes itself.

Schubert M. Ogden understands God's being as historical being in another way.[45] God's eternity is not to be conceived as his timelessness following the metaphysical tradition, but rather as his eminent temporality, his historicity.[46] God is a God who acts, as he is known in the Bible; his self must therefore be conceived in strict analogy with the human self, and anthropomorphic language about God is entirely appropriate. Just as man is not an isolated I, neither is God. Without the universe, without the world, his creation, God is not. To this extent he not only stands in relation to the world, but is dependent upon it. But this dependence is actual, i.e. it is actualized in his own free decisions as well as in the free decisions, which correspond to his own, of the creatures that constitute his world. As answer to God's deci-

---

[42] For criticism of Troeltsch, cf. Gogarten, pp. 114–116.

[43] *Harvard Theological Review* 55, 1962, pp. 1–20.

[44] Jonas, of course, also sees the dialectic between the relation to the world and the relation to God, and says that we encounter the eternal in the temporal, especially in the decisions in which eternity and nothingness meet in one in that the now of the decision is always to be understood as the final moment of time granted us. That means in fact to understand the end in a light from beyond time.

[45] *Journal of Religion* 43, 1963, pp. 1–19.

[46] Cf. M. Heidegger, *Being and Time*, tr. J. Macquarrie and E. Robinson (London, 1962), p. 499, n. xiii: "If God's eternity can be 'construed' philosophically, then it may be understood only as a more primordial temporality which is 'infinite.'"

sions which arise from unbounded love, the latter themselves contribute to God's self-creation.

This all certainly sounds astonishing at first hearing. Is not God, as we learned from Psalm 90, he who was there before the mountains were brought forth and the earth and the world created, God from everlasting to everlasting? Indeed he is! But we understand Ogden when we comprehend how he endeavors to free the idea of the eternity of God from the metaphysical conception of God as the unmoved mover, the *"causa sui,"*[47] and to conceive the eternity of God as historical without giving up thinking of God as creator. If, according to the biblical tradition, God is a person, so is he historical. In support of the view that God is not, apart from the world, the creator is not, apart from the creation, Ogden is able to invoke John 1:1–3, that remarkable assertion that in the beginning was the word, and the word of creation at that, through which everything came into being. This word in the beginning was with God, indeed the word was God. That is no different from what Ogden intends to say. And when we reflect on the word "before" in the Psalm, it is to be said that already for the Psalmist the meaning of "before" is not exhausted in the chronological sense, but that it means the creative superiority, the creative origin. This origin did not occur once as *prima causa*, out of which world history then unfolded in time; on the contrary, this origin is always present.

With this we come back to the assertion that for modern man the idea of a God above or beyond the world is either no longer viable or is perverted in a religiosity which would like to escape from the world. By no means! Only the idea of God which can find, which can seek and find, *the unconditional in the conditional*, the beyond in the here, the transcendent in the present at hand, as possibility of encounter, is possible for modern man.

It then remains to keep oneself open at any time for the *encounter with God in the world, in time*. It is not the acknowledgment of an image of God, be it ever so correct, that is real faith in God; rather, it is the readiness for the eternal to encounter us

[47] Cf. M. Heidegger, *Identität und Differenz* (Pfullingen, 1957), pp. 70f. Cf. *Essays in Metaphysics: Identity and Difference*, tr. Kurt F. Leidecker (New York: Philosophical Library, 1960), pp. 64f.

at any time in the present—at any time in the varying situations of our life. Readiness consists in openness in allowing something really to encounter us that does not leave the I alone, the I that is encapsulated in its purposes and plans, but the encounter with which is designed to transform us, to make us ever new selves. The situation can be heartening just as well as disheartening, can be challenging as well as requiring endurance. What is demanded is selflessness, not as a pattern of moral behavior, but as the readiness not to cling to our selves, but to receive our authentic selves ever anew. This readiness can be interrogative, but it can also be completely naïve. For surprisingly God can encounter us where we do not expect it.[48]

We have thus perhaps come to an understanding of what is

[48] That is evidently also the intention of Herbert Braun, whose avoidance of the word "God" in his delineation of what the New Testament has to say to me (*Gesammelte Studien zum Neuen Testament und seiner Umwelt*, Tübingen, 1962, p. 297) has offended and evoked criticism (cf. especially H. Gollwitzer, *Die Existenz Gottes im Bekenntnis des Glaubens* [*Beitrage zur Evangelischen Theologie* 34], Munich, 1963, pp. 26–29). Cf. Gollwitzer, *The Existence of God as Confessed by Faith* (Philadelphia: Westminster Press, 1965). Braun's purpose is to emphasize, over against an ideological theism, that God is not "the one who exists for himself," but rather is "the whence of my being agitated" (p. 341; = "The Problem of a New Testament Theology," *Journal for Theology and the Church*, number 1, pp. 169–183, pp. 182f.) This being driven about is understood by Braun as determined by the "I may" and "I ought." It might be asked how this dialectic (if it may be called that) relates to the dialectic between worldliness and a believing relation to transcendence. But, in any case, the relation to transcendence is understood in the New Testament, according to Braun, as an event, and indeed, as he formulates it, as an "unexpectable" event (275). The believing self-understanding awakened in such an event is not theoretical knowledge, but "an event which occurs again and again" (277). The truth of the relation to transcendence understood in this sense is "bound to its being perpetually proclaimed anew" (277) and to its being heeded (297), to its being heard (298), respectively. The self-understanding awakened by such hearing is actualized in concrete human community. Braun is thus able to put it very sharply: "Man as man, man in relation with his fellow man, implies God" (341; = *Journal for Theology and the Church*, 1, p. 183). R. G. Smith also emphasizes the importance of community ("A Theological Perspective," p. 22): "Man is (*scil.* man) insofar as he receives. He is (*scil.* man) only so far as he is whole. And this wholeness is found only in relation to others. Man's being is being in relation. This simply cannot be arranged or planned. It happens, it is an event in which man's being is disclosed in the presence of the other." The problem of the relation of law and gospel also belongs here; see Ebeling, e.g., *Word and Faith*, pp. 143f.

meant by the "transformations of God." All of us are probably acquainted with sagas and legends, pagan as well as Christian, in which the profound idea of the transformation of God has been concealed in the mythological representation of the metamorphosis of the deity or of gods, who visit a mortal *incognito* and unrecognized. How the one visited receives the god determines his destiny.

The New Testament contains the most striking proclamation of the "transformations" of God, and oddly enough in the picture which Jesus sketches of the last judgment (Matt. 25:31–46). The judge of the world assembles all men before his throne, some to the right, some to the left. To those on the right he says: "I was hungry and you gave me food, I was thirsty and you gave me drink, I was a stranger and you welcomed me . . . ." And when those so addressed inquire in astonishment, "When did we do all this?" the Lord will answer, "What you did to one of the least of these my brethren, you did to me!" The dialogue with those on the left runs correspondingly: "I was hungry and you gave me no food, I was thirsty and you gave me no drink . . . ." And when they ask, "Lord, when did we see thee hungry or thirsty . . . and did not minister to thee?" then they must face the answer, "What you did not do to the least of these, you did not do to me either!" This picture thus contains the two doctrines, which belong together, of the "transformations" of God and of the presence of eternity in time.

Simone Weil

[1900–1943]

BORN A JEW, buried as a Catholic, Simone Weil was a passionate and brilliant child of her time.[1] At her graduation from the Ecole Normale in Paris, 1931, she was known as the "red virgin"; although of middle-class origin, she threw herself into the labor movement. After a year as a factory worker in 1935, she taught philosophy at the University of Bourges, but when the civil war broke out in Spain she left to fight for the Republic.

An intellectual of decidedly rational temper, she was unprepared for the experience of that war, with its glaring discrepancies between ideology and behavior, its betrayals, its sheer brutality and cruelty. To come to some terms with these realities, she turned to metaphysics and to an intense preoccupation with Christ. Most of her writings consist of compact meditations like those that follow here.

Simone Weil was a "free spirit" in the Nietzschean sense, but her supreme act of freedom was a decision to restrict her diet out of sympathy for her countrymen during the Nazi occupation of France. Maurice Friedman has called her a "modern gnostic" for her extreme asceticism, which led to her death from malnutrition.

Despite the keen ardor of her religious sensibility, she refused to be baptized because she felt this would divide her from the rest of mankind. She had no impulse to persuade others to her belief, but had to understand theirs as well as her own. A contemporary of Sartre and Camus, she shared their existentialism

---

[1] See Richard Rees, *Simone Weil: A Sketch for a Portrait* (Southern Illinois University Press, 1966).

and their dedication to the Resistance movement. Her comments on atheism, written as a devotee of Christ, are both self-explanatory and reflect an extraordinary insight into the twentieth-century mind. It hardly needs saying that her own mind was extraordinary, as was her brief life as a revolutionary anarchist, pacifist, fighter and saint.

Atheism as a Purification

A case of contradictories which are true. God exists. God does not. Where is the problem? I am quite sure that there is a God in the sense that I am quite sure my love is not illusory. I am quite sure that there is not a God in the sense that I am quite sure nothing real can be anything like what I am able to conceive when I pronounce this word. But that which I cannot conceive is not an illusion.

There are two atheisms of which one is a purification of the notion of God.

Perhaps every evil thing has a second aspect, a purification in the course of progress toward the good, and a third which is the higher good.

We have to distinguish carefully between these three aspects, because it is very dangerous for thought and for the effective conduct of life to confuse them.

Of two men who have no experience of God, he who denies him is perhaps nearer to him than the other.

The false God who is like the true one in everything, except that we cannot touch him, prevents us from ever coming to the true one.

We have to believe in a God who is like the true God in everything, except that he does not exist, since we have not reached the point where God exists.

The errors of our time come from Christianity without the supernatural. Secularization is the cause—and primarily humanism.

Religion, insofar as it a source of consolation, is a hindrance to true faith: in this sense atheism is a purification. I have to be atheistic with the part of myself which is not made for God. Among those men in whom the supernatural part has not been awakened, the atheists are right and the believers wrong.

A man whose whole family had died under torture, and who had himself been tortured for a long time in a concentration camp. Or a sixteenth-century Indian, the sole survivor after the total extermination of his people. Such men if they had previously believed in the mercy of God would either believe in it no longer, or else they would conceive of it quite differently than before. I have not been through such things. I know, however, that they exist: so what is the difference?

I must move toward an abiding conception of the divine mercy, a conception which does not change whatever event destiny may send upon me, and which can be communicated to no matter what human being.

V

THE NEW
CHRISTIANITY

Dietrich Bonhoeffer

[1906–1945]

BORN IN BRESLAU, Bonhoeffer was six when his father was appointed professor of psychiatry at the University of Berlin. At eighteen, Bonhoeffer enrolled there in theological studies. This was an unusual step that rather surprised other members of the family, for the Bonhoeffers' ties to the church were polite but slack.[1] Socially, his family was upper-middle-class, with more than a few connections in the power structure. Its cultural outlook was fairly conventional, a fact that is mirrored in the literary references in Bonhoeffer's own writings, not to mention his tastes in music. His favorite authors were all men of the eighteenth and nineteenth centuries, none of them well known outside Germany. Such contemporaries as Mann, Hesse and Brecht were not part of his sheltered world.[2]

Bonhoeffer's contacts were far-reaching, but they were all within the framework of the church and related institutions, as when he served as pastor to German congregations in Barcelona and London. He was one of the very few Christians to speak out publicly against anti-Semitism after Hitler came to power, an act that may be partly explained by the fact that his twin sister was married to a Jew.

Most of Bonhoeffer's writings are only of retrospective interest. For the most part they display nothing more than an alert grasp of the neo-orthodox "theology of the Word" expounded by Karl

[1] This is not to ignore the fact that his grandfather was a chaplain to the Kaiser, or that his maternal great-grandfather was a noted church historian, Carl von Hase. But none of Bonhoeffer's six brothers and sisters and neither of his parents were more than conventionally religious.
[2] There has been so much glib eulogizing of Bonhoeffer for his "involvement" that it seems to me relevant to point this out.

Barth. His mature books, *The Cost of Discipleship* and *Life Together*, dating respectively from 1937 and 1939, reflect courage and commitment but also a high degree of naïveté and cloistered piety. Even after his imprisonment, he never engaged in the asceticism implied in his concept of discipleship, and he was apparently unaware of the agonizing privations of the concentration camps.[3]

Bonhoeffer visited the United States in 1931 and 1939. On the second occasion he chose deliberately to return to Germany and carry on the fight against Nazism. Now for the first time he utilized his ecumenical contacts for secular purposes, acting as courier for a conspiracy of German generals who attempted to assassinate Hitler in July 1944. Bonhoeffer was seized in April 1943 on suspicion of his involvement, but only after the event was he packed off to maximum-security confinement, and executed in April 1945. The fact of his execution is pivotal to the impact his writings later had, particularly with the American publication of his prison letters in 1954 under the flamboyant and inaccurate title *Prisoner for God.*

Bonhoeffer was not imprisoned for his faith, although he could have been, as was Martin Niemöller. He was executed for a quite secular activity. But he commands attention because he was an articulate and well-known theologian, and because of the direction his thinking took while imprisoned. With the exception of a couple of notes to his parents, the letters cover a period of about sixteen months—the first such period in Bonhoeffer's life in which he was cut off from both home and his customary religious environment. There is a great deal of religious parochialism in all of these letters, and nothing of real interest until the last four months. It is the letters and papers from that brief period that represent a radical turn, a new assessment of the relationship between the church and the world, and a number of provocative questions affecting the future of Christianity.

The selections that follow encompass these writings in their entirety, beginning with Bonhoeffer's first intimations to his friend Eberhard Bethge that his thinking had taken a new turn. Omitted

---

[3] In prison he had many privileges and amenities, which presumably ceased when he was transferred to the camps, but his correspondence ceased too.

are topical remarks and digressions from the main theme. They give little hint of what sort of world Bonhoeffer expected to emerge in the years ahead. In a sense, they are letters addressed to the church from a churchman isolated from the ecclesiastical orbit, reporting on his jarring contact with the world outside that orbit. From his outpost in this religionless world he discerns the need for revolutionary changes in the church's *modus operandi*, in its self-image and self-understanding. There are theological inferences, too—a tacit discovery of the inefficacy and irrelevance of the God of traditional theism, and a number of striking new images of incarnation, such as "the beyond in the midst of our life" and "the man for others."

There is much here that is paradoxical, such as the notion of a "religionless Christianity" shunning demythologizing and carried on by the church, albeit with radically new forms of organization. There is a clear repudiation of secular humanism and at the same time a strong impulse to make Christianity both secular and humanistic while retaining a strictly biblical theology of the Word. What makes the Bonhoeffer legacy so valuable is its tentativeness and incompleteness. The last prison letters represent a bold thrust in a new direction, a leap from bourgeois Christendom into the uncharted regions of a future that is now the present. In short, they comprise an invitation, *carte blanche*, to move forward from Barthian neo-orthodoxy. The direction in which they point may be toward a Feuerbachian or a Tillichian confrontation with secularity, or toward some new synthesis. Bonhoeffer's striking phrases are validated not by theological astuteness but by the eschatological optimism and radical seriousness of one "man for others" about to die for the secular consequences of his faith. The existential testimony of Bonhoeffer's life as a man struggling to secular maturity and articulating his own "secret discipline" of "worldly holiness" is the key to his enduring influence. In the United States, response to *The Cost of Discipleship* coincided with the involvement of Barthian seminary students in the racial crisis of the 1960s. Directly or indirectly the freedom movement first tested their resources for spiritual discipline and then dramatically confronted them with the same kind of "worldly" questions that Bonhoeffer addresses in his prison letters. Likewise,

Bonhoeffer looms as a major influence within the church in East Germany, which has had to uproot itself from the cozy bourgeois assumptions on which it rested before the Communists took over.[4] Here as in America, Bonhoeffer opens the way for engagement and survival. Herein lies the crux of Bonhoeffer's significance. In German, the title of his last writings is *Widerstand und Ergebung* —"resistance and submission." The phrase is drawn from a letter of February 21, 1944:

> It is impossible to define the boundary between resistance and submission in the abstract. Faith demands this elasticity of behavior. Only so can we stand our ground in each situation as it comes along and turn it to gain.[5]

This statement and the burden of the following writings are not addressed to the general public. They do not seek to convert secular man but to convert avowed Christians to a new type of Christianity. Any further influence must be that of action and example.

Last Letters from a Nazi Prison[1]

April 30, 1944

. . . You would be surprised and perhaps disturbed if you knew how my ideas on theology are taking shape. This is where I miss you most of all, for there is no one else who could help me so much to clarify my own mind. The thing that keeps coming back to me is, what *is* Christianity, and indeed what *is* Christ, for us today? The time when men could be told everything by

---

[4] The most comprehensive study of Bonhoeffer's theology is a massive book by a professor at Humboldt University in East Berlin: Hanfried Müller, *Von der Kirche zur Welt* (Leipzig: Koehler & Amelang, 1961).

[5] Dietrich Bonhoeffer, *Letters and Papers from Prison* (New York: Macmillan, 1962), p. 138. This translation is often hasty and inaccurate, and a new one is in preparation.

[1] From *Widerstand und Ergebung* (München: Chr. Kaiser, 1951), trans. Reginald Fuller, *Letters and Papers from Prison* (New York: Macmillan, 1962).—Ed.

means of words, whether theological or simply pious, is over, and so is the time of inwardness and conscience, which is to say the time of religion as such. We are proceeding toward a time of no religion at all: men as they are now simply cannot be religious any more. Even those who honestly describe themselves as "religious" do not in the least act up to it, and so when they say "religious" they evidently mean something quite different. Our whole nineteen-hundred-year-old Christian preaching and theology rests upon the "religious premise" of man. What we call Christianity has always been a pattern—perhaps a true pattern— of religion. But if one day it becomes apparent that this *a priori* "premise" simply does not exist, but was an historical and temporary form of human self-expression, i.e. if we reach the stage of being radically without religion—and I think this is more or less the case already, else how is it, for instance, that this war, unlike any of those before it, is not calling forth any "religious" reaction?—what does that mean for "Christianity"?

It means that the linchpin is removed from the whole structure of our Christianity to date, and the only people left for us to light on in the way of "religion" are a few "last survivals of the age of chivalry," or else one or two who are intellectually dishonest. Would they be the chosen few? Is it on this dubious group and none other that we are to pounce, in fervor, pique, or indignation, in order to sell them the goods we have to offer? Are we to fall upon one or two unhappy people in their weakest moment and force upon them a sort of religious coercion?

If we do not want to do this, if we had finally to put down the western pattern of Christianity as a mere preliminary stage to doing without religion altogether, what situation would result for us, for the Church? How can Christ become the Lord even of those with no religion? If religion is no more than the garment of Christianity—and even that garment has had very different aspects at different periods—then what is a religionless Christianity? Barth, who is the only one to have started on this line of thought, has still not proceeded to its logical conclusion, but has arrived at a positivism of revelation which has nevertheless remained essentially a restoration. For the religionless workingman, or indeed, man generally, nothing that makes any real difference is gained by that. The questions needing answers would surely be: What is the significance of a Church (church, parish, preaching, Christian life) in a religionless world? How do we speak of God without religion, i.e. without the temporally influenced presuppositions of metaphysics, inwardness, and so on? How do we speak (but perhaps we are no longer capable of speaking of such things as we used to) in secular fashion of God? In what way are we in a religionless and secular sense Christians, in what way are we the *Ekklesia*, "those who are called forth," not conceiving of ourselves religiously as specially favored, but as wholly belonging to the world? Then Christ is no longer an object of religion, but something quite different, indeed and in truth the Lord of the world. Yet what does that signify? What is the place of worship and prayer in an entire absence of religion? Does the secret discipline, or, as the case may be, the distinction (which you have met with me before) between penultimate and ultimate, at this point acquire fresh importance? . . .

The Pauline question whether circumcision is a condition of justification is today, I consider, the question whether religion is a condition of salvation. Freedom from circumcision is at the same time freedom from religion. I often ask myself why a Christian instinct frequently draws me more to the religionless than to the religious, by which I mean not with any intention of evangelizing them, but rather, I might almost say, in "brotherhood." While I often shrink with religious people from speaking of God by name—because that Name somehow seems to me here not to ring true, and I strike myself as rather dishonest (it is especially bad when others start talking in religious jargon: then I dry up completely and feel somehow oppressed and ill at ease)—with people who have no religion I am able on occasion to speak of God quite openly and as it were naturally. Religious people speak of God when human perception is (often just from laziness) at an end, or human resources fail: it is really always the *Deus ex machina* they call to their aid, either for the so-called solving of insoluble problems or as support in human failure—always, that is to say, helping out human weakness or on the borders of human existence. Of necessity, that can only go on until men can, by their own strength, push those borders a little further, so that

God becomes superfluous as a *Deus ex machina*. I have come to be doubtful even about talking of "borders of human existence." Is even death today, since men are scarcely afraid of it any more, and sin, which they scarcely understand any more, still a genuine borderline? It always seems to me that in talking thus we are only seeking frantically to make room for God. I should like to speak of God not on the borders of life but at its center, not in weakness but in strength, not, therefore, in man's suffering and death but in his life and prosperity. On the borders it seems to me better to hold our peace and leave the problem unsolved. Belief in the Resurrection is not the solution of the problem of death. The "beyond" of God is not the beyond of our perceptive faculties. The transcendence of theory based on perception has nothing to do with the transcendence of God. God is the "beyond" in the midst of our life. The Church stands not where human powers give out, on the borders, but in the center of the village. That is the way it is in the Old Testament, and in this sense we still read the New Testament far too little on the basis of the Old. . . .

May 5, 1944

. . . A bit more about "religionlessness." I expect you remember Bultmann's paper on the demythologizing of the New Testament? My view of it today would be not that he went too far, as most people seem to think, but that he did not go far enough. It is not only the mythological conceptions, such as the miracles, the ascension and the like (which are not in principle separable from the conceptions of God, faith and so on), that are problematic, but the "religious" conceptions themselves. You cannot, as Bultmann imagines, separate God and miracles, but you do have to be able to interpret and proclaim *both* of them in a "nonreligious" sense. Bultmann's approach is really at bottom the liberal one (i.e. abridging the Gospel), whereas I seek to think theologically.

What do I mean by "interpret in a religious sense"? In my view, that means to speak on the one hand metaphysically, and on the other individualistically. Neither of these is relevant to the Bible message or to the man of today. Is it not true to say that individualistic concern for personal salvation has almost completely left us all? Are we not really under the impression that there are more important things than bothering about such a matter? (Perhaps not more important than the matter itself, but more than bothering about it.) I know it sounds pretty monstrous to say that. But is it not, at bottom, even biblical? Is there any concern in the Old Testament about saving one's soul at all? Is not righteousness and the kingdom of God on earth the focus of everything, and is not Romans 3.14ff., too, the combination of the view that in God alone is righteousness, and not in an individualistic doctrine of salvation? It is not with the next world that we are concerned, but with this world as created and preserved and set subject to laws and atoned for and made new. What is above the world is, in the Gospel, intended to exist *for* this world—I mean that not in the anthropocentric sense of liberal, pietistic, ethical theology, but in the Bible sense of the creation and of the incarnation, crucifixion, and resurrection of Jesus Christ.

Barth was the first theologian to begin the criticism of religion —and that remains his really great merit—but he set in its place the positivist doctrine of revelation which says in effect, "Take it or leave it": Virgin Birth, Trinity or anything else, everything which is an equally significant and necessary part of the whole, which latter has to be swallowed as a whole or not at all. That is not in accordance with the Bible. There are degrees of perception and degrees of significance, i.e. a secret discipline must be reestablished whereby the *mysteries* of the Christian faith are preserved from profanation. The positivist doctrine of revelation makes it too easy for itself, setting up, as in the ultimate analysis it does, a law of faith, and mutilating what is, by the incarnation of Christ, a gift for us. The place of religion is taken by the Church—that is, in itself, as the Bible teaches it should be—but the world is made to depend upon itself and left to its own devices, and that is all wrong.

I am thinking over the problem at present how we may reinterpret in the manner "of the world"—in the sense of the Old Testament and of John 1.14—the concepts of repentance, faith, justification, rebirth, sanctification and so on. I shall be writing to you again about that. . . .

May 25, 1944

. . . We have to keep men out of their one-track minds. That is a sort of preparation for faith, although it is only faith itself that can make possible a multidimensional life. . . .

Weizsäcker's book on the world-view of physics is still keeping me busy. It has brought home to me how wrong it is to use God as a stopgap for the incompleteness of our knowledge. For the frontiers of knowledge are inevitably being pushed back further and further, which means that you only think of God as a stopgap. He also is being pushed back further and further, and is in more or less continuous retreat. We should find God in what we do know, not in what we don't; not in outstanding problems, but in those we have already solved. This is true not only for the relation between Christianity and science, but also for wider human problems such as guilt, suffering and death. It is possible nowadays to find answers to these problems which leave God right out of the picture. It just isn't true to say that Christianity alone has the answers. In fact the Christian answers are no more conclusive or compelling than any of the others. Once more, God cannot be used as a stopgap. We must not wait until we are at the end of our tether; he must be found at the center of life: in life, and not only in death; in health and vigor, and not only in suffering; in activity, and not only in sin. The ground for this lies in the revelation of God in Christ. Christ is the center of life, and in no sense did he come to answer our unsolved problems. From the center of life certain questions are seen to be wholly irrelevant, and so are the answers commonly given to them—I am thinking for example of the judgment pronounced on the friends of Job. In Christ there are no Christian problems. . . .

May 30, 1944—Evening

. . . I wonder if we have become too rational? When you have deliberately suppressed every desire for so long, it burns you up inside, or else you get so bottled up that one day there is a terrific explosion. The only alternative is the achievement of complete selflessness. I know better than anyone else that that has not happened to me. I expect you will say it's wrong to suppress one's desires, and you would be quite right. . . .

June 8, 1944

The movement beginning about the thirteenth century (I am not going to get involved in any arguments about the exact date) toward the autonomy of man (under which head I place the discovery of the laws by which the world lives and manages in science, social and political affairs, art, ethics and religion) has in our time reached a certain completion. Man has learned to cope with all questions of importance without recourse to God as a working hypothesis. In questions concerning science, art, and even ethics, this has become an understood thing which one scarcely dares to tilt at any more. But for the last hundred years or so it has been increasingly true of religious questions also: it is becoming evident that everything gets along without "God," and just as well as before. As in the scientific field, so in human affairs generally, what we call "God" is being more and more edged out of life, losing more and more ground.

Catholic and Protestant historians are agreed that it is in this development that the great defection from God, from Christ, is to be discerned, and the more they bring in and make use of God and Christ in opposition to this trend, the more the trend itself considers itself to be antichristian. The world which has attained to a realization of itself and of the laws which govern its existence is so sure of itself that we become frightened. False starts and failures do not make the world deviate from the path and development it is following; they are accepted with fortitude and detachment as part of the bargain, and even an event like the present war is no exception. Christian apologetic has taken the most varying forms of opposition to this self-assurance. Efforts are made to prove to a world thus come of age that it cannot live without the tutelage of "God." Even though there has been surrender on all secular problems, there still remain the so-called ultimate questions—death, guilt—on which only "God" can furnish an answer, and which are the reason why God and the

Church and the pastor are needed. Thus we live, to some extent, by these ultimate questions of humanity. But what if one day they no longer exist as such, if they too can be answered without "God"? We have of course the secularized offshoots of Christian theology, the existentialist philosophers and the psychotherapists, who demonstrate to secure, contented, happy mankind that it is really unhappy and desperate, and merely unwilling to realize that it is in severe straits it knows nothing at all about, from which only they can rescue it. Wherever there is health, strength, security, simplicity, they spy luscious fruit to gnaw at or to lay their pernicious eggs in. They make it their object first of all to drive men to inward despair, and then it is all theirs. That is secularized methodism. And whom does it touch? A small number of intellectuals, of degenerates, of people who regard themselves as the most important thing in the world and hence like looking after themselves. The ordinary man who spends his everyday life at work, and with his family, and of course with all kinds of hobbies and other interests too, is not affected. He has neither time nor inclination for thinking about his intellectual despair and regarding his modest share of happiness as a trial, a trouble or a disaster.

The attack by Christian apologetic upon the adulthood of the world I consider to be in the first place pointless, in the second ignoble, and in the third unchristian. Pointless, because it looks to me like an attempt to put a grown-up man back into adolescence, i.e. to make him dependent on things on which he is not in fact dependent any more, thrusting him back into the midst of problems which are in fact not problems for him any more. Ignoble, because this amounts to an effort to exploit the weakness of man for purposes alien to him and not freely subscribed to by him. Unchristian, because for Christ himself is being substituted one particular stage in the religiousness of man, i.e. a human law. Of this more later.

But first a word or two on the historical situation. The question is, Christ and the newly matured world. It was the weak point of liberal theology that it allowed the world the right to assign Christ his place in that world: in the dispute between

Christ and the world it accepted the comparatively clement peace dictated by the world. It was its strong point that it did not seek to put back the clock, and genuinely accepted the battle (Troeltsch), even though this came to an end with its overthrow.

Overthrow was succeeded by capitulation and an attempt at a completely fresh start based on consideration of the Bible and Reformation fundamentals of the faith. Heim sought, along pietist and methodist lines, to convince individual man that he was faced with the alternative "either despair or Jesus." He gained "hearts." Althaus, carrying forward the modern and positive line with a strong confessional emphasis, endeavored to wring from the world a place for Lutheran teaching (ministry) and Lutheran worship, and otherwise left the world to its own devices. Tillich set out to interpret the evolution of the world itself—against its will—in a religious sense, to give it its whole shape through religion. That was very courageous of him, but the world unseated him and went on by itself; he too sought to understand the world better than it understood itself, but it felt entirely *mis*understood, and rejected the imputation. (Of course the world does need to be understood better than it understands itself, but not "religiously," as the religious socialists desired.) Barth was the first to realize the mistake that all these efforts (which were all unintentionally sailing in the channel of liberal theology) were making in having as their objective the clearing of a space for religion in the world or against the world.

He called the God of Jesus Christ into the lists against religion, "*pneuma* against *sarx*." That was and is his greatest service (the second edition of his Epistle to the Romans, in spite of all its neo-Kantian shavings). Through his later dogmatics, he enabled the Church to effect this distinction in principle all along the line. It was not that he subsequently, as is often claimed, failed in ethics, for his ethical observations—so far as he has made any—are just as significant as his dogmatic ones; it was that he gave no concrete guidance, either in dogmatics or in ethics, on the nonreligious interpretation of theological concepts. There lies his limitation, and because of it his theology of revelation becomes positivist, a "positivism of revelation," as I put it.

The Confessing Church[2] has to a great extent forgotten all about the Barthian approach, and lapsed from positivism into conservative restoration. The important thing about that Church is that it carries on the great concepts of Christian theology, but that seems all it will do. There are, certainly, in these concepts the elements of genuine prophetic quality (under which head come both the claim to truth and the mercy you mention) and of genuine worship, and to that extent the message of the Confessing Church meets only with attention, hearing and rejection. But they both remain unexplained and remote, because there is no interpretation of them.

People like, for instance, Schütz, or the Oxford Group, or the Berneucheners, who miss the "movement" and "life," are dangerous reactionaries, retrogressive because they go straight back behind the approach of revelation theology and seek for "religious" renewal. They simply do not understand the problem at all, and what they say is entirely beside the point. There is no future for them (though the Oxford people would have the biggest chance if they were not so completely devoid of biblical substance).

Bultmann would seem to have felt Barth's limitations in some way, but he misconstrues them in the light of liberal theology, and hence goes off into the typical liberal reduction process (the "mythological" elements of Christianity are dropped, and Christianity is reduced to its "essence"). I am of the view that the full content, including the mythological concepts, must be maintained. The New Testament is not a mythological garbing of the universal truth; this mythology (resurrection and so on) is the thing itself—but the concepts must be interpreted in such a way as not to make religion a precondition of faith (cf. circumcision in St. Paul). Not until that is achieved will, in my opinion, liberal theology be overcome (and even Barth is still dominated by it, though negatively), and, at the same time, the question it raises

---

[2] The Confessing Church was an organization formed by Protestants who chose to affirm their faith in Jesus Christ rather than acquiesce in the ideology of Nazism. It was based on the Barmen Declaration of 1934. Karl Barth was among its most prominent leaders.—Ed.

be genuinely taken up and answered—which is not the case in the positivism of revelation maintained by the Confessing Church.

The world's coming of age is then no longer an occasion for polemics and apologetics, but it is really better understood than it understands itself, namely, on the basis of the Gospel, and in the light of Christ.

You ask whether this leaves any room for the Church, or has it gone for good? And again, did not Jesus himself use distress as his point of contact with men, whether as a consequence the "methodism" I have so frowned upon is not right after all? I'm breaking off here, and will write more tomorrow.

June 30, 1944

. . . I began by saying that God is being increasingly edged out of the world, now that it has come of age. Knowledge and life are thought to be perfectly possible without him. Ever since Kant, he has been relegated to the realm beyond experience.

Theology has endeavored to produce an apologetic to meet this development, engaging in futile rear-guard actions against Darwinism, etc. At other times it has accommodated itself to this development by restricting God to the so-called last questions as a kind of *Deus ex machina*. God thus became the answer to life's problems, the solution of its distresses and conflicts. As a result, if anyone had no such difficulties, if he refused to identify himself in sympathy with those who had, it was no good trying to win him for God. The only way of getting at him was to show that he had all these problems, needs and conflicts without being aware of it or owning up to it. Existentialist philosophy and psychotherapy have both been pretty clever at this sort of thing. It is then possible to talk to a man about God, and methodism can celebrate its triumph. If, however, it does not come off, if a man won't see that his happiness is really damnation, his health sickness, his vigor and vitality despair; if he won't call them what they really are, the theologian is at his wits' end. He must be a hardened sinner of a particularly vicious type. If not, he is a case of bourgeois complacency, and the one is as far from salvation as the other.

You see, this is the attitude I am contending against. When Jesus blessed sinners, they were real sinners, but Jesus did not make every man a sinner first. He called them out of their sin, not into their sin. Of course, encounter with Jesus meant the reversal of all human values. So it was in the conversion of St. Paul, though in his case the knowledge of sin preceded his encounter with Jesus. Of course Jesus took to himself the dregs of human society, harlots, and publicans, but never them alone, for he sought to take to himself man as such. Never did Jesus throw any doubt on a man's health, vigor or fortune, regarded in themselves, or look upon them as evil fruits. Else why did he heal the sick and restore strength to the weak? Jesus claims for himself and the kingdom of God the whole of human life in all its manifestations.

. . . Let me briefly summarize what I am concerned about: it is, how can we reclaim for Christ a world which has come of age?

July 8, 1944

. . . When God was driven out of the world, and from the public side of human life, an attempt was made to retain him at least in the sphere of the "personal," the "inner life," the private life. And since every man still has a private sphere, it was thought that he was most vulnerable at this point. The secrets known by a man's valet, that is, to put it crudely, the area of his intimate life—from prayer to his sexual life—have become the hunting ground of modern psychotherapists. In this way they resemble, though quite involuntarily, the dirtiest gutter journalists. Think of the newspapers which specialize in bringing to light the most intimate details about prominent people. They practice social, financial and political blackmail on their victims: the psychotherapists practice religious blackmail. Forgive me, but I cannot say less about them.

From the sociological point of view this is a revolution from below, a revolt of inferiority. Just as the vulgar mentality is never satisfied until it has seen some highly placed personage in his bathing attire, or in other compromising situations, so it is here. There is a kind of malicious satisfaction in knowing that everyone has his weaknesses and nakednesses. In my contacts with the outcasts of society, its pariahs, I have often noticed how mistrust is the dominant motive in their judgments of other people. Every act of a person of high repute, be it never so altruistic, is suspected from the outset. Incidentally, I find such outcasts in all ranks of society. In a flower garden they grub around for the dung on which the flowers grow. The less responsible a man's life, the more easily he falls a victim to this attitude.

This irresponsibility and absence of bonds has its counterpart among the clergy in what I should call the "priestly" snuffing around in the sins of men in order to catch them out. It is as though a beautiful house could only be known after a cobweb had been found in the furthermost corner of the cellar, or as though a good play could only be appreciated after one had seen how the actors behave offstage. It is the same kind of thing you find in the novels of the last fifty years, which think they have only depicted their characters properly when they have described them in bed, or in films where it is thought necessary to include undressing scenes. What is clothed, veiled, pure and chaste is considered to be deceitful, disguised and impure, and in fact only shows the impurity of the writers themselves. Mistrust and suspicion as the basic attitude of men is characteristic of the revolt of inferiority.

From the theological point of view the error is twofold. First, it is thought that a man can be addressed as a sinner only after his weaknesses and meannesses have been spied out. Second, it is thought that man's essential nature consists of his inmost and most intimate background, and that is defined as his "interior life"; and it is in these secret human places that God is now to have his domain!

On the first point it must be said that man is certainly a sinner, but not mean or common, not by a long chalk. To put the matter in the most banal way, are Goethe or Napoleon sinners because they were not always faithful husbands? It is not the sins of weakness, but the sins of strength, which matter here. It is not in the least necessary to spy out things. The Bible never does so.

(Sins of strength: in the genius, *hybris*, in the peasant, the breaking of the order of life—is the Decalogue a peasant ethic?—in
the bourgeois, fear of free responsibility. Is this correct?)

On the second point it must be said that the Bible does not
recognize our distinction of outer and inner. And why should it?
It is always concerned with *anthropos teleios*, the *whole* man,
even where, as in the Sermon on the Mount, the Decalogue is
pressed home to refer to inward disposition. It is quite unbiblical
to suppose that a "good intention" is enough. What matters is the
whole good. The discovery of inwardness, so-called, derives from
the Renaissance, from Petrarch perhaps. The "heart" in the biblical sense is not the inward life, but the whole man in relation
to God. The view that man lives just as much from outward to
inward as from inward to outward is poles apart from the view
that his essential nature is to be understand from his intimate
background.

This is why I am so anxious that God should not be relegated
to some last secret place, but that we should frankly recognize
that the world and men have come of age, that we should not
speak ill of man in his worldliness, but confront him with God at
his strongest point, that we should give up all our clerical subter-
fuges, and our regarding of psychotherapy and existentialism as
precursors of God. The importunity of these people is far too
unaristocratic for the Word of God to ally itself with them. The
Word of God is far removed from this revolt of mistrust, this
revolt from below. But it reigns. . . .

July 16, 1944

. . . Now a few more thoughts on our theme. I find it's very
slow going trying to work out a nonreligious interpretation of
biblical terminology, and it's a far bigger job than I can manage
at the moment. On the historical side I should say there is *one*
great development which leads to the idea of the autonomy of
the world. In theology it is first discernible in Lord Herbert
of Cherbury, with his assertion that reason is the sufficient instrument of religious knowledge. In ethics it first appears in Mon-

taigne and Bodin with their substitution of moral principles for the Ten Commandments. In politics, Machiavelli, who emancipates politics from the tutelage of morality, and founds the doctrine of "reasons of state." Later, and very differently, though like Machiavelli tending toward the autonomy of human society, comes Grotius, with his international law as the law of nature, a law which would still be valid, *etsi deus non daretur*. The process is completed in philosophy. On the one hand we have the deism of Descartes, who holds that the world is a mechanism which runs on its own without any intervention of God. On the other hand there is the pantheism of Spinoza, with its identification of God with nature. In the last resort Kant is a deist, Fichte and Hegel pantheists. All along the line there is a growing tendency to assert the autonomy of man and the world.

In natural science the process seems to start with Nicolas of Cusa and Giordano Bruno with their "heretical" doctrine of the infinity of space. The classical cosmos was finite, like the created world of the Middle Ages. An infinite universe, however it be conceived, is self-subsisting *etsi deus non daretur*. It is true that modern physics is not so sure as it was about the infinity of the universe, but it has not returned to the earlier conceptions of its finitude.

There is no longer any need for God as a working hypothesis, whether in morals, politics or science. Nor is there any need for such a God in religion or philosophy (Feuerbach). In the name of intellectual honesty these working hypotheses should be dropped or dispensed with as far as possible. A scientist or physician who seeks to provide edification is a hybrid.

At this point nervous souls start asking what room there is left for God now. And being ignorant of the answer they write off the whole development which has brought them to this pass. As I said in an earlier letter, various emergency exits have been devised to deal with this situation. To them must be added the *salto mortale* back to the Middle Ages, the fundamental principle of which however is heteronomy in the form of clericalism. But that is a counsel of despair, which can be purchased only at the cost of intellectual sincerity. It reminds one of the song:

It's a long way back to the land of childhood
But if only I knew the way!

There isn't any such way, at any rate not at the cost of deliberately abandoning our intellectual sincerity. The only way is that
of Matthew 18.3, i.e. through repentance, through *ultimate* honesty. And the only way to be honest is to recognize that we have
to live in the world *etsi deus non daretur*. And this is just what
we do see—before God! So our coming of age forces us to a true
recognition of our situation *vis-à-vis* God. God is teaching us that
we must live as men who can get along very well without him.
The God who is with us is the God who forsakes us (Mark 15.34).
The God who makes us live in this world without using him as a
working hypothesis is the God before whom we are ever standing.
Before God and with him we live without God. God allows himself to be edged out of the world and onto the cross. God is weak
and powerless in the world, and that is exactly the way, the only
way, in which he can be with us and help us. Matthew 8.17
makes it crystal-clear that it is not by his omnipotence that Christ
helps us, but by his weakness and suffering.

This is the decisive difference between Christianity and all
religions. Man's religiosity makes him look in his distress to the
power of God in the world; he uses God as a *Deus ex machina*.
The Bible, however, directs him to the powerlessness and suffering of God; only a suffering God can help. To this extent we may
say that the process we have described by which the world came
of age was an abandonment of a false conception of God, and
a clearing of the decks for the God of the Bible, who conquers
power and space in the world by his weakness. This must be the
starting point for our "worldly" interpretation.

July 18, 1944

. . . "Christians range themselves with God in his suffering;
that is what distinguishes them from the heathen." As Jesus asked
in Gethsemane, "Could ye not watch with me one hour?" That
is the exact opposite of what the religious man expects from God.

Man is challenged to participate in the sufferings of God at the hands of a godless world.

He must therefore plunge himself into the life of a godless world, without attempting to gloss over its ungodliness with a veneer of religion or trying to transfigure it. He must live a "worldly" life and so participate in the suffering of God. He *may* live a worldly life as one emancipated from all false religions and obligations. To be a Christian does not mean to be religious in a particular way, to cultivate some particular form of asceticism (as a sinner, a penitent or a saint), but to be a man. It is not some religious act which makes a Christian what he is, but participation in the suffering of God in the life of the world.

This is *metanoia*. It is not in the first instance bothering about one's own needs, problems, sins, and fears, but allowing oneself to be caught up in the way of Christ, into the Messianic event, and thus fulfilling Isaiah 53. Therefore, "believe in the Gospel," or in the words of St. John the Baptist, "Behold the lamb of God that taketh away the sin of the world." (By the way, Jeremias has recently suggested that in Aramaic the word for "lamb" could also mean "servant"—very appropriate, in view of Isaiah 53). This being caught up into the Messianic suffering of God in Jesus Christ takes a variety of forms in the New Testament. It appears in the call to discipleship, in Jesus' table fellowship with sinners, in conversions in the narrower sense of the word (e.g. Zacchaeus), in the act of the woman who was a sinner (Luke 7), an act which she performed without any specific confession of sin, in the healing of the sick (Matthew 8.17, see above), in Jesus' acceptance of the children. The shepherds, like the wise men from the east, stand at the crib, not as converted sinners, but because they were drawn to the crib by the star just as they were. The centurion of Capernaum (who does not make any confession of sin) is held up by Jesus as a model of faith (cf. Jairus). Jesus loves the rich young man. The eunuch (Acts 8), Cornelius (Acts 10) are anything but "existences over the abyss." Nathanael is an Israelite without guile (John 1.47). Finally, Joseph of Arimathaea and the women at the tomb. All that is common between them is their participation in the suffering of God in Christ. That is their faith. There is nothing of religious asceticism here. The religious act is always something partial, faith is always some-thing whole, an act involving the whole life. Jesus does not call men to a new religion, but to life. What is the nature of that life, that participation in the powerlessness of God in the world? More about that next time, I hope.

Just one more point for today. When we speak of God in a nonreligious way, we must not gloss over the ungodliness of the world, but expose it in a new light. Now that it has come of age, the world is more godless, and perhaps it is for that very reason nearer to God than ever before.

July 21, 1944[3]

During the last year or so I have come to appreciate the "worldliness" of Christianity as never before. The Christian is not a *homo religiosus*, but a man, pure and simple, just as Jesus was a man, compared with John the Baptist anyhow. I don't mean the shallow this-worldliness of the enlightened, of the busy, the comfortable or the lascivious. It's something much more pro-found than that, something in which the knowledge of death and resurrection is ever-present. I believe Luther lived a this-worldly life in this sense. I remember talking to a young French pastor at A. thirteen years ago. We were discussing what our real pur-pose was in life. He said he would like to become a saint. I think it is quite likely he did become one. At the time I was very much impressed, though I disagreed with him, and said I should prefer to have faith, or words to that effect. For a long time I did not realize how far we were apart. I thought I could acquire faith by trying to live a holy life, or something like it. It was in this phase that I wrote *The Cost of Discipleship*. Today I can see the dangers of this book, though I am prepared to stand by what I wrote.

Later I discovered and am still discovering up to this very moment that it is only by living completely in this world that one learns to believe. One must abandon every attempt to make something of oneself, whether it be a saint, a converted sinner,

[3] Written after the news of the failure of the attempt to assassinate Hitler on the 20th July.

a churchman (the priestly type, so called!), a righteous man or an unrighteous one, a sick man or a healthy one. This is what I mean by worldliness—taking life in one's stride, with all its duties and problems, its successes and failures, its experiences and helplessness. It is in such a life that we throw ourselves utterly in the arms of God and participate in his sufferings in the world and watch with Christ in Gethsemane. That is faith, that is *metanoia*, and that is what makes a man and a Christian (cf. Jeremiah 45). How can success make us arrogant or failure lead us astray, when we participate in the sufferings of God by living in this world? . . .

OUTLINE FOR A BOOK[4]

I should like to write a book not more than a hundred pages long, and with three chapters.
　1. A Stocktaking of Christianity.
　2. The Real Meaning of the Christian Faith.
　3. Conclusions.

Chapter 1 to deal with:
　(*a*) The coming of age of humanity (along the lines already suggested). The insuring of life against accident, ill fortune. If elimination of danger impossible, at least its minimization. Insurance (which although it thrives upon accidents, seeks to mitigate their effects) a Western phenomenon. The goal, to be independent of nature. Nature formerly conquered by spiritual means, with us by technical organization of various kinds. Our immediate environment not nature, as formerly, but organization. But this immunity produces a new crop of dangers, i.e. the very organization.

[4] This was enclosed with Bonhoeffer's letter of August 3, 1944. In the three letters that followed in the same month—the last he was to write except two to his parents—he referred to the fact that he was at work on this book. His final words on the subject are from the last letter to Bethge, August 23: "I am often shocked at the things I am saying, especially in the first part, which is mainly critical. I shall be glad when I get to the more positive part. But the whole subject has never been properly thrashed out, so it sounds very undigested. However, it can't be printed at present anyhow, and it will doubtless improve with waiting."—Ed.

Consequently there is a need for spiritual vitality. What protection is there against the danger of organization? Man is once more faced with the problem of himself. He can cope with every danger except the danger of human nature itself. In the last resort it all turns upon man.

(*b*) The decay of religion in a world that has come of age. "God" as a working hypothesis, as a stopgap for our embarrassments, now superfluous (as already intimated).

(*c*) The Protestant Church. Pietism as the last attempt to maintain evangelical Christianity as a religion. Lutheran orthodoxy—the attempt to rescue the Church as an institution for salvation. The Confessing Church and the theology of revelation. A δὸς μοὶ ποῦ στῶ over against the world, involving a "factual" interest in Christianity. Art and science seeking for a foundation. The over-all achievement of the Confessing Church: championing ecclesiastical interests, but little personal faith in Jesus Christ. "Jesus" disappearing from sight. Sociologically, no effect on the masses—interest confined to the upper and lower middle classes. Incubus of traditional vocabulary, difficult to understand. The decisive factor: the Church on the defensive. Unwillingness to take risks in the service of humanity.

(*d*) Public morals—as evidenced by sexual behavior.

Chapter 2

(*a*) "Worldliness" and God.

(*b*) What do we mean by "God"? Not in the first place an abstract belief in his omnipotence, etc. That is not a genuine experience of God, but a partial extension of the world. Encounter with Jesus Christ, implying a complete orientation of human being in the experience of Jesus as one whose only concern is for others. This concern of Jesus for others the experience of transcendence. This freedom from self, maintained to the point of death, the sole ground of his omnipotence, ominiscience and ubiquity. Faith is participation in this Being of Jesus (incarnation, cross and resurrection). Our relation to God not a religious relationship to a supreme Being, absolute in power and goodness, which is a spurious conception of transcendence, but a new life for others, through participation in the Being of God. The transcendence consists not in tasks beyond our scope and power, but in the nearest thing[5] to hand. God in human form, not, as in other religions, in animal form—the monstrous, chaotic, remote and terrifying—nor yet in abstract form—the absolute, metaphysical, infinite, etc.—nor yet in the Greek divine-human of autonomous man, but man existing for others, and hence the Crucified. A life based on the transcendent.

(c) This is the starting point for the reinterpretation of biblical terminology. (Creation, fall, atonement, repentance, faith, the new life, the last things.)

(d) *Cultus.* (Details to follow later, in particular on cultus and religion.)

(e) What do we really believe? I mean, believe in such a way as to stake our whole lives upon it? The problem of the Apostles' Creed? "What must I believe?" the wrong question. Antiquated controversies, especially those between the different confessions. The Lutheran *versus* Reformed, and to some extent, the Catholic *versus* Protestant controversy. These divisions may at any time be revived with passion, but they no longer carry real conviction. Impossible to prove this, but necessary to take the bull by the horns. All we can prove is that the faith of the Bible and Christianity does not stand or fall by these issues. Barth and the Confessing Church have encouraged us to entrench ourselves behind the "faith of the Church," and evade the honest question, What is our real and personal belief? Hence lack of fresh air, even in the Confessing Church. To say "It's the Church's faith, not mine" can be a clericalist subterfuge, and outsiders always regard it as such. Much the same applies to the suggestion of the dialectical theologians that we have no control over our faith, and so it is impossible for us to say what we do believe. There may be a place for such considerations, but they do not release us from the duty of being honest with ourselves. We cannot, like the Catholics, identify ourselves *tout court* with the Church. (This incidentally explains the popular complaint about Catholic insincerity.) Well then, what do we really believe? Answer, see (b), (c) and (d).

---

[5] *Nächste.* Perhaps better translated "nearest person."—Ed.

Chapter 3
Consequences

The Church is her true self only when she exists for humanity. As a fresh start she should give away all her endowments to the poor and needy. The clergy should live solely on the free-will offerings of their congregations, or possibly engage in some secular calling. She must take her part in the social life of the world, not lording it over men, but helping and serving them. She must tell men, whatever their calling, what it means to live in Christ, to exist for others. And in particular, our own Church will have to take a strong line with the blasphemies of *hybris*, power-worship, envy and humbug, for these are the roots of evil. She will have to speak of moderation, purity, confidence, loyalty, steadfastness, patience, discipline, humility, content and modesty. She must not underestimate the importance of human example, which has its origin in the humanity of Jesus, and which is so important in the teaching of St. Paul. It is not abstract argument, but concrete example which gives her word emphasis and power. I hope to take up later this subject of example, and its place in the New Testament. It is something we have well-nigh forgotten. Further: the question of revising the creeds (the Apostles' Creed). Revision of Christian apologetics. Reform of the training for the ministry and the pattern of clerical life.

All this is very crude and sketchy, but there are certain things I want to say simply and clearly, things which we so often prefer to ignore. Whether I shall succeed or not is another matter, and I shall certainly find it difficult without your help. But I hope in this way to do something for the sake of the Church of the future.

John Arthur Thomas Robinson

[b. 1919]

ARTHUR W. ROBINSON was born in an Anglican vicarage in 1856,
At the age of sixty he became residentiary canon of Canterbury
Cathedral. Two years later he married the daughter of his late
predecessor. Their first child was named John. In the nine years
before the elderly canon died, young John thrived in the liberal
environment of the cathedral close. These were the days of William Temple, and the Robinson household was in accord with it.
Canon Robinson was familiar with the writings of Strauss, Renan,
Harnack and the Oxford Hegelians, and it was with revolutionary
enthusiasm that he greeted the publication of William James' *The
Varieties of Religious Experience*. The scope of his interests is
suggested by some of the books he wrote—*The Trend of Thought
in Contemporary Philosophy*, *The Christ of the Gospels* and *The
New Learning and the Old Faith*.

 After his father's death it was his mother who provided John
Robinson with "a breadth and a depth and a largeness of spirit
to which I owe more than I know or can say."[1] Two dominant
influences were Phillips Brooks and the founder of Christian
socialism, Frederick Denison Maurice. When he went away to
school, first at Marlborough College and then at Cambridge, he
first studied the Classics, then moved toward the philosophy of
religion, warming to the religious existentialism of Kierkegaard,
Berdyaev and Buber. He spent the war years at Cambridge,

---

[1] Quoted in Richard P. McBrien, *The Church in the Thought of Bishop John
Robinson* (London: SCM Press, 1966), p. 5. From a sermon, "Ascendancy,"
Andover Newton Quarterly, n.s. 5, 1964.

receiving his B.A. in 1942 with a first in theology, his M.A. in 1945, when he entered the ministry, and his Ph.D. in 1946. It was then that he first read Karl Barth and Thomas Aquinas, and found in Emil Brunner's *The Divine-Human Encounter* a Christian counterpart of Buber's philosophy, which formed the basis of his doctoral dissertation.

It was under the postwar Labor government that Robinson served in his first pastorate, St. Matthew's Church in the industrial parish of Moorfields, in Bristol. The impress of this encounter is evident in his books, especially *The Body* (1952), *On Being the Church in the World* (1960) and *The New Reformation?* (1965). His concern for social issues earned him the soubriquet "Bolshie Bishop" when he was appointed suffragan bishop of Woolwich eleven years after his curacy at St. Matthew's.[2] During those years, he embarked on a distinguished academic career, first as chaplain and lecturer at Wells Theological College in his ancestral shire of Somerset. It was here that he became interested in the personalist writings of John MacMurray and H. H. Farmer, and it was here that he explored the "house church" and other renewal movements.[3]

In 1951, after three years at Wells, Robinson became dean of the chapel at Clare College, Cambridge. His chief preoccupation as a lecturer was with New Testament studies. It was in this connection that he encountered Bultmann's *Theology of the New Testament* when it appeared in English in 1952 and 1955, and that he gained an international reputation. He was chosen as one of the translators of *The New English Bible* and served on its New Testament Panel. He visited the United States in 1955 and 1958, lecturing respectively at Harvard and at Union Theological Seminary in Richmond, Va.

Just as he was embarked on a major study of the sources and history of the Johannine writings, he was called to the episcopate. He would be suffragan bishop under Mervyn Stockwood, his

[2] Thus Hugh Montefiore in his *Observer* review of *The New Reformation?*: "A bolshie bishop is so rare that he cannot go unnoticed, and Dr. Robinson is a twentieth-century Lollard airing truths without which the Church must soon suffocate."

[3] See *On Being the Church in the World* (Philadelphia: Westminster, 1962), pp. 83–95.

former vicar at St. Matthew's and now Bishop of Southwark. After five months' deliberation he accepted and in 1959 moved to the old cathedral in Blackheath, southeast London.

Robinson's book, *Honest to God*, was published in 1963, kicked off with a full-page *Observer* article titled "Our Image of God Must Go." The book, which has subsequently sold over a million copies, draws together several strands of thought that had been in Robinson's mind for some time. He became acquainted with Tillich's *Systematic Theology*, I, in 1960, when preparing a series of lectures for the Southwark ordination course for industrial priest-workers, a program he developed; but as early as 1949 he had used Tillich's *The Shaking of the Foundations* in his lectures at Wells, and he had met Tillich during his 1955 visit to Harvard. He had read excerpts from Bonhoeffer's prison letters when they appeared in *The Ecumenical Review* in 1952. What triggered the writing of *Honest to God* was an illness that in 1962 curtailed his usual activities; it was then that he read the Bonhoeffer material in full for the first time and discovered a vital affinity with the latter's blend of churchmanship and worldliness.

Honest to God is not an original book; it is scarcely even an interpretation, but is rather an enthusiastic presentation of certain motifs from Bonhoeffer, Tillich and Bultmann, in that order of emphasis, and a showcase also for the creative thinking of a number of English writers such as John Wren-Lewis, Ronald Gregor Smith, Daniel Jenkins and Alec Vidler.

The book nevertheless placed its author at the center of a storm of controversy. Encouraged by the response, Robinson further developed the implications of *Honest to God* in a series of lectures given the following year in the United States, at Cornell and at Hartford Seminary, subsequently published as *The New Reformation?* (1965). Among the responses to *Honest to God* was a trenchant critique by Alasdair MacIntyre in *Encounter*, which suggested that both Tillich and Robinson were, in fact, atheists. No doubt because of this, Robinson was invited to speak at the opening of an Exhibition on Atheism, Eastern and Western, held in November 1964 at the University of Frankfurt. The following selection is this lecture. It is significant not so much for its originality, nor even for a consistent radicalism, but chiefly as a popularly oriented document of the on-going ferment in the church.

Can a Truly Contemporary Person Not Be an Atheist?

A bishop lecturing on atheism still strikes people, in England at any rate, as incongruous—though since I have freely been called "the atheist bishop" (as well as plenty of other things!) many will simply assume that I have now reached my proper level. Indeed, I have discovered at least one virtue in what I believe to be the unhappy German title of *Honest to God, Gott ist Anders* (God is Different). A friend of mine found that he was able to take as many copies as he liked to East Germany— they thought it was atheistic propaganda!

In fact I want to treat the question of atheism as a very serious one for those of us who would call ourselves Christians. So I have deliberately posed it, for myself as well as for you, in the form: "Can a truly contemporary person *not* be an atheist?" For I believe there is an important sense in which a person who is fully a man of our times *must*—or, at any rate, *may*—be an atheist before he can be a Christian. That is to say, there is so much in the atheist's case which is true that for many people today the only Christian faith which can be valid *for them* is one that takes over *post mortem dei*, after the death of God as "God" has traditionally been understood. I put this strongly—and can afford to put it strongly—as I shall insist equally strongly on the faith. But it is a faith which I suspect for increasing numbers of our contemporaries will only be possible through, and out the other side of, the atheist critique. The Christian should therefore take atheism seriously, not only so that he may be able to "answer" it, but so that he himself may still be able to be a believer in the mid-twentieth century.

With this in mind, I would ask you to expose yourselves to the three thrusts of modern atheism. These are not so much three types of atheism—each is present, in varying degree, in any representative type—so much as three motives which have impelled men, particularly over the past hundred years, to question the God of their upbringing and ours. They may be represented by three summary statements: 1. God is intellectually superfluous; 2. God is emotionally dispensable; 3. God is morally intolerable. Let us consider each of them in turn.

1. GOD IS INTELLECTUALLY SUPERFLUOUS

"I have no need of that hypothesis": so Laplace, the great astronomer, replied to Napoleon, when asked where God fitted into his system. Within the terms of an astronomical system, he was clearly correct. To bring in God to fill the gaps in our science or to deal with life at the point at which things get beyond human explanation or control is intellectual laziness or practical superstition. And yet, ever since the scientific and technological revolution which created our modern world, the defence of Christianity has in fact been bound up with staving off the advance of secularization, whose effect is precisely to close the gaps in the circle of explanation and control. Bonhoeffer put it accurately enough in the well-known passage in his *Letters*:

> Man has learned to cope with all questions of importance without recourse to God as a working hypothesis. In questions concerning science, art, and even ethics, this has become an understood thing which one scarcely dares to tilt at any more. But for the last hundred years or so it has become increasingly true of religious questions also: it is becoming evident that everything gets along without "God," and just as well as before. As in the scientific field, so in human affairs generally, what we call "God" is being more and more edged out of life, losing more and more ground. . . .
>
> Christian apologetic has taken the most varying forms of opposition to this self-assurance. Efforts are made to prove to a world thus come of age that it cannot live without the tutelage of "God." Even though there has been a surrender on all secular problems, there still remain the so-called ultimate questions—death, guilt—on which only "God" can furnish an answer, and

which are the reason why God and the Church and the pastor are needed. . . . But what if one day they no longer exist as such, if they too can be answered without "God"?[1]

One has only to raise this question to recognize the threat that most churchmen instinctively feel and the vested interest which we still have in the "God of the gaps." Indeed, when we hear it from the atheist, we take it as the attack for which it is clearly intended. Here, for instance, is Sir Julian Huxley:

> The god hypothesis is no longer of any pragmatic value for the interpretation or comprehension of nature, and indeed often stands in the way of better and truer interpretation. . . .
> It will soon be as impossible for an intelligent, educated man or woman to believe in a god as it is now to believe that the earth is flat, that flies can be spontaneously generated, that disease is a divine punishment, or that death is always due to witchcraft.[2]

God is an x in the equation whom we cannot get on without, a cause, controller or designer whom we are bound to posit or allow room for—this hypothesis seems to men today more and more superfluous. There is nothing indeed that *disproves* it. It is simply, in the words of Anthony Flew, the linguistic philosopher, being "killed by inches"; it is dying "the death of a thousand qualifications." And he vividly illustrates how this happens in the parable[3] from which Paul van Buren starts his *Secular Meaning of the Gospel*:

> Once upon a time two explorers came upon a clearing in the jungle. In the clearing were growing many flowers and many weeds. One explorer says, "Some gardener must tend this plot." The other disagrees. "There is no gardener." So they pitch their tents and set a watch. No gardener is ever seen. "But perhaps he is an invisible gardener." So they set up a barbed-wire fence. They electrify it. They patrol it with bloodhounds. . . . But no

[1] *Letters and Papers from Prison*, pp. 145–146.
[2] *Religion without Revelation*, 2d ed. (London: Max Parrish, 1957), pp. 58, 62.
[3] *New Essays in Philosophical Theology*, ed. A. G. N. Flew and A. C. Mac-Intyre (London: SCM Press; and New York: Macmillan, 1955), pp. 96–7.

shrieks ever suggest that some intruder has received a shock. No movement of the wire ever betrays an invisible climber. The bloodhounds never give cry. Yet still the Believer is not convinced. "But there is a gardener, invisible, intangible, insensible to electric shocks, a gardener who has no scent and makes no sound, a gardener who comes secretly to look after the garden which he loves." At last the Skeptic despairs, "But what is left of your original assertion? Just how does what you call an invisible, intangible, eternally elusive gardener differ from an imaginary gardener or even from no gardener at all?"[4]

And what is true at the level of explanation is equally true at the level of control. Neither to account for sickness nor to deal with it does it occur to men today to bring in "God." Or if it does occur to them, it is when they have reached the end of their tether and "turn to prayer." But this simply confirms the judgment of Werner Pelz that "When we use the word 'God' we are talking about something which no longer connects with anything in most people's life, except with whatever happens to be left over when all the vital connections have been made."[5] Most of us today are practical atheists. The "god-hypothesis" is as irrelevant for running an economy or coping with the population explosion as it was for Laplace's system. As a factor you must take into account in the practical business of living, God is "out"— and no amount of religious manipulation can force him back in. He is peripheral, redundant, incredible—and therefore *as God* displaced: in Julian Huxley's words, "not a ruler, but the last fading smile of a cosmic Cheshire Cat."[6]

I am very far from saying this is the whole truth or that all the atheist's arguments on this front, or any other, are valid (many of them reflect a very superficial or crudely tendentious understanding even of the traditional theology). What I am urging is that we allow ourselves to feel the full force of this attack rather than spend our time looking for yet another hole in the wire fence.

[4] Paul M. van Buren, *The Secular Meaning of the Gospel* (New York: Macmillan, 1963), p. 3.
[5] *Prism*, April 1963, p. 23.
[6] *Op. cit.*, p. 58.

2. GOD IS EMOTIONALLY DISPENSABLE

The reference earlier to Bonhoeffer's theme of man come of age shows the close connection. Man is discovering that he no longer *needs* God or religion. He finds he can stand on his own feet without having to refer constantly to Daddy in the background or to run to Mummy's apronstrings.

According to this line of attack religion is a prop or a sop. It is not merely something incredible and superfluous: it is a dangerous illusion which can prevent men facing reality and shouldering responsibility. This lies at the heart of the Freudian critique of religion as the universal neurosis or the Marxist attack on it as "the opium of the people." God and the gods are the projection of men's fears, insecurities and longings. They act as a debilitating crutch which men must have the courage to discard if they are to grow up and shake off the sense of helplessness which religion both induces and sanctions.

The call of atheism here is to man to cut the strings, to move out of the shadow of the Father figure, to cease treating God as a peg, or a refuge, or a compensation for miseries which he should be fighting. Secularization means that man must accept responsibility for his own destiny, neither trying to blame it on the gods nor expecting some providence to relieve him of it or see him through.

Again I believe we must recognize the essential truth of this attack. Whatever as Christians we may wish to add or come back with, we should not be caught trying to defend this God or save him from death by artificial respiration. This was the strength of Bonhoeffer's courageous acceptance of the edging out of the "God of religion": unless a man is prepared to be "forsaken" by that God, he cannot find what Jesus is showing us on the Cross. But are we prepared to let that God go? In varying degrees we all *need* religion, and nowhere more than here is the thrust of atheism seen as a threat. The tearing down of the traditional structure in which "the good Lord provides" and surrounds the whole of life with the protective comfort of the womb is viewed as an act of sacrilege which must be withstood, if not for our own sake, at any rate for the sake of the weaker brethren to whose pastoral care we hasten. Or, as an alternative line of defense, we seek to dismiss those who try, as someone has put it, to "destroy my grandmother's religion with my grandfather's science." But if we are honest, our "grandmother's religion" probably plays a much larger role in our conscious and unconscious life than we care to admit.

Consider, for instance, the quite central belief in Providence. The trust that in and through and despite everything there meets one a love, stronger than death, from which nothing can separate us is fundamental to the Christian confidence. But I am sure there are some forms of belief in providence which merely pander to emotional immaturity. And these are the forms which secretly retain God in the gaps of our ignorance or fears, or which see him as a celestial manipulator rearranging, interrupting, or taking over from, the forces which would otherwise be at work. And when these forces are those of human responsibility their "providential overruling" can quickly lead to the debilitation, the superstition, and even the fatalism, of which the atheists accuse the religious.

Each time I go to London Airport I am met by a large notice, greeting me with the assurance: "BOAC takes good care of you." What are we to make of this declaration of secular providence? If it fails, whom are we to blame—BOAC or God? When first I flew, I used to indulge in additional "cover" for those tense thirty seconds of takeoff as one waits to see whether the plane will make it and leave the ground. Did my prayer in the gap—when somehow a little supernatural "lift" would always be welcome—do credit to my trust in God? I think not. I suspect that this is where a Christian *ought* to be a practical atheist—and trust the pilot. If this is the sort of God he believes in—and logically he should only believe in him if he is a God who *does* take over—then the protest of the atheist is valid. Men need to be weaned, however painfully, from refusal to accept the burden of responsibility. A God who relieves them of this requires killing.

This clamor for the death of a God who keeps men languid and dispossessed, associated with Feuerbach before Marx, Engels and Freud developed it in their different ways, leads directly into the even more strident protest which expresses itself in the third statement.

3. GOD IS MORALLY INTOLERABLE

This reverses Voltaire's dictum that "If God did not exist, we should have to invent him." It says rather, "If God did exist, we should have to abolish him." This is the tradition that derives again from Feuerbach, and runs through Bakunin, Proudhon and Nietzsche to Camus and Sartre. It represents the real quick of twentieth-century atheism, in contrast with its dying nerves—if one may dare to thus speak of Marxism, as I think one can, as somewhat dated. It is what Jacques Maritain has called "positive atheism."[7] It centers in the determination that God must *die* if man is to *live*. It is not content with accepting the negative absence of God and carrying on as though everything remained the same. It is concerned positively in living in "a world without God"—creating the justice and the meaning and the freedom which God, the great bloodsucker, has drained away.

But we should be careful not to state it in too emotive language. It would be easy to discredit this whole protest as the titanism of a Nietzsche or the outburst of a few intellectuals. But if this was once true, it is certainly true no longer. Camus spoke for an entire emerging generation. There is a dispassionate quality about modern atheism, of a piece with our whole urban-secular civilization. It is not vindictive or despairing, and it is noticeably losing its overtones of an anti-religion. A speaker can deliberately ask to be introduced on the television, as happened in my presence, as an "atheist" rather than an "agnostic" without any sense of defiance. And this I believe is a healthy development. For in "the secular city" constructive debate will only become possible if atheism, like Christianity, can discover what it means to be "religionless," and the various competing "ologies" and "isms" are "desacralized."

This is not in the least to suggest that this particular form of

[7] "The Meaning of Contemporary Atheism," *The Listener*, March 9, 1950.

atheism, above all, should lapse into indifferentism. It has a moral nerve which must not be cut, if it is to continue to purge and purify. For it draws its strength from the seriousness with which it takes the problem of evil. A God who "causes" or "allows" the suffering of a single child is morally intolerable. So the debate ranges, back and forth, in some of the great dialogues of modern literature—in Dostoevsky's *Brothers Karamazov*, in Camus's *The Plague* and, most recently, in Peter de Vries's *The Blood of the Lamb*[8] (describing the agony of a father watching his girl die of leukemia). But, of course, this is no intellectuals' debate. It is the root of atheism in most ordinary people, and today it is openly asserted even by the young. Here, for instance, is a girl of nineteen interviewed in the *Daily Mirror*:

> "Do you believe in God?"
>
> "No. I used to, but not now. I don't see how there can be a benevolent God. There are too many tragedies—personal and in the world. . . . RELIGION IS DISGUSTING."[9]

Religion is disgusting. God does not solve the problem of suffering: he only magnifies it. To push off evil onto God simply makes him into a Devil—and in any case represents a cowardly evasion. Men must carry the can and refuse the temptation to dissociation or transference.

I believe that this is a profoundly moral response, and one that must be taken with the utmost seriousness. Any glib notion of a God who "causes" cancer or "sends" the streptococcus *is* a blasphemy. Most traditional theodicy, so far from justifying the ways of God to man, has the effect of strengthening atheism. "Whatever your sickness is," the priest is instructed to say in the seventeenth-century Anglican Book of Common Prayer, "know certainly that it is God's visitation." Who could speak like that today? Atheism has done its purifying work. For there is nothing that provokes our generation to doubt or blasphemy more than the idea of a Being who sends such events into the lives of individuals. One of the liberating effects of secularization is that *this* idea of divine

[8] Boston: Little, Brown and Co.; and London: Gollancz, 1961.
[9] In a brilliant piece of reporting by Marjorie Proops, "For These Girls, It's All Happening," March 5, 1964.

causation has at any rate been discredited. People rightly look for natural rather than supernatural causes. *But they still assume that Christians teach otherwise*—and their God is dismissed with them with indignation and disgust.

AFTER THE DEATH OF GOD

Can a truly contemporary person *not* be an atheist? It is a very real question. Not all people will feel the force of each of these thrusts. Their God may survive any or indeed all of them. I would certainly not want to suggest that a contemporary Christian *must* go through the mill of first being an atheist. But I firmly believe that he *may*, and that increasingly many will.

But *post mortem dei*, what? Is, in fact, faith possible out the other side? I believe that it is, and that not merely despite the death of God but even because of it. For this, after all, is no new situation for the people of God. The faith of Abraham, the father of faith, was born, as St. Paul reminds us, out of "contemplating his own body, now as good as dead, and the deadness of Sarah's womb."[10] The faith of Job was possible to him only after all that he trusted in had first been removed. Even Jesus himself had to go through the process of the death of God—of the One who allowed it all to happen, "with a million angels watching, and they never move a wing."[11] But, above all, Christianity itself was "born in the grave" (some of you may know the remarkable little sermon of that title in Tillich's *Shaking of the Foundations*[12]): it could only come into being at all *post mortem dei*. And for each one of us in some degree the Resurrection can only happen after the death of God. Though it looks as if everything is taken away—even the body of the Lord—yet this is not the destruction of Christianity but its liberation.

For—with all metaphysical security shattered, with even the word "God" of doubtful currency, with no theodicy of our own that we can establish[13]—we find that we still cannot get shot of

[10] Romans 4.17–25.
[11] From *Friday Morning*, in 9 *Carols or Ballads* by Sydney Carter. (Clarion Photographic Services Ltd., London, 1964).
[12] New York: Scribner, 1948; and London: SCM Press, 1949, pp. 164–168.
[13] Romans 10.3.

God: after his death he is disturbingly alive. No one that I know has wrestled through this problem more compellingly in our day than William Hamilton of Colgate Rochester Divinity School, New York. His *New Essence of Christianity* seeks in an age of theological "reduction" to lay claim to those few things that are certain, and in a chapter called "Belief in a Time of the Death of God" he writes:

> In one sense God seems to have withdrawn from the world and its sufferings, and this leads us to accuse him of either irrelevance or cruelty. But in another sense, he is experienced as a pressure and a wounding from which we would love to be free. For many of us who call ourselves Christians, therefore, believing in the time of the "death of God" means that he is there when we do not want him, in ways we do not want him, and he is not there when we do want him.[14]

Is not the situation of many of us today that we feel we *must* be atheists, and yet we *cannot* be atheists? God as we have been led to posit him *is* intellectually superfluous, *is* emotionally dispensable, *is* morally intolerable—and yet, in grace and demand, he *will not* let us go. The hound of heaven still dogs us, the "beyond in our midst" still encounters us, when all the images, all the projections, even all the words for God have been broken.

Can a truly contemporary person *not* be an atheist? In one sense, he can hardly fail to be. There is no going back to the presecular view of the world, where God is always "there" to be brought in, run to, or blamed. Yet, in another sense, he may find that he *cannot* be an atheist, however much he would like to be. For on the Emmaus road, on the way back from the tomb, the risen Christ comes up with him and he knows himself constrained.

What then, in the last analysis, remains the difference between the atheist and the one who cannot finally rest in that name? In *Honest to God* I wrote:[15]

---

[14] William Hamilton, *The New Essence of Christianity* (New York: Association Press, 1961), p. 69.
[15] John A. T. Robinson, *Honest to God* (Philadelphia: Westminster Press, 1963), pp. 47–48.

So conditioned for us is the word "God" by association with a Being out there [with all, in other words, that the anti-theist finds superfluous, dispensable or intolerable] that Tillich warns us . . . "You must forget everything traditional you have learned about God, perhaps even that word itself."[16] Indeed, the line between those who believe in God and those who do not bears little relation to their profession of the existence or non-existence of such a Being. It is a question, rather, of their openness to the holy, the sacred, in the unfathomable depths of even the most secular relationship. As Martin Buber puts it of the person who professedly denies God, "When he, too, who abhors the name, and believes himself to be godless, gives his whole being to addressing the Thou of his life, as a Thou that cannot be limited by another, he addresses God."[17]

There, I suggest, lies the clue to the real difference. Let me use a familiar analogy. In dealing with other people it is possible for us to treat them simply as things—to use them, control them, manipulate them. This is what John Macmurray calls the *instrumental* relationship.[18] Or, if for no other reason than that we soon discover they are not wholly amenable to such treatment, we can relate ourselves to them in what he calls the *functional* relationship, of cooperation with them. This is the most common relation we have with others, in which we treat them often as means to an end but never merely as means. But, thirdly, we can give ourselves to them in pure *personal* relationship, responding to them in love and trust for their own sakes. And ultimately it is only in this relationship that we can know them—and we ourselves be known—*as persons*.

To transfer this analogy to the universe, to life as a whole, we can respond to it in a purely instrumental, scientific relationship—at the level of its mathematical regularities. We can regard reality as ultimately nothing more than a collocation of atoms, and we can even try to run history as a piece of social engineering. But there are few purely mechanistic materialists today. Much more common are those whose ultimate frame of reference is a func-

16 *The Shaking of the Foundations*, p. 64.
17 *I and Thou*, tr. R. Gregor Smith (Edinburgh: T. & T. Clark; and New York: Scribner, 1937), p. 76.
18 In *Interpreting the Universe* (London: Faber and Faber, 1936).

tional one—humanists, whether dialectical, evolutionary or ideal-istic. And the atheist is the man who in his attitude to life stops there—for whom nothing finally is absolute or unconditional, for whom all is a means (though not merely a means).

The man who finds himself compelled to acknowledge the re-ality of *God*, whatever he may call him or however he may image him, is the man who, through the mathematical regularities and through the functional values, is met by the same grace and the same claim that he recognizes in the I-Thou relation with another person. It may come to him through nature, through the claims of artistic integrity or scientific truth, through the engagements of social justice or of personal communion. Yet always it comes with an overmastering givenness and demand such as no other thing or person has the power to convey or the right to require. Like the child Samuel in the Temple, confusing the call of God with the voice of Eli, he may think at first that it can simply be identified with or contained within the finite relationship by which it is mediated. He may not be able to tell what to make of it, he may find it profoundly disturbing, but he knows it in the end to be inescapable and unconditional. In this relationship, too, he discovers himself known and judged and accepted for what ultimately he is. He finds in it for himself the way, the truth and the life. And if he is a Christian, he recognizes and acknowl-edges this grace and claim supremely in the person of Jesus Christ, the definition at one and the same time of a genuinely human existence and of this intangible, ineffable reality of "God." He agrees, passionately, with the atheist that such a reality can-not be *used* or *needed*. A God like that *is* superfluous, dispensa-ble, intolerable. In fact it is *no God*. And then, when that God is dead, the Lord appears.

The Lord appears—not as one who is needed, nor as one who intrudes, forcing men's freedom or curtailing their responsibility, but as one who "makes as though he would go further."[19] Like the disciples on the road to Emmaus, we find ourselves faced with the bewildering double adjustment of learning at one and the same time to live in a world without God and in a world with God. It is a new situation, a post-resurrection world, in

[19] Luke 24.28.

which the old *is* dead. There is no question of introducing that God again by the back door or of returning to the *status quo ante*. Yet, despite the irreversibility of that change, there is the constraint of the other reality with which to come to terms. How, then, does it stand in relation to three thrusts we examined before?

In the first place, God remains intellectually superfluous, in the sense that he does not need to be "brought in." There is no "place" for him in the system—or for that matter on its edge. The ring has been closed in which before an opening was left for God. Secularization must be gladly accepted—and no attempt made to find another hole in the fence or to reinstate him outside it.

There is a parallel here, to return to our previous analogy, with attempts to "locate" the element of the distinctively personal— the free, spiritual reality of "I" and "Thou"—in our description of human behavior. Clearly this does not depend on establishing gaps in the chemistry or the psychology. Efforts to secure a place for freedom and the spirit in that way are foredoomed. Nor is there any more hope in representing it as external to a closed system, which a free spirit, depicted as a sort of supernatural self, controls and directs from the outside—though such a model has been a common presupposition both in psychology and theology. To know a man as a person is not to posit another invisible factor between or beyond the regularities which the scientist investigates. It is to respond to a total reality which engages one in, through and under the regularities, which in no way denies them and yet is related to them like another dimension.

Similarly with God. As a factor introduced to make the system work he is redundant. In that sense it is possible to answer every question without God—even the ones that before were thought to admit only of a religious solution. And at the level of control things get along, for good or for ill, just as well without him. It is not necessary to bring him in.

But in another sense it is not possible to leave him out—any more than it is possible to run an economy or cope with the population explosion without in the last analysis treating persons as persons, without reckoning with the dimension of the "Thou." God is a reality of life whom one cannot ultimately evade.

Huxley, quite legitimately, may not need him as a hypothesis, nor Flew be able to trap him in his mesh. Like the scientist or philosopher who looks in vain for the "Thou" in the person he is analyzing without addressing, the searcher for God finds himself in the position of Job:

> Behold, I go forward, but he is not there;
> and backward, but I cannot perceive him;
> on the left hand I seek him, but I cannot behold him;
> I turn to the right hand, but I cannot see him.[20]

But then he adds, aware of the presence by which all the while he is being explored:

> But he knows the way that I take.

The one who is superfluous as a hypothesis becomes all too present as a subject in encounter.

Then, secondly, God continues to be emotionally dispensable. The returning Lord does not come as compensation for the gap left by the God of the gaps. There is no solace to restore the old relationships. The crutches are broken, and it remains "good for you that I go away."[21] Nothing relieves of responsibility those who have to live by the Spirit.

Yet man come of age is still called to be a son. It is a mark of our religious immaturity that the "Father" image inextricably suggests emotional dependence, if not domination. The son never seems to grow up. Yet in fact the New Testament "sonship" is a figure for freedom and stands precisely for man who has passed out of his minority and come of age.[22] The Christian faith, so far from seeking to keep men in strings, calls them to maturity, not the maturity of the adolescent revolting *against* a father, but of the "full-grown man" entering into the responsible freedom of the son and heir.

There is nothing in the God of the New Testament—nor indeed in the God who said to the prophet, "Son of man, stand upon your feet and I will speak with you"[23]—which would keep men lan-

[20] Job 23.8–10.
[21] John 16.7.
[22] See especially John 8.31–8 and Galatians 4.1–7.
[23] Ezekiel 2.1.

guid or dispossessed. The call is to bear and to share the terrible freedom of love. And faith in the fatherly reality to which sonship is the response is not a belief in anything that undercuts this. Speaking of a mature trust in providence, Tillich writes:

> The man who believes in providence does not believe that a special divine activity will alter the conditions of finitude and estrangement. He believes, and asserts with the courage of faith, that no situation whatsoever can frustrate the fulfillment of his ultimate destiny, that nothing can separate him from the love of God which is in Jesus Christ.[24]

And again:

> Providence means that there is a creative and saving possibility implied in every situation, which cannot be destroyed by any event.[25]

The prayer that is immature is the prayer that cannot trust this, but resorts to reliance on physical or mental interference. True prayer is not for additional "cover" that, if the worst comes to the worst, the controls may be taken over by celestial manipulation. True prayer is prayer for the pilot, and by the pilot, that his responsibility may be heightened, not diminished, by trusting the love his life exists to serve and from which not even "the worst" can separate it.

This brings us, lastly, to the third charge, that God is morally intolerable. Again, it is a charge that stands. A Being who "sends" the worst into the lives of individuals or who stands aside to "permit" it is a God who must die. But that is precisely what the Christian faith proclaims happened at Calvary. The God who could have sent "twelve legions of angels" and did not is exposed as the God who failed even his Son. The obituary read by the atheist is valid, even if sometimes shrill.

Nothing in the Christian faith implies the rehabilitation of that God. Yet the Christian, as he looks back on the Cross from the other side of the Resurrection, sees not a world without God at its borders but a world with God at its center. What it means

[24] *Systematic Theology*, I, p. 296.
[25] *The Shaking of the Foundations*, p. 106.

to believe in love as the final reality is to be discerned not in the absentee controller who allows the suffering but in the crucified transfiguring figure who bears it. The New Testament "answer" to the problem of evil is given not majestically out of the whirlwind[26] but agonizingly out of the darkness. As Bonhoeffer saw, in that situation "only a suffering God can help."[27] The God of the Christian faith, who alone can be "our" God, can ultimately be revealed and responded to only as love which *takes* responsibility for evil—transformingly and victoriously.

For men to adjust to life in a world with that as its central reality is no intellectual exercise: it is, in Bonhoeffer's words again, to "range themselves with God in his suffering."[28] That is the test he saw distinguishing Christians from unbelievers. And even among professed unbelievers there may at the point of dereliction, where the choice of our ultimate allegiance stands forth most starkly, be many who find that they cannot rail.

"For Christians, heathens alike he hangeth dead."[29] Such is the reality Bonhoeffer recognized as the common presupposition of our age—replacing what he called "the religious premise." Atheists and Christians start there together. And on their walk from the tomb, sharing the disenchantment of other more facile hopes, the dialogue can begin.

[26] Job 38.1.
[27] *Letters and Papers from Prison*, p. 164.
[28] *Ibid.*, p. 166.
[29] From his last poem, "Christians and Unbelievers," *ibid.*, pp. 166–167.

William Hamilton

[b. 1924]

THE SON of an electrical engineer, William Hughes Hamilton Jr. was born in Evanston, near Chicago. At nineteen he left Oberlin College to serve as a gunnery officer on an LST in World War II, taking his B.A. in absentia after his discharge in 1946. Like many of his generation, after an exploratory year at Princeton's graduate school he enrolled at Union Theological Seminary in New York "to find out if he was a Christian." Here he earned his B.D. degree and was ordained a Baptist minister. Subsequent study led to a Ph.D. from the University of St. Andrews in Scotland, the land of his ancestors, and to an academic career at Colgate Rochester Divinity School.

Hamilton's first book, *The Christian Man* (1955), reflects the strong influence of Karl Barth and of Martin Luther, and he sees the "radical theology" that first emerged in his *The New Essence of Christianity* (1961) as a direct outgrowth, "a normal extension of neo-orthodoxy."[1] He describes Bonhoeffer as "an ordinary square sort of theologian, except for a few poems, a few letters, the fragment of a drama." He doubts that Bonhoeffer would have endorsed radical theology but believes that in appropriating the later prison letters "we legitimately misuse him."

Hamilton today still cherishes "large chunks" of Barth's pivotal study, *The Epistle to the Romans*, as well as Barth's *Church Dogmatics*, I/2 and IV/2. His interpretation of the "secular" Bonhoeffer is backed up by his own secular involvements, both in wartime and during a decade of television work while a professor of theology. Although the television programs on which he

---

[1] This and subsequent quotations, unless otherwise identified, are from personal correspondence.

worked were religious, the producers, directors and actors represented for him a "community of men who did not need God, men
come of age, for whom certain kinds of talk worked and for
whom certain kinds did not." Other important influences are
Dostoevsky and Camus, "the first living so horribly under the
pressure of the enemy God, the hound of heaven I had hoped
to make my peace with, the second living so cannily without
him."

Bonhoeffer raised the question of a Christianity without religion. In the process of thinking out the implications of this problem, the question of the disappearance or death of God became
pivotal to Hamilton. As the following selection shows, Hamilton
defers to Altizer in the explication of the death of God. For
Hamilton it is not the central issue but rather is one of three
themes characteristic of the radical movement, the others being
"obedience to Jesus" and "a new optimism."[2]

Like the Bultmann selection in this volume, Hamilton's is as
much a survey of other men's thought as it is an exposition of his
own. Radical theology, for Hamilton, is not likely to produce a
settled body of doctrine like Tillich's *Systematic Theology* or
Barth's *Church Dogmatics*. In his own writings one detects a fast-
paced process of development. The Bonhoefferian motif of "waiting" that concludes Hamilton's survey has already yielded, as he
indicates in a set of unpublished *Questions and Answers on the
Radical Theology*, to "an increased confidence in those nontheistic
forms of explanation of man's experiences of moral obligation,
need of judgment, longing for healing or community that the arts
and sciences provide us with."

In these *Questions and Answers*, Hamilton makes it unmistakably clear that the God who has died is not only the "God of
religion or culture," but the God of faith, specifically Christian
faith. The death of God is, in one sense, simply an honest consequence of pressing demythologization beyond the limits set for
it by Bultmann. Yet this does not point to a flatly rationalistic
perspective. Modern man can and should accept the experience
of "wonder, awe and reverence," not explain it away. "For the

[2] William Hamilton, "The Shape of a Radical Theology," *The Christian
Century*, October 6, 1965, p. 1222.

radical Christian, Jesus' death is sacred in a godless sense: it bears the full meaning of Jesus' own life and work, and it shows the way man is to stand in his world."[3] One of the challenges facing the radical Christian is to find new images by which to interpret the dimension of mystery, tragedy and holiness. The image of God is no longer relevant here, but that of Jesus decidedly is. The death of God is therefore a necessary Christian event, stripping away what is unessential so that man may respond freely to Jesus.

Hamilton conceives his role as twofold—in addition to developing his own theological perspective, he sees himself not as the founder of a new cult but as the initiator of a new movement. It was Hamilton who brought together a diverse group of thinkers for the first conference on radical theology, a three-day affair held at the University of Michigan in October 1966. Among the new voices thus introduced there were Henry Malcolm, who is developing a new theology illumined by such twentieth-century minds as Freud, Marshall McLuhan and Herbert Marcuse and is much concerned with the liberation of man from repression; Maynard Kaufmann, who insists that our era is post-Christian, post-God, post-religious and requires a totally new outlook, "beyond Christianity"; and John A. Phillips, who seeks not only to demythologize but to "detheologize" Jesus Christ in the light of the death of God.[4] These are men we may expect to hear more from in the future—and it is one of Hamilton's purposes to keep them in dialogue with one another, through a proposed journal, further conferences and other means.

What happens next in the open-ended process remains to be seen. Hamilton sees, to the left, a Marxist or Freudian atheism; to the right, intensified dialogue with the "secular theology" of Harvey Cox and the "new Reformation" outlook of John A. T. Robinson; or a third way that will emphasize "the positive requirements for living as a Christian without God," exploring the meaning of loyalty to Jesus in the context of human community (an unacknowledged Buberian point) in contrast to divine sanctions. There is an inherently pragmatic and eclectic element in

[3] *Questions and Answers.*
[4] A volume containing the papers from this conference is in preparation.

Hamilton's thought; he does not disdain to embrace insights from Feuerbach, Tillich, Pasternak and others if they can contribute to the liberating result that justifies the "new optimism" of a Christianity without God. A note of humility, Hamilton would suggest, is in order. From Camus and others we know that belief in God is not indispensable to integrity or the good life. It remains for Christians to demonstrate, for their own sake, the vital relevance of Jesus in a world from which God has irretrievably vanished.

The Death-of-God Theology[1]

Complacencies of the peignoir, and late
Coffee and oranges in a sunny chair,
And the green freedom of a cockatoo
Upon a rug mingle to dissipate
The holy hush of ancient sacrifice.
She dreams a little, and she feels the dark
Encroachment of that old catastrophe. . . .

What is divinity if it can come
Only in silent shadows and in dreams?
Shall she not find in comforts of the sun,
In pungent fruit and bright, green wings, or else
In any balm of beauty of the earth,
Things to be cherished like the thought of heaven?
Divinity must live within herself. . . .
          —WALLACE STEVENS, "Sunday Morning"

We have been aware for some time that modern atheism has become a subject of special theological concern to Christians, but only recently has it moved so close to the center of theology and faith itself. The British publication of Bishop Robinson's *Honest to God* partly created and partly released forces that may well be

[1] From *The Christian Scholar*, Spring, 1965.—Ed.

coming together into a new theological movement in that country.[2] And there is an American counterpart to this British movement, though it goes back in time a bit before *Honest to God.* I am going to call this American movement the death-of-God theology. It is a movement, though until quite recently there was no communication between the participants. But they are beginning to talk to each other and to discover that there are a handful of people here and there who one day may all contribute to a common theological style. Right now, the American death-of-God movement seems to be more radical than the British "radicals," more radical on each of the three main points of *Honest to God—* God, ethics, and the church. To the death-of-God theologian, Robinson is far too confident about the possibility of God-language. To use Paul van Buren's terms, Robinson is perfectly right to reject objectified theism, but he is wrong to think that his nonobjectified theism is any more satisfactory. Van Buren would claim, I suspect, that modern philosophy has done away with both possibilities.

But unlike many American theologians, the death-of-God people do not patronize *Honest to God.* They take its publication as an important event in the life of the church, and they note particularly its enthusiastic reception by the laity as a sign that they may have a theological vocation in the church after all, in spite of the fact that their writing has up to now given more ecclesiastical offense than they expected. In any case, the purpose of this essay is not to study the British radicals but to describe this American death-of-God theological tradition and to ask under what condi-

[2] Ronald Gregor Smith's *The New Man* (1956) was perhaps the first piece of secular theology in the British tradition. In the debate over *Honest to God* the most significant representatives of the "radical theology" (as it is being called) come from a group of laymen which already includes scientists like John Wren Lewis and James Mark, and journalists like Monica Furlong and Christopher Driver. Mark's material in the Theological Colleges Department (SCM) brochure "The Death of the Church" is worth study.

The radical theology in Britain is well enough established that it has started to get patronized, and that from all quarters; the modern churchmen and high churchmen seem equally disturbed, as are the secularists who apparently, as in this country, like their theology orthodox and thus obviously irrelevant.

tions it might become part of the very lively theological discussion going on right now in this country.[3]

There are two important representatives of this movement that I would like to mention fairly briefly before I add my own notes and comments: Prof. Thomas J. J. Altizer of Emory and Prof. Paul van Buren of Temple.[4] Before we have a look at their work, a word about the phrase "death of God" is called for. What is meant by it? Altizer likes to say, for example, that the death of God is a historical event, that it has happened in our time, and that we should welcome, even will it, not shrink from it. But if

[3] In a recent series of lectures (entitled "Is God Dead?" and "God Is Not Dead") published in *The Voice* (Crozier Theological Seminary), Dr. Langdon Gilkey of the University of Chicago has made a provisional exposition and criticism of this theological position. Gilkey is in a kind of horrified sympathy with the death-of-God theology, and he has made a number of shrewd criticisms and raise some important questions. [An adaptation of these lectures appears in Langdon Gilkey, *The Relevance of God-Language* (Indianapolis: Bobbs-Merrill, 1967).—Ed.]

[4] In selecting these two writers, I am by no means suggesting that they are alone in their emphasis. Gabriel Vahanian of Syracuse has done some important work in his *The Death of God* and *Wait Without Idols*, in "Beyond the Death of God," *Dialog*, Autumn, 1962, and in "The Future of Christianity in a Post-Christian Era," *The Centennial Review*, Spring 1964. John Cobb of Claremont has an excellent descriptive article, by no means in sympathy with the movement, in "From Crisis Theology to the Post-Modern World," *The Centennial Review*, Spring 1964. Mention should also be made of the work of the New Testament scholars Robert Funk and Edward Hobbs; of the work of the Jewish scholar Richard L. Rubenstein, especially his excellent "Person and Myth in the Judaeo-Christian Encounter," *The Christian Scholar*, Winter, 1963. Rudolf Bultmann himself has written, not perhaps at his best, on this tradition in "Der Gottesgedanke und der moderne Mensch," *Zeitschrift für Theologie und Kirche*, December, 1963. [See page 250 of this anthology.—Ed.]

Altizer's position can best be studied in his book *Mircea Eliade and the Dialectic of the Sacred* (Westminster), and in a series of articles. The best of them is probably "America and the Future of Theology," which appears together with "Theology and the Death of God" in Altizer and Hamilton, *Radical Theology and the Death of God* (Indianapolis: Bobbs-Merrill, 1966). See also "Nirvana and the Kingdom of God" in Marty and Peerman, eds., *New Theology No. 1* (Macmillan, 1964).

The influential, fascinating, and somewhat baffling book by Paul van Buren, *The Secular Meaning of the Gospel*, should be consulted, though it is almost fatally easy to misconstrue this book as a study in the relation of British philosophical movements to theology. A book of mine, *The New Essence of Christianity* (Association, rev. ed. 1966), is perhaps relevant to the general movement.

we call it an event, it is so in a special or odd sense, for it has not been experienced in any regular or ordinary way.[5]

What does it mean to say that God is dead? Is this any more than a rather romantic way of pointing to the traditional difficulty of speaking about the holy God in human terms? Is it any more than a warning against all idols, all divinities fashioned out of human need, human ideologies? Does it perhaps not just mean that "existence is not an appropriate word to ascribe to God, that therefore He cannot be said to exist, and He is in that sense dead"? It surely means all this, and more. The hypothetical meanings suggested still all lie within the safe boundaries of the neo-orthodox or biblical-theology tradition, and the death-of-God group wants clearly to break away from that. It used to live rather comfortably there, and does so no longer.[6] Perhaps we can put it this way: the neo-orthodox reconstruction of the Christian doctrine of revelation seems to have broken down for some. It

[5] [Nietzsche's parable of the madman is of key relevance. See page 138 of this anthology.—Ed.] An important recent study of Nietzsche which places "the death of God" at the center of his thought can be found in the April 1964 *Encounter*: "The Importance of Nietzsche" by Erich Heller.

[6] Dr. Gilkey has clearly observed the senses in which the death-of-God theology is not a return to liberalism, and has a very interesting remark on the connections between it and neo-orthodoxy:

> From Barth this movement has accepted the radical separation of the divine and the secular, of God and ordinary experience, and so of theological language and philosophy; and it approves his further separation of Christianity and religion, and the consequent centering of all theological and religious concerns solely on Jesus Christ. From Tillich it has accepted the campaign against theism, and against personalist and mythological language about God. From Bultmann it has absorbed the polemic against ancient "mythological" categories in theology, which polemic needed only to be enlarged to include biblical-kerygmatic as well as objective-interventionist theological language about God to become very radical indeed. It also agrees with Bultmann that objective ontological and dogmatic language about God is impossible, with the consequence that theological language is reduced to language about the figure of Jesus Christ and about man's self-understanding. (*Op. cit.*, p. 4.)

This is a very shrewd observation by an observer who probably knows as much about what is really happening in American theology today as anybody. This passage shows the connections between the death-of-God movement and some of the left-wing Bultmannians who have not advanced to metaphysics.

used to be possible to say: we cannot know God but He has made himself known to us, and at that point analogies from the world of personal relations would enter the scene and help us out. But somehow, the situation has deteriorated; as before, we cannot know, but now it seems that He does not make himself known, even as enemy. This is more than the old protest against natural theology or metaphysics; more than the usual assurance that before the holy God all our language gets broken and diffracted into paradox. It is really that we do not know, do not adore, do not possess, do not believe in God. It is not just that a capacity has dried up within us; we do not take all this as merely a statement about our frail psyches, we take it as a statement about the nature of the world and we try to convince others. God is dead. We are not talking about the absence of the experience of God, but about the experience of the absence of God.[7] Yet the death-of-God theologians claim to be theologians, to be Christians, to be speaking out of a community to a community. They do not grant that their view is really a complicated sort of atheism dressed in a new spring bonnet. Let us look more carefully at their work.

I

Thomas Altizer's book, *Mircea Eliade and the Dialectic of the Sacred*, was published late in 1963 and has so far attracted very little attention. It does not have the snappiest of titles, and in the book Altizer has not decided whether to do a book on Eliade (to whom he owes a profound debt) or an original piece of theological exposition. He comes up with a little of both, so the book is not structurally satisfactory. But it is a brilliant book in many ways and an important piece of material in the movement we're studying.

Altizer begins by declaring that his basic presupposition is the

[7] Thus, we are moving in quite a different direction from the rather vague remark by Heidegger: "The phrase 'God is dead' means that the supersensible world is without effective force." *Holzwege* (Frankfurt: Klostermann, 1957), p. 200.

death of God in our history, for us, now. A theology of the word can ignore this death, he says, but only by keeping the word quite untouched by the reality of modern existence. So Altizer lays out the problems raised for him by the death of God in terms of the sacred and the profane, and this enables him to make interesting use of Eliade's studies of the meaning of the sacred in archaic and modern religion. Altizer's question becomes, then, how to recover that connection with the sacred that modern men have lost. He grants that gnosticism, the negation of the profane, is a powerful temptation at this point, and he tries very hard to reject it. We must not, he says, seek for the sacred by saying "no" to the radical profanity of our age, but by saying "yes" to it. Thus, he writes, "the task of the theologian becomes the paradoxical one of unveiling religious meaning in a world that is bathed in the darkness of God's absence."[8]

This statement suggests that Altizer, like Nietzsche, finds it a painful thing to have to affirm the death of God, and it is clear that he wishes things were otherwise. But he refuses to follow Eliade's tempting advice to return to some sort of precosmic primitivism and to recover the sacred in the way archaic religion did. How does the sacred become a possibility for a man who refuses to think himself out of his radically profane contemporary existence, who refuses in other words to archaize himself, with Eliade into primitivism or with Barth into the strange new world of the Bible?

Apparently the answer comes in Altizer's use of the Kierkegaardian idea of dialectic, or—what comes to the same thing— in his reading of Eliade's version of the myth of the coincidence of opposites. This means that affirming something passionately enough—in this case the full reality of the profane, secular, worldly character of modern life—will somehow deliver to the seeker the opposite, the sacred, as a gift he does not deserve. At times, Altizer walks very close to the gnostic nay-sayer whose danger he ordinarily perceives. His interest in the religious writing, such as it is, of Norman O. Brown, is a sign of his own

[8] Thomas J. J. Altizer, *Mircea Eliade and the Dialectic of the Sacred* (Philadelphia: Westminster Press, 1963), pp. 19–20.

religious-gnostic temptations. Brown not only mounts an undialectical Freudian attack on the profane and the secular, he sees both history and ordinary genital sexuality as needing to be radically spiritualized and transcended. His religious vision, both at the end of *Life Against Death* and in his more recent thought, is mystical, spiritual, and apocalyptic. This temptation is not a persistent one in Altizer, and in one important section of his book he makes the most ungnostic remark that the sacred will be born only when Western man combines a willing acceptance of the profane with a desire to change it.[9]

For the most part Altizer prefers mystical to ethical language in solving the problem of the death of God, or, as he puts it, in mapping out the way from the profane to the sacred. This combination of Kierkegaard and Eliade makes rather rough reading, but his position at the end is a relatively simple one. Here is an important summary statement of his views:

> If theology must now accept a dialectical vocation, it must learn the full meaning of Yes-saying and No-saying; it must sense the possibility of a Yes which can become a No, and of a No which can become a Yes; in short, it must look forward to a dialectical *coincidentia oppositorum*. Let theology rejoice that faith is once again a "scandal," and not simply a moral scandal, an offense to man's pride and righteousness, but, far more deeply, an ontological scandal; for eschatological faith is directed against the deepest reality of what we know as history and the cosmos. Through Nietzsche's vision of Eternal Recurrence we can sense the ecstatic liberation that can be occasioned by the collapse of the transcendence of Being, by the death of God . . . and, from Nietzsche's portrait of Jesus, theology must learn of the power of an eschatological faith that can liberate the believer from what to the contemporary sensibility is the inescapable reality of history. But liberation must finally be effected by affirmation. . . .[10]

This is an astonishing statement, ebullient, crotchety, full of linguistic and logical difficulties. Some of Altizer's Kierkegaardian or Nietzschean or gnostic uneasiness in the presence of the vulgar

[9] *Ibid.*, pp. 69ff.
[10] Altizer, "Theology and the Death of God," *op. cit.*, pp. 143–144.

historical can be seen in it. But it is also a powerful and poetic statement, with a good deal of the radical eschatological message of the New Testament in it, calling men out of the world into the presence of Jesus.

For Altizer men do not solve the problem of the death of God by following Jesus, but, it seems, by being liberated from history by him. In spite of his insight, already noted, that ethics (or transforming the profane) can be a real way of handling the problem of the ambiguity of the profane realm, Altizer ultimately prefers the categories of neither Christology nor ethics but of mysticism. Thus his vision, beginning with man accepting, affirming, even willing the death of God in a radical sense, ends with man willing to participate in the utter desolation of the secular or the profane, willing to undergo the discipline of darkness, the dark night of the soul (here Altizer's affinity with the religious existentialists, who may not have God but who don't at all like not having Him, is clearest), while the possibility of a new epiphany of the sacred, a rebirth of the possibility of having God once more is awaited. Sometimes Altizer would have us wait quietly without terror; more often it seems he would have us attack the profane world with a kind of terrible hostility so that it might give up its sacred secret.

Altizer's vision is a tremendously exciting one, logically imprecise, calculated to make empiricists weep, but imaginatively and religiously it is both sophisticated and powerful.[11]

11 In "America and the Future of Theology," Altizer makes one point not found so strongly in his other writings, and it is a point that the death-of-God writers tend to have in common. It is that America has a theological vocation today that is likely to be quite separate from the European experience. The group has a strong sense of being in a particular place, urban America, and at a particular time; born in the twenties, just old enough (usually) to get into World War II, products of the affluent society, very conscious of being white. This intense, and perhaps overemphasized, Americanism should not be dismissed as chauvinism, nor should it be passed off as some sort of guilt for having loved Barth or Bultmann too much. All of us have drawn from many non-American sources, not the least important of which is the later Bonhoeffer. But this special sense of a vocation to America should be noted, and it is no doubt part of the whole post-existentialist self-consciousness so characteristic of the group.

See the important article by Robert Funk, "Colloquium on Hermeneutics," *Theology Today*, October, 1964.

II

The work of Paul van Buren is much discussed today and thus it needs little more than a mention at this point. It says something about the rather strange sense of community that one finds in the death-of-God group that two such different personalities as van Buren and Altizer could have a common theological vocation. Altizer is all élan, wildness, excessive generalization, brimming with colorful, flamboyant, and emotive language. Van Buren is ordered, precise, cool. Indeed, I would venture a guess that van Buren and Altizer are so different temperamentally that they probably don't care much for each other's work. But they belong together, whether they like it or not.

While van Buren has certainly moved beyond the position of his book, it is in fact his book, *The Secular Meaning of the Gospel*, that has placed him firmly in the death-of-God camp, and we must briefly recall its major emphases.

Van Buren begins by citing Bonhoeffer's plea for a nonreligious interpretation of the Gospel, appropriate to the world come of age. The title of his book reflects this Bonhoefferian concern, though the book as a whole does not, and the Bonhoeffer introduction is really extraneous to his argument.

He next moves on to a consideration of the method he proposes for his nonreligious theology, and it turns out to be a certain species of linguistic analysis. The work of Hepburn, Hare, Ramsey, and Flew seems to interest him the most, and one feels in van Buren's very careful methodological work a rather deliberate reaction against the logical and methodological carelessness of Schubert Ogden's powerful book *Christ Without Myth*, with which in some ways van Buren's book has an affinity. The theological context within which van Buren puts his method to work is, after all, that created by Bultmann and his demythologizing project, and van Buren very clearly sees the sense in which Bultmann, taken seriously, means the end of the rhetoric of neo-orthodoxy and the so-called biblical theology.

> The mythological view of the world has gone, and with it went the possibility of speaking seriously of a *Heilsgeschichte*: a his-

torical "drama of salvation," in which God is said to have acted at a certain time in this world to change the state of human affairs.[12]

He rejects Barth, who is described as forfeiting the world as we live in it today (precisely the reason for Altizer's rejection of the theologies of the word), and he rejects also the left-wing Bultmannians who have, he justly remarks, given up the historical basis of faith for an idea of authentic existence. In van Buren's debate with a left-wing Bultmannian like Schubert Ogden we can see what he is after. What he attacks in Ogden (pp. 64ff.) is the belief that there is *any* trustworthy language about God at all, either analogical language or retranslations such as the odd one Ogden uses: God as "experienced non-objective reality."

Van Buren is inclined to assume that analytical philosophy has made all language about God impossible. He is not talking about the deterioration of our experience of God, and he is not talking about the loss of the sacred. He is talking about words, and how hard it is to find the right ones. "Simple literal theism" is out, he says, but so is the kind of sophisticated and qualified nonobjective theism that he finds in Ogden, Tillich, Karl Jaspers, and that he ought to find, if he doesn't, in Bishop Robinson.

It is not necessary to raise the question as to whether van Buren is guilty of taking this philosophical tradition too seriously, of receiving the impressive blows it is able to deliver with too radical a retreat. The fact remains that he has set about to do his theological work without God. There is something remaining in the vacated space, and perhaps the idea of one's historical perspective or point of view can be used to rebuild the old notion of faith as *assensus* and *fiducia* before God. Perhaps. But apart from this, we do without God and hold to Jesus of Nazareth.

Thus, the urbane and methodologically scrupulous van Buren joins hands with Altizer, the ecstatic and complex proclaimer of the death of God. The tone of voice is quite different; indeed the languages are not the same, but the meaning is unmistakable in both: God is dead. For Altizer the disappearance of the sacred is a sort of cosmic event; for van Buren it can be more precisely

[12] *The Secular Meaning of the Gospel*, pp. 11–12.

described: the rise of technology and modern science, the need in our thinking to stick pretty close to what we can experience in ordinary ways. Both, be it noted, are referring to something that has happened to them, not to someone else or to modern man in some generalized sense, and they are willing to admit it.

Altizer comes finally to depend on mystical categories to deal with the death of God, to save himself from undialectical atheism. Van Buren is too loyal an erstwhile Barthian to want to use mystical categories: for him ethical terms will do. When the theisms have gone, literal or fancy, as they must, and after faith has been Ramseyed and Hared, Christianity still stands as an ethic, public and private, and its character is largely derived from the sovereign freedom of Jesus the Lord. The Christian without God is a waiting man for Altizer, daring to descend into the darkness, grappling with all that is profane to wrest from it its potential sacral power. The Christian without God for van Buren is Jesus' man, perfectly free lord of all, subject to none.[13]

Altizer and van Buren thus may be said to share a common

---

[13] It is worth noting that the contemporary religious philosopher perhaps closest to van Buren, in mood at least, is Alasdair MacIntyre in "God and the Theologians," *Encounter*, September 1963. MacIntyre's essay is an extended review of *Honest to God*, a valedictory to the Christian faith, and an interesting and confused piece of work. His chief gimmick is the insistence that all three of Robinson's theologians, Bonhoeffer, Bultmann, and Tillich, are atheists, which he apparently defines as any rejection of literal objectifiable theism.

What MacIntyre has done is to swallow the apologetic strategy of Karl Barth without a murmur. Barth has always loved to dangle the threatening figure of Feuerbach before the faces of anyone interested in the self, modern man, or despair, and to say, in effect, "Look out, gentlemen; if you leave my protection and go down the slippery path toward Bultmann or Tillich you will be unable to stop until you arrive at Feuerbach, who was at least honest in his atheism." MacIntyre has apparently been beguiled by this device. Using the same tools that van Buren uses, he has declared for overt atheism rather than the death of God, and also, with Feuerbach, has chosen the historical fate of man and his freedom in this world, to salvation and the next. It is, incidentally, unfortunate that modern Protestants have trusted Barth as an interpreter of Feuerbach. Robert Tucker has pointed out (*Philosophy and Myth in Karl Marx*, p. 93) that Feuerbach mistakenly assumed that his foe, Christianity, was identical with Hegelianism. Since he was unable to see how deeply anti-Christian Hegelianism really was, his inversion of Christianity was really an inversion of Hegelian Christianity and thus, to say the least, more Christian in substance than Hegelianism ever was.

vision which we have been calling the death of God, though this actual phrase is doubtless more congenial to the fiery Altizer than to the lucid van Buren. Both men, furthermore, deny that this vision disqualifies them as religious or Christian men. It may cripple, it may weaken or threaten, but they are both inside the circle. And each uses a different strategy to deal with the problem raised by the vision: Altizer, as we have seen, uses images from the world of mysticism: waiting, darkness, a new epiphany, the dialectic of opposites; van Buren does without and does not really need God, preferring to point to Jesus as a way of standing before the neighbor. We will meet later in this essay this distinction between mysticism and a christological ethic as different ways of living in the time of the death of God.

III

I would like to move now from the fairly invulnerable task of reporting the views of others, to the task of laying out my own point of view, which I believe belongs in this general tradition. If Altizer begins with the cosmic event of the disappearance of the sacred, and if van Buren begins with the language problem, my starting point may be said to have two parts, one negative, the other positive.

The negative part is the perception, already referred to, of the deterioration of the portrait of the God-man relation as found in biblical theology and the neo-orthodox tradition. This theological tradition was able to portray a striking and even heroic sort of faith, a sort of holding on by the fingernails to the cliff of faith, a standing terrified before the enemy-God, present to man as terror or threat, comforting only in that He kept us from the worse terrors of life without Him. This God, we used to say, will never let us go. But He has, or we have Him, or something, and in any case this whole picture has lost its power to persuade some in our time.

But our negations are never very important or interesting. There is a positive affirmation or starting point by which I enter into the country inhabited by the death-of-God settlers. It has to do with the problem of the Reformation or being a Protestant today. This is what I mean. At the end of the last century the Reformation was interpreted as a victory for the autonomous religious personality, freed from the tyranny of hierarchy and institution, while man's relation to God was described as unmediated and available to all. This is what the Reformation means; for example, in Adolf von Harnack's *What is Christianity?* it was characteristic of liberal Protestantism as a whole, and it achieves its symbolic expression in Luther, standing alone at Worms, refusing to go against his conscience.

As the century wore on, and wars, depressions, bombs and anxieties came our way, we found ourselves seeing the Reformation in a new light. The old approach was not wrong, it was just that the new approach fitted our experience better. In this new approach, which we might call yesterday's understanding of the Reformation, the central fact was not the autonomous religious personality; it was the theological discovery of the righteous God. In that portion of our century when men and nations knew trouble, sin, and guilt, we needed to receive this theological truth of the Reformation, just as earlier the psychological truth needed to be heard. Thus, we learned to say that the Reformation was a theological event, it centered in Luther's discovery of the meaning of justification or forgiveness, and its symbol proved to be Luther, storming about his room in Wittenberg, cursing the God who demands righteousness of men.

Today we may need to look at the Reformation in a third sense, no more or less true than the earlier approaches, but perhaps needing special emphasis just now and fitting new experiences in both church and world. This approach is more ethical than psychological or theological, and its focus is not on the free personality or on justification by faith, but on the movement from the cloister to the world. Of course, there is no specific event in Luther's life that can be so described, but the movement is there in his life nonetheless, and it is a movement we need to study. From cloister to world means from church, from place of protection and security, of order and beauty, to the bustling middle-class world of the new university, of politics, princes, and peasants. Far more important than any particular ethical teaching of Luther is this fundamental ethical movement. Here I touch some of Altizer's concerns, but I am not as anxious to recover the sacred, since I am starting with a definition of Protestantism as a movement away from the sacred place.

This view of the Reformation, along with my preliminary negative comment, does allow a kind of picture of faith. It is not, this time, holding on by the fingernails, and it is not a terror-struck confession before the enemy-God. It is not even, one can almost say, a means of apprehending God at all. This faith is more like a place, a being with or standing beside the neighbor. Faith, one might suggest, has almost become collapsed into love, and the Protestant is no longer defined as the forgiven sinner, the *simul justus et peccator*, but as the one beside the neighbor, beside the enemy, at the disposal of the man in need. The connection between holding to the neighbor and holding to Jesus will be dealt with in a moment.

At this point I am inclined to reflect the later Bonhoeffer more than either van Buren or Altizer want or need to. The Protestant I am describing has no God, has no faith in God, and affirms both the death of God and the death of all the forms of theism. Even so, he is not primarily a man of negation, for if there is a movement away from God and religion, there is the more important movement into, for, toward the world, worldly life, and the neighbor as the bearer of the worldly Jesus. We must look more carefully at these two movements: toward the world and away from religion.

IV

We need to be very careful in how we put this Protestant "yes" to the world. It is not the same kind of "yes" that one finds in that tradition of theology of culture today that makes use of the world as illustrations for its doctrines of sin and redemption. This "yes" is also in considerable tension with a number of themes in modern literature. Recently, Lionel Trilling called attention to Thomas Mann's remark that all his work was an effort to free himself from the middle class, and to this Trilling added the comment that all truly modern literature can be so described. Indeed, he goes on, modern literature is not only asking for a freedom from the middle class, but from society itself. It is this conception of the modern, I am saying, that should be opposed by the Protestant. Who are the characteristically modern writers in this sense I am criticizing? Any such list would surely include Henry James, Eliot, Yeats, Pound, Joyce, Lawrence, Kafka, Faulkner, Beckett. Is it possible to affirm the value of the technological revolution, the legitimacy of the hopes and claims of the dispossessed, most of all, of the moral centrality of the Negro revolution in America today—is it possible to affirm all these values and still to live comfortably in the modern world as these writers portray it? Surely not, in some important senses.

When I state that there is something in the essence of Protestantism itself that drives us into the world, it is not into the world of these "modern" writers, but in many ways it is into the world they reject—the world of technology, power, money, sex, culture, race, poverty, and the city. Lawrence's protest against the mechanization of life now seems a bit archaic and piquant, and his aristocratic hostility to the democratic ethos of Christianity is rather more than piquant, it is irrelevant and false. In a way, I am describing not a move away from Puritanism, but a move to it, and to the middle class and to the city. Perhaps the time has come when Protestants no longer need to make ritual acts of hostility to Puritanism, moralism, and to all the hypocrisies and prohibitions of middle-class culture. The chronicle of middle-class hypocrisy may well be complete, with no more work on it necessary. There are those in our world today who would like to be a little closer to the securities of middle-class existence so they too might become free to criticize them, and who must indeed be granted political, economic, and psychological admission to that world. Attacks on the silliness of middle-class morality have almost always had an antipolitical character, and it is to that element in the modern sensibility that the Protestant takes exception. Thus the worldliness affirmed by Protestantism has a postmodern, pro-bourgeois, urban and political character. This may mean a loosening of the ties between the Protestant intellectual and avant-garde modernism, and it might even mean the start of some interesting work in the shaping of a radical ethic today.

The Protestant protest against religion is related to, but it must not be confused with, this affirmation of the world. (Both are clearly implied by our formula, from church to world.) Assertions that Protestantism is against religion, or that Christianity or revelation is an attack on religion, have, of course, been with us for a considerable time now, and nearly everybody has had a word to say on the subject. Karl Barth's long discussion of the subject in *Church Dogmatics* I/2 has had a massive and perhaps undeserved influence. Barth defines religion, in his attack on it, as something like man's arrogant and grasping attempt to become God, so it is hard to see what all the posturing is about. If by definition religion equals sin, and you then say revelation ought to be against religion, you may cause some shuddering frissons of delight among careless readers, but you have not forwarded theological clarity very much.

More immediate in influence, of course, is the plea for a religionless Christianity in the prison letters of Bonhoeffer. We really don't know what Bonhoeffer meant by religion, though long articles have been written on the subject, and our modern study of the problem of religionlessness must be carried on quite independent of the task, probably fruitless, of establishing just what Bonhoeffer meant.

There are two schools of interpretation of Protestant religionlessness. One might be called the moderate, Honest-to-God, ecclesiastical interpretation. In this, religion generally means "religious activities" like liturgy, counseling, going to church, saying your prayers. To be religionless in this sense is to affirm that the way we have done these things in the past may not be the only way, or may not be worth doing at all, and that radical experiments ought to be attempted in the forms of the church and ministry. Bishop Robinson's book *The New Reformation?* is an able presentation of this moderate radicalism. A good deal of the material out of New York, Geneva, and the denominational headquarters on the church and ministry reflects this promising line, and a good many religious sociologists and radical religious leaders on the race issue tend to use Bonhoeffer and religionlessness in this way.

This is an important trend, and we need more and not less experimentation on these matters of the ministry, for we are well into the opening phase of the breakdown of organized religion in American life, well beyond the time when ecumenical dialogues or denominational mergers can be expected to arrest the breakdown.

The religionlessness I wish to defend, however, is not of this practical type. At no point is the later Bonhoeffer of greater importance to the death-of-God theology than right here, in helping us work out a truly theological understanding of the problem of religionlessness. I take religion to mean not man's arrogant grasping for God (Barth) and not assorted Sabbath activities usually performed by ordained males (the moderate radicals), but any system of thought or action in which God or the gods serve as fulfiller of needs or solver of problems. Thus I am asserting with Bonhoeffer the breakdown of the religious a priori and the coming of age of man.

The breakdown of the religious a priori means that there is no way, ontological, cultural, or psychological, to locate a part of the self or a part of human experience that needs God. There is no God-shaped blank within man. Man's heart may or may not be restless until it rests in God. It is not necessarily so. God is not in the realm of the necessary at all; he is not necessary being, he is not necessary to avoid despair or self-righteousness. He is one of the possibles in a radically pluralistic spiritual and intellectual milieu.

This is just what man's coming of age is taken to mean. It is not true to say, with Luther, *entweder Gott oder Abgott*. It is not true to say, with Ingmar Bergman, who probably didn't mean it, "Without God, life is an outrageous terror." It is not true to say that there are certain areas, problems, dimensions to life today that can only be faced, solved, illumined, dealt with, by a religious perspective.

I am defining religion as the assumption in theology, preaching, apologetics, evangelism, counseling, that man needs God, and that there are certain things that God alone can do for him. I am denying that religion is necessary and saying that the movement from the church to the world that we have taken as definitive of Protestantism not only permits but requires this denial. To assert that we are men moving from cloister to world, church to world, to say that we are secular men, is to say that we do not ask God to do for us what the world is qualified to do. Really to travel along this road means that we trust the world, not God, to be our need fulfiller and problem solver, and God, if he is to be for us at all, must come in some other role.

This combination of a certain kind of God-rejection with a certain kind of world-affirmation is the point where I join the death-of-God movement. At this point, I would like to formulate a question directed against what I have been saying. What distinguishes this position I have been sketching out from ordinary Feuerbachian atheism? Earlier we distinguished between mysticism and christological ethics as ways of handling the historical experience of the death of God. I think both of these responses are valid and useful, and in answering the question about atheism I would like to propose my version of them.

I am in full sympathy with much of the mystical imagery used by Altizer, perhaps most of all with the idea of "waiting." There is an element of expectation, even hope, that removes my position from classical atheisms and that even removes from it a large amount of anguish and gloom. In addition to the idea of waiting for God, I am interested in the search for a language that does not depend on need or problem. Perhaps the Augustinian distinction between *frui* and *uti* will prove to be helpful. If God is not needed, if it is to the world and not God that we repair for our needs and problems, then perhaps we may come to see that He is to be enjoyed and delighted in. Part of the meaning of waiting for God is found in this attempt to understand what delighting in Him might mean.

To the valid theme of the christological ethic worked out by van Buren I am adding the emphasis on Protestant worldliness both as an interpretation of the Reformation and as an attack on certain forms of modern sensibility.

By way of a provisional summary: the death of God must be affirmed; the confidence with which we thought we could speak of God is gone, and our faith, belief, experience of Him are very poor things indeed. Along with this goes a sharp attack on religion, which we have defined as any system using God to meet a need or to solve a problem, even the problem of not having a

God. Our waiting for God, our godlessness, is partly a search for a language and a style by which we might be enabled to stand before Him once again, delighting in His presence.

In the time of waiting we have a place to be. It is not before an altar, it is in the world, in the city, with both the needy neighbor and the enemy. This place really defines our faith, for faith and love have come together in the interim of waiting. This place, as we shall see, is not only the place for the waiting for God, it is also a way to Jesus Christ.[14]

V

I wish presently to draw a number of these themes—death of God, waiting, enjoyment, holding fast to Jesus Christ, Jesus as the neighbor, faith moving into love, movement to the world, city, politics—into a coherent theological position. But before I do this, I should like to make a somewhat odd attempt to clarify what I am doing theologically by using some nontheological models. This is what I propose to claim: American theological thought and action has been, for perhaps thirty years, in what might be called an Oedipal phase, and the time has come for it to move into its post-Oedipal situation. The hero of the new situation must no longer be Oedipus at all, but Orestes. In other terms, the postmedieval hero of the Christian consciousness has been Hamlet, and we have all made our struggle for faith in his shadow. But we must move beyond Hamlet, and the Shakespearean hero that can guide us is Prospero. Let me briefly illustrate

[14] This combination of waiting, enjoyment, and a Christological ethic brings my position fairly close to that of Hanfried Müller, the East Berlin theologian and author of the best book to date on Bonhoeffer, *Von der Kirche zur Welt*. Müller's basic theological principle is the theology of the cross, and as he interprets this—no present experience of Incarnation or resurrection, etc. —it is close to, but not perhaps as extreme as what I have been calling the vision of the death of God. But to the *theologia crucis* Müller adds, and this is a real source of interest and distinguishes him from Kierkegaard, a social-political optimism which, in his case of course, is derived from Marxism. One wonders whether the Negro revolution in America may not provide a context for a similar combination of the cross and optimism. Cf. J. M. Lochman's essay on Müller, "From the Church to the World," in Marty and Peerman, eds., *New Theology No. 1* (Macmillan, 1963).

what I mean by this double movement, from Oedipus to Orestes and from Hamlet to Prospero.

It is interesting to observe how Orestes has come to fascinate writers of widely different perspectives today. O'Neill has treated the whole saga in *Mourning Becomes Electra*. Eliot in *The Family Reunion* and Sartre in *The Flies* have each left their stamp on the Greek hero, and today even Jack Richardson in *The Prodigal* has brought Orestes into the world of modern experimental theater. In a fascinating article, Herbert Fingarette has suggested that Orestes has the power to become the hero in the modern world of ego psychology and identity crisis.[15] This may or may not be the case, but it is true, I believe, that Orestes can serve as a symbolic theological guide. What does this mean?

Oedipal theology today asks such questions as these: "Who is my Father? Is rebellion against the Father permissible, or must I submit? What can I love in the loveless world? Where is the true locus of authority? Is there any Father for me to love?" And it is a theology based on a sense of sin: "I am a sinner, I love my mother and I desire to kill my Father." The Oedipal believer, we might add, is a man standing still and alone in a desolate place. He is looking up to the heavens, he has no eyes of flesh, only eyes of faith, and he is crying out his questions to the heavens.

Psychologically, as Fingarette shows, Oedipus stands for the individual as he moves into his central crisis of growth, as he solves the problems of his adolescence or coming of age. Orestes, on the other hand, is the individual having moved beyond this crisis. Oedipus shows us the individual's psychological bondage, Orestes shows us his freedom and struggle for harmony. Orestes, as Aeschylus portrays him, returns from exile to his royal home. He comes back to the place where his father was murdered and where his mother took up her liaison with Aegisthus, who aided her in the murder. Now grown, Orestes comes back to the Oedipal situation. He could have remained in exile, but he did not. He chose to return. Unlike Oedipus, he does not perform his acts out of fate, but out of a destiny. Unlike Oedipus, he has a direction. Orestes had made a vow to Apollo to take up his

[15] Herbert Fingarette, "Orestes: Paradigm Hero and Central Motif of Contemporary Ego Psychology," *The Psychoanalytic Review*, Fall, 1963.

responsibility as son and heir. It is not fate, but his own free vow to Apollo that binds him. As he returns, he comes to see that he must destroy the faithless mother.

Oedipus inadvertently kills the father, while Orestes chooses to kill the corrupt mother, out of loyalty to the father. Psychologically, we are in a new world beyond the Oedipal state, and religiously we are in a new world as well. Out of loyalty both to the gods and to the memory of the murdered father, the mother must be destroyed, the mother who represents security, warmth, religion, authority, but who has become corrupt and an evil bearer of all that she is supposed to represent.

This readily points to the theological task of post-Oedipal, Orestean theology. To be freed from the parents is to be freed from religion, the religious a priori, religion as necessary, God as meeter of needs and solver of problems. Orestean theology means the end of faith's preoccupation with inner conflict, of the struggle of faith, of the escape from the enemy-God, of the careful confession of sin. When the believing man can thus abandon this mode of introspective self-scrutiny, "then the center of a man's existence is himself as a man among men, a man *of* the real world and not merely in it." Fingarette goes on to say:

> . . . a man of the world, in the sense here intended, is a man at last open to the world and to his fellow men as his fellows. And, although in a certain sense men's existence is the center, this does not imply, either in the play or in life, a denial of the marvelous, both holy and profane.[16]

At the close of the Aeschylean trilogy, Athena sets Orestes free, and Apollo and Orestes leave the center of the action, and the city, the *polis*, dominates our attention at the end. Orestes has returned home in obedience to a vow, has cleansed the state of the evil infecting it (which happened to be his own mother), and takes up his role as prince and ruler. The psychological interpretation of the hero refers to the need for mastering and accepting our anxiety and finding a constructive role in society. Theologically, we must also claim Orestes as our paradigmatic hero, for we too must reject the mother. Unlike Orestes, who kills the

16 *Ibid.*, pp. 102f.

mother because of a loyalty to the father, we must kill the mother in order to discover the as yet unformed meaning of our loyalty to the father. In order to overcome the death of the father in our lives, the death of God, the mother must be abolished and we must give our devotion to the *polis*, to the city, politics, and our neighbor. Waiting for God, expecting the transcendent and the marvelous, searching for a means of enjoying them, we go out into the world and the city and, working, wait there.

Thus, Protestant men, Protestant churches, and, most important here, Protestant theology, belong in the street if they are to be truly Orestean. The academy and the temple can, for now, no longer be trusted as theological guides. Not only our action but our thought belong with the world of the city, which in our time means power, culture, art, sex, money, the Jew, the Negro, beauty, ugliness, poverty and indifference. Thought and action both must make the move from Oedipus to Orestes from self and anxiety and crying out to the enemy-God, to the neighbor, the city, the world.

But the movement from Oedipus to Orestes has an Elizabethan counterpart. It is also the move from Hamlet to Prospero. What does it mean to say that Hamlet-theology is at an end and that we need to discern some clues in Prospero? Hamlet-theology, like that of his spiritual ancestor Oedipus, is about authority and about the father. Is the ghost really the father, and should he be obeyed? Shall I acquiesce in his demand, even though it is for blood revenge, or shall I rebel against the father? The Hamlet theology, thus, is one in which man is largely alone, in which he is obsessed by his own and his people's rottenness, and in which he, in his solitariness, wonders about God and what God wills. If there is any action (or ethics) that emerges from such a theology, it is fairly arbitrary, and does not proceed out of interior soliloquy at all, but comes rather in response to surface stimuli. To mark the end of solitariness as a theological posture, of obsessive senses of sin, of crying out to God, absent or present, is to mark the end, in Protestant circles at least, of the existentialist mood.

But to move beyond Hamlet is to come to sit before Prospero. What does this mean? The Prospero I am interested in, and that I would propose as a model, is not the forgiver but the man who gives up his magic, his charismatic power, and releases Ariel. We hear him say, "this rough magic I here abjure" (Act V, scene 1) and "Now my charms are all o'erthrown" (Epilogue). Prospero is the man who leaves the place of mystery and magic and returns to his dukedom in Milan. He moves from the sacred, from magic, from religion, to the world of the city. Prospero's abjuring of magic is parallel to Orestes' killing of the faithless mother, and his return to his rightful dukedom is parallel to Orestes' return to Argos and his princely duties.

In these comments on Greek tragedy and on Shakespeare, I am far from proposing that my remarks constitute anything like literary criticism. I am rather using familiar literary material to express in an image a theological shift and emphasis, already hinted at and explained. We must now make a final summary in ordinary prose.

VI

I must now attempt to draw some of the themes of this essay together, so that I may be attacked and assented to for the proper reasons, and so this death-of-God tradition may have as good a chance as possible of taking on a theological life of its own along with the other theological styles and visions that we are beginning to discern in this new post-existentialist, post-European period.[17] In a recent critical review of Julian Huxley's *Essays of a Humanist*, Philip Toynbee makes an attack on all psychologically inclined Christians, biologists who listen to Bach, mystical astronomers and humane Catholics. What can we put in their place? he asks.

---

[17] Professor Gilkey (*op. cit.* p. 6) has listed five works of the death-of-God tradition, and they should perhaps be set down: (1) the problematic character of God and of man's relation to him today, (2) the acceptance of the secular world as normative intellectually and ethically good, (3) the restriction of theological statements to what one can actually affirm oneself, and with this the rejection of certain traditional ideas of tradition and authority, (4) the centrality of Jesus as one who calls us into the world to serve him there, (5) uneasiness with mythological, super-historical, eschatological, supernatural entities or categories.

Gilkey goes on to note how each of these five points is a direct attack on a certain portion of the neo-orthodox tradition.

And the answer? Simply to wait—on God or whatever it may be, and in the meantime to leave the general alone and to concentrate all our natural energies and curiosities on the specific, the idiosyncratic, the personal.[18]

This combination of waiting and attention on the concrete and personal is precisely the theological point I have been trying to make. Waiting here refers to the whole experience I have called "the death of God," including the attack on religion and the search for a means by which God, not needed, may be enjoyed. We have insisted all along that "death of God" must not be taken as symbolic rhetoric for something else. There really is a sense of not having, of not believing, of having lost, not just the idols or the gods of religion, but God Himself. And this is an experience that is not peculiar to a neurotic few, nor is it private or inward. Death of God is a public event in our history, we are saying.

Thus we wait, we try out new words, we pray for God to return, and we seem to be willing to descend into the darkness of unfaith and doubt that something may emerge on the other side. In this way, we have tried to interpret and confirm the mystical images that are so central to the thought of Altizer.[19]

But we do more than play the waiting game. We concentrate our energy and passion on the specific, the concrete, the personal. We turn from the problems of faith to the reality of love. We walk away from the inner anguish of a Hamlet or an Oedipus, and take up our worldly responsibility with Prospero and Orestes. As Protestants, we push the movement from church to world as

---

[18] *The Observer* (London), March 22, 1964.

[19] This emphasis on a passive and letting-be attitude to the world will suggest, to some readers, several other related themes in current theological thought; for example, it can be found in a quite different, and most interesting form, in some of the recent work of Heinrich Ott and of others working with the problem of the theological use of the later Heidegger. The theme is also found in the emerging reaction against existentialism in the post-Bultmannians. Ernst Käsemann has written: "The cardinal virtue of the historian and the beginning of all meaningful hermeneutic is for me the practice of hearing, which begins simply by letting what is historically foreign maintain its validity and which does not regard rape as the basic form of engagement." ("Zur Thema der urchristlichen Apokalyptik," *Zeitschrift für Theologie und Kirche*, LIX, 1962, pp. 262ff.)

far as it can go and become frankly worldly men. And in this world, as we have seen, there is no need for religion and no need for God. This means that we refuse to consent to that traditional interpretation of the world as a shadow-screen of unreality, masking or concealing the eternal which is the only true reality. This refusal is made inevitable by the scientific revolution of the seventeenth century, and it is this refusal that stands, as a troublesome shadow, between ourselves and the Reformation of the sixteenth. The world of experience is real, and it is necessary and right to be actively engaged in changing its patterns and structures.

This concentration on the concrete and the worldly says something about the expected context of theology in America today. It means, I think, that the theological work that is to be truly helpful—at least for a while—is more likely to come from worldly contexts than ecclesiastical ones, more likely to come from participation in the Negro revolution than from the work of faith and order. But this is no surprise, for ever since the Civil War, ever since the Second Inaugural of Lincoln we might even say, the really creative American theological expressions have been worldly rather than ecclesiastical: the work of Walter Rauschenbusch and the work of Reinhold Niebuhr are surely evidence for this.[20]

The death-of-God Protestant, it can be seen, has somewhat inverted the usual relation between faith and love, theology and ethics, God and the neighbor. We are not proceeding from God and faith to neighbor and love, loving in such and such a way because we are loved in such and such a way. We move to our neighbor, to the city and to the world out of a sense of the loss of God. We set aside this sense of loss or death, we note it and

[20] It is not yet clear how the civil rights movement is going to take on its theological significance, but it clearly is beginning to already, as the radical southern Negro student comes out of the movement to seminary. He brings a passionate interest in the New Testament doctrines of discipleship and following Jesus, for example, and very little interest in the doctrine of sin. One of the most pressing intellectual responsibilities of the Negro student and minister today is that of working out some of the ethical and theological clues that the Negro revolution is teaching him and us all.

allow it to be, neither glad for it, nor insistent that it must be so for all, nor sorry for ourselves. And, for the time of our waiting we place ourselves with our neighbor and enemy in the world.

There is something more than our phrase "waiting for God" that keeps this from sheer atheist humanism. Not only our waiting but our worldly work is Christian too, for our way to our neighbor is not only mapped out by the secular social and psychological and literary disciplines, it is mapped out as well by Jesus Christ and his way to his neighbor. Our ethical existence is partly a time of waiting for God and partly an actual christology. Our being in the world, in the city, is not only an obedience to the Reformation formula, from church to world, it is an obedience to Jesus himself. How is this so? How is Jesus being disclosed in the world, being found in the world in our concrete work?

First, Jesus may be concealed in the world, in the neighbor, in this struggle for justice, in that struggle for beauty, clarity, order. Jesus is in the world as masked, and the work of the Christian is to strip off the masks of the world to find him, and, finding him, to stay with him and to do his work. In this sense, the Christian life is not a longing and is not a waiting, it is a going out into the world. The self is discovered, but only incidentally, as one moves out into the world to tear off the masks. Life is a masked ball, a Halloween party, and the Christian life, ethics, love, is that disruptive task of tearing off the masks of the guests to discover the true princess.

In the parable of the last judgment (Matt. 25:34ff.) the righteous did not know it was Jesus they were serving. The righteous today don't need to know it either, unless they are Christian, in which case they will say that what they are doing is not only service, work, justified for this and that structural reason; it is also an act of unmasking, a looking for, a finding, and a staying with Jesus.

In this first sense, the Christian life, ethics, love, is public, outward, visible. It is finding Jesus in your neighbor: "as you did it to one of the least of these my brethren, you did it to me" (Matt. 25:40).

There is another form of the presence of Jesus Christ in the world. Here, we no longer talk about unmasking Jesus who is out there in the world somewhere, we talk about becoming Jesus in and to the world. Here, the Christian life, ethics, love, is first a decision about the self, and then a movement beyond the self into the world.

The form, if not the content, of the parable of the Good Samaritan, should be recalled. Jesus is asked a question: Which one, among all the many claimants out there, is my neighbor? Jesus answers the question with one of his characteristic non-answers: "Don't look for the neighbor, be one." Or, to put the form of his answer to work on our problem: "Don't look for Jesus out there, in scripture, tradition, sacraments, Ingmar Bergmann movies, in the world behind a mask—become Jesus." Become a Christ to your neighbor, as Luther put it.

In this form, the Christian life is not a looking outward to the world and its claims, it is first a look within in order to become Jesus. "For me to live," cried Paul in one of his most daring utterances, "is Christ." Ethics and love are first a dangerous descent into the self. And in this form, the Christian life, ethics, love, are not so active or worldly. At this point the Christian is the passive man, and doubtless tempted into all the easily noted dangers of confusing the self with Jesus.

The Christian life as the discernment of Jesus beneath the worldly masks can be called work or interpretation or criticism; while the Christian life as becoming Jesus looks a little different. At this point the Christian is the sucker, the fall guy, the jester, the fool for Christ, the one who stands before Pilate and is silent, the one who stands before power and power structures and laughs.

Whichever of the paths one takes to find or define Jesus in the world, and perhaps some of us are called to choose both ways, and some only one, the worldliness of the Protestant can never, because of this, have an utterly humanistic form. I may be proposing a too simple marriage between christology and ethics, a too narrowly ethical approach to christological problems, but it should at least be noted that however acute the experience of the death of God may be for us, however much silence and loneliness are entailed during our time of waiting for the absent God, we are not particularly cast down or perplexed by this. A form of obedience remains to us in our time of deprivation. We de-christianize no one, we make no virtue of our defects, and we even dare to call men into the worldly arena where men are in need and where Jesus is to be found and served.

Gabriel Vahanian

[b. 1927]

BORN IN MARSEILLES, Vahanian's childhood in France was intricately involved with the Bible and the church. "Long before I was ten," he says, "the story of Jacob cheating Esau, my sympathy for the latter and my mother's unsatisfactory explanations"[1] had a decisive influence on his religious development, as did his adolescent experience of "the church's unfaithful separation from the world, that very world which 'God so loved.'" His mother, with her "disastrous superabundance of faith and hope against hope in God," was the one individual who decided him on a religious career. He studied at Grenoble and the Sorbonne before coming to the United States under a scholarship from the World Council of Churches. He earned master's and doctor's degrees at Princeton Theological Seminary and was for three years an instructor at Princeton University before becoming assistant professor of religion at Syracuse University.

Both in his writing and in the classroom, Vahanian displays a broad sophistication in literature, history and philosophy as well as in theology. Like William Hamilton, he is alert to such literary voices as Eliot, Camus, Dostoevsky and Beckett. In theology, however, Vahanian represents the diametrical opposite of Hamilton. Unthinking journalists have conscripted him into the fold of radical theology when, in fact, his perspective is a conservative one, rooted in the thought of Kierkegaard and Barth, with their insistence on the transcendence and "otherness" of God.

For Vahanian, as for Barth, faith is man's relation to God. The

[1] Quotations, unless otherwise specified, are from personal correspondence.

reality of God is subject to ambiguity through man's interpretation—that is, to errors of perception. It is the task of theology
to offset these errors, to correct the distorted perception—and
this task has assumed staggering proportions in a time when
Western culture has ceased to be Christian. "The Death of God,"
says Vahanian, "makes sense and is a liberating event only when
it is considered as a cultural phenomenon."[2] A seminal influence
in Vahanian's outlook here is the seventeenth-century French
philosopher Pierre Bayle, whose delineation of the frontiers of
faith and reason is implicit in much of Vahanian's thought. "If
more people had read Bayle," he says, "some of the nonsense
that pervades so much of the present controversy about atheism
and the death of God would be avoided."

Both Vahanian and the radicals appear to agree on certain
fundamentals in their diagnosis of the present situation and its
historical origins. The French Revolution brought deicide along
with regicide, inaugurating a new era both godless and democratic. To Vahanian, this meant the toppling of idols, not the
demise of the true and living God; and the work of Schleiermacher represented the first in a series of mistaken attempts to
accommodate Christianity to an increasingly post-Christian culture. Hamilton and Vahanian would both lament the degeneration of the Christian tradition into a vapid bourgeois religiosity,
and both would call for a Kierkegaardian seriousness in response
to this degeneration. Both might even agree to Vahanian's statement that the death of God "has alienated us both religiously
and culturally from the biblical conception of God."[3] But for
Vahanian, religion is what the shell is to the egg—not a source
of salvation but a necessary container of faith. Religiosity becomes worthless when it becomes an *empty* shell, and it may
be harmful when it contains the right faith in the wrong way
or when it conceals a rotten faith. The right faith remains that
of the gospel; it must not be adulterated or modified. The problem that the cultural death of God poses is that modern man
loses his bearings, settles for an adulterated or even poisonous

[2] Gabriel Vahanian, "Swallowed Up By Godlessness," *The Christian Century*, December 8, 1965, p. 1505.
[3] *Ibid.*, p. 1506.

faith—or an empty shell. The problem for the Christian, then, is one of purification, of getting back to the "iconoclastic" faith of the Gospel. Vahanian has had little to say directly about Bonhoeffer, but the following rebuke surely fits him as well as Hamilton, Altizer and others:

> Putting the gospel upside down or inside out results not in a reli-
> gionless Christianity, much less in a godless Christianity, but in
> an ersatz that is not less religious for being godless.[4]

He sees, perhaps accurately, that such a perspective must logi-
cally result in atheism, and he will not allow that a Christian atheism could be possible; it can only end in capitulation to the world and its stunted values.

His book *The Death of God* (1961) offers a sensitive critique of post-Christian culture, from the viewpoint of a "defense of faith" that may be described as neo-Barthian. In *Wait Without Idols* (1964) he proceeds to assess the difficulties involved in the Christian task of *restoring* the primacy of faith. His perspective is conservative, not reactionary. He does not wish to preserve the tottering relationship between faith and Western culture—
the true and living God transcends this culture and all others. In his third book, *No Other God* (1966), he turns to Calvin's *Institutes of the Christian Religion,* affirming a rigorously Christo-
centric, "Word of God" and church-based theology which con-
tends that knowledge itself is theonomous—the word of man implies the word of God.

As Vahanian points out in the following selection, part of the problem is exacerbated by the fact that Western culture is immunized against Christianity. It has not only lost its sacral dimension in the process of secularization, but because it *is* post-Christian it is disposed to identify the very concept of a sacral dimension with its own experience of the past. Acceptance of the cultural "death of God" means facing the fact that Christian assumptions have been rendered unintelligible; Christian religiosity has yielded or is yielding to a new, post-Christian religiosity that no longer points to the living God but to idols that present man with delusive self-images. To "wait without

[4] *Ibid.*

idols" is to resist the seductions of idolatry, to repudiate God as a supernatural prop or as a natural force. The task ahead is to clarify the biblical concept of God and to achieve a new cultural synthesis, on a world scale, that can recover this lost concept and gain access to the reality it represents.

Christianity in a Post-Christian Era[1]

> *Le Monde est beau, et hors*
> *de lui point de salut.*
> —ALBERT CAMUS, *Noces.*

God is man's failure. Never does this become so manifest as in periods of transition, like ours, which are essentially periods of spiritual *interregnum.* Throughout the ages, Christian or not, pre-Christian and post-Christian, God has been man's failure. And in the death of his gods, man both fails and overcomes his failure.

It is not sacrilegious to speak of the death of God, or of God as the chief failure of man. After all, the concept of God is a cultural—not to say ethnolatrous—concept, and God often is nothing other than some sort of constant accessory of culture. Concepts can be valid only so long as they spearhead the spontaneous expression of a particular human experience; they can live only as long as their cultural framework lasts. But a culture is also materialized by institutions, and these tend to overwhelm and atrophy the human experience, until they have invalidated it. By thus defrauding the concept, institutions objectify and ultimately transform into an empirical datum the human reality they are supposed to incarnate.

In the Gospel of John, the incarnation means the constantly unique event through which destiny is improvised once and for all, and not its objectification. Human existence, because it can never be rehearsed, is not an institution but a necessary improvisation of destiny. Admittedly, institutions too are born of the

---

[1] From *Wait Without Idols* (New York: Braziller, 1964).—Ed.

necessity of improvisation, but they freeze it, they codify it, just as dogmas and religion betray faith by codifying the acts of faith—through which they are improvised—forgetting that existence itself, as a spontaneous act of faith, is an impertinent improvisation on the theme of God's reality, of the presentness of God.

Unfortunately, organized religion with its variegated paraphernalia, by trying to show how pertinent faith is, blunts it and mummifies it. No improvisation thus lasts beyond the moment when it is conceived, and the concept that results from it leads finally to the institutionalization of religion, or to the cultural annexation of God, or the deliquescence of faith into religiosity. To cite Karl Barth, man can only formulate concepts that are not identical with God; there is no adequacy between God and our concepts of God.[2] Religion and its gods are, consequently, so many screens, so many obstacles between the living God and man. No wonder, according to biblical thought, God in whose image man is created is imageless. And we may, quite appropriately, paraphrase Faulkner's sentence when he writes in *The Sound and the Fury*, "it was men invented virginity, not women,"[3] by saying: it was men invented religion, not God. It was men invented the God that dies.

Indeed, men take pleasure in inventing religions, if not quite to the point of patenting them, at least to that of "incorporating" them. This stricture is not directed against certain American denominations only; every Christian confession is similarly reprehensible whether it is established officially as territorial or unofficially as cultural church, or whether it is incorporated in Vatican State. Christianity itself, as a whole, comes under this judgment insofar as it has *de facto* become the trademark of Western culture.

To speak of the death of God means, then, that finally at the end of the Christian phase of Western culture, the reality of the living God is freed from the cultural concepts and other institu-

---

[2] Karl Barth, *Fides quaerens intellectum: Anselms Beweis der Existenz Gottes* (München, 1931), ch. I/3.
[3] William Faulkner, *The Sound and the Fury* (New York: Modern Library), p. 97.

tions that attempt to objectify and domesticate it. The death of God marks the end of Christian culture and, especially, of its attempt to assimilate *the other God*, the living God of whom our religion as well as our diffuse religiosity is a desperate caricature. This means that, man being a religious animal, we are groping for a new concept of God and a new attitude, a mode of being congruous with it; that a new religiosity is dawning. And a new era begins when a new religiosity appears, rises from the empty tomb of the dead God.

It was Montesquieu who said, a couple of centuries ago, that Protestantism was bound to disappear, but that, when it has disappeared, Catholicism will have become Protestant. This might well happen. But what will Christianity itself have become by that time? Will it not have fully and plainly become what it already seems to be—nothing more than the bed of a new religiosity, whether this be the threefold religiosity of America's three-religions-and-no-faith, or the cultural, ethnolatrous theology of the West against its rivals for world domination? Montesquieu overlooked the fact that Christianity (ever since it baptized the pagan, syncretistic religiosity of the Mediterranean world) was creating its own religiosity, just as the craving for a drug replaces the illness it was meant to cure. Thalidomide, meant to ease some pains, resulted in "monsters." Christianity "eased the pains" of the world into which the Word was made flesh, but the religious monstrosity it conceived has now become our torment or the object of our disdain.

The dissolution of Christianity into religiosity is what Montesquieu failed to see. (We must not blame him for that. After all, is it not true that we can only wear the face of our religion and that religion can only wear the face of the culture it masks?) Between Montesquieu and ourselves, the death of God has marked this transition from a Christianity resting on the Christianized religiosity of the Roman Empire to our post-Christian religiosity which rests on the ruins of the Christian era.

Thus the death of God has also resulted in the unmasking of the latent, diffuse religiosity to which man is, by nature, inclined. It may well be, therefore, as Mircea Eliade remarks, that the present period will go down in history as the first to have rediscovered "diffuse religious experiences," to have recovered the relevance of raw diffuse religiosity, once overcome by the triumph of Christianity.[4]

But this post-Christian religiosity may also force Christianity out of its Western cage, enable it to break through the walls of Occidentalism and develop into a new historic reality and into a new possibility as individual existence. Doubtless, there are concrete obstacles hindering such expectations for the survival of Christianity. And what if the Christian tradition were check-mated by these obstacles? Such an eventuality is not impossible: it is becoming more and more evident if not absolutely inescapable.

Nonetheless, everything still depends on the ultimate effect of the transition from radical monotheism to radical immanentism and of the leveling down of transcendental values to immanental ones. Either this effect will consist in the recovery of our classic, transcendental categories, according to which God is distinct from, wholly other than his creation. Or else, God has been, so to speak, *renaturalized*, into an immanental force, animating the compulsory ideology of the classless society, at one end of the spectrum, and our most democratic pretensions to deity at the other end. Either way, one thing is clear: man is not an atheist, except by contrast with an established theism, whether it be monotheism or polytheism. As Jean Guitton has said, man is essentially an idolater or an "iconoclast," but not an atheist.[5] But this aspect of the problem cannot concern us at this point, except insofar as it helps us to stress the iconoclastic element peculiarly inherent in the biblical view of existence, or the icono-clastic nature of man's obligation to God.

Our present crisis stems from the fact that we have changed the biblical iconoclasm of the Christian tradition into the idola-trous post-Christian religiosity of our cultural institutions, be they social, political, economic, or ecclesiastical.

And let us not pretend that Christianity has never been *really*

---

[4] Mircea Eliade, "Note pour un humanisme," *Nouvelle Revue Française*, November 1961.

[5] Cf. Henri Fesquet, *Le Catholicisme, religion de demain* (Paris, 1962), p. 105.

tried. It is dishonest to do so after nearly twenty centuries of Christian apologetics, intellectually or ethically, religiously or institutionally as well as culturally. Besides, that same claim could be made for all the dead religions that are now preserved in the religious wax museum of mankind. To pretend that Christianity has never been really tried can only imply, not that its ideals have been much too difficult and demanding for mortal men to realize, but that we are seeking dubious excuses to conceal the fact (as Teilhard de Chardin has rightly observed) that, because Christianity is neither pure nor demanding enough, it can command our allegiance no longer. The death of God is, after all, not a divine failure but the failure of Christian man, like other human failures in history.[6] "Splendid results attained by Christendom!" exclaimed Kierkegaard as he remarked that unfaith, the impossibility or "inability to believe" was now "the sign of a deeper nature."[7]

The repudiation of Christianity does not, of course, entail the repudiation of religion. It does imply, however, that mythological Christianity has given way to a technological religiosity; or that, in Berdyaev's terms, religion used to play a *symbolic* role in the shaping of Western culture, but has now become pragmatic and utilitarian. Technological religiosity simply corroborates the increasing irrelevance of Christianity now become the syndrome of the death of God. In plain words, Christianity was regressing even while it brought about the cultural development that presided over the birth of our technological society.

And yet the de-divinization of nature (as necessitated by biblical thought) need not have resulted in the "deconsecration" or secularization of the world. Secularity, or involvement in the world for the sake of God's glory, need not have slipped into secularism. Fostered by Christianity, secularism has been the best expression of the immanentist religiosity that has succeeded the radical monotheism of classical Christianity, when nature, de-divinized, was still conceived of as made for grace. Man's preeminence over the creation was an act of faith. His conquest of the universe is today a technological act of prowess if not

---

[6] Nicholas Berdyaev, *Le sens de l'histoire* (Paris, 1948), pp. 182ff.
[7] Kierkegaard, *The Sickness Unto Death* (New York: Anchor Books), p. 246.

simply a technical problem. This deterioration had already set in when in the modern period "reason was cultivated at the expense of spirit."[8] No wonder, then, that today we cultivate religiosity at the expense of faith in God. That is why we can reverse Kierkegaard's statement and claim that Western culture is the misfortune of Christianity. And that is also why Christianity has remained a Western if not a strictly European phenomenon.

At this point, the question becomes: Can Christianity disentangle itself from the present crisis of Western culture? In other words, is Christianity regressing or developing?

It must be borne in mind that any development of Christianity is by necessity a matter of faith. Unlike economic goals, it will not be achieved through any sort of five-year plan. Insofar as one can distinguish Christianity from its religious and cultural institutions, it is not an empirical datum but the expression of an act of faith. In order to develop, Christianity must, accordingly, dissociate itself from those institutions of Western culture that are catalyzing the present spiritual crisis. And by doing this Christianity would be truly iconoclastic, smashing its own golden calf. To paraphrase St. Vincent of Lerins, the task is to say all things in a new way without proclaiming insidious novelties. The time has come to proclaim the Gospel in a new, bold manner, yet without proclaiming a new gospel. Never easy, this kind of task is still more difficult today, and the future quite precarious, what with all the newfangled ideologies that compete with Christianity—and not always unsuccessfully—both at home and abroad.

As we have said, Christianity has until now been almost exclusively a European or Western phenomenon. But the realities of the present world have forced Europe and America to realize that the destiny of the West must include non-Western countries. The era of geographic narcissism has gone—whether that be a good thing or not. The fact is that the ideological gigantism of the modern world and its economic, political, social, religious, and philosophical ramifications will burst through the frame of

[8] Wilhelm Röpke, *Die Gesellschaftskrisis der Gegenwart* (Erlenbach-Zürich, 1942), pp. 24–25.

"European" Christendom, and dislocate Christianity—unless, of course, Christianity should choose to become solely the home-grown religion of the West, for internal use only.

As an empirical datum Christianity has regressed, and this precisely because it has fulfilled itself in Western culture, or, more accurately, in the Christian or Constantinian phase of Western culture. This judgment is based on the claim—I should prefer to say, on the fact—that culturally, if not theologically, there has been a Christian era. Though every age is in need of God's grace and accordingly no age is Christian from a strict theological point of view, the fact remains that our cultural institutions, from the church to our democratic ideals, are unmistakably Christian and not Buddhist or what-have-you; Christianity has become an empirical datum.

We may, therefore, and must, in fact, consider our problem in terms of Christianity in this light. Before inquiring into its three main aspects, i.e., theological, ecclesiastical-institutional, and cultural, let us state our premises. If God is dead, then it follows that as an empirical datum Christianity is regressing. It follows, too, that such a situation makes it culturally impossible to become a Christian under the present circumstances. But it does not follow that no act of faith, no new proclamation of the kerygma (i.e., the core of the Gospel) can never take place and overcome this self-invalidation of Christianity.

The future of Christianity depends, in other words, upon a cultural reconversion. This is exactly what I understand Tillich to mean when he writes: "The destruction of the ontological argument is not dangerous. What is dangerous is the destruction of an approach which elaborates the possibility of the question of God. This approach is the meaning and truth of the onto-logical argument."[9] With such a statement we are already deal-ing with the first of the three aspects I have mentioned, the theological.

It is a truism to say that the critical moments of Western history have also involved the greatest theological activity. And there is no self-congratulation—no delusion either—in claiming

[9] Paul Tillich, *Systematic Theology*, I (University of Chicago Press, 1951), p. 208. [See p. 242 of this anthology.—Ed.]

that in this period of crisis, too, we are witnessing a theological work of such magnitude that it can be advantageously compared with the best examples of the past. From Karl Barth to Father Teilhard, including Tillich and D'Arcy, Niebuhr and Maritain as well as, of course, Rudolf Bultmann, there has emerged a constellation of thinkers who are, as the above quotation from Tillich shows, in no sense lagging behind the times. Nor are they, as some did when Christianity was faring in better circumstances, accommodating the Christian faith to the exigencies of the *Zeitgeist*, even while they cope with them. This is not the place to review their work individually, or to assess the impact of their thought upon contemporary intellectual life. Like the sociologists, we must content ourselves with generalities, and concern ourselves with empirically observable facts.

Let us, then, admit that it would be a sign of intellectual impotence to chide our theologians for any lack of comprehension of our spiritual and philosophical problems. Christian theological activity has seldom been quite so alive. But this activity seems to take place mostly in the areas of Christian existence that are less, if at all, governed by the institutionalism of our ecclesiastical organizations. Indeed, nothing resists so much the institutionalism of Christian confessions as does Barth's *Kirchliche Dogmatik* (ecclesiastical dogmatics). And Teilhard's work is published without the *imprimatur*. There is some irony in pointing out that for the first time we have theologians without churches or theological systems without their corresponding ecclesiastical apparatus.

Without doubt, it is permissible to consider today's theological renewal as a part and preparation or even a precondition of the cultural reconversion without which there can be no further Christian development, no new Christian historical departure. At the same time, one must also point out, it seems, that our Christian institutions have not yet proved themselves worthy of such a magnificent renewal. To put the matter differently and, perhaps, in theologically more accurate terms, it is as if we had arrived at the point where one can still sense in our institutions the presence of the Christian tradition, but it does not coincide with contemporaneous Christian thought. Conversely, the best

Christian thinking is today cut off from the tradition as represented by its institutions. Which means, in the words of Isaiah, that

> We have become like those thou hast never ruled, like those who are not called by thy name.

The theological evidence thus points to the practical possibility of God's absence. And even stranger is the fact that the reality of God is eclipsed by the very institutions of the Christian tradition.

This brings us to the ecclesiastical-institutional aspect of the problem. Christianity lives on under the form of secularism; for this reason, the demarcation line between regression and development is here almost imperceptible. As a result, most of what is left of Christianity flirts with pluralism, while the rest of it has degenerated into a thoroughgoing syncretism. As Dostoevsky said, when the gods lose their indigenous character they die, and so do their people. A few believers, of course, survive, headed against the stream of "churchgoers," those ardent supporters of the perennial institutionism of the Christian churches. But the thing that draws our attention, without surprising us really, is that institutionalism and secularism always seem to go hand in hand. And yet, it is to the sclerotic institutions of Christianity that some have invited us to turn "with some hope," claiming as does Martin Marty that "we already possess the institutions we need to undertake the religious task set before" us.[10] Possibly, a certain degree of hopefulness is permissible, but we should not neglect to use caution, lest these institutions be like the lips with which we honor God while our hearts are far from him. To cite Isaiah again: "because this people draw near with their mouth and honor me with their lips, while their hearts are far from me . . . the wisdom of their wise men shall perish, and the discernment of their discerning men shall be hid."[11]

Peter Berger reminds us that the Church is an article of faith,

---

[10] Martin Marty, *The New Shape of American Religion* (New York, 1959), p. 122.
[11] Isaiah 29/13-14; Mark 7/6-7. (R.S.V.).

not an empirical datum. He writes: "Now, it is certainly true that no human culture is so designed as to facilitate conversion. The Jewish culture of Jesus' own time was not so designed. Neither was the Graeco-Roman into which the Christian message was carried by Paul. In other words, the Christian faith will always be in tension with the world. What is characteristic of our situation is that the religious establishment itself obscures this tension and produces the illusion that what tension there is can be understood as growing pains."[12]

Indeed, to be less iconoclastic than those outside the Church would be the greatest treason of Christianity. Nor can one force happiness down other people's throats, let alone faith; and yet this is exactly what our institutions have generally attempted to do. Or over and over again they keep fighting old battles not only in theological matters but also in the spheres of politics and economics—if a battle is engaged in at all. For example, it is doubtful whether the separation of Church and State is a valid theological issue of our time. Our ecclesiastical factions waste their energy, it seems, either when they argue radically in favor of it, or when, casuistically, they defend the principle while at the same time they seek, if they do not actually draw, support from the State for various purposes, such as education. The real problem is what the principle of Church-and-State separation has come to mean today; the fact is that the State no longer needs the Church, being itself a sort of clerical organization that has taken over many responsibilities that used to be ecclesiastical.

Incidentally, let us make it clear, if we must, that none of this is meant to minimize the importance of the Ecumenical Movement or of the worldwide council that is being held at the Vatican. Whether they are any indication that the Christian tradition may yet enjoy a new lease on life depends, of course, on whether they are dominated by the institutionalism of the various Christian confessions they represent. Are they not in fact part of the process toward gigantism so characteristic of our age? To be sure, there is nothing intrinsically evil about gigantism,

[12] Peter Berger, *The Noise of Solemn Assemblies* (Garden City: Doubleday, 1961), p. 117.

whether or not it is a necessity of the modern world. But when Christianity sanctions this particular trend, the danger is that it may be doing so for merely social and institutional reasons, for the sake of maintaining its status. Should this be the case, not only the Christian ecumenical concern would be misplaced or misguided; it would serve to accelerate the petrifying grip of institutionalism and sanction the definitive surrender of the Christian tradition.

It is more likely, however, that the leaders of both the World Council of Churches and the Vatican Council have sensed the danger that faces the Christian tradition. In this case, they should also realize that the divisions of Christianity rest, in the last analysis, on a conception of faith and existence that is descriptive of, and dependent on, the world-view of the so-called Christian era. That is to say, even granting that these divisions were at one time valid for theological reasons, today they have become purely social and institutional: they have lost their theological justification. Nothing less than a radical about-face, such as, for example, an adjustment of dogmas to the realities of our post-Christian era, would convince us of an unsuspected vitality on the part of the Christian tradition. In a post-Christian era, the sociological divisions of Christianity make no sense. They should not be sanctified, but denounced. True iconoclasm begins with oneself, with the smashing of one's own idols, i.e., of one's super-annuated conception of God, of faith and religious allegiance.

We come now to the third aspect of Christianity as an empirical datum, the cultural. Actually, all that has been said so far has been largely determined by this aspect. Instead, then, of a repetitious elaboration, we shall rather try to sharpen our focus, and for that we must be ready for paradoxes.

On the one hand, our cultural incapacity for God stems from the radical immanentism that informs human experience today. On the other hand, we are no less religious today than those of the previous era. Religiosity, in other words, has set in, sometimes merely concealing religious anarchy and sometimes hardly concealed by religious pluralism, under the guise of tolerance. But pluralism is a misnomer. Really, should we not, instead, characterize the present phenomenon and plethora of religious experiences as the subtle expression of henotheism? Doubtless, it is not here a question of national henotheism. The gigantism of the modern world would prevent this. But we may legitimately speak of cultural henotheism, whether it be in terms of the legacy of the Judaeo-Christian tradition to the West, or in terms of a more diffuse reality that actually rests on roughly economic, social, political, or ideological allegiances. Is not denominationalism but a concealed form of the modern version of henotheism —not to mention the latest fad, the tripartite religiosity of democracy?

Clearly, I am not advocating religious bigotry and intolerance. But tolerance need not be syncretistic or lead to that institutional pluralism for which God is a social commodity—as was exemplified in the emperor cult of the dying Roman empire. And like the syncretism of the Graeco-Roman world before the rise of the Christian tradition, in the last analysis pluralism can only be an interlude. It often represents nothing other than the lack of vision on the part of a people that is religiously tired, whose God is dead. Obviously, then, if any hope is left that Christianity might somehow recover certain attributes that will make it again relevant to the future of Western culture, it must first of all substitute new cultural patterns for the old ones with which it is identifying itself without any theological justification. Nothing less than a cultural renovation of Christian institutions—and that means a radically new approach to the question of Christianity's cultural embodiment—is necessarily prescribed if any theological renascence is to have some effect outside the walls of the Church as well as within.

That is why, as we have already underlined, an iconoclastic reconversion, a cultural revolution, is sorely needed, and all the more urgently because neither institutions nor cultural patterns in general are so "designed as to facilitate conversion" to Christianity, if they are not, as they seem to be today, so designed as to make it altogether superfluous. By comparison, a much easier task, indeed, confronted the early Christians. To begin with, they were not immobilized nor was their vision obscured by already existing institutions, not to mention the fact that the non-Christian institutions were not only religious but also sacral, at least supernatural in their significance, while our culture has lost its sacral dimension. It follows, therefore, that the survival of the Christian tradition is handicapped rather than helped by the existence of cultural structures that are Christian in name only. It was doubtless easier to make the conversion from pre-Christian to Christian than it is from post-Christian to Christian, and the reasons for this are obviously not merely chronological, as we have attempted to show in the preceding theological essays on literature.

The conclusions we have reached may be summarized in the following manner:

First, in its deepest recesses, Western culture is practically immunized against Christianity. Conversely, there has occurred what we might call a cultural neutralization of the Christian tradition. This means that the once powerful and culturally pregnant symbols of the God-man, of the real presence of God's transcendent immediacy, of communion, are now become words of a forgotten language. Our customs still exhale a Christian flavor, but our hearts are not Christian.[13]

Second, assuming that it was Christianity that began to kill the pagan gods of nature, by de-divinizing nature, until modern science simply confirmed their death, it is possible that, in the last analysis, the death of God means the death of those pagan deities that had somehow survived in the Christian cultural conception of God. Accordingly, the absence of God, as the only divine reality that can be experienced today, may yet enable Christianity further to clarify the biblical concept of God as the Wholly Other, because he is the Creator and not a natural force.

Third, the era of Western religious narcissism is gone, and this certainly, is a significant contribution of our post-Christian era to the Christian tradition. The national egotism of emergent countries will perhaps force Christianity to become more kerygmatic at home as well as abroad, that is to say, to help bring about or to awaken us to the need for a cultural renovation by becoming iconoclastic again and, thus, relevant to the culture of the West.

Fourth, the exposing of religious obscurantism and the absence

[13] Alain, *Propos sur la religion* (Paris, 1957), p. 41.

of supernatural crutches may equally force us to formulate what Berdyaev refers to as our "cultural will," whether as Christians or not, but certainly not as pseudo-Christian Westerners or as pseudo-Western Christians.

Our final point will be made by way of a question borrowed from St. Augustine: "How could the City of God," he asked, ". . . either take a beginning or be developed, or attain its proper destiny, if the life of the saints were not a social life?"[14] How can the Christian tradition survive or develop without a concomitant, congruous, cultural reality manifest in all realms of the spirit from theology to art and literature as well as on all levels of life from morality to economics and politics?

In short, the Christian tradition has been regressing insofar as it has not been relevant to the present crisis of our cultural situation. On the other hand, Christian thought has been developing, but it is no longer relevant to the situation of our post-Christian age and its cultural postulates—nor will it be relevant as long as it is tied down by its institutions and by the dogmas of a forgotten language. And should Christianity perchance survive the dishabilitation of its institutions, the least that still must be said is that Western culture is not "ready" for it, as the pre-Christian world once was ready for the Christian gospel.

[14] St. Augustine, *De civitate dei,* 19/5.

Thomas Jonathan Jackson Altizer

[b. 1927]

A DESCENDANT of Civil War General Stonewall Jackson, Thomas Altizer was born in Cambridge, Massachusetts, and grew up in Charleston, West Virginia. From early childhood, he had a passionate and enduring interest in religion, which at one time led him to undergo "a brief and devastating 'test' of a monastic vocation in an Episcopalian Benedictine monastery in Michigan,"[1] and subsequently to attempt "a full Catholic devotional life."

At the age of eighteen, Altizer interrupted his education to serve in the U.S. Army Air Force and was briefly stationed in Japan shortly after World War II. Returning home, received his B.A. from the University of Chicago in 1948. For a time, Marxism became the focus of his religious outlook, and he counts "radical political beliefs and activities" as having asserted a decisive influence on his subsequent intellectual development, as did his discovery of Freud. "I cannot conceive of meaningful discourse in our world," he says, "apart from the mythical-symbolical language of Marxism and Freudianism." It is hardly accidental that he is also indebted to Paul Tillich, whom he regards as "the modern father of radical theology," although he found Tillich's theological conclusions "not yet radical enough."[2]

Altizer enrolled in the University of Chicago Divinity School with the intention of entering the parish ministry of the Episcopal

---

[1] Quotations, unless otherwise specified, are from personal correspondence.
[2] Thomas J. J. Altizer, *The Gospel of Christian Atheism* (Philadelphia: Westminster, 1966), p. 10.

Church, and he served as a student pastor in an interracial Chicago mission, but he decided against ordination and took an M.A. in theology before going on to a Ph.D. in the history of religions, which he studied under Joachim Wach. Like many of his generation, Karl Barth was for him an important theological influence but one that eventually yielded to others. "In a certain sense," says Altizer, "Nietzsche has been my most influential teacher." Admitting to such a variety of mentors, he adds that he has never been attracted to positivism or analytic philosophy, and for many years he has "not been able to look upon the language of our theologians with anything approaching seriousness."

His quest for a new and suitable language has paralleled his steady drift away from the church. Although he retains "a certain basic loyalty to both its active and its dormant expressions," its vision of ultimate truth became increasingly provincial in the light of his studies of Oriental mysticism, which began to yield new insight into the significance of Jesus Christ. It was in this context and through a study of Mircea Eliade's work that the genesis of a new, radical theology began to take shape, and this was given exciting impetus by Altizer's discovery of William Blake in 1963.

Some eight months of intensive study, embracing Blake's complete works but with particular attention to his great epics *Milton* and *Jerusalem*, convinced Altizer that Blake held the key to a uniquely Christian interpretation of man's destiny. Or perhaps it would be truer to say that the radical vision of Blake—a vision reflected in different form in Hegel's dialectic of the spirit—comprises a further step in the process left incomplete in the New Testament. The way out of the impasse of modern Christianity lay not, as for Vahanian, in regaining the lost transcendence of the primal God of the Old Testament, but in accepting the loss as part of a forward-moving eschatological process. Altizer discovered that Blake's apocalypse was the exact reverse of Hindu and other quietistic cosmologies and mysticisms—that in Blake the dialectic between sacred and profane is summed up in such a phrase as "All that lives is holy," which expresses dialectically the *meaning* of life and holiness. For life is a matter of energy, of a process of expansion and fulfillment, and holiness is a new innocence achieved only through the dynamic of experience. As man becomes fulfilled, growing toward the maturity of his eschatological or ultimate vision of total reality, the wholly other God of the past becomes emptied of that very meaning which is flowing into human consciousness. For Altizer, if not for Blake, the incarnation in Jesus is not an isolated cosmic event but the inauguration of the eschatological process, which has entered its final phase in the modern world with the ossification and irreversible negation of the God of the primordial past.

The nature of vision can be better understood if we realize that for Blake it is always revelatory, a source of new disclosures about reality; and by the same token Blake regards memory as its opposite. When religious faith is "the remembrance or repetition of a past or primordial reality,"[3] says Altizer, it cannot be a living faith. The crisis of contemporary theology is that it has become an unavailing effort of memory that succeeds only in isolating the divine Word from present reality. "Whatever contemporaneity is present in modern theology," he insists, "derives from its mute witness to the death of God."[4] The only legitimate alternative to this silence is an affirmation of the Incarnate Word predicated on an acceptance of the finality of the death of the transcendent God. Altizer rejects Buber's notion of an "eclipse" of God as a nostalgic evasion. He tacitly repudiates Vahanian's view of the event as a cultural phenomenon. In his careful essay "The Self-Annihilation of God," Altizer performs what he considers an essential task of theology that is specifically Christian, a task of "creative negation" that does not reluctantly accept the death of God but affirms it as the dialectical precondition or consequence of the incarnation. What is distinctively Christian is that the divine Word has moved from eternity into time; it is no longer primordial and transcendent. "We Christians are called upon to be loyal only to Christ, only to the Incarnate Word who

---

[3] Altizer, "William Blake and the Role of Myth in the Radical Christian Vision," *Centennial Review*, Fall, 1965, p. 479. This essay is adapted from a forthcoming book, Thomas J. J. Altizer, *The New Apocalypse: The Radical Christian Vision of William Blake* (East Lansing: Michigan State University Press, 1967).
[4] Altizer, "Creative Negation in Theology," *The Christian Century*, July 7, 1965, p. 865.

has appeared in our flesh, and therefore we should already have been prepared for the appearance of Christ without God. We know that Christ is present in the concrete actuality of our history or he is not truly present at all."[5] To proclaim the death of God is thus to recognize that there is no possibility of return to a long-lost innocence. It is to affirm joyously that man's redemption occurs not in the abstract but in the fulfillment of life here and now, through experience. The Bible is neither closed nor sacrosanct; it has validity as part of an unfolding series of disclosures or discoveries of the Word, which continues to live and grow among men. The historical epoch of the secular, in which man has achieved the vision of the death of God, is as decisive as that in which the Gospel first made its appearance. The emergence of a new Christianity from the ruins of the old is comparable to the rise of a "new Israel" among the first followers of Jesus. The kenotic Christ of today is not a relic of antiquity but is the "divine humanity" in process of self-realization.

Altizer's achievement is remarkable as a synthesis and systematic commentary on Blake's vision, suffused and illumined with a masterful grasp of the Hegelian dialectic. It is the fullest and most sustained theological statement of the new Christianity that has yet been attempted. Yet it has elicited more sympathy than endorsement, and it remains to be seen whether Altizer can meet the challenge of such critics as Charles Long, who asserts: "The eschatological mythology which Altizer proposes is not rooted in that basic contact with reality which is the touchstone of every myth. It presents us with a rich exterior and a glorious future, but it has no interiority . . ."[6] Both Blake's rich and insightful symbolism and Altizer's interpretation of it are not sufficiently engaged with actual history. What are the implications of the new Christianity for the freedom movement in the United States, for the dialogue between East and West—in terms of pragmatic occasions? How does a man live as a Christian in today's and tomorrow's world? In a sense, Altizer's thinking remains too narrowly theological. It will be tested as it is related

[5] Ibid., p. 866.
[6] Charles H. Long, "The Ambiguities of Innocence." This is a chapter from a book in progress.

to the specific contours of experience. For Altizer's own part, the style of thought toward which he is now moving is "more Nietzschean than Blakean." Given also his familiarity with Marxist and Freudian thought, there is every reason to expect that in future he will be engaged in active and fruitful dialogue with his critics.

The Self-Annihilation of God[1]

What can it mean to speak of the death of God? Indeed, how is it even possible to speak of the death of God, particularly at a time when the name of God would seem to be unsayable? First, we must recognize that the proclamation of the death of God is a Christian confession of faith. For to know that God is dead is to know the God who died in Jesus Christ, the God who passed through what Blake symbolically named as "Self-Annihilation" or Hegel dialectically conceived as the negation of negation. Only the Christian can truly speak of the death of God, because the Christian alone knows the God who negates himself in his own revelatory and redemptive acts. Just as a purely religious apprehension of deity must know a God who is transcendent and beyond, so likewise a purely rational and nondialectical conception of deity must know a God who is impassive and unmoving, or self-enclosed in his own Being. Neither the religious believer nor the nondialectical thinker can grasp the God whose actuality and movement derives from his own acts of self-negation. Thus it is only the radical, or the profane, or the nonreligious Christian who knows that God has ceased to be active and real in his preincarnate or primordial reality.

Nevertheless, it is essential that the radical Christian make clear what he means by his confession, eliminating so far as possible all that confusion and ambiguity arising from the language of the death of God, and clearly establishing both his Christian claim and his repudiation of all forms of religious Christianity.

[1] From *The Gospel of Christian Atheism* (Philadelphia: Westminster, 1966). —Ed.

To confess the death of God is to speak of an actual and real event, not perhaps an event occurring in a single moment of time or history, but notwithstanding this reservation an event that has actually happened both in a cosmic and in a historical sense. There should be no confusion deriving from the mistaken assumption that such a confession refers to an eclipse of God or a withdrawal of God from either history or the creation. Rather, an authentic language speaking about the death of God must inevitably be speaking about the death of God himself. The radical Christian proclaims that God has actually died in Christ, that this death is both a historical and a cosmic event, and, as such, it is a final and irrevocable event, which cannot be reversed by a subsequent religious or cosmic movement. True, a religious reversal of the death of God has indeed occurred in history, is present in the religious expressions of Christianity, and is now receding into the mist of an archaic, if not soon to be forgotten, past. But such a religious reversal cannot annul the event of the death of God; it cannot recover the living God of the old covenant, nor can it reverse or bring to an end the progressive descent of Spirit into flesh. Religious Christians may know a resurrected Lord of the Ascension, just as they may be bound to an almighty and distant Creator and Judge. Yet such a flight from the finality of the Incarnation cannot dissolve the event of the Incarnation itself even if it must finally impel the Christian to seek the presence and the reality of Christ in a world that is totally estranged from Christianity's established vision of the sacred.

Once again we must attempt to draw a distinction between the original or primal death of God in Christ and the actualization or historical realization of his death throughout the whole gamut of human experience. Remembering the radical Christian affirmation that God has fully and totally become incarnate in Christ, we must note that neither the Incarnation nor the Crucifixion can here be understood as isolated and once-and-for-all events; rather, they must be conceived as primary expressions of a forward-moving and eschatological process of redemption, a process embodying a progressive movement of Spirit into flesh. At no point in this process does the incarnate Word or Spirit assume a final and definitive form, just as God himself can never be wholly or simply identified with any given revelatory event or epiphany, if only because the divine process undergoes a continual metamorphosis, ever moving more deeply and more fully toward an eschatological consummation. While the Oriental mystic knows an incarnational process whereby the sacred totally annihilates or transfigures the profane, a process providing us with our clearest image of the primordial reality of the sacred, it is Christianity alone which witnesses to a concrete and actual descent of the sacred into the profane, a movement wherein the sacred progressively abandons or negates its particular and given expressions, thereby emptying them of their original power and actuality. Radical Christianity knows this divine or incarnational process as a forward-moving Totality. Neither a primordial God nor an original garden of innocence remains immune to this process of descent: here all things whatsoever are drawn into and transfigured by this cosmic or total process of metamorphosis. This movement from "Innocence" to "Experience" is potentially or partially present at every point of time and space, and in every epiphany of the divine process: thus we could even say that God dies in some sense wherever he is present or actual in the world, for God actualizes himself by negating his original or given expressions. Yet we truly know this divine process of negativity only by knowing God's death in Christ.

Estranged as we are from our Christian heritage, and distant as we most certainly are from the actual faith of the earliest disciples, what can the contemporary Christian know of the original epiphany of God in Christ? Initiated as we are, moreover, into a historical consciousness that has unveiled a whole new world of New Testament thought and imagery, a world that is subject neither to theological systemization nor to translation into modern thought and experience, how can we hope to ascertain the fundamental meaning for us of the original Christian faith? Let us openly confess that there is no possibility of our returning to a primitive Christian faith, and that the Christ who can become contemporary to us is neither the original historical Jesus nor the Lord of the Church's earliest proclamation. Given our historical situation in the twilight of Christendom, we have long since died to the possibility of a classical or orthodox Christian belief, and must look upon both the New Testament and early Christianity as exotic and alien forms of religion. Nevertheless, and here we continue to have much to learn from the radical Christian, we cannot neglect the possibility that it is precisely our alienation from the religious world of primitive Christianity which can make possible our realization of the fundamental if underlying meaning of the earliest expressions of the Christian faith. For if a religious movement necessarily embodies a backward movement of involution and return, then the very fact that we have died to the religious form of early Christianity can make possible our passage through a reversal of religious Christianity, a reversal that can open to us a new and fuller participation in the forward movement of the Incarnation.

We know that the proclamation of both Jesus and the earliest Palestinian churches revolved about the announcement of the glad tidings or the gospel of the dawning of the Kingdom of God. But thus far neither the theologian nor the Biblical scholar has been able to appropriate the eschatological symbol of the Kingdom of God in such a manner as to make it meaningful to the modern consciousness without thereby sacrificing its original historical meaning. It is scarcely questionable, however, that this symbol originally pointed to the final consummation of a dynamic process of the transcendent's becoming immanent: of a distant, a majestic, and a sovereign Lord breaking into time and space in such a way as to transfigure and renew all things whatsoever, thereby abolishing the old cosmos of the original creation, and likewise bringing to an end all that law and religion which had thus far been established in history. The very form of Christianity's original apocalyptic proclamation rests upon an expectation that the actualization of the Kingdom of God will make present not the almighty Creator, Lawgiver, and Judge, but rather a wholly new epiphany of the deity, an epiphany annihilating all that distance separating the creature from the Creator. Despite Paul's conviction that the victory which Christ won over the powers of sin and darkness had annulled the old Israel and initiated the annihilation of the old creation, to say nothing of his assurance that God will be all in all, both Paul and the early Church were unable fully or decisively to negate the religious forms of the old history, or to surmount their bondage to the transcendent and primordial epiphany of God. Consequently, early Christianity was unable either to negate religion or to absorb and fully assimilate an apocalyptic faith, with the result that it progressively became estranged from its own initial proclamation.

Already we have seen that the modern radical Christian has evolved an apocalyptic and dialectical mode of vision or understanding revolving about an apprehension of the death of God in Christ, and it is just this self-negation or self-annihilation of the primordial reality of God which actualizes the metamorphosis of an all-embracing Totality. Can we not make the judgment that it is precisely this vision of the death of God in Christ that can make possible for us a realization of the deeper meaning of the Christian and eschatological symbol of the dawning of the Kingdom of God? Thereby we could know that the victory of the Kingdom of God in Christ is the fruit of the final movement of God into the world, of Spirit into flesh, and that the Christian meaning of the Kingdom of God is inseparable from an abolition or reversal of all those preincarnate forms or epiphanies of Spirit. By so conceiving the underlying meaning of the original Christian proclamation, we can also see that it is the religious vision of early Christianity which reverses the Christian reality of the Kingdom of God. Inevitably, the orthodox expressions of Christianity abandoned an eschatological ground, and no doubt the radical Christian's recovery of an apocalyptic faith and vision was in part occasioned by his own estrangement from the dominant and established forms of the Christian tradition. Such a contemporary appropriation of the symbol of the Kingdom of God can also make possible our realization of the Gospel, or the "good news," of the death of God: for the death of God does not propel man into an empty darkness; it liberates him from every alien and opposing other, and makes possible his transition into what Blake hailed as "The Great Humanity Divine," or the final coming together of God and man.

Whether or not we choose to so understand the original Christian gospel of the dawning of the Kingdom of God, it is clear that the radical Christian affirms that God has died in Christ, and that the death of God is a final and irrevocable event. All too obviously, however, we cannot discover a clear and decisive witness to the meaning of this event in either the Bible or the orthodox teachings and visions of Christianity. But the radical Christian envisions a gradual and progressive metamorphosis of Spirit into flesh, a divine process continually negating or annihilating itself, as it ever moves forward to an eschatological goal. While the Christian proclaims that this process is triumphant in Christ, or that it is inaugurated in its final form by the events of the Incarnation and the Crucifixion, it does not follow that the process itself ceases to move forward in all that history following the death of Christ. Simply by noting the overwhelming power and the comprehensive expression of the modern Christian experience of the death of God, we can sense the effect of the ever fuller movement of the Word or Spirit into history, a movement whose full meaning only dawns with the collapse of Christendom, and in the wake of the historical realization of the death of God. A contemporary faith that opens itself to the actuality of the death of God in our history as the historical realization of the dawning of the Kingdom of God can know the spiritual emptiness of our time as the consequence in human experience of God's self-annihilation in Christ, even while recovering in a new and universal form the apocalyptic faith of the primitive Christian. Insofar as the kenotic or negative movement of the divine process is a movement into the actuality of human experience, it can neither be isolated in a given time and place nor be understood as wholly occurring within a given moment. On the contrary, the actualization of the metamorphosis of the Word into flesh is a continual and forward-moving process, a process initially occurring in God's death in Christ, yes, but a process that is only gradually and progressively realized in history, as God's original self-negation eventually becomes actualized throughout the total range of human experience.

Once again we have detected a Christian religious reversal of God's act in Christ: for a faith that isolates the sacred events of Christ's passion from the profane actuality of human experience must inevitably enclose Christ within a distant and alien form and refuse his presence in the immediacy of our existence. Every

Christian attempt to create an unbridgeable chasm between sacred history and human history gives witness to a refusal of the Incarnation and a betrayal of the forward-moving process of salvation. We can discover a reversal of the kenotic movement of the Word in the very insistence of the religious Christian that faith has for once and for all been given, that it is fully and finally present in the Scriptures, the liturgies, the creeds, and the dogmas of the past, and can in no sense undergo a development or transformation that moves beyond its original expression to new and more universal forms. All such religious claims not only attempt to solidify and freeze the life and movement of the divine process, but they foreclose the possibility of the enlargement and evolution of faith, and ruthlessly set the believer against the presence of Christ in an increasingly profane history, thereby alienating the Christian from the actuality of his own time. The radical Christian calls upon his hearer to open himself to the fullness of our history, not with the illusory belief that our history is identical with the history that Jesus lived, but rather with the conviction that the death of God which has dawned so fully in our history is a movement into the total body of humanity of God's original death in Christ. Once we grasp the radical Christian truth that a radically profane history is the inevitable consummation of an actual movement of the sacred into the profane, then we can be liberated from every preincarnate form of Spirit, and accept our destiny as an occasion for the realization in the immediacy of experience of the self-emptying or self-annihilation of the transcendent and primordial God in the passion and death of Christ.

From this perspective it would even be possible to understand Christendom's religious reversal of the movement of Spirit into flesh as a necessary consequence of the Incarnation, preparing the way for a more comprehensive historical realization of the death of God by its progressive banishment of the dead body of God to an ever more transcendent and inaccessible realm. If we conceive of the Word or Spirit as moving more and more fully into the body of the profane in response to the self-negation of God in Christ, then we can understand how the Christian God gradually becomes more alien and beyond, receding into a lifeless and oppressive form, until it finally appears as an empty and vacuous nothingness. The God who is progressively manifest in human experience as an empty and alien other is the inevitable consequence of the Spirit who descends ever more deeply into flesh. Not only does the distant and alien God witness to the historical actualization of the Word in the flesh, but his epiphany as a vacuous and empty formlessness dissolves the possibility of a living and actual faith in God, thus impelling the Christian to seek a new epiphany of Christ in the world. Let the contemporary Christian rejoice that Christianity has evolved the most alien, the most distant, and the most oppressive deity in history: it is precisely the self-alienation of God from his original redemptive form that has liberated humanity from the transcendent realm, and made possible the total descent of the Word into the fullness of human experience. The God who died in Christ is the God who thereby gradually ceases to be present in a living form, emptying himself of his original life and power, and thereafter receding into an alien and lifeless nothingness.

The death of God in Christ is an inevitable consequence of the movement of God into the world, of Spirit into flesh, and the actualization of the death of God in the totality of experience is a decisive sign of the continuing and forward movement of the divine process, as it continues to negate its particular and given expressions, by moving ever more fully into the depths of the profane. A faith that knows this process as a self-negating and kenotic movement, as both embodied and symbolically enacted in the passion of Christ, knows that it becomes manifest in the suffering and the darkness of a naked human experience, an experience banished from the garden of innocence, and emptied of the sustaining power of a transcendent ground or source. So far from regarding the vacuous and rootless existence of modern man as the product of an abandonment of faith, the radical Christian recognizes the spiritual emptiness of our time as the historical actualization of the self-annihilation of God, and despite the horror and anguish embedded in such a condition of humanity, the radical Christian can greet even this darkness as a yet more comprehensive embodiment and fulfillment of the original passion of Christ. Hence a radical faith claims our contemporary condition as an unfolding of the body of Christ, an extension into the fullness of history of the self-emptying of God. No evasion of an autonomous human condition is possible for the Christian who confesses his participation in a Word that has negated its primordial and transcendent ground: the Christian who lives in a fully incarnate Christ is forbidden either to cling to an original innocence or to yearn nostalgically for a preincarnate Spirit. Indeed, it is precisely the Christian's life in the kenotic Word which impels him to accept and affirm a world in which God is dead as the realization in history of God's self-annihilation in Christ.

Once the Christian has been liberated from all attachment to a celestial and transcendent Lord, and has died in Christ to the primordial reality of God, then he can say triumphantly: God is dead! Only the Christian can speak the liberating word of the death of God because only the Christian has died in Christ to the transcendent realm of the sacred and can realize in his own participation in the forward-moving body of Christ the victory of the self-negation of Spirit. Just as the primitive Christian could call upon his hearer to rejoice in the Crucifixion because it effected the advent of the Kingdom of God, the contemporary Christian can announce the glad tidings of the death of God, and speak with joy of the final consummation of the self-annihilation of God. True, every man today who is open to experience knows that God is absent, but only the Christian knows that God is dead, that the death of God is a final and irrevocable event, and that God's death has actualized in our history a new and liberated humanity. How does the Christian know that God is dead? Because the Christian lives in the fully incarnate body of Christ, he acknowledges the totality of our experience as the consummation of the kenotic passion of the Word, and by giving himself to the Christ who is present to us he is liberated from the alien power of an emptied and darkened transcendence. Rather than being mute and numb in response to the advent of a world in which the original name of God is no longer sayable, the Christian can live and speak by pronouncing the word of God's death, by joyously announcing the "good news" of the death of God, and by greeting the naked reality of our experience as the triumphant realization of the self-negation of God. What can the Christian fear of the power of darkness when he can name our darkness as the fulfillment of the self-emptying of God in Christ?

Harvey Gallagher Cox Jr.

[b. 1929]

BORN IN CHESTER COUNTY, Pennsylvania, Harvey Cox majored
in history at the University of Pennsylvania (B.A., 1951). This
interest continued when he turned to theological studies at Yale
Divinity School, where he received his B.D. degree in 1955 and
was ordained a Baptist minister. In the ten years that followed,
he joined the faculty of Andover Newton Theological School
as assistant professor of theology and culture and became actively
involved with the Blue Hill Christian Center and its work in
the Negro ghetto of Roxbury, Massachusetts, where he chose
to live. He continued his studies at Harvard toward a Ph.D. in
history and philosophy of religion, which was conferred in 1963
on his return from a sabbatical year of study at the Free University of Berlin. As a teen-ager at the end of World War II, Cox
had worked aboard UNRRA cattle and relief ships bound for
Poland and Germany, and while in Germany during 1962 and
1963 he served as a fraternal worker for the Gossner Mission in
East Berlin. Since 1965, he has been professor of church and
society at Harvard Divinity School.

For some years, Cox has shown an outstanding gift for writing
knowledgeably about both churchly and worldly concerns. "Miss
America and the Cult of the Girl" (*Christianity and Crisis*) and
"Rome, Delhi and the Council" (*Commonweal*) are articles
dating from 1961 that suggest two facets of his interest. Another,
"Dialogue Among Pickets" (*Commonweal*), describes his participation in a civil-rights campaign during which he spent five
days in jail in 1963, soon after his return from Europe.

Few Protestant scholars of today can match Cox's familiarity
with both theology and sociology. Perhaps his most brilliant

scholarly work to date is an article that appeared in the Spring 1965 issue of *The Christian Scholar*, "Sociology of Religion in a Post-Religious Era," in which he proposes a "sociology of theology" drawing upon the work of such diverse thinkers as Max Weber, Emile Durkheim, Georg Lukacs, Maurice Merleau-Ponty and others not often found in theological discourse. Both academic studies and his own sense of identity as a secular, urban man have kept him attuned to the dialectic between ultimate questions and empirical realities.

Cox's first book[1] was written in 1963 as a series of lectures given at a nationwide Baptist Student Conference, just after the historic March on Washington, in which Cox participated. Titled *God's Revolution and Man's Responsibility*, it draws heavily from Cox's experiences in East Germany and consists largely of an approach to "secularizing the gospel" along Bonhoefferian lines through linguistic clarifications. Here are sample remarks:

> The God of the Bible was and is a God who is only secondarily interested in nature. He is first and foremost interested in political events. . . . The word used for the "service of God" in the Old Testament is also used to refer to the service of a soldier or a citizen in the army of the king.
>
> Perhaps it is our task as Christians in the twentieth century, at the end of what Bonhoeffer calls the "religious era," to begin now to despiritualize all of these words, to give them back their gritty, earthy, political significance.[2]

The Secular City is quite a different sort of book, an ambitious, imaginative exposition of theology in relation to contemporary culture and social structures. In it he discusses such problems of urban life as bureaucracy, mass communications, the nature of technology and work, and sexual alienation. Accepting our emerging "technopolitan" culture, he discerns a new type of "I-You" relation developing in contrast to the more intimate and

[1] Although published later in the same year, 1965, this book preceded *The Secular City* in the writing and should be regarded as a preliminary work.
[2] Harvey Cox, *God's Revolution and Man's Responsibility* (Valley Forge: Judson, 1965), pp. 22–24 *passim*.

familial "I-Thou" of which Feuerbach and Buber speak. Perhaps today, says Cox, man's relation to God is best understood as a sharing in common tasks. Perhaps, too, "our English word *God* will have to die,"[3] but this is a linguistic problem rather than a theological one. At the present time, at least, Cox retains a basic theological loyalty to Karl Barth, despite evident sympathies with the "death of God" theologians. William Hamilton has more wittily than wisely labeled Cox's viewpoint as "pop Barth." Actually, Cox is closer to Buber's notion of "eclipse," the idea of a present but hidden transcendence. He is far less concerned, however, with "tongue-tied verbosity, of empty and ambiguous words,"[4] than with the pragmatics of experience.

The following selection is adapted from a talk given in March 1966 at the University of California in Santa Barbara. It is of twofold interest for its psychosocial critique of the "death of God" theology and for highlighting some of the new directions in theology that may point toward a new Christianity. What is radical in Cox's perspective is different from that in Hamilton and Altizer. Whether it represents real divergence remains to be seen as each of their styles develops and interacts.

The Death of God and the Future of Theology[1]

In one sense there is no future for theology in an age of the "death of God," but in another sense we cannot be certain of this until we know what the phrase means and what the function of theology is. For "death of God" is sometimes used to mean different things, even by the same writer in a single paragraph. My own investigation has isolated three distinct meanings.

---

[3] Cox, *The Secular City* (New York: Macmillan, 1965), p. 265.
[4] *Ibid.*
[1] An unedited version of this essay originally appeared in *El Gaucho*, newspaper of Associated Students, University of California, Santa Barbara, March 23, 1966. The present version was prepared especially for this anthology.—Ed.

The first is nontheistic or atheistic. As Paul van Buren has said, "Christianity is about man and not about God." For van Buren it is futile to say anything at all about "God," since the word has no viable empirical referent. We must therefore construct some form of theology in which we stop talking about God. Religious devotion and even religious language may remain, but the referents are entirely changed.

Van Buren's methodology is borrowed from the rigorous techniques of British and American philosophical analysis. A very different viewpoint is that of Thomas Altizer, who seems to be informed by certain Buddhist and Hegelian themes that have led him to assert that there once was a transcendent, real God, but that this God became immanent in Jesus and finally died in his crucifixion. In contrast to van Buren, Altizer insists that we must not only use the word "God," but we must make the announcement of his death central to our proclamation today. He is not puzzled by the word; he not only knows what it means but is willing to say more about the history of God than most Christian theologies have said in the past. Furthermore, Altizer insists that "only the Christian can experience the death of God." Experiencing the death of God is, for Altizer, close to what has traditionally been associated with conversion.

The second sense in which the phrase "death of God" is used occurs in the context of cultural analysis. For Gabriel Vahanian and sometimes William Hamilton, it simply means that the culturally conditioned ways in which people have experienced the holy have become eroded. Religious experience is learned in any culture just as other experience is learned, in the unspoken assumptions and attitudes which children absorb from their parents and from their closest environment. Our forebears learned from their forebears to expect the experience of the holy in socially defined ways, whether in the sunset, in a camp-meeting conversion or in holy communion. This experience was structured by a culture of residual Christendom, still bearing traces of what Paul Tillich calls "theonomy." But the coming of modern technology and massive urbanization shook the structures of traditional society and thereby dissipated the cultural ethos within which the holy had been experienced. Hence the "God" of Christendom is "dead." For most modern writers the phrase is metaphorical, but in a culture strongly influenced by pietism, where the reality of God is identified with the experience of God, the phrase may be taken literally as a somber and threatening event.

The third sense in which "God" is "dead" is one that I discussed in the last chapter of my book *The Secular City*, and it is in some respects similar both to Vahanian's and van Buren's viewpoints. For me, the idea of the "death of God" represents a crisis in our religious language and symbol structure, which makes the word "God" ambiguous. It is not that the word means nothing to "modern man," as van Buren contends, but that it means so many things to different people that it blurs communication rather than facilitating it.

For years the doctrine of God has been in trouble. Paul Tillich, who assailed the very idea that God "is" (in his *Systematic Theology*), would never have settled for an undialectical nontheism, although his attempt to move "beyond theism" (in *The Courage to Be*) probably contributed to the present situation in theology. Karl Barth's christological positivism may also have prepared the way. The "death of God" movement is an interitance from them, dramatizing the bankruptcy of the categories we have been trying to use. It is more the symptom of a serious failure in theology than a contribution to the next phase.

Modes of religious experience are, as we have noted, shaped by cultural patterns. When social change jars the patterns, conventional ways of experiencing the holy disappear. When the thickly clotted symbol system of a pre-urban society is replaced by a highly differentiated and individuated urban culture, modalities of religious experience shift. When this happens gradually, over a long span of time, the religious symbols have a chance to become adapted to the new cultural patterns. The experience of the death of the gods, or of God, is a consequence of an abrupt transition which causes the traditional symbols to collapse, since they no longer illuminate the shifting social reality.

The "death of God" syndrome can only occur where the controlling symbols of the culture have been more or less uncritically fused with the transcendent God. When a civilization collapses and its gods topple, theological speculation can move either toward a God whose being lies beyond culture (Augustine, Barth), toward some form of millenarianism or toward a religious crisis that takes the form of the "death of God."

In our own period, which is marked by man's historical consciousness reaching out and encompassing everything in sight, the nooks and crannies formerly reserved for the transcendent have all been exposed. Pluralism and radical historicism have become our permanent companions. We know that all doctrines, ideals, institutions and formulations, whether religious or secular, arise within history and must be understood in terms of their historical milieu. How then do we speak of a God who is somehow present in history, yet whose being is not exhausted by the limits of history? How, in short, do we maintain an affirmation of transcendence within the context of a culture whose mood is relentlessly immanentist? Perhaps a rediscovery of the millenarian tradition, a reappropriation of eschatology tradition, is the way we must go.

The crisis in our doctrine of God is a serious one. This cannot be denied. Nevertheless, our continued and correct insistence on the need to encounter God in *all* of life and not just in a "religious" or cultic precinct fails to express anything that really transcends "history," the source of our experiential reference for what we usually talk about. Some theologians, like Schubert M. Ogden, have responded to the present impasse by going back to the only significant constructive work that has been done in recent decades in American theology—the thought of Charles Hartshorne and Henry Nelson Wieman—and to the philosophy of Alfred North Whitehead. This tactic may eventually produce results, but so far it has not really resolved any of the radical criticisms raised by the "death-of-God" writers.

My own response to the dead-end signaled by the "death of God" mood is to continue to move away from any spatial symbolization of God and from all forms of metaphysical dualism. I am trying to edge cautiously toward a secular theology, a mode of thinking whose horizon is human history and whose idiom is "political" in the widest Aristotelian sense of that term, i.e. the context in which man becomes fully man.

As I move in this direction, there are certain traps I want to try to avoid. First, though it may be satisfactory for some, I want to steer clear of the mystical-atheistic monism of Thomas Altizer. From the perspective of the science of religion, mysticism and atheism have always been similar. Both lack the elements of encounter with an "Other," a confrontation that is characteristic of most forms of theism. In Altizer this structural similarity has come to explicit expression. Second, I want to avoid the uncritical empiricism of Paul van Buren. I think his methodological starting point, derived from contemporary British and American linguistic analysis, is too constrictive. It does not take sufficient account of the nonempirical functions of many modes of human speech, the open and changing character of all languages, and the place of any language within a larger universe of symbolic, metaphorical, and poetic modes of expression. Kenneth Burke, in *The Rhetoric of Religion*, has laid out a type of religious-language analysis which does embrace these larger cultural dimensions, thus offering a corrective to the analysts' presuppositions.

Finally, I want to steer clear of the inverse pietism of William Hamilton, whose perceptive analysis of the cultural mood[2] is sometimes confused with the theological task itself. Since he often deduces the mood of the culture from a description of his own moods and beliefs, the basis of his theology is extremely experiential. This may be good, especially in view of the unjustly severe disparaging of "experience" which was so characteristic of the followers of Karl Barth, but theology cannot become experiential in this sense without courting the danger of becoming subjective. Thus, while I can accept his diagnosis of the cultural *élan*, which is often correct, I decline to enlarge it into a properly theological claim.

Let me make it clear that I do not condemn the men I have just named. I do not wish to belittle their contributions. As Gordon Kaufman has suggested, many of us are engaged in

---

[2] See his essay "The New Optimism" in Hamilton and Altizer, *Radical Theology and the Death of God* (Indianapolis: Bobbs-Merrill, 1966).

different "experiments in thought," pushing ahead to think
through the implications of this or that set of premises.[3] This
theological diversity is a mark of strength, not of weakness. Let
me make it clear, too, that if I regard undialectical religious
atheism as too easy a way out, I also find most available "theistic"
options equally unattractive. The road ahead often seems narrow,
dark and perilous, yet we can neither retreat nor stand still.
The best I can do now is to try to indicate where I hope a break-
through might be found, to point in the direction I want to go,
not to a spot where I have arrived.

For me, the way out of the "death of God" miasma which
leads forward rather than backward is lighted, however flicker-
ingly, by two of the seminal minds of our era, Pierre Teilhard
de Chardin and Ernst Bloch. Both of these men are intellectual
vagabonds; neither belongs to the theological club. But if our
present decrepitude teaches us anything, it is that the club needs
massive transfusions of new blood if it is to survive at all. I
believe it is only by listening to such outsiders as these that any
new health will come to the faltering enterprise of theology.

Teilhard's theology is only accidentally scientific, in the narrow
sense. It is really a Christian cosmology, the first that has really
engaged the imagination of modern man. Teilhard correctly saw
that for modern man the question of God would focus on the
question of man. It would appear in, with and under the issue
of man's place in the enormously expanded world of modern
science. Teilhard's complex theories about the role of centrifugal
and centripetal forces in evolution, the new kind of heredity
seen in man as a culture-bearing animal, and the crucial role
man's consciousness of evolution will play in that evolution—
these cannot be discussed here. The point which they suggest,
however, is that any thinking about God from now on must
begin with the recognition that man now sees himself as the
one who can and must carry through many of the responsibilities
which men of earlier millennia have assigned to their gods.

Between Teilhard, the maverick Catholic, and Bloch, the rene-
gade Marxist, there are many differences; but one cannot help

[3] See Gordon D. Kaufman, "Theological Historicism as an Experiment in
Thought" in *The Christian Century*, March 2, 1966, p. 268.

noticing the similarities. Both of them discuss transcendence in terms of the pressure exerted by the future on the present. Both see the future as that pressure on the present which is only possible where there is a creature who can orient himself toward the future and relate himself to reality by this orientation, in short a "creature who can hope." They both regard reality as a radically open-ended process. Teilhard detected in the logic of evolution an ever deepening humanization of man and "hominization" of the universe. Bloch concerned himself with "man-as-promise" and mapped out what he called "the ontology of the not-yet."

Teilhard's world of discourse was the breathtakingly massive universe and the appearance within it of the phenomenon of man, that point where the cosmos begins to think and to steer itself. Bloch's place of philosophizing is human history, exhumed from its burial in timelessness and launched on a journey into the future by the "birth of the hope," an orientation introduced into the world by the biblical faith but now lost sight of by Christians. Both Bloch and Teilhard affirmed the centrality of what the Germans now call the *Impuls der Erwartung*, or impulse of expectancy. The one examined the way cosmic space and geological time seem to dwarf man, the other how history seems to buffet him. But neither became discouraged; both saw hope in man's growing capacity to apply science and critical reflection to the shaping of his own destiny.

We need a no-nonsense "leveling" in theological discourse. I think that if we can affirm anything real which also transcends history, it will be the future as it lives in man's imagination, nurtured by his memory and actualized by his responsibility. Some theologians have already begun to explore the implications this would have for traditional ideas of eschatology and incarnation. Although I think Teilhard's legacy will increasingly help us in working out this new direction, it is Bloch who I believe will be more influential.

Bloch's massive book, *Das Prinzip der Hoffnung* (*The Principle of Hope*), first published in 1954, though difficult and often unclear, supplies the only serious alternative to Martin Heidegger's even more opaque *Sein und Zeit* (*Being and Time*) of 1927 as a philosophical partner for theology. Heidegger senses life to be hemmed in and radically finite, but he still fiercely presses the desperate question of the *Sein des Seienden*, the meaning of the being of that which is. Heidegger's influence on modern theology has been enormous, but as I argued in *The Secular City*, it seems to me almost wholly deleterious. Bloch presses the same difficult questions that Heidegger raises, but he does so within an ontology that seeks to question and subvert the tight finitude of Heidegger's constricted human world.

Thus while Heidegger plumbs the caliginous depths of anxiety, care and *Sein zum Tode* (being toward death), Bloch deals with that "infatuation with the possible" without which human existence is unthinkable. "The basic theme of philosophy," argues Bloch, "is that which is still not culminated, the still unpossessed homeland," and instead of anxiety and death "philosophy's basic categories should be 'frontier,' 'future,' 'the new' and the '*Traum nach vorwärts.*' "[4] Like Heidegger, Bloch considers himself to be an atheist. But just as many theologians, such as Rudolf Bultmann, Herbert Braun and Heinrich Ott, have found ideas of worth and interest in Heidegger, so a new group has already begun to find promising hints in the works of Ernst Bloch. Thus Jürgen Moltmann's recent book, *Theology of Hope*,[5] obviously owes much to Bloch, as does Gerhard Sauter's *Zukunft und Verheissung*.[6]

One point of continuing interest for the theologians is that Bloch not only engages in a brilliant analysis of man as "the creature who hopes," he also postulates a correspondence between man as the being who hopes and dreams and the historical world itself. He sees this correspondence (*Entsprechung*) between the "subjective of hope" and the "objectively possible," and he even tries (often unsuccessfully) to describe and elucidate it. The relationship between "subjective" and "objective" hope raises in Bloch's mind the question of an "identity" between

[4] Bloch, *Das Prinzip der Hoffnung* (Berlin: Suhrkampf Verlag, 1954), p. 83. Bloch's expression *Traum nach vorwärts* is simple enough German, but a literal translation would be "dream toward forward" rather than "dream toward the future," which is our closest idiomatic equivalent.
[5] New York: Harper & Row, 1967.
[6] Zurich: Zwingli Verlag, 1965.

man-who-hopes and a structure of reality which supports and nourishes such hope.

Here the Christian naturally thinks of qualities sometimes attributed to God. Bloch is not unaware of the similarity; indeed he describes the identity between subjective spontaneity and historical possibility as the "demythologized content of that which Christians have revered as God." He therefore insists that atheism is the only acceptable stance today because the Christian God has been imprisoned in the categories of a static ontology.

There are many questions to be asked about Bloch's work from a biblical perspective. He does not provide us with a clear-cut way out of the "death of God" morass. At many points in his argument Bloch's commitment to radical historicism, along with residual traces of his Marxist materialism, seems to collide with his passionate desire to picture a radically open world in which at least the possibility of something "wholly other" is not excluded in principle. There are several places where, for example, he insists that all possibility is already incipiently present in what is, thus betraying an Aristotelian teleological bias. But his main thesis cannot be easily dismissed.

I agree with Wolf-Dieter Marsch's remark that so long as Christians cling to the static "is" as the normative predicate for God, such thinkers as Bloch must rightly continue to regard themselves as atheists. But if theology can leave behind the God who "is" and begin its work with the God who "will be" (or in biblical parlance "He who comes"), an exciting new epoch in theology could begin, one in which Ernst Bloch's work would be extraordinarily important.

If the present wake is for the God who *is* (and now *was*), this may clear the decks for the God who *will be*. I cannot say for sure that the opening of such a path will lead anywhere, but the task of opening it would first require a thorough reworking of our major theological categories. We would see Jesus, for example, not as a visitor to earth from some supraterrestrial heaven, but as the one in whom precisely this two-story dualism is abolished for good, and who becomes the pioneer and first sign of the coming New Age. We would see the community of faith as those "on the way" to this promised reality, "forgetting what is behind and reaching out for that which is ahead." (Phil. 3:14). Radical theology would have more radical social consequences than the so-called radical theology of the death of God has produced so far.

The doctrine of God would become theology's answer to the seemingly irrefutable fact that history can only be kept open by "anchoring" that openness somewhere outside history itself, in this case not "above" but *ahead*. Faith in God would be recognized, for our time, in that hope for the future Kingdom of Peace that frees men to suffer and sacrifice meaningfully in the present. Still, I would be the worst of imposters if I pretended that in the God of Hope we can immediately affirm the one who will appear when the corpse of the dead God of metaphysical theism is finally interred. He may not appear at all, and our efforts to work out a new and viable doctrine of God for our time may be fated to fail from the beginning. But before any of us throws in the towel, I hope we will exercise the freedom given us by the present *Götterdämmerung* of the divinities of Christendom, and use this freedom to think as candidly and as rigorously as possible about where we go from here.[7]

The only future that theology has, one might say, is to become the theology of the future. Its attention must turn to that future which God makes possible but for which man is inescapably responsible. Traditionally, it is prophecy that has dealt with the future. Hence the fate of theology will be determined by its capacity to regain its prophetic role. It must resist the temptation of becoming an esoteric specialty and resume its role as critic and helper of the faithful community as that community grapples with the vexing issues of our day.

The "death-of-God" syndrome signals the collapse of the static orders and fixed categories by which men have understood themselves in the past. It opens the future in a new and radical way. Prophecy calls man to move into this future with a confidence

[7] Since writing this article I have read Leslie Dewart's brilliant new book, *The Future of Belief: Theism in a World Come of Age* (New York: Herder, 1966). It is a splendid example of a new possibility in theism once we have divested ourselves of static metaphysical categories. Dewart stresses the "presence" rather than the existence of God.

informed by the tradition but transformed by the present. Theology helps prophecy guide the community of faith in its proper role as the avant-garde of humanity. This community must clarify the life-and-death options open to *homo sapiens*, devote itself unsparingly to the humanization of city and cosmos, and keep alive the hope of a kingdom of racial equality, peace among the nations and bread for all. One should never weep for a dead god. A god who can die deserves no tears. Rather we should rejoice that, freed of another incubus, we now take up the task of fashioning a future made possible not by anything that "is" but by "He who comes."

Suggestions for
Further Reading

ALTIZER, THOMAS J. J., ed., *Toward a New Christianity: Readings in the Death of God Theology* (New York: Harcourt, Brace & World, 1967).

ARNOLD, MATTHEW, *Literature and Dogma*.

BROWN, NORMAN O., *Life Against Death* (Middletown, Conn.: Wesleyan University Press, 1959).

————, *Love's Body* (New York: Random House, 1966).

COBB, JOHN B., *Living Options in Protestant Theology* (Philadelphia: Westminster Press, 1962).

COOPER, JOHN C., *The Roots of the Radical Theology* (Philadelphia: Westminster, 1967).

COCKSHUT, A. O. J., *The Unbelievers: English Agnostic Thought, 1840–1890* (New York: New York University Press, 1966).

DEWART, LESLIE, *The Future of Belief: Theism in a World Come of Age* (New York: Herder and Herder, 1966).

FLEW, ANTONY, *God and Philosophy* (New York: Harcourt, Brace & World, 1966).

FROMM, ERICH, *You Shall Be As Gods* (New York: Holt, Rinehart & Winston, 1966).

GILKEY, LANGDON, *The Relevance of God-Language* (Indianapolis: Bobbs-Merrill, 1967).

GROENBECH, VILHELM, *Religious Currents in the Nineteenth Century* (Lawrence, Kansas: University of Kansas Press, 1966).

HAMILTON, KENNETH M., *God Is Dead* (Grand Rapids: Eerdmans, 1966).

HELLER, ERICH, *The Artist's Journey into the Interior* (New York: Random House, 1965).

HERZOG, FREDERICK, *Understanding God: The Key Issue in Present-Day Protestant Thought* (New York: Charles Scribner's Sons, 1966).

HOCKING, WILLIAM ERNEST, *The Meaning of God in Human Experience* (New Haven: Yale University Press, 1912).

HORDERN, WILLIAM, ed., *New Directions in Theology Today*, Vol. I (Philadelphia: Westminster Press, 1966).

ICE, JACKSON, and CAREY, JOHN J., *The Death of God Debate* (Philadelphia: Westminster, 1967).

JAMES, RALPH, *The Concrete God* (Indianapolis: Bobbs-Merrill, 1967).

JAMES, WILLIAM, *Pragmatism and Other Essays* (New York: Meridian Books, 1965).

JENKINS, DANIEL, *Guide to the Debate About God* (London: SCM Press, 1965).

JUNG, CARL GUSTAV, *Modern Man in Search of a Soul* (New York: Harcourt, Brace & World, 1933).

MARCUSE, HERBERT, *Eros and Civilization* (Boston: Beacon Press, 1955).

————, *One-Dimensional Man* (Boston: Beacon Press, 1964).

MEHTA, VED, *The New Theologian* (New York: Harper & Row, 1966).

MELAND, BERNARD, *The Secularization of Modern Cultures* (New York: Oxford University Press, 1966).

MILLER, J. HILLIS, *The Disappearance of God* (Cambridge: Harvard University Press, 1964).

MILLER, WILLIAM ROBERT, *Christianity Here and Now* (New York: Avon Books, 1967).

MUNBY, D. L., *The Idea of a Secular Society* (New York: Oxford University Press, 1963).

MURCHLAND, BERNARD, ed., *Death of God Anthology* (New York: Random House, 1966).

NOVAK, MICHAEL, *Belief and Unbelief* (New York: Macmillan, 1965).

OGDEN, SCHUBERT M., *Christ Without Myth* (New York: Harper & Row, 1961).

————, *The Reality of God* (New York: Harper & Row, 1966).

OGLETREE, THOMAS W., *The Death of God Controversy* (Nashville: Abingdon Press, 1966).

PAUL, LESLIE, *Alternatives to Christian Belief* (Garden City: Doubleday, 1967).

RICHARDSON, ALAN, *Religion in Contemporary Debate* (London: SCM Press, 1966).

RICHARDSON, HERBERT W., *Toward an American Theology* (New York: Harper & Row, 1967).

ROBINSON, JOHN A. T., *Exploration into God* (Stanford University Press, 1967).

RUBENSTEIN, RICHARD L., *After Auschwitz* (Indianapolis: Bobbs-Merrill, 1966).

SMITH,. RONALD GREGOR, *The New Man* (New York: Harper & Row, 1956).

————, *Secular Christianity* (New York: Harper & Row, 1966).

TILLICH, PAUL, *Perspectives on Protestant Theology* (New York: Harper & Row, 1967).

VAHANIAN, GABRIEL, *No Other God* (New York: Braziller, 1966).

————, ed., *The God Is Dead Debate* (New York: McGraw-Hill, 1967).

VAN BUREN, PAUL, *The Secular Meaning of the Gospel* (New York: Macmillan, 1963).

WOOLF, LEONARD, *After the Deluge* (London: Hogarth Press, 1953).

THIS BOOK WAS SET IN

CALEDONIA AND BULMER TYPES BY

MARYLAND LINOTYPE.

IT WAS PRINTED BY

THE MURRAY PRINTING COMPANY

AND BOUND BY

H. WOLFF BOOK MFG. CO., INC.

TYPOGRAPHY AND DESIGN ARE BY

LARRY KAMP AND BARBARA LIMAN